Contents

Acknowledgements
Notes on contributors
Foreword by Ram A. Cnaan

Acknowledgements

The research presented in this book was funded by the EU 7th Framework Programme (7FP) FACIT project ('Faith-based organisations and exclusion in European cities', Grant agreement no 217314). Along with the various partners of the consortium we are very grateful for the support aand the work that made both the research and this volume happen.

One of the chapters contained in the volume has appeared in print elsewhere, albeit with a different introduction and some minor textual changes. We would like to thank the editorial board and referees at *Geoforum* for their role in the production of Cloke, P., Johnsen, S. and May, J. (2007) 'Ethical citizenship? Volunteers and the ethics of providing services for homeless people', *Geoforum*, vol 38, pp 1089-01, which became Chapter Six in this volume. Thanks also go to Elsevier Publishing for granting permission to reproduce the original article.

Two of the contributions to the book (Chapters Two and Three) would not have come to fruition if it had not had been for the enthusiasm, diligence and professionalism shown by Agatha Herman and José Luis Romanillos, who came into the process late in the day as short-term contract researchers. Thanks go to colleagues at the Personnel and Organisation Department of the University of Groningen, the Netherlands, for making their contracts a reality against the odds.

Due to a series of issues relating to the completion of the project and the difficulties of reconciling diverse epistemologies of researching the 'f' word in faith-based organisations (FBOs), it took a tremendous amount of time and effort to submit the final typescript. We would like to thank, in particular, Commissioning Editor, Emily Watt, along with her colleagues, Laura Vickers and Rebecca Tomlinson, at The Policy Press, for their understanding, forbearance and support.

Justin, on a personal note, would like to thank the continued and unconditional love and support of his family in the UK, without which none of the work contained here would have come about or have had any significance or meaning. The same applies for Nell, Albert and others close to him in the delightful northern Dutch city of Groningen. Pepe and Dunya – his two cats! – kept the process very much grounded in what really matters, and where always great fun.

Paul, as always, would like to thank his wonderful family – Viv, Liz and Will (and Ringo the dog) for their amazing context of love, support, agape and caritas, which is the foundation for his participation in this and other research. Heartfelt thanks also to Andy and Samwise, for being such excellent companions on this particular research journey, and to Mike and Peter for friendship that has helped make sense of the 'f' word in different postsecular and psychogeographical contexts.

Notes on contributors

Justin Beaumont is assistant professor in the Department of Spatial Planning and Environment at the University of Groningen, the Netherlands. He has developed new enquiries on social interventions within postsecular cities, as well as faith-based organisations, and on social justice in urban areas. He is currently undertaking research on problems of the postsecular and the ethical turn in urban theory. He is co-editor of *Exploring the postsecular: The religious, the political and the urban* (Brill, 2010), *Postsecular cities: Space, theory and practice* (Continuum, 2011) and *Spaces of contention: Spatialities of social movements* (Ashgate, 2012).

Paul Cloke is professor of human geography at the University of Exeter, UK. Over the last decade he has been involved in research that takes a new look at the geographies of ethics, focusing in particular on responses to homelessness, the new politics of ethical consumption and the growing significance of 'theo-ethics' in contemporary society. He is currently engaged in research on postsecularism and faith-based interventions in a range of social and caring arenas. His latest books (co-authored) include *Swept up lives? Re-envisioning the homeless city* (Wiley-Blackwell, 2010) and *Globalizing responsibility: The political rationalities of ethical consumption* (Wiley-Blackwell, 2011).

Ram A. Cnaan is professor and senior associate dean at the University of Pennsylvania, School of Social Policy and Practice, USA. He is director of the Program for Religion and Social Policy Research and past president of ARNOVA (Association for Research on Nonprofit Organizations and Voluntary Action). He received his doctorate from the School of Social Work at the University of Pittsburgh, and his bachelor's degree in social work and master's in social work from the Hebrew University, Jerusalem, Israel. Professor Cnaan has published numerous articles in scientific journals on a variety of social issues and serves on the editorial boards of nine academic journals. He is the author or editor of eight books, including: *The other Philadelphia story: How local congregations support quality of life in urban America* (University of Pennsylvania Press, 2006). He is considered an international expert in the areas of volunteering, re-entry, faith-based social care and social policy. He lectures widely and teaches regularly in four countries.

Maarten Davelaar is researcher at the Verwey-Jonker Instituut in Utrecht, the Netherlands, with a background in political science. His research interests cover urban policy and governance, with a particular focus on issues concerning homelessness, the participation of socially excluded people, the role of the voluntary sector in general and of faith-based organisations in particular. Much of his research has been pursued in a comparative European context, including involvement in a number of cross-national research projects. He has been involved in cross-national research on urban policy and citizen participation and on local social policy and participated in the EU-FACIT project on faith-based organisations and social exclusion in cities. He is research adviser for the European Observatory on Homelessness (linked to FEANTSA, the European Federation of National Organisations working with the Homeless). Before joining the Verwey-Jonker Institute he worked as a campaigner and project manager in the faith-based and voluntary sector, supporting local and national networks working on issues like social exclusion, homelessness, integration and immigration and sustainable urban development.

Nynke de Witte works at the Audit Office of the Dutch government in The Hague, the Netherlands. She has an MPhil in political and social sciences from the University of Pompeu Fabra, Barcelona and bachelor and master's degrees in human geography from the Radboud University Nijmegen. She worked as a researcher for the Spanish case in the EU 6FP project EMILIE, 'A European approach to multicultural citizenship'. Between 2008 and 2009 she was a junior researcher for the Dutch case in the EU 7FP FACIT project.

Danielle Dierckx is assistant professor at the Research Group OASeS (Centre on Inequality, Poverty, Social Exclusion and the City) of the University of Antwerp, Belgium, with a PhD thesis in political and social sciences on poverty policies in Flanders. Her academic activities consist of policy-oriented research in the field of poverty and social exclusion. These activities focus on the understanding of the main social challenges as well as on the strategies and instruments governments use for issues relating to multidimensional poverty policies. Danielle was the project manager of FACIT.

Ingemar Elander is professor emeritus at Örebro University, Sweden. His research interests cover urban governance in a broad sense as exemplified in publications on cities and climate change, environment and democracy, faith-based organisations and social exclusion in European cities, urban partnerships and public health. He is currently involved in research projects on sustainable development and neighbourhood renewal. He is co-editor of *Urban governance in Europe* (Eckardt and Elander, 2009), and co-author of *Faith-based organisations and social exclusion in Sweden* (Elander and Fridolfsson, 2011)

Jürgen Friedrichs studied sociology, social psychology and philosophy at the Universities of Berlin and Hamburg in Germany. He took his PhD in Hamburg, was assistant professor at the University of Hamburg, and in 1974 became full professor at the Institute of Sociology at the University of Hamburg, where he founded the Institute for Comparative Urban Analyses. In 1991 he was appointed to the University of Cologne, holding a chair in sociology and directing the Research Institute of Sociology, founded in 1919. He is senior editor of the *Kölner Zeitschrift für Sociology* and is on the advisory board of *Housing Studies* and the *European Journal of Housing Policy*. He has published on urban sociology, research methods and rational choice theory, has conducted many projects on urban problems and urban development, and participated in several European Union projects. In 2007 he became professor emeritus at the Research Institute of Sociology in Cologne, Germany.

Agatha Herman is lecturer of human geography in the School of Geography, Earth and Environmental Sciences at Plymouth University, UK. Her research interests include geographies of justice, ethics and alternative economic and political spaces. Her recent research has explored ethical discourses within the South African wine industry, spaces of postsecular ethics, the impact of the economic recession on charity shops in the UK and post-institutional social re-integration.

Sarah Johnsen is senior research fellow in the Institute for Housing, Urban and Real Estate Research (IHURER) at Heriot-Watt University, Edinburgh, UK. She has previously worked at Queen Mary, University of London, the University of York and The Salvation Army, all in the UK. Most of her research focuses on aspects of homelessness and street culture (begging, street drinking and street-based sex work). She was co-author of *Swept up lives? Re-envisioning the homeless city* (Wiley-Blackwell, 2010), and has published chapters based on work with faith-based organisations in *Religion and change in modern Britain* (Routledge, 2012) and *Innovative methods in the study of religion* (Oxford University Press, forthcoming).

Wendy Kerstens studied sociology and was a junior researcher at the Research Group OASeS (Centre on Inequality, Poverty, Social Exclusion and the City) of the University of Antwerp, Belgium, during the EU 7FP FACIT project. Her main interest was the role of faith-based organisations in fighting social exclusion.

Jennifer Klöckner studied sociology, psychology and pedagogy at the University of Cologne, Germany, graduating with a Master of Arts. She was a junior researcher at the Institute of Sociology at the University of Cologne in 2007, where she participated in a DFG (*Deutsche Forschungsgemeinschaft*) project on poverty neighbourhoods. She is currently working on her PhD, which focuses on the differences between Islamic and Christian members of faith-based organisations in motivations for volunteering activities. In 2008 she was a junior researcher in the EU 7FP FACIT project.

Jon May is professor of geography at Queen Mary, University of London, UK. His work draws on ethnographic approaches to explore issues of inequality and social justice in an era of rapid social, economic and urban change. Research with Paul Cloke and Sarah Johnsen has sought to extend narrow accounts of the 'revanchist' city to explore instead the various and complex experiences of and responses to street homelessness in a context of neoliberal welfare 'reform'. Work with colleagues in the Global Cities at Work team at Queen Mary explored the processes behind and characteristics of the 'migrant division of labour' in London's low wage economy. He is the co-author or co-editor of a number of books, including, most recently: *Swept up lives? Re-envisioning the homeless city* (Wiley-Blackwell, 2010) and *Global cities at work: New migrant divisions of labour* (Pluto, 2010).

José Luis Romanillos is lecturer in human geography at the School of Geography, College of Life and Environmental Sciences, University of Exeter, UK. His research interests include sociospatial theory, contemporary political subjectivities and the geographies of death and finitude.

Mustafa Şen is lecturer at the Middle East Technical University (METU) in Ankara, Turkey, in the field of the sociology of religion. He has had published research on Islam and conflicts in Europe and his research interests also include: solidarity networks of immigrants in Berlin; activities of the Directorate of Religious Affairs and Turkish Islamic organisations in Germany; and the social, cultural and political formation of poverty in urban Turkey. He has a long-standing interest in social theory and philosophy.

Samuel Thomas is research assistant in the School of Geography at the University of Exeter, UK, as well as a worker for Exeter YMCA. His doctoral work involved a series of ethnographic studies of incarnational communities in the UK, and he is currently preparing a thesis on faith and performance in the incarnational geographies of faith-based organisations.

Jan Vranken is professor emeritus at University of Antwerp, Belgium, and is founder and former director of OASeS (Centre on Inequality, Poverty, Social Exclusion and the City). He has been conducting research on poverty and related matters since 1970. He coordinated a number of European projects (three successive projects of the 'Preparatory Actions' for 'Poverty 4' of the European Commission:'A model to evaluate actions and policies on social exclusion', 1999, 'Policy-relevant databases on poverty and social exclusion', 2000 and 'Non-monetary indicators of social exclusion and social inclusion', 2001) and the FP5 project UGIS, and participated in several others, such as URBEX. He is currently the Belgian representative in the management committee of COST A26 on City Regions. He was the Belgium representative for the peer review on the 'Rough Sleeping Strategy' in England (2004).

Andrés Walliser received his PhD in sociology at Instituto Juan March in Madrid, and is currently an associated professor at New York University in Madrid and visiting professor at Hertie School of Governance in Berlin. He has a wide experience as a basic and applied researcher and consultant in urban issues such as neighbourhood regeneration, social exclusion, citizen participation, community development, governance and participatory planning in Spain and Europe. He collaborates on a regular basis with Ecosistema Urbano Arquitectos developing innovative participatory tools and programmes.

Andrew Williams is associate research fellow in the School of Geography at the University of Exeter, UK. His interests lie in the intersections of religion, politics and postsecularism, particularly with regard to the neoliberal contextualisation of faith-based welfare in the UK and elsewhere. His PhD research was based on ethnographic studies of Christian drug treatment providers in the UK, focusing on the varied ethics of care and experiences of service-users. He is currently working on a project examining the uneven impact of recent institutional and socioeconomic changes on small towns in the UK.

Foreword

Faith-based organisations (FBOs), especially in the European context, are both interesting and understudied. A century ago, Max Weber noted that religious organisations must face the dilemma of administrative versus higher authority. They are unique as they are placed between the state and the people they serve yet they are committed to follow their faith values. In his quest to understand power and organisations he was puzzled by these organisations that, on the one hand, had to function rationally like all other organisations and accumulate resources, maintain staff and interact with their environment, while on the other hand, they were constrained as they had to follow a semi-strict religious doctrine. The tension arising from attempting to comply with these two authorities can cause serious conflict and threaten the faith-based organisation's ability to function. In one of my studies I came across a religious school that was offered by the state a large sum of money to run an afterschool programme, which would be required to include sex education. The school desperately needed the money but found the stipulation of teaching sex education in contradiction to their religious beliefs. After lengthy debates the school declined the money and offered a much more limited version of an afterschool programme.

The administrative sides of FBOs are changing rapidly as a response to changes in society, technology, political power and members' preferences and willingness to pay; their faith side has become more robust and at times in conflict with their administrative side. This dilemma is emphasised in welfare-related FBOs. The quest to evangelise and instill a strict moral code as well as care for others as an actualisation of the dictum 'care for thy neighbour' is strong among most religions and is often one of the main motivations behind the existence of FBOs. In many Western democracies, FBOs operating in the welfare arena have to collaborate with governments, keep faith separate from service, apply universalist principles of eligibility, operate according to state laws and, in the process, may find it challenging to keep their commitment to their higher authority.

The welfare state that emerged after the Second World War was the greatest social promise in the history of the human race. It was intended to cover all human and economic needs from cradle to grave and to protect all members of society against all social falls and ills. It set a new dimension in relationships between the state and citizens and cast a shadow over the need for religion and religious-based organisations. The post-1945 massive involvement of Western democracies in welfare provision created a situation of crowding out in which previous welfare providers, most notably FBOs, left the welfare arena and relinquished it to powerful governments. It was widely assumed that FBOs and other charitable organisations were no longer needed, that they were anachronistic and would soon disappear.

However, two generations after the Second World War, there was a major retrenchment in the welfare state. Since the days of Margaret Thatcher in the

UK and Ronald Reagan in the US during the 1980s, neoliberalism became the preferred ideological social policy in most advanced democracies. Governments at that time found it impossible to pay for the ambitious social welfare programmes formed in the two to three decades after the Second World War, and citizens are unwilling to carry the financial burden needed for maintaining such a comprehensive welfare state. Consequently, in the years since the first serious retrenchment of welfare states, first in the US and now all over Europe, eyes are increasingly set on the faith community to come back and reassume its historical role of providing care for the poor and needy in society. But the faith community cannot assume the same role played in the early days of the 20th century. FBOs have been called to supplant state services and to lower the cost of public welfare. They act as shadow government, if one still believes in the responsibility of governments for the welfare of citizens, or as free agents reclaiming their historical role in a postmodernist society. Calling FBOs to help in the welfare arena creates new realities for society and for the faith community that demand new scrutiny and understanding. FBOs in the early part of the 21st century are significantly different than those that operated 70 years ago when most members of society were associated with religious organisations and governments did not claim the role of serving their citizenry.

In the US, the shift from public social services to FBOs was planned and has taken place over the past two decades, and it may serve as a knowledge base for European countries. It was not a Republican ploy, however, as many people wanted to believe. The two main political parties both compete over who will be more faith friendly and who will reach out to congregations for collaboration and support. Using FBOs as shadow government in the US was part of the 1996 legislation known for massive cuts in helping poor single mothers (welfare reform). Linking these two policies (enhancing the use of FBOs and cutting welfare as we know it) tainted the 'faith-based initiative' as a fig leaf for public welfare retrenchment. The many studies that followed this initiative are split regarding its success, and are often ideologically driven. Some claim that it brought services to people at the community level and that clients were highly satisfied when assisted by FBOs. Others contend that FBOs failed to be more effective than public or private services and that they helped blur church–state separation. Regardless, they are currently part of the US scene and serve a major role in caring for poor people, immigrants and under-served communities. Interestingly, US FBOs, while contracting with governments, also raise funds for their services from members, supporters and foundations, and charge clients for some services. As such, they can offer more services with a variety of faith components in addition to the services contracted directly by government. However, only large and rich religious organisations, congregations and FBOs are able to amass enough income to provide alternative services. We found in the US that most FBOs were heavily financed by the state and that only a few that were more fundamentalist in nature avoided public money. These latter organisations preferred to be able to select the clients they cared for, to demand spiritual participation and growth, and to 'kick out' those who did not really believe.

Learning for the US is often unwise and inapplicable. The US is quite religious, with a large segment of its population attending houses of prayer on a regular basis – people are used to supporting religious activities. In fact, in our studies of congregations, we found that more than four fifths of a congregation's income came from members' contributions, and when the congregation undertook a new social mission, even if it was carried through a separate non-profit religious organisation, members would support the initiative. Furthermore, as a result of Supreme Court ruling on the separation of church and state, the state is intentionally detached from telling religious organisations what to do and has limited control over them. Congregations and many FBOs are exempt from reporting to the government and are independent as long as they do not violate the law. Within this context religion is flourishing in the US, and the role of religion in society is central. Unlike in the US, however, in Europe religious organisations are subjected to the state and are required to report about their operations. Many studies demonstrate a striking decrease in religious beliefs and participation in European countries – while Europe has witnessed a trend of secularisation, FBOs and the denominations that sponsor them still exist. While faith communities and FBOs have lost in centrality and have seen a decrease in public support, they are still capable of playing an important role the welfare arena, If called upon, they will rise to the challenge as they did in past eras.

The changing environment in Europe has seen numerous changes that have had a large-scale impact on FBOs and their role in society. Growing secularisation in many countries, the formation of a unified European Union (EU), the creation of the euro as a cross-country currency and enhanced democratic forces throughout Europe have posed a serious challenge to organised religion, and FBOs in particular. The concept of the postsecular has therefore attracted considerable attention in the European context, although the process of secularisation is not equal in all countries and to all segments of society. While mainstream religions in most countries have seen a decline in membership and impact, ethnic religions have experienced a significant rise, and their ability to form new FBOs is impressive. Furthermore, religion is a dynamic social phenomenon and even the same faith traditions in the same society evolve over time in diverse manners. Two FBOs of the same denomination in the same locale can overtime be very different in their religious strictness, clients served, reliance on the denomination, and relationships with the state. The way one FBO or religious congregation in the same social ecology has emerged may show important differences reflected in how they react to new calls for welfare involvement. How each faith tradition within a specific locality reacts to the challenge of poverty and exclusion is a major theme of this volume, and one that still mystifies many scholars.

Emerging neoliberalism has left the welfare arena open for FBOs to step in and reclaim some of their traditional role, and in each country a new set of FBOs are working with poor people and with new immigrants, many of them of religions that were previously unheard of and as such should now be highlighted and studied.

Justin Beaumont and Paul Cloke, the editors, and the other contributors to this volume, set the bar high; their aim was to produce a volume that studied the role played by FBOs in combating poverty and social exclusion in countries across Europe. Realising that in the 21st century governments are no longer the central and sole problem solvers, juxtaposed with the varied historical and political arrangements across Europe, the rise in the centrality of FBOs is not a universal process. What works in Turkey, where official secularism was always in the shadow of deep public affinity to Islam, is dramatically different from what takes place in the post-Lutheran Scandinavian welfare regime Sweden. Europe is complex and many welfare-religious narratives are emerging. Weaving them together and demonstrating their intricacy along trends is the key contribution of this volume. Furthermore, given the complexity of the role that higher authority plays from wishing to convert to instilling new moral principles, the quest to serve acquires many faces within and between cities and countries. This volume is the first attempt to document and analyse these trends in a comprehensive yet insightful manner.

Many of the authors in this volume have discussed the degree to which FBOs collaborate with other organisations. In the US studies, FBOs and congregations were much more collaborative than anyone predicted – many scholars and practitioners expected them to be isolationist and to ignore other organisations in their environment, but this was not the case. Neither in the US nor in Europe did faith organisations that served the poor act alone. Also of relevance to this volume, in the US there were few distinctions between which faith tradition served the poor. The differences were in explaining the motivation (duty versus actualising faith) and areas of involvement (feeding versus educational programmes). Surprisingly, very few programmes contained proselytising elements. While all hoped for clients to find God, they all noted that helping the poor did not bring faith. In the words of one clergy, "my service to the poor is one small nail in the building of their faith." These issues may take a different expression in the European context and this volume provides the first answers, and in a comparative perspective.

The editors and contributors in this volume focus on a set of cities from all over Europe, namely: Belgium, the Netherlands, Germany, the UK, Turkey, Spain and Sweden. Questions are raised that were hardly discussed in the US but that should have been discussed. Based on the US experience, will the emerging reliance on FBOs in Europe enhance expectation for individual responsibility at the expense of entitlements, or will faith-based social services coexist with the culture of entitlements? Assessing the degree to which FBOs and especially those from non-traditional religions contribute to social cohesion and help reduce social exclusion poses new challenges to many European countries – are they state agents or threats to state cohesion? What challenges does the combination of evolving technologies of virtual communication and reliance on traditional beliefs pose for policy makers and public officials? Religion is enormously powerful and can be used equally to heal or to incite to kill – how can European nations make sure that the focus is on healing? We know that houses of prayer and FBOs tend to enhance bonding social capital, but their ability to contribute bridging social capital is questionable and should be part of the social and political discourse. These and many other discourses are ripe and awaiting a solid platform. This volume provides the needed platform and will serve as a foundation for many studies to follow. Mission accomplished.

Ram A. Cnaan
Professor and Senior Associate Dean
Director, Program for Religion and Social Policy Research
School of Social Policy and Practice
University of Pennsylvania, USA

Introduction to the study of faith-based organisations and exclusion in European cities

Justin Beaumont and Paul Cloke

Introduction

This book on faith-based organisations (FBOs) and exclusion in European cities has a long history. The core idea came about in 2000 when one of us (Justin Beaumont) first came across and was immediately gripped by Norman Lewis' *The honoured society* (Lewis, 1984). The British travel writer's non-sensationalist yet sensitive and acutely aware handling of the Sicilian mafia sparked the ideas that over time developed and matured, culminating in this book. In one particularly astounding chapter, Lewis reveals the compelling story of Padre Camelo, the 80-year-old Capuchin (Franciscan) priest, and his fellow monks from the city and commune Mazzarino, in the province of Caltanissetta, Sicily, Italy, who in the 1950s and 1960s terrorised local inhabitants with extortion rackets, violent threats at the confessional box and murder.

The case of the 'Mazzarino Friars', as it became popularly known (see Polara, 1989), was a hotly debated controversy during the early 1960s at a time of intense conflict between clerical and anti-clerical political forces. The clerics, namely the Democrazia Cristiana Church and other Catholic institutions led by Palermo Archbishop Ernesto Ruffini, waged war against their various opponents who felt the sinister Mafiosi monks rightly deserved to be punished for their crimes. Later the errant friars were indeed sentenced to 30 years imprisonment, but the decision was later commuted. The leniency of the court decision outraged many jurists and citizens at the time.

For those familiar with the longer history of bandit and robber monks riding with outlaw bands and attacking lonesome travellers and isolated farms in rural Sicily, the Mazzarino scandal probably came as little surprise. What was striking, however, was the complex *interpenetration* of seemingly distinct forces – the church, the state, religion, politics, government, people – in a country ravished by scarce resources, financial and political corruption, and extreme and debilitating poverty.[1]

This book at an abstract level studies the interpenetration between religion and politics, church and state, between officialdom and more informal channels of interaction between institutions and the people they profess to govern. It does so in empirical and theoretical terms via a *comparison of FBOs and their actions against poverty and social exclusion across various European cities*. We neither offer an analysis of the present-day mafia and the religious influences therein, nor do we engage in detailed excavations of the political actions of religiously motivated figures throughout history. The book is also a far cry from any form of normative defence of religious extremism and fundamentalism, as with the 'Mazzarino Friars' or others like them. We also vehemently resist any normative apology for neoliberal global restructuring of welfare services and care. *Instead we are concerned with the ordinary and everyday progressive actions of faith-motivated individuals and their organisations in their ethical and political quest for social justice in European cities.*[2]

The volume, therefore, while value-laden in terms of the subject matter of urban social justice, is neither theologically, religiously nor politically normative in nature per se. The inherent diversity of epistemological, theoretical and methodological positions contained within it testifies to this neutrality. The volume reflects a bifurcation between those seeking to critically reveal the contribution of the 'f-word' in FBOs in the various struggles against injustice in European cities, with those who see FBOs as a particular manifestation of an otherwise general process of engagement with poverty and exclusion within civil society. We return this contentious matter in the Conclusion at the end of the book.

At the time of writing this Introduction (August 2011), the global community is still reeling from the twin horrors of the 2011 Norway attacks[3] and the England riots.[4] The combined reactions to these events within political circles and the media are arguably indicative of a sharpened critical public consciousness towards: (1) reasons for deep-rooted poverty, exclusion and deprivation among an enduring underclass of citizens in Europe's cities; (2) problematic relations between religious and ideological fanaticism, resulting in the violent murder of innocent people; and (3) a perceived lack of love, compassion and understanding of 'the other' at a time of heightened neoliberal globalisation, transnational migration and economic crisis.

The various contributions to this volume aim to discern the difference the 'f-word' in FBO makes for augmenting social justice in urban areas, albeit in different ways. This fundamental objective leads us to recall the influence of Albert Camus. The French author, journalist and philosopher, often mentioned in discussions of existentialism and the 'absurd', claimed in *The rebel* (*L'homme révolté*) (Camus, 1971) that acts of rebellion (take, for instance, the rioting in London; religious-motivated acts of compassion in the face of poverty; protest and revolt of various kinds) spring from a basic human rejection of normative justice in societies, especially Western Europe. In their disenchantment with contemporary systems of justice, people rebel as a result of the tension between an innate striving for clarity and understanding on the one hand, and the rampant meaningless and absurdity of an unjust world on the other. Our book engages with an alleged re-enchantment of the possibility of social justice, here and now, through the ordinary, everyday, largely overlooked and sometimes progressive actions of FBOs in European cities.

Our volume complements and advances debates set forth in the stream of titles currently available at The Policy Press scrutinising the faith dimensions of contemporary society, welfare and care (see, for example, Farnell et al, 2003; Furbey et al, 2006; Ashencaen Crabtree et al, 2008; Dinham et al, 2009; Furness and Gilligan, 2009; see also Milligan and Conradson, 2006) by adding a European comparative perspective. We begin in this Introduction with the objectives and methodologies of the FACIT project, then we proceed to a discussion of what FBOs are and why they are important, subsequently laying down a contextual canvas for analysing FBOs in various national and urban contexts that moves beyond an Anglo-American bias within academic discourses of political theory. We then detail some of the key FBO questions that render this volume topical, and set down the driving intellectual challenges from the recent academic literature. We conclude with a summary of the various chapter contributions that constitute the volume as a whole.

The FACIT project

In the European Union (EU) 7th Framework Programme (7FP) Faith-based organisations and exclusion in European cities (FACIT) project (2008-10) we explored FBOs and exclusion in European cities in six member states (the Netherlands, Belgium, the UK, Germany, Spain and Sweden) and in one candidate state (Turkey). This volume is a direct result of the research undertaken for that project, with the chapter by Cloke et al (Chapter Five) on ethical citizenship a mildly edited version of a paper that was previously published in an Economic and Social Research Council (ESRC) research project on emergency services for street homelessness in the UK. Most books stemming from EU-funded projects offer a country-by-country, blow-by-blow account of the research involved. We deliberately depart from that model in order to provide an incisive and intellectually robust volume that emphasises particular strands of transversal findings, offering research examples from across the European spatial range of the study.

In what follows we provide a short account of the main ideas of the FACIT project, the background, methodologies and case study rationale (see also Beaumont, 2008b, 2008c; and the FACIT description of work). The research concerned the present role of FBOs in matters of poverty and other forms of social exclusion (such as homelessness or undocumented people) in cities. The project defined FBOs as *any organisation that refers directly or indirectly to religion or religious values, and functions as a welfare provider or as a political actor*. The central assumption is that FBOs tend to fill the gap left after the supposed withdrawal of the welfare state in several domains of public life, particularly in social welfare and in social protection. At first sight, this looks like a return to the charity of former times, when such associations occupied the fore of social help in many countries. But we might as well witness the beginning of a new type of welfare regime with a stronger focus on local policies and strategies and new interplays between local authorities and civil society organisations.

Questions that arose included: What is the position of FBOs in combating poverty and other forms of social distress cities? How has this role changed over time and how do these activities contribute to combating social exclusion and promoting social cohesion? What are the implications for policies and the governance of European cities? From both scientific and policy perspectives, there is a great need for better empirical and comparative data on what is going on in European cities in matters of poverty and exclusion policies and, in particular, the contribution of FBOs in the reduction (or deepening) of the problems. FBOs have direct entrance to the 'poor side' of cities because of (1) their activities in deprived urban neighbourhoods and among excluded groups and (2) as in the case of many FBOs with a non-Western background, because their members often belong to these deprived and excluded groups themselves.

Objectives of FACIT

The objective of the FACIT project was fourfold. To assess the:

- significance of FBOs from a variety of faiths (Christian, Islamic and others) in the policy and practice of urban social policy in general, combating social exclusion and promoting social cohesion in particular;
- institutional and political conditions under which FBOs have become increasingly present in urban social policies;
- extent to which FBOs have been informed and are operating in a context of a shadow state formed by the retrenchment of welfare states; and
- relations that FBOs have developed, formally and informally, with other non-governmental organisations (NGOs) and with national and local public authorities.

Theoretical conceptualisation and mapping of the present situation served each objective and was realised during the first nine months of the project. A survey, qualitative data collection and transnational comparison were conducted to assess and evaluate the role of FBOs, their relation to other NGOs, the political and institutional conditions and the context of welfare state retrenchment. Results were translated in terms of policy implications and were disseminated at the end of the project. These objectives were measurable, in that we required ourselves to select a number of cities, to have a number of interviewees in our survey and to interview a number of key people in the cross-evaluation.

Contribution of FACIT

Little is known on the precise nature, the complex and variable internal and external organisational geographies and sociologies of FBOs and the political implications for poverty reduction and the achievement of social justice in the urban context. The FACIT research provides knowledge that helps policy makers at the local, national and European level to identify the opportunities that reside within FBOs when they are better integrated into forms of (urban) governance aiming at combating social problems at that level – but also of the threat they could become when developing and implementing their own agenda.

We examined how the role of FBOs in tackling poverty and achieving social justice can be illuminated and perhaps explained by current developments in the social welfare realm in different countries. More specifically, we studied the impact of the constitutional separation between church and state on the options of FBOs. In many countries, many civil associations, including FBOs, are at the sharp end in dealing with the most vulnerable, marginalised and deprived people in urban society, such as immigrants, asylum-seekers and undocumented people, moving through intricate transnational networks in an increasingly globalised world. Research in different European countries therefore prioritised both the extent of 'deprivatisation' of FBOs and demands for values, ethics and the rise of FBOs in anti-poverty and social justice politics.

Policy implications of changing relations between the state and FBOs, as part of a wider process of recasting the position of the third sector and the restructuring of the state and state welfare, are crucial. Understanding the policy connections between FBOs and urban exclusion contributes to the building of social capital, community capacity and confidence, social coherence, that all, one way or another, relate to current urban policy conventions. The comparative dimension of our research critically addresses how FBOs relate to competitiveness, cohesion and governance agendas, while assessing in concrete terms implications for policy beneath conventional policy narratives.

In sum, the FACIT research was designed to increase knowledge about urban forms of increasing social exclusion and decreasing social cohesion in a context of retreating welfare states; to uncover the more prominent role of FBOs in combating poverty and exclusion in cities and in Europe; to identify a European dimension of the position of FBOs in relation to poverty and exclusion in cities, bearing in mind dynamic relations between national and local diversity and common European characteristics; and to construct a common framework for the analysis and evaluation of the policy and governance implications of FBOs, aiming to augment their European characteristics.

Research questions and hypotheses

This conceptual design was supported by a number of hypotheses and research questions that drove our research. In terms of data and comparative perspective, our research was fashioned by two broad questions:

- What is the geographical and sociological map of FBOs in Europe? Our approach here implied description leading to a database that was updated periodically on the project website
- What different kinds of FBOs are operating in the city, implying the need for a typology?

Four closely related hypotheses and research questions developed the project from this starting point:

Hypothesis 1: On the relation between FBOs and the welfare state

Globalisation, neoliberal reforms and the retreat of the welfare state open spaces for NGOs in general and FBOs in particular to engage in economic, social and political actions with vulnerable, excluded and marginalised citizens; types of activities of FBOs depend on the welfare regime in question:
- Is there a relationship between welfare state retrenchment and the growth of activities of FBOs?
- Does the scope and type of activity of FBOs differ by welfare state regime?
- What role do FBOs have in contemporary processes of welfare reform across a variety of welfare regimes? How does the local/national embeddedness of FBOs translate into the ways in which they can and do operate as service delivery agencies and as political actors?
- What are the relationships and differences between secular NGOs and FBOs where they fulfil similar functions in relation to social need?

Hypothesis 2: On the changing position of FBOs

FBOs (like NGOs in general) have to re-invent the roles that are connected to these positions, as well with respect to the state, with respect to each other and to their 'clientele' in combating various forms of exclusion in cities:
- What accounts for the ideological and political ambiguity of FBO activity in the social welfare realm and their changes in time (conservative and even fundamentalist versus progressive, emancipating)?
- Are there differences in strategy between FBOs addressing exclusion and NGOs without a religious background?
- What are the ethnic target groups of FBOs?
- How do FBOs describe their role in combating exclusion in the past and how is this role likely to develop in the future?

Hypothesis 3: On FBOs with respect to policy and governance

In developing new forms of governance for the implementation of social policies involving FBOs, account has to be taken of the changing relations between FBOs and welfare states and their own changing positions; participation of

FBOs in social policies depends on whether public authorities follow a rather top-down or bottom-up approach towards governance:

– To what extent are FBOs governed by the conditions set by government on funding schemes, audit objectives and broader (dis)approval of their work in the city?

– How do FBOs seek freedom-to-act by working outside of government restrictions, or by working to set the policy agendas that govern these restrictions?

– How do the variable legislative frameworks and tax exemption issues have an impact on the position, activities and effectiveness of FBOs in relation to other actors?

– How can we account for the centralising tendencies within some parts of welfare state policies in combination with contradictory localisation of social policies and disciplining of the poor and marginalised?

Hypothesis 4: About the urban context

The hypothesised processes above are said to congeal and intensify in urban environments, the specific form will depend on the urban welfare regime and the city has the social scale that permits the gathering of sufficient numbers of like-minded, faith-motivated and action-oriented people:

– To what extent are FBOs implicated in urban policies – by their participation or by challenging or contesting their premises, at least in some policy areas, for example, treatment of refugees and asylum-seekers?

– How do we explain the changing role of FBOs in treating exclusion in cities and its variation by socio-institutional context?

Overall research strategy

Our approach may be summarised as a specific and somewhat innovative form of triangulation in which multiple methods were deployed in order to triple check our results. The idea here was that one can be more confident if different methods lead to the same results. In short, our approach had the following characteristics:

• *It stands on shoulders:* review of relevant literature
• *It is conceptually sound:* desk research on the definitions, concepts and terminology
• *It is descriptive:* mapping the field of FBOs
• *It is comparative:* a selection of countries and cities

Review of relevant literature

Since the significance of FBOs in Europe has been sufficiently documented, we first explored secondary information through academic journals, books, edited volumes, official publications, newspapers and magazines. Linking and cross-referencing the main strands of work from urban governance and politics, church–state relations, welfare theory and FBOs as social and political agents led to further coherence of our conceptual and theoretical framework.

Data collection

The project engaged in data collection from urban cases from different European cities, including a number of new or candidate member states. A brief pilot or descriptive study was conducted on these cases. Face-to-face interviews were conducted with key informants, actors and representatives of main institutions (public, private, semi-public), as well as leading figures in civil society.

Mapping of FBOs: their context and their structure

Each participant explored the case of their own country including constituent cities therein, and, moreover, wrote a brief report on one additional country, which provided us with a broad picture on what was going on in about half of the EU member states (see Table 1.1). Special attention was paid to the situation in Central Europe. Some months after the start of the project, we selected another Central European country on the basis of our preliminary findings. The idea was to ensure that we covered the complete geographical spread of European countries in the mapping exercise, also allowing us to write an interesting overview of what was going on in Europe (see www.facit.be).

Table 1.1: Participants, urban cases and additional reports

Participant	Urban cases	Additional report
Belgium	Antwerp, Brussels, Ghent	France
The Netherlands	Amsterdam, Rotterdam, Tilburg	Poland
Germany	Cologne, Hamburg, Leipzig	Austria
UK	London, Manchester, Bristol	Ireland
Turkey	Ankara, Istanbul, Konya	Bulgaria
Spain	Madrid, Barcelona, Guadalajara	Greece
Sweden	Stockholm, Göteborg, Malmö	Denmark

Case study comparison

The research focused on a number of countries, with different settings regarding planning practices, political environments and the involvement of 'third sector' organisations. Our selection of case cities in the participating countries allowed exploration of conceptual issues at the urban level, focusing on relations between governance actors at diverse spatial scales through a multilevel, geographical analysis. The focus on governance issues in an urban setting mitigates scale differentials between cities. This approach would incorporate 'cases–within–cases' at neighbourhood and project levels.

Case comparison permits a manageable empirical focus for conceptual ideas, providing a descriptive basis for the explanation of social phenomena. Such an approach yields theoretical, conceptual and policy insights through analysis rather than a merely descriptive juxtaposition of cases. When this type of research pays attention to underlying assumptions of causality, the analytical content of the approach strengthens considerably.

Qualitative data collection

The partners studied urban cases; they used a mix of in-depth analysis, strategic semi-structured interviews and focus groups. The initial idea was to include participant observation, whereby the researchers would volunteer within FBOs as part of the data collection. This idea was later rejected in favour of the survey. The project thus adopted certain qualitative methods to collect and analyse textual data such as interview transcripts, policy documents and organisations' websites.

The survey

To explore the sociodemographic characteristics, motivations, activities and the benefits derived from participation in FBOs, postal surveys of members and volunteers of FBOs were conducted. In order to achieve a solid empirical basis, three FBOs were studied in ten cities of the total sample of cities. Results allowed us to specify which faith drove their activities and how homogeneous these motives were in a given organisation. Since we knew little about FBOs in European countries, results of these surveys yielded their precise characterisation.

Cross-evaluation

Cross-evaluation was used to assess the role and relations of FBOs at different levels (at the neighbourhood and city level) and their impact on poverty policies. 'Cross-evaluation' meant that an international team – consisting of the coordinator and of a changing group of other foreign experts from the research consortium – visited the cities in a given country and interviewed a selection of policy makers. The visit (four to five days) was prepared and organised by the national team. It also provided the informative basis for these interviews, which consisted of the traditional national report and the results of interviews with key informants (such as field workers) who had experienced the workings of FBOs in their daily work and life. The interviews were structured according to a series of items, information on which was needed to answer the research questions.

Data analysis

Paying attention to corroborating evidence from a number of respondents and at the point of theoretical saturation ensured an important degree of validity of the findings. A combination of tape recording and note taking accompanied the interviews. Annotated transcripts of interviews were coded and analysed and additional interviews and telephone calls with key respondents were conducted where necessary to garner further information and clarify existing data. Analysis sometimes involved an innovative systematic approach such as Qualitative Comparative Analysis (QCA). QCA uses Boolean methods of logical comparison to represent all cases as a combination of causal and outcome conditions and is well suited for comparing a middle sized number of cases. These combinations can be compared with each other and then logically simplified through a bottom-up process of paired comparison. Particular care was taken to differentiate between bottom-up and top-down products as the result of the method. In the end, however, this comparative dimension of the project was not exploited to the extent initially envisaged, although several transnational comparative reports were produced. The qualitative research was supplemented (and in parts tested) by quantitative survey results.

Organisation of work

All partners were involved in each of the work packages that comprised the project, with one or more selected as work package leaders. At least one member of the Consortium Management Group (CMG) was involved in each of the work packages. Work package leaders prepared templates for country reports in dialogue with all partners. All country reports were synthesised for the work package reports and the comparative analysis.

What are faith-based organisations?

After our engagement with the methods of the FACIT project, we now address some conceptual discussions that pervaded the project. While something of a neologism from the 1970s and notoriously difficult to define in relation the 'faith' element, FBOs are organisations that embody some form of religious belief in the mission statements of staff and volunteers. Many of the studies of FBOs have emerged in the US and, as a result of the politics of the White House Office of Faith-Based and Community Initiatives (see Beaumont, 2004, 2008a, 2008b), tend to reflect Christian beliefs. These studies show that FBOs are important within charitable activities and also within contracted-out public services such as caring for the infirm and elderly, advocating justice for the oppressed and playing a major role in humanitarian aid and international development efforts. Examples in the US include the Compassion Capital Fund, Mentoring Children of Prisoners and Access to Recovery, the latter focusing on increasing the availability of drug and alcohol treatment programmes. Critical questions over the role of proselytisation within these FBOs remain largely unanswered.[5]

Defining FBOs is therefore contentious, and as Clarke (2006) and Clarke and Jennings (2008) note in the frame of international development, FBOs are a complex set of actors that remain inadequately understood. There are differences between those more traditional, evangelistic and controlling FBOs, those more innovatively dedicated to reconciling virtue with difference and those acting as umbrella organisations for faith-motivated and secular people within a contested and differentiated postsecular context (see Chapter Three, this volume, for a detailed engagement with the concept of the postsecular). As a relatively unproblematic point about the inherent variety of FBOs that defies straightforward definition, these differences also suggest the need for typologies that are sufficiently sensitive to cater to this variety. It would appear, however, that there are almost as many typologies of FBOs as there are studies. We caution over the use of ideal-type categorisations (see Chapters Two and and Three, this volume).

We consider FBOs as providers of basic, emergency social services but also as the basis for political action, mobilisation and contestation. Recalling the FACIT project that defined FBOs as *any organisation that refers directly or indirectly to religion or religious values, and that function as a welfare provider and/or as a political actor*, while there are other possible definitions, our approach is sufficiently broad to contribute to contemporary research on FBOs and to help sharpen new definitions and understandings in the European context.

It is important to note that FBOs are not merely churches or other official religious institutions per se, but rather parastatal or para-religious associations that exist as independent legal entities, such as registered charities. Their roles typically relate to a combination or hybridity of approaches based on community development, social facilities and service provision on the one hand, and lobbying/ political participation activities on the other. Thus in the UK context there is a strong tendency for national-level FBOs to combine a particular functional purpose with a related lobbying activity. For example, Traidcraft promotes the consumption of fair trade goods in local communities but also lobbies government on trade justice issues; also Faithworks sponsors local service provision, such as schools and community centres, and sits on a governmental advisory group for tackling social exclusion in 'hard-to-reach' communities. There is also a wide range of FBOs at the local level across Europe responding to urban injustices in a multitude of ways.

Clearly, FBOs should not be regarded as homogeneous in their motivation or approach, and we should guard against any sweeping generalisations about their activities and impacts. For example, again in the UK context, the Varley Trust has established new urban schools along what would appear strict evangelical lines which have an impact on the curriculum, the moral expectations of students, codes of discipline and religious activity in the schools concerned. By contrast, Faithworks has similarly been active in the establishment of such schools, but claims to work in a more multicultural way that embraces diversity and difference in ethnicity and religion. In the homelessness sector, some FBOs restrict participation to those sharing a particular faith position, while others, including Nightshelter and the Julian Trust, welcome volunteers regardless of faith background or motivation (Cloke et al, 2005, 2010; see also Chapter Six, this volume).

It is vital to differentiate in this way and stress the inherent political and ideological variety of FBOs so that our research can avoid misrepresenting FBOs as legitimising certain neoliberal subjectivities (for example, of homeless people: see Del Casino Jr and Jocoy, 2008; cf Peck and Tickell, 2002), and as a consequence, circumventing themselves as a constitutive element of what Jamie Peck (2006) calls the 'new urban right' (see also Uitermark and Duyvendak, 2008, on urban revanchism in Rotterdam). Rather, the aim is to couch the rich diversity of FBOs in cities as simultaneously part and parcel of neoliberal urbanism *and* inherent sites of resistance, subversion and contestation (cf Ramsay, 1998; May et al, 2005; see also Chapter Eight, this volume). Chapter Six in this volume deals with faith-motivated volunteering and portrays FBOs as part of a landscape of care that prompts an alternative narrative of the 'charitable city' that needs to be placed alongside existing hypotheses about the 'revanchist' and 'post-welfare' city (see also Cloke et al, 2010).

Writing from an explicitly US perspective, Cnaan et al (1999) point to six categories of religious service organisations: (1) local congregations (or houses of worship); (2) inter-faith agencies and ecumenical coalitions; (3) citywide or region-wide sectarian agencies; (4) national projects and organisations under religious auspices; (5) para-denominational advocacy and relief organisations; and (6) religiously affiliated international organisations (see also Cnaan and Dilulio, 2002; Cnaan, 2006). While useful in drawing attention to diverse social functions, the typology does not say a great deal about the faith dimension of FBOs. Smith (2002) draws our attention to an alternative typology developed in the US (Working Group on Human Needs, Faith-Based and Community Initiatives, 2002) that advances six categories with explicit relation to the 'f-word': *faith-saturated, faith-centred, faith background, faith-related, faith–secular partnership* and *secular*. Our approach pays respect to these US typologies while following a new European orientation.

James (2009) offers us some useful pointers for thinking through characteristics of FBOs in the European scene (see also Beaumont et al, 2010). According to him, many FBOs of a Christian orientation tend to keep quiet about their faith identity, for fear of escalations of problems, prejudices and discriminatory attitudes, especially in relation to funding. Often FBOs wish to pragmatically distance themselves from the worst negativities of faith association. Part of the reason for this pragmatism stems from the wish to avoid any perception from others of 'arrogance' or 'self-righteousness' (in relation to 'doing good' for others), and just as importantly, to maintain levels of professionalism to access secular funding regimes, to hold staff and volunteers together and to support partners from multi-faith and no-faith backgrounds. On the whole, James finds that Muslim FBOs are more open about their faith identity as they tend to be younger, homogeneously staffed and less dependent on public – and therefore secular – funds, with differences between nations. His research indicates that faith identity can have profound organisational implications in terms of internal operation such as the leadership, relationships, culture and policies of the FBOs. Broad agreement over the meaning of faith identities among staff and volunteers for practices within the organisation are crucial.

Throughout the FACIT project we emphasised the need to avoid reductionist thinking when analysing FBOs. Simple binary oppositions such as progressive versus reactionary, evangelical versus 'no strings attached', do not help us grasp the realities of FBOs on the ground. FBOs are complex and diverse. Using *The poor side of the Netherlands* social movement as an example, Beaumont and Nicholls (2007) show that it was the progressive actions of dissenting Christians in key FBOs at the national level – and not the FBOs themselves – that were instrumental in mobilising support among a range of stakeholders and anti-poverty movement constituents during the peak moments of activisms in the 1980s and 1990s. The Christian Aid and Resources Foundation (CARF), also in the Netherlands, illustrates similar ambiguities inherent in FBOs.[6] The executive director has fought a high profile media campaign for the rights of African women brought to the Netherlands as sex slaves. Yet, as the Reverend of the House of Fellowship in the deprived Bijlmer (or Bijlmermeer) neighbourhood in Amsterdam South East, the same man vehemently opposes homosexuality on religious grounds, refusing to support gay men and lesbian women in the community.

Why context matters

Not only is it the case that FBOs themselves represent a heterogeneous mix of theology, organisational structure and practical aims, but the context in which FBOs are placed is also crucial. Context matters, both in terms of academic discourse and also the practicalities of FBO activities over space and time. In the popular imagination and sometimes even outside it is often assumed that FBOs are mostly related either to the Christian evangelical right in the US or the most extreme expressions of Islamic fundamentalism and 'radicalisation'. The Christian right, the Christian Coalition of America and the Moral Majority neatly fit these stereotypes given their role as lobby organisations for the Republican Party.

Conflating FBOs with these forms of cultural and political expression, however, would gloss over the range of more progressive FBOs at the local level in the US (for example, The Simple Way of new monastic 'ordinary radicals' in North Philadelphia; see Claiborne, 2006[7]). It would also ignore similar evangelical networks in other countries. Take the Evangelical Alliance in the Netherlands, for instance, a country usually considered a far cry from the US in religious and political terms. Clearly there is a great deal of variety over space and time, across and within different country contexts.

Temporal framing

Within the academic discourses of political theory there are traditions of thought in the US and the UK that shed light on differences between state–civil society relations. The discourses equally provide an historical, temporal and diachronic canvas for the analysis of contemporary FBOs in these countries (see also Chapter Twelve, this volume). The US pluralist approach to political democracy, importantly influenced by de Tocqueville's *Democracy in America* (de Tocqueville, 1945), refers to various works, claiming that democratic politics are sustained by a wider society where plural forms of representation and influence are institutionalised and maintained (Hirst, 1994). Less concerned with formal representative mechanisms of participation, this approach stresses the importance of numerous autonomous associations in civil society, including churches, religious institutions and FBOs, that mediate between the individual and the state (cf Chapter Seven, this volume). Aiming to ensure against the tyranny of majoritarian democracy – for the US pluralists, partly the outcome of Rousseau's social contract formulation (Rousseau, 1973) – these intermediary organisations disperse opinion and influence more or less equally throughout society given a relative egalitarian distribution of power. A polity is democratic when composed of many competing minority factions, none able to exert inordinate influence at any one time.

Developed formally in US political science since the 1940s (Truman, 1951; Parsons, 1969), the most important work was Dahl's *A preface to democratic theory* that constructed a theoretical model of the conditions a polity must satisfy to ensure 'polyarchy', the plural and successive influence of interest groups (Dahl, 1966; cf his famous 1961 *Who governs* work on New Haven, Connecticut in the US). Seymour Martin Lipset was another important influence, whose insights (see Lipset, 1960), taken together with Dahl's work, constitute a pluralist approach to political theory and power. Under these conditions FBOs would act as one of a number of organisations between the individual and the state, with government mediating between various interest groups.

Several important titles in recent years have been published at the Real Utopias Project at Verso that continue this line of thinking about politics and power, with implications for FBOs as progressive and emancipatory agents within a polyarchic governance arrangement characteristic of but not confined to the US. Tracing lines of inquiry at the interface between dreams of alternative futures and political practice, these include *Associations and democracy* (Wright, 1995), *Deepening Democracy* (Fung and Wright, 2003) and *Envisioning real utopias* (Wright, 2010; cf 2006). FBOs like other actors in civil society can contribute to progressive social change and not merely to more conservative forces of reaction.

The English tradition of political pluralism flourished in the early part of the 19th century, only to fade soon after, but has experienced a recent resurgence (see Hirst, 1994; see also the work of the political theologian David Nicholls, 1994). Rather than argue for the diffusion of power as an empirical fact – as with the US pluralists – this variant became more of a critique of state structure and the authority of the state. Challenging unlimited state sovereignty and the unitary, centralised and hierarchical structure of this conception of the state, English pluralists – like the legal historian F.W. Maitland, the Anglican clergyman and monk John Neville Figgis, and socialists G.D.H. Cole and Harold J. Laski – stress the importance of voluntary associations of people in civil society for democracy. As with the US pluralist tradition, it is relatively straightforward to imagine how FBOs as an example of such associations contribute to democratic governance on this view.

Following a somewhat normative template (interestingly, like the Real Utopias Project today) this strand of thinking urged the state to pluralise in order to complement and reflect the needs of these associations in a democratic polity. This pluralisation entails the necessity for devolution of authority and power to self-governing associations in civil society – such as FBOs and other religiously inspired actors – as perhaps the most appropriate way to represent the specificity and diversity of will and opinion within and across the populace. Institutions of traditional representative democracy are simply unable to deal with this diversity. These institutions should be replaced with a functional form of democracy based on industrial guilds and other networks of association, with the implication that FBOs could and perhaps should be key institutions of service delivery, political engagement and democratic governance.

The Church of England in the UK, to take a pertinent example for our study, has been influential in this way. The *Faith in urban regeneration* and *Faithful cities* reports in the UK revives academic and policy attention to the role of FBOs and faith communities more generally in urban policies (Farnell et al, 2003; Commission on Urban Life and Faith, 2006; cf Baker, 2007). It is now over 20 years since a similar report, *Faith in the city*, exposed the realities of many of the social ills afflicting UK inner cities – rooted primarily in structural unemployment, poverty and deprivation – and the role of churches and other faith-based actors in addressing those problems (Faith in the City, 1985). The report met with political controversy as it pointed the finger at neoliberal Thatcherite policies as leading to the decline of inner cities in the UK.

It is unclear what precisely has changed in terms of the policies and actions of FBOs on urban social problems since the mid-1980s in the UK, especially with growing attention to faith communities and the Big Society legislative programme of the Conservative-Liberal Democrat Coalition Agreement (see Chapters Two, Three and Eight, this volume). Timescales vary in different places, and it is vital to differentiate the longstanding presence of some faith actors prior to welfare state consolidation in the postwar period (see the Preface to this volume) and new faith groups from the 1980s onwards. Examples include The Salvation Army, initially established by the Methodist minister, William Booth, in Whitechapel in London's East End as the Christian Revival Society in 1865, then the Christian Mission and formalising as The Salvation Army along military rather than voluntary lines in 1878 (Booth, 1997, 2006; Winston, 2000; Walker, 2001). The Salvation Army combines charity with social services for the poor as part of the Christian church. The more recent intensification of processes of neoliberalisation, restructuring of welfare systems and transnational movements of people from diverse cultures under globalisation have dramatically altered the contexts in which FBOs situate and operate.

One should also bear in mind that various strands of Christianity are historically significant in cities as well, such as the largely Catholic liberation theology movement that views Jesus Christ as the redeemer but also the liberator of poor and oppressed people (see Rowland, 1999; Guttierrez, 2001; cf Freire, 1972), but also expressions of social Christianity and the doctrine of the Social Gospel. The historic significance is evident both in the longstanding local work of particular national organisations such as The Salvation Army, and in the sheer presence of key faith groups or churches who have been active in social ministry over many decades.

On the basis of our nuanced analysis of different types of FBOs in the previous section and the changing historical contexts within which FBOs operate, we suggest a four-point differentiation based on timelines: FBOs as charity re-entering into discourse of faith-motivated action on social problems, such as the Barnardo's organisation in the UK which lobbies on issues relating to children in poverty; longstanding FBOs like The Salvation Army that predate the welfare state; new forms of FBOs filling welfare gaps under neoliberalism, such as recently constituted anti-homelessness organisations like the St Petrocs Trust in the UK; and inter-faith and multi-faith activities as a vast arena in its own right, such as the Interfaith Alliance in the US and similar networks in other countries.

Spatial variety

The largely Anglo-American orientation of the preceding discussion on political theory clearly does not do justice to the range of governance contexts across Europe, with differential implications for FBOs (see Chapter Four, this volume). One way to capture a sense of spatial variety across Europe relies on a tradition of work on welfare regimes and also church–state relations across Europe (see Chapter Two, this volume). The following two chapters deal with the variety of governance and welfare contexts in more detail. It suffices now to provide some snapshots of this multiplicity.

Differences between nations in terms of 'welfare regime' (Esping-Andersen, 1990, 1996) and 'welfare mix' (Ascoli and Ranci, 2002) are crucial for determining the impacts of neoliberal restructuring and prospects and constraints for FBOs in specific contexts (see also Beaumont, 2008a, 2008b, 2008c). Despite notable exceptions (see, for example, Noordegraaf and Volz, 2004; see also Bäckström, 2005; Yeung, 2006a, 2006b; Bäckström and Davie, 2010, 2011), welfare regimes and mix discussions are relatively silent on church–state relations and the position of various religions and faiths in secularising welfare contexts (see also Madeley and Enyedi, 2003). Attention to these contextual dimensions enhances our understanding of the hypothesised formal/informal and political/spiritual interpenetrations between FBOs and the state in questions of social welfare provision.

The empirical analysis of the introduction of welfare provisions, such as pensions, health and unemployment insurance, shows both for the period around 1900 and 1962-89 that Catholic countries have not promoted welfare provision; instead workers have fought against the religious elite. Lutheran countries were 'welfare pioneers' and introduced state welfare provisions at an earlier time than reformist countries (see also de Swaan, 1988).

Manow's (2004) and van Kersbergen and Manow's (2009) modification of Esping-Andersen's typology of three welfare regimes is important. They argue that Esping-Andersen did not sufficiently differentiate the middle group, the conservative (European) regime. Countries in this category should be differentiated first by a Catholic–Protestant divide, and in addition Protestants into Lutheran and reformist. For Heidenheimer (1983), what we have amounts to a delayed westward spread of the welfare state. Applying these findings and the corresponding differentiation to our study, we assume non-state welfare provisions – hence, FBOs – to be most prominent in the UK, the Netherlands and Switzerland, and the least so in Germany and Sweden.

While in some welfare states FBOs are an important force in welfare issues and urban politics more generally, it is expected that this role is secondary to the state in other countries displaying a strong statist tradition in governance (Prochaska, 2006). In these countries, FBOs perform a cradling function as the 'underside' of traditional social democratic welfare provision (Beaumont and Dias, 2008). Processes of neoliberal globalisation, state restructuring and the impact on cities, however, are potentially revealing multiple, complex and differentiated spaces for FBOs to enter the fray of political and ethical action against injustices (see Chapter Two, this volume). Less statist welfare regimes, such as Italy and other southern European welfare countries (Ferrera, 1984, 1996), display historically significant local civil organisational presence, with specific reference to Catholic Church (caritas, Opus Dei) activities *in place* of the state (for example, Milan, Lombardy).

Taking Turkey as an example of a candidate, non-Christian and non-Western country with elements of corporatism (but less a welfare *state* as in other countries), the question of the functions of a welfare state, rights of labour unions and poverty policies remain unclear. The reality of an expanding Europe (Byrnes and Katzenstein, 2006) augments the topicality of the Turkish case. The ramifications for FBOs are therefore complex (see Chapter Ten, this volume). While the current government of Turkey, the Justice and Development party (AKP[8]), sometimes identifies itself as one operator of the welfare state, the regime is also estimated as a liberal-conservative one. While a decline in welfare provisions in cities has been a reality in Turkey, the role of civil society and especially FBOs are comparatively new issues in the country. The gaps emerging from some of the social functions of the state are being replaced by certain clear examples of local government populism. But it is unclear how civil society and some early emerging FBOs are filling these gaps in practice. Some current NGOs can probably be considered as FBOs that enjoy a degree of popularity, but their power and effectiveness in addressing poverty are still under debate.

Muslim FBOs play a role in combating poverty and exclusion in Turkey.[9] The Deniz Feneri (Lighthouse) Association was founded in 1996 via the Islamic-based television channel (Channel 7) through which people are selected and some aid is provided as a result of particularly hard and distressing images of poverty. The organisation provides fiscal and non-fiscal aid, household items, charcoal, education courses, accommodation and healthcare services. Deniz Feneri organises primarily in major cities, such as Istanbul and Ankara, but also has branches in Northern and Eastern Anatolia, cross-border projects in Europe and in some Muslim countries such as Indonesia. Their approach is 'help from everybody to everybody' and this philosophy is embedded in Islamic religious values.

The Cansuyu Association was founded in 2005 and while not as powerful or popular as Deniz Feneri, follows a similar way of operating through television. Some people claim that these organisations are organically connected with the political parties of AKP and Saadet Partisi (SP).[10] Cansuyu has branches in major cities and in some peripheral cities, as well as cross-border projects in Palestine. Religious references are more overt than in Deniz Feneri. Questions about clientelistic relations between the beneficiaries of Deniz Feneri and Cansuyu and the AKP and SP remain largely speculative and under-investigated.

Topicality of the volume

The collection of chapters offered here is highly topical at a time of heightened neoliberal globalisation and crisis, welfare state retrenchment and processes of desecularisation. It promises to have a direct impact on distinctly European postsecular controversies over immigration, integration and paranoia over perceived religious-based 'radicalisation'. We follow a multidisciplinary approach rooted explicitly in social science that neither reflects nor adopts a normative theological, religious or political perspective as we are committed to understanding new developments on the ground in an intellectually robust fashion.

Claims are increasingly made these days within academic, political and media circles about the possibilities of religions and faiths in general and FBOs in particular for tackling social issues in an era of intensified neoliberal globalisation (Molendijk et al, 2010; Beaumont and Baker, 2011; Cloke and Beaumont, 2011). Around the same time as the appearance of Charles Taylor's (2007) magnum opus, *A secular age*, the online journal *Eurozine* published a series of articles, including contributions by Jürgen Habermas, José Casanova and Danièle Hervieu-Léger, on the rather contested notions of postsecularism and postsecular society,[11] while *The Economist* published a special report devoted to religion and public life across the globe (Habermas, 2002, 2006; McLennan, 2007). Combined with recent governments in the US and the UK revalorising FBOs in matters of social policy, urban regeneration and social cohesion in state-regulated urban policies (the Big Society initiative in the UK is relevant here: see Chapters Three and also Eight, this volume), the European public sphere is dense with unresolved questions about the ways religion and faiths are imbricated in the social and political concerns of the day.

Discussions on the role of religion in an expanding Europe (Byrnes and Katzenstein, 2006) and the alleged distinction between the religious US and secular Europe (Berger et al, 2008) stand to gain from detailed empirical investigations on FBOs in European cities that stress the two-way reconfiguration of relations between state, market and civil society. While research on FBOs, welfare and social services in the US is voluminous, particularly that relating to (urban) congregations and affiliated groups more generally in the frame of the Olavsky-inspired compassionate conservatism and charitable choice (Beaumont, 2004, 2008a, 2008b, 2008c), and a growing body of work on these issues across European countries, in which the contexts of governance, welfare and religious culture vary significantly (see Bäckström, 2005; Yeung, 2006a, 2006b; Bäckström and Davie, 2010, 2011),[12] our volume focuses specifically on FBOs and exclusion in the European urban context.[13] These are times where debates in the UK and the US on the revalorising of FBOs in matters of poverty reduction, welfare/social/care services and urban regeneration have taken hold. We critically confront recent pronouncements, like that of President Barack Obama, who stated '[t]he fact is, the challenges we face today – from saving our planet to ending poverty – are simply too big for government to solve alone. We need all hands on deck.'[14] We foresee an increasing emphasis on FBOs in the provision of social services in the European context, and therefore our volume sits at the vanguard of academic, policy and political attention to this important, highly contentious and relatively under-explored arena.[15]

The dominance of women in terms of faith-based volunteering and welfare services in Europe – combined with their relative absence in more technical and organisational roles, and in the higher levels of decision making – provide a vital link to questions of the gendered nature of care (see Chapter Four, this volume; see also Bäckström and Davie, 2010, 2011; Edgardh, 2011). The project started from the assumption that concepts such as 'cultural identities' and 'values', with the gender dimension a prime issue of concern, were best understood in practice. The project therefore examined in detail who offered what in terms of services, and for what reasons, as indicative of values in any given context across Europe.

Alongside the WREP and WaVE projects, our volume continues a parallel line of enquiry on the social and political value of FBOs in cities under alleged conditions of postsecular society. *Exploring the postsecular: The religious, the political and the urban* (Molendijk et al, 2010) represents one of the first attempts to address the re-emergence of the religious in the secular domains of cities. Based on a conference that took place in Groningen, in November 2008, this innovative coming-together of geographers, urbanists, sociologists, philosophers and theologians asked what we might mean by the postsecular and assumed the alleged shifts from the secular to the postsecular were most visible in the spheres of urban space, governance and civil society. The various contributions conversed across discussions of public religion, deprivatisation of religion and theorisations of multiple modernities. The actions of FBOs in cities are an important but secondary focus of the volume, which in the first instance aims for theoretical engagement across disciplines rather than detailed and critical empirical enquiry. Notable exceptions include chapters by Luke Bretherton, Paul Cloke, and Candice Dias and Justin Beaumont.

Hot on the heels of this initial inquiry, *Postsecular cities: Space, theory and practice* (Beaumont and Baker, 2011) attempts to deepen the idea of *rapprochement* (Cloke, 2010; see also Chapter Three, this volume) to trigger critical dialogue between human geography, theology and sociology to address the multiplicities that constitute contemporary urban life. The contributions address what we mean by postsecular cities and the editors call for new theorisations of the urban that place religion, the role of FBOs and the value of spiritual capital centre stage. The collection presents a wide range of contributions that vary in their degree of theoretical, philosophical and empirical emphasis, but welded in their appeal to cross-over thinking and new approaches. One of the areas identified for further inquiry concerns '[t]he role of religion in social justice narratives … [in general and] … more specifically in the quest for the right to the city and the just city' (Baker and Beaumont, 2011, p 264).

Processes of neoliberal globalisation raise further issues about poverty and injustice and the links between faiths, FBOs and political action. The relations between neoliberalism and radical protest movements involving FBOs and other actors in cities are relevant in this regard. FBOs can be placed in the context of justice movements and social movements more generally. Studies by Beaumont and Nicholls (Beaumont and Nicholls, 2007; Nicholls and Beaumont, 2004a, 2004b) reveal that FBOs sometimes enter the fray as active partners in progressive and in some instances neo-Alinsky style multiorganisational social justice coalitions (Warren, 2001; Chambers, 2003; Bretherton, 2010; see Chapter Three, this volume)[16] and other approaches inspired by liberation theology. This body of work stands to gain from deeper insights into the factors that determine as well as limit FBO involvement in social justice coalitions (see Chapters Three and Eight, this volume). Research can equally contribute to a better understanding of how intentional and incarnational communities, based on neoanarchist ethical and political commitments (see Chapters Five and Eleven, this volume), can help augment progressive social change.[17] The Het Jeanette Noëlhuis/ Amsterdam Catholic Worker intentional community in Amsterdam South East, the Netherlands, is an example of the nexus of neoanarchism, pacifism and social justice in practice.

Swept-up Lives? Re-envisioning the homeless city (Cloke et al, 2010) challenges conventional accounts of urban revanchism and the purification of public space in the UK, indicating instead the role of FBOs among others in resisting and reworking neoliberal regulation of homeless people through the development of spaces of *caritas* and *agape* in the city. Through detailed ethnographies and institutional analyses, the authors reveal the rich geographies of homelessness, the governance of neoliberal voluntarism and spaces of caring and active citizenship in the UK. Their research points to the direct experience of individuals reacting to desperately impoverished 'others' in cities, with spiritual sensitivity at the root of our humanity, as part of hope and desire for social equality and justice. While many FBOs are active agents in emergency services for homeless people in the UK, the book does not interrogate the 'f-word' in FBO directly.

Emerging from this work one might ask about the ways faith-based involvement is relevant in how spaces of care are performatively brought into being, through micro-examples of particular services (for example, work on homeless shelters) (see Chapter Nine, this volume). In turn one can address how people relationally practice faith and thereby (re)produce affects and material outcomes of care as new areas of inquiry. Similarly, we can ask about faith-based responses to social exclusion in the city that provide a pathway for people of faith to demonstrate their faith in practice (for example, by volunteering, or working full time in what is often a low-paid and insecure form of employment), thereby expressing a form of citizenship that is more ethical than political (Chapters Five and Six, this volume).

One way of assessing FBO activity is to assume an insider/outsider binary opposition among voluntary organisations of the 'shadow state' (Wolch, 1990; Lipsky and Smith, 1993; Salamon and Anheier, 1996) with implications for FBOs (see Chapter Six, this volume). Central in this kind of analysis lies a distinction between insider and outsider organisations, with the former financed in line with government policies and the latter often running on a shoestring, rooted in basic human concern and external to (but often an example for) government policy. This distinction can be illustrated, for example, in the work by May et al (2005) on homelessness in the UK city of Bristol, in which FBOs providing night shelters, soup runs and drop-in centres fall outside of the para-state system of funding because they are deemed to provide services that keep homeless people on the streets. Other such FBOs, whose role is provision of long-term accommodation or rehabilitation, have attained insider status as they are eligible for government funding and the associated legitimacy in connection with the task of keeping homeless people off the streets. Clearly, however, this insider/outsider distinction is only one aspect of the more complex positioning of FBOs in networks of governance and politics – a complexity demonstrated in *Swept-up Lives?* with respect to FBOs and homelessness, and in Williams' chapter (Chapter Eight, this volume) in the context of workfare policy.

FBOs might in certain instances actually deepen social exclusion of their own membership (see Chapter Seven, this volume), or are at least accused in the public debate or by local authorities of doing so. The assumption is that FBOs might only serve fellow members of their faith or belief system (for a contrasting view, see Chapters Three, Five, Six and Twelve, this volume). Pertinent examples include, again, the contested policies towards charity soup runs for street sleepers in London in the UK as well as the general suspicion and distrust felt towards the social and political role of mosques in various European urban contexts these days. The debate on the role of Afro-Christian churches in addressing the needs of their members in the Netherlands and elsewhere is another area of contention.

Predating these recent books and edited volumes by a couple of years are two collections of articles within journals that brought together a range of scholarship on FBOs in relation to urban social issues and human geography. The special issue 'Faith-based organisations and urban social issues' in *Urban Studies* (see Beaumont, 2008a, 2008c) called for new perspectives on the city that derive inspiration from Christian anarchist thought in the vein of Kiekegaard, Thoreau, Tolstoy and the radical theosophy of Nikolai Berdyaev. Chapters Three, Five and Six, as well as Chapters Eight and Eleven, this volume, provide crucial pointers for a new line of research waiting to be done in this fascinating and under-explored area.

The dossier 'FBOs and human geography' at the Tijdschrift voor Economische en Sociale Geografie (TESG) (Beaumont, 2008a; cf Beaumont and Dias, 2008) identified three areas for further research. First, deeper theorisation of faiths and FBOs from an urban geographical perspective – a 'geo-political-economy' perspective on FBOs would be an important advance, particularly how various organisations are implicated in government-valorised social policies and also within progressive multiagency alliances. Second, more philosophically inspired and theoretical work can deal with religion, politics and implications for cities with a postsecular society. Finally, there is a need to deepen international comparative analyses on FBOs in cities. Much is known about FBOs in the US and also countries of the Global South,[18] but far less across the European continent. This current volume makes an attempt to advance the debates on these thematics, while contributing to new areas for internationally relevant research in the years to come.

The contributions

The volume is structured into two thematically driven parts – Defining relations of faith-based organisations and Sectoral studies – with a strategic Introduction and Conclusion by the editors.

Following this Introduction, Part I begins with Chapter Two, where José Luis Romanillos, Justin Beaumont and Mustafa Şen investigate how state–religion relations and the diversity of welfare regimes in Europe shape the social and political engagement of FBOs in social issues in European countries. This chapter provides an introduction to the key terms, concepts and debates useful for the conceptualisation of the political and ethical engagements of FBO activity. In particular, the chapter explores how the multiplicity of FBO activities signal a broader set of (re)configurations of state–religion relations across different European contexts. As the chapter demonstrates, within a predominantly secular Europe, these activities raise a series of questions over the meaning of secularism, welfare, the public realm and citizenship, as well as the kinds of rationality mobilised by traditional social scientific accounts of social exclusion.

In Chapter Three, Agatha Herman, Justin Beaumont, Paul Cloke and Andrés Walliser address directly the concept of the postsecular, with reference to emergent spaces of postsecular praxis, where faith-based and secular interests collaborate in particular, and differentiated forms of *rapprochement* to embody and enact transformational forms of social justice. The authors engage with the contemporary literature on the postsecular city. They adopt a notion of *postsecular ethics*, a highly contextual concept enacted through a dialogue, which ensures a performed virtue ethics based on recognition of an intersubjective community. The authors argue that despite different national framings of FBO engagements in urban spaces, FBOs are not simply puppets of neoliberalism. These issues are addressed with reference to the empirical examples of London Citizens in the UK, as well as Exodus Amsterdam and CARF in the Netherlands. The case material helps position FBO engagements at the nexus of post-political neoliberalism and spaces and ethics of postsecular engagements in cities. The empirical cases weave through the chapter's exploration of the political and ethical promise of FBOs in urban spaces, through their creation of collaborative and connected communities.

In Chapter Four, Ingemar Elander, Maarten Davelaar and Andrés Walliser take issue with the relations between FBOs, urban governance and welfare state retrenchment in various contexts across Europe. Their chapter provides an analysis of FBOs and their relationship to central–local government and related changes in welfare provision aimed at combating social exclusion in the Netherlands, Spain and Sweden. The central questions addressed are: why are FBOs of interest in times when financial and economic crises trigger governments at all levels to reconsider their responsibilities as providers and protectors of social welfare? How do FBOs in different welfare regimes operate at the local level in the context of welfare retrenchment and/or redesign? What are their (faith-motivated) interests and strategies? Are FBOs a substitute or a complement as welfare providers, that is, are they in a process of replacing public authorities as welfare providers, or are they, at best, capable and willing to give complementary support at the margin? The chapter ends on a speculative note on the likely current and future role of FBOs in cities under conditions of global economic crisis.

In Chapter Five, Paul Cloke, Samuel Thomas and Andrew Williams explore the changing theological landscape of Christian faith motivation with reference to the UK. The questions they pose, are, first, how do we explain the increasing capacity of governance within society to embrace, or at least to tolerate, the involvement of faith groups in issues of justice, welfare and care? Second, what factors help explain the increasing propensity for some faith groups to become involved in this way? The authors pay particular attention to this second question through the specific lens of Christian faith motivation and involvement in action for social justice in the UK. They argue that there is a significant move from faith simply as personal belief to faith-as-practice, a change influenced by a variety of theological perspectives such as evangelicalism, radical orthodoxy and postmodern theology. They show that rather than emphasise stereotypical notions of extremism or fundamentalism, 'radicalisation' refers as much if not more to ordinary faith-motivated people who have become determined to act on social issues.

Chapter Six by Paul Cloke, Sarah Johnsen and Jon May draws on evidence from interviews with faith-motivated volunteers to question the precise role that faith plays in their participation in providing services for homeless people and the performance of care therein. Following a qualitative and participatory methodology, the authors argue that religious groups are important social networks within which the validity of faith-motivated works can be taught and reinforced, and the gap between rhetoric of caring for others and practical action may be bridged. Interconnections between such religious networks and FBOs can be very significant at the local level, and in turn, local FBOs often form an available device through which theo-ethical impulses to volunteer can be satisfied. Often their activities represent a way of living out their faith in obedient service rather than opportunities for out-and-out conversion of others to faith. In this way, the authors argue that faith can inspire a form of ethical citizenship that goes beyond conventional explanations of identity building and moral selving. These performances provide evidence for significant postsecular rapprochement at the ground level in European cities.

Part II begins in Chapter Seven by Danielle Dierckx, Jan Vranken and Ingemar Elander, who deal with how FBOs participate – and therefore ostensibly influence and change – poverty policies with specific reference to the Belgian and Swedish cases. The authors argue that promoting participation in decision making has entered the agenda as a cure against many problems/shortcomings of the polity in modern societies. Shortcomings in those participatory processes, however, have been identified. It concerns more general ones such as the relation between decision making outside and within the structure resulting from the formal electoral system. More specifically, the middle-class bias of decision-making processes remains a problem, resulting in the (in)voluntary exclusion of groups such as single mothers/parents, minority ethnic groups and the less educated in general. The introduction of the faith dimension further complicates the picture. On the one hand, if FBOs are close to the population (especially excluded groups), then they can improve their chances of participation. On the other hand, particular value systems lead to the exclusion of certain groups from participating in FBOs and strong intra-group cohesion excludes others in society at large.

In Chapter Eight, Andrew Williams critically examines welfare-to-work 'ethics' in the UK in the context of the current policy regime of the Big Society and the ways that FBOs challenge those ethics towards more progressive conceptions of social justice. From a broadly defined governmentality perspective, he shows how, in certain instances, FBOs work in and with government policy in order to simultaneously subvert those regimes to tackle social justices in European cities. Through the case study of Pathways Ltd in South London, the author reveals that the ethical agency of staff bringing alternative rationalities and technologies into workfare programmes can, in certain instances, carve out a space for resistance against neoliberal formulations of welfare-to-work by simultaneously working inside and outside government logics.

In Chapter Nine, Maarten Davelaar and Wendy Kerstens explore the various ways that FBOs provide relief services for homeless people. Against the discursive background of post-revanchist theorising about emergency services and care for homeless people, the authors assess the importance of third sector involvement, and especially that of FBOs, with respect to service provision for the homeless across countries from the FACIT project. The data presented considers the role of FBOs in organising help for the homeless; the authors take a look at their characteristics and the services they provide. This analysis is followed by an in-depth discussion of the strategies that FBOs use to guarantee access to different types of services. Across this canvas the authors argue that FBOs have become significant actors in the care of homeless people, and that as well as being cost-effective, they also provide accessible and often trusted services that contribute more generally to the development of the charitable city.

In Chapter Ten, Jürgen Friedrichs, Jennifer Klöckner, Mustafa Şen and Nynke de Witte compare Turkish Islamic organisations in Germany, the Netherlands and Turkey. Five million migrants from Turkey live in European countries and their number is increasing. Among them, Turkish people are the largest immigrant group in both Germany and the Netherlands. However, both countries differ markedly in their integration strategies. This chapter assesses these strategies and their social and political implications. While in Germany the main issue for Islam organisations is to get legally accepted as a religion, in the Netherlands Diyanet and Millî Görüş are both part of the Contact Body for Muslims and Government; within the Dutch Millî Gorüs movement there has been internal strife between more conservative and liberal leaders about the future of policy. The authors specifically study the links and influence between European Millî Görüş and Diyanet, and furthermore the relationship of Millî Görüş with the Justice and Development Party in Turkey. A major question underlying their analyses is whether migrant problems are transformed into religious problems and the problem of institutionalisation of Islam in Europe. The authors derive several policy implications.

In Chapter Eleven, Samuel Thomas presents findings from his research on Christian convictional communities in socioeconomically deprived areas in the UK. While most FBOs establish an organisational presence among the socially marginalised, there has been a recent move towards a more incarnational personal presence among such people. Thomas shows that this faith-motivated praxis involves choosing to live in among the excluded, serving as a close neighbour rather than as a volunteer, or worker, who vocationally breezes in and out of these areas. Drawing on three short case studies Thomas examines how Christians in the UK have responded differently to certain discourses, including: incarnation, community and mission. The motivational distinctiveness of these discourses helps draw out comparisons with their non-faith-based NGO counterparts. With reference to a more in-depth case study, the chapter highlights how these discourses are variously translated into action, embedded into a local geographic context, and in turn enmeshed into emergent ethical spaces.

Finally, in Chapter Twelve, Paul Cloke and Justin Beaumont conclude with a summary of the central thematics of state/society/religion relations addressed by the volume in its entirety. The authors allude to the 'FBO phenomenon' as something that evokes a series of dilemmas and difficulties, but also a fascinating and hitherto under-explored area of research in Europe. They provide eight propositions that emerge from the summary of these findings.

It would appear that we have come a long way from Padre Camelo, the 'Mazzarino Friars' and their violent misdemeanours that opened the chapter. As Sir Herbert Read noted in his foreword to *The rebel*: '... rebellion cannot exist without a strange form of love' (Camus, 1971, p 10). Our fascination in the *spirit of the FBO phenomenon* presented in this volume is something that infuses to a greater or lesser extent all the contributions. It is our hope that the book will shape new, innovative and exciting research on FBOs across nations and urban contexts in the years to come.

Notes

[1] Countless other high profile and politically damaging images of this interpenetration of religion, politics and the misuse of power exist. Perhaps the most worrying in the public consciousness concerns child sexual abuse in the US but also elsewhere in the world. The highly acclaimed documentary film *Deliver us from evil* (2006) addresses the true story of Catholic priest Oliver O'Grady, who molested and raped around 25 children in Northern California between the late 1970s and early 1990s. The film reveals the reluctance on the part of the Catholic hierarchy at various scales to deal publicly with the atrocities and also the subsequent cover-up by then Archbishop Roger Mahony, among others.

[2] We are fully aware that not all FBOs are progressive and that a great many could easily be labelled conservative or reactionary with regards to their social and political orientations. These issues are discussed in more detail in the following section.

[3] The 2011 Norway attacks were two terrorist attacks against the government (within Regjeringskvartalet, the executive government quarter of Oslo) and the civilian population at a summer camp (on the island of Utøya in Tyrifjorden, Buskerud, organised by AUF, the youth division of the ruling Norwegian Labour Party [AP]) on 22 July 2011. The 32-year-old Norwegian Christian fundamentalist, Islamophobe and right-wing extremist, Anders Behring Breivik, was arrested and subsequently charged for both attacks. One public opinion survey displays that every fourth inhabitant in Norway personally knows someone (relative, friend) who was hit by the attacks (*Dagens Nyheter* [*Swedish Daily*], 2011, p 7) (email correspondence with Ingemar Elander, 24 August 2011).

[4] The 2011 England riots refer to the widespread rioting, looting and arson that took place in parts of England during 6-10 August 2011. Following a peaceful march protesting against the fatal shooting of Mark Duggan by Metropolitan Police Service firearms officers on 4 August 2011, troubles started in Tottenham, North London, with unrest spreading across several parts of the city and also to other urban areas of England. Reasons for the rebellion were manifold and complex, including: (1) poverty, social exclusion and an enduring underclass; (2) opportunistic criminality; and (3) individualism, consumerism and social irresponsibility, combined with an alleged lack of compassion for others and strangers.

[5] *Proselytisation* refers to the process whereby individuals, groups and institutions make attempts, covertly as well as overtly, to convert people to another worldview and in particular an alternative religion or belief system in exchange for services rendered. Debates are emerging over what could be termed post-evangelicism where 'few strings' or 'no strings' services and support are increasingly the norm (see Chapters Six and Twelve, this volume).

[6] CARF is an Amsterdam-based organisation founded around 1990 dedicated to the rescue and rehabilitation of victims of the sex 'slave trade'. The organisation 'helps women, mostly from Africa, who are brought to the Netherlands by a syndicate of women traffickers to work against their will in the prostitution industry (interview with Executive Director, 30 July 2009). See also Chapter Three, this volume.

[7] The Simple Way is an example of an intentional Christian community of people who, having been highly motivated by their faith, have begun to seek out non-violent and counter-cultural responses to the plight of socially excluded people. High profile actions, such as taking over a cathedral to provide shelter for homeless people, and visiting Iraq to stand alongside local people when the bombs fell, are coupled with myriad lower profile actions that perform the biblical injunction to 'love thy neighbour'.

[8] The Justice and Development Party is the mainstream new right party coming from an Islamic tradition. It identifies itself as 'conservative democrat' and has been in power since 2002.

[9] In *The Economist*, 1 November 2007, 'Faith and politics: The new wars of religion' (www.economist.com/opinion/displaystory.cfm?story_id=10063829), the article 'Back to the Ottomans: why Turkey matters so much to Islam' showed how Turkey matters to important debates on religion and public life, and discusses: (1) the compatibility of Islam with modernity; (2) the universal issue of drawing the line between religion and the modern state; and (3) balances and tensions between secularism, modernity and Islam.

[10] Saadet Partisi (SP) is the Islamic tradition where the current government, AKP, comes from. While defending traditional rules and Islamic identity, SP sets itself more strictly than AKP. In 2002 elections, SP could not participate in the parliament but is still a powerful rival of AKP and is an efficient political actor of religious conservatism in Turkey.

[11] The articles address postsecular tendencies and religion in the new Europe, asking about public and private realms of religion, European Islam and European identities and solidarities in the context of transnational migration and religious diversity (see www.eurozine.com/articles/2007-10-19-leggewie-en.html).

[12] These publications reflect the findings of two EU projects: (1) 'Welfare and religion in a European perspective' (WREP) (2003-06), which analysed the role of majority churches as actors within the social economy from a European perspective, and 'Welfare and values

in Europe' (WaVE) (2006-09), on religious, minority and gender-related values that have an impact on social change in European society. Both projects were coordinated at Uppsala University in Sweden.

[13] The WREP project drew on empirical studies in eight medium-sized towns in Sweden, Norway, Finland, Germany, England, France, Italy and Greece, and addressed a number of questions on the relationship between religion and welfare. There are, indeed, parallels to the FACIT project, although there are also differences. For example, the conceptual framework of WREP leant more towards a sociology of religion and general welfare theory, the FACIT framework is rather more about urbanism. Another difference is that WREP had a particular focus on majority churches, when FACIT also examines the role of religious minorities, in particular Muslim immigrant congregations. On the other hand, FACIT lacks the explicit gender perspective penetrated in the WREP study (Edgardh, 2011).

[14] See http://my.barackobama.com/page/community/post/amandascott/gG5xY3

[15] The ESRC/Arts and Humanities Research Council (AHRC) Religion and Society programme has funded closely related projects. Relevant examples include Sarah Johnsen's work on the difference that faith makes, particularly non-Christian faith, in the provision of services for homeless people in the UK (see Johnsen, 2009), Betsy Olson's research on marginalised spiritualities and Gill Valentine and Kevin Ward's forays into sexuality and global faith networks (see www.religionandsociety.org.uk).

[16] Saul Alinsky was a US community organiser and writer, generally regarded as the founder of modern community organising on the non-socialist left (see Alinsky, 1989). His approach emphasised organising the poor for social action in deprived communities across North America. People from diverse class, racial, ethnic, cultural and religious identities would be brought together in broad-based alliances to build mass power.

[17] Intentional communities are purposively orchestrated residential communities based on a high level of teamwork and mutual interaction and support. In the context of FBOs, usually members of these communities share a common social, political, religious and/or spiritual vision, rooted in an alternative lifestyle that shares responsibilities and resources among marginalised people. While examples include cohousing communities, ecovillages and housing cooperatives, *incarnational communities* are those where the Christian notion of 'incarnation' – the descent of a god, or divine being in human form on Earth – manifests as faith-in-praxis over faith-in-dogma through ethically dwelling in spaces of need.

[18] Another article in *The Economist* special report, 'Bridging the divide', shows how India, the birthplace of Buddhism, Jainism, Sikhism and Hinduism, continues to struggle with religious politics: (1) externally with Pakistan; (2) internally with a Hindu majority and sizeable Muslim minority; and (3) fierce debates about religion in the public sphere, religious movements within Hinduism and differences between Vedanta (closer to

Congress) and Hindutva (closer to the Bharatiya Janata Party) strains, as well as their differences towards voluntarism and welfare.

References

Alinksy, S. (1989) *Rules for radicals: A pragmatic primer for realistic radicals*, New York: Vintage Books.

Ascoli, U. and Ranci, C. (eds) (2002) *Dilemmas of the welfare mix: The structure of welfare in an era of privatization* (Nonprofit and Civil Society Studies), New York: Kluwer Academic/Plenum Publishers.

Ashencaen Crabtree, S., Husain, F. and Spalek, B. (2008) *Islam and social work: Debating values, transforming practice*, Bristol: The Policy Press.

Bäckström, A. (ed) (2005) *Welfare and religion: A publication to mark the fifth anniversary of the Uppsala Institute for Diaconal and Social Studies*, Diakonivetenskapliga instiutets skriftserie, nr 10, Uppsala: Slut.

Bäckström, A. and Davie, G. (with N. Edgardh and P. Pettersson) (eds) (2010) *Welfare and religion in 21st century Europe, Volume 1: Configuring the connections*, Farnham: Ashgate.

Bäckström, A., Davie, G., Edgardh, N. and Pettersson, P. (eds) (2011) *Welfare and Religion in 21st Century Europe, Volume 2: gendered, religious and social change*, Farnham: Ashgate.

Baker, C. (2007) *Hybrid church in the city*, Farnham: Ashgate.

Baker, C. and Beaumont, J. (2011) 'Afterword: postsecular cities', in J. Beaumont and C. Baker (eds) *Postsecular cities: Space, theory and practice*, London: Continuum, pp 254-66.

Beaumont, J.R. (2004) 'Workfare, associationism and the "underclass" in the United States: contrasting faith-based action on urban poverty in a liberal welfare regime', in H. Noordegraaf and R. Volz (eds) *European churches confronting poverty: Social action against social exclusion*, Bochum: SWI Verlag, pp 249-78.

Beaumont, J.R. (2008a) 'Dossier: faith-based organizations and human geography', *Tijdschrift voor Economishe en Sociale Geografie*, vol 99, no 4, pp 377-81.

Beaumont, J.R. (2008b) 'Faith action on urban social issues', *Urban Studies*, vol 45, no 10, pp 2019-34.

Beaumont, J.R. (2008c) 'Introduction: faith-based organizations and urban social issues', *Urban Studies*, vol 45, no 1, pp 2011-17.

Beaumont, J.R. and Baker, C. (eds) (2010) *Postsecular cities: Space, theory and practice*, London: Continuum.

Beaumont, J.R. and Dias, C. (2008) 'Faith-based organizations and urban social justice in the Netherlands', *Tijdschrift voor Economishe en Sociale Geografie*, vol 99, no 4, pp 382-92.

Beaumont, J.R. and Nicholls, W.J. (2007) 'Between relationality and territoriality: investigating the geographies of justice movements in the Netherlands and the United States', *Environment and Planning A*, vol 39, no 11, pp 2554-74.

Beaumont, J.R., Carta, G., Cloke, P., Davelaar, M., van den Toorn, J., Thomas, S. and Williams, A. (2010) *Transnational comparison of the religious dimension*, Internal Working Paper for the EU 7FP FACIT project: 'Faith-based organisations and exclusion in European cities', November.

Berger, P., Davie, G. and Fokas, E. (2008) *Religious America, secular Europe? A theme and variations*, Farnham: Ashgate.

Booth, W. (1997) *In darkest England and the way out*, Glenridge, NJ: Patterson Smith.

Booth, W. (2006) *Purity of heart*, Liskeard: Diggory Press.

Bretherton, L. (2010) 'Religion and the salvation of urban politics: beyond cooption, competition and commodification', in A.L. Molendijk, J. Beaumont and C. Jedan (eds) *Exploring the postsecular: The religious, the political and the urban*, Boston, MA/Leiden: Brill, pp 207-21.

Byrnes, T.A. and Katzenstein, P.J. (eds) (2006) *Religion in an expanding Europe*, Cambridge: Cambridge University Press.

Camus, A. (1971) *The Rebel* (translated by Anthony Bower, foreword by Sir Herbert Read), London: Penguin, in association with Hamish Hamilton.

Chambers, E.T. (2003) *Roots for radicals: Organizing for power, action, and justice*, New York, NY: Continuum International Publishing Group.

Claiborne, S. (2006) *Irresistible revolution: Living as an ordinary radical*, Grand Rapids, MI: Zondervan.

Clarke, G. (2006) 'Faith matters: faith-based organizations, civil society and international development', *Journal of International Development*, No 18, pp 835–48.

Clarke, G. and Jennings, M. (2008) *Development, civil society and faith-based organizations*, Basingstoke: Palgrave Macmillan.

Cloke, P. (2010) 'Theo-ethics and radical faith-based praxis in the postsecular city', in A.L. Molendijk, J. Beaumont and C. Jedan (eds) *Exploring the postsecular: The religious, the political and the urban*, Boston, MA/Leiden: Brill, pp 223-41.

Cloke, P. and Beaumont, J. (2012) 'Geographies of postsecular rapprochement in the city', *Progress in Human Geography*, see http://phg.sagepub.com/content/early/2012/04/18/0309132512440208.abstract

Cloke, P., Johnsen, S. and May, J. (2005) 'Exploring ethos? Discourses of charity in the provision of emergency services for homeless people', *Environment and Planning A*, vol 37, pp 385-402.

Cloke, P., May, J. and Johnsen, S. (2010) *Swept-up Lives? Re-envisioning the homeless city*, Oxford: Wiley-Blackwell.

Cnaan, R.A. (2006) *The other Philadelphia story: How local congregations support quality of life in urban America*, Philadelphia, PA: Penn Press.

Cnaan, R.A. and Dilulio, J. (2002) *The invisible caring hand: American congregations and the provision of welfare*, New York, NY: NYU Press.

Cnaan, R.A., Wineburg, R.J. and Boddie, S.C. (1999) *A newer deal: Social work and religion in partnership*, New York, NY: Columbia University Press.

Commission on Urban Life and Faith (2006) *Faithful cities: A call for celebration, vision and justice*, Peterborough: Methodist Publishing House.

Dagens Nyheter [*Swedish Daily*] (2011) '*Norge samlades för att minnas och samla kraft*' ['Norway got together to remember and gather strength'], 22 August.

Dahl, R. (1961) *Who governs: Democracy and power in an American city*, New Haven, CT: Yale University Press.

Dahl, R. (1966) *A preface to democratic theory*, New Haven CT: Yale University Press.

de Swaan, A. (1998) *In care of the state: Health care, education and welfare in Europe and the USA in the modern era*, Cambridge: Polity Press.

Del Casino, Jr, V.J. and Jocoy, C.L. (2008) 'Neoliberal subjectivities, the "new" homelessness, and struggles over spaces of/in the city', *Antipode*, vol 40, no 2, pp 192-9.

de Tocqueville, A. (1945) *Democracy in America*, 2 vols, New York: Vintage.

Dinham, A., Furbey, R. and Lowndes, V. (eds) (2009) *Faith in the public realm: Controversies, policies and practices*, Bristol: The Policy Press.

Edgardh, N. (2011) 'A gendered perspective on welfare and religion in Europe', in A. Bäckström and G. Davie (with N. Edgardh and P. Pettersson) (eds) *Welfare and religion in 21st century Europe, Volume 2: Gendered, religious and social change*, Farnham: Ashgate, pp 61-106.

Esping-Andersen, G. (1990) *The three worlds of welfare capitalism*, Cambridge: Polity Press.

Esping-Andersen, G. (ed) (1996) *Welfare states in transition: National adaptations in global economies*, London: Sage Publications.

Faith in the City (1985) *Faith in the city: A call for action by church and nation*, Report of the Archbishop of Canterbury's Commission on Urban Priority Areas, London: Church House Publishing.

Farnell, R., Furbey, R., Shams Al-Haqq Hills, S., Macey, M. and G. Smith (2003) *Faith in urban regeneration: Engaging faith communities in urban regeneration*, Bristol: The Policy Press.

Ferrera, M. (1984) *Il welfare state in Italia: Sviluppe e crisi in prospettuia comparata*, Bologna: Il Mulino.

Ferrera, M. (1996) 'The "southern model" of welfare in social Europe', *Journal of European Social Policy*, vol 6, no 1, pp 17-37.

Freire, P. (1972) *Pedagogy of the oppressed*, Harmondsworth: Penguin.

Fung, A. and Wright, E.O. (2003) *Deepening democracy: Innovations in empowered participatory governance* (The Real Utopias Project, Vol 4), London: Verso.

Furbey, R., Dinham, A., Farnell, R., Finneron, D. and Williamson, C.G. (with C. Howarth, D. Hussain and S. Palmer) (2006) *Faith as social capital: Connecting or dividing?*, Bristol: The Policy Press.

Furness, S. and Gilligan, P. (2009) *Religion, belief and social work: Making a difference*, Bristol: The Policy Press.

Guttierez, G. (2001) *A theology of liberation* (15th anniversary edn), New York: Orbis Books.

Habermas, J. (2002) *Religion and rationality: Essays on reason, God, and modernity*, Cambridge, MA: The MIT Press.

Habermas, J. (2006) *Time of transitions* (translated by Gareth Schott), Cambridge: Polity Press.

Heidenheimer, A.J. (1983) 'Secularization patterns and the Westward spread of the welfare state, 1883-1983: two dialogues about how and why Britain, the Netherlands, and the United States have differed', *Comparative Social Research*, vol 6, pp 3-65.

Hirst, P. (1994) *Associative democracy*, Cambridge: Polity Press.

James, R. (2009) *What is distinctive about faith? How European FBOs define and operationalize their faith*, Praxis Paper 22, Oxford: INTRAC.

Johnsen, S. (with S. Fitzpatrick) (2009) *The role of faith-based organisations in the provision of services for homeless people*, York: Centre for Housing Policy.

Lewis, N. (1984) *The honoured society: The Sicilian mafia observed* (Epilogue by Marcello Cimino), London: Eland.

Lipset, S.M. (1960) *Political man: The social bases of politics*, Garden City, NY: Doubleday & Company, Inc.

Lipsky, M. and Smith, S.R. (1993) *Nonprofits for hire: The welfare state in the age of contracting*, Cambridge, MA: Harvard University Press.

McLennan, G. (2007) 'Towards postsecular sociology?', *Sociology*, vol 41, pp 857-70.

Madeley, J.T.S. and Enyedi, Z. (eds) (2003) *Church and state in contemporary Europe: The chimera of neutrality*, London: Frank Cass Publishers.

Manow, P. (2004) *The good, the bad, and the ugly: Esping-Andersen's regime typology and the religious roots of the western welfare state*, Max-Planck Institute for the Study of Societies Working Paper 04/3, Cologne: MPIfG.

May, J., Cloke, P. and S. Johnsen (2005) 'Re-phasing neo-liberalism: New Labour and Britain's crisis of street homelessness', *Antipode*, vol 37, pp 703-30.

Milligan, C. and Conradson, D. (eds) (2006) *Landscapes of voluntarism: New spaces of health, welfare and governance*, Bristol: The Policy Press.

Molendijk, A.L., Beaumont, J. and Jedan, C. (eds) (2010) *Exploring the postsecular: The religious, the political and the urban*, Leiden/Boston, MA: Brill.

Nicholls, D. (1994) *The pluralist state: The political ideas of J.N. Figgis and his contemporaries* (2nd edn), London: Macmillan in association with St. Anthony's College Oxford.

Nicholls, W.J. and Beaumont, J.R. (2004a) 'Guest editorial: the urbanisation of justice movements?', *Space & Polity*, vol 8, no 2, pp 107–18.

Nicholls, W.J. and Beaumont, J.R. (2004b) 'The urbanization of justice movements? possibilities and constraints for the city as a space for contentious struggle', *Space & Polity*, vol 8, no 2, pp 119–36.

Noordegraaf, H. and Volz R. (eds) (2004) *European Churches confronting poverty: Social action against social exclusion*, Bochum: SWI Verlag.

Parsons, T. (1969) *Politics and social structure*, New York: Free Press.

Peck, J. (2006) 'Liberating the city: between New York and New Orleans', *Urban Geography*, vol 27, no 8, pp 681-713.

Peck, J. and Tickell, A. (2002) 'Neoliberalizing space', *Antipode*, vol 34, no 3, pp 380-404.

Polara, G.F. (1989) *La terribile istoria dei Frati di Mazzarino* [*The terrible history of the Mazzarino Friars*] (2nd edn), Palermo: Sellerio.

Prochaska, F. (2006) *Christianity and social service in modern Britain: The disinherited spirit*, Oxford: Oxford University Press.

Ramsay, M. (1998) 'Redeeming the city', *Urban Affairs Review*, vol 33, no 5, pp 595-626.

Rousseau, J.-J. (1973) *The social contract and discourses* (translation and introduction by G.D.H. Cole, revised and augmented by J.H. Brumfitt and J.C. Hall), London: J.M. Dent Ltd.

Rowland, C. (ed) (1999) *The Cambridge companion to liberation theology*, Cambridge: Cambridge University Press.

Salamon, L.M. and Anheier, H.K. (1996) *Defining the nonprofit sector: A cross-national analysis*, Manchester: Manchester University Press.

Smith, G. (2002) *Faith in the voluntary sector: A common or distinctive experience of religious organisations*, Mimeo, London: Centre for Institutional Studies, University of East London.

Taylor, C. (2007) *A secular age*, Cambridge, MA: Harvard University Press.

Truman, D.B. (1951) *The governmental process*, New York: Alfred Knopf.

Uitermark, J. and Duyvendak, J.-W. (2008) 'Civilizing the city: populism and revanchist urbanism in Rotterdam', *Urban Studies*, vol 45, no 7, pp 1485-503.

van Kersbergen, K. and Manow, P. (eds) (2009) *Religion, class coalitions and welfare state regimes*, Cambridge: Cambridge University Press.

Walker, P.J. (2001) *Pulling the devil's kingdom down: The Salvation Army in Victorian Britain*, Berkeley, CA: University of California Press.

Warren, A. R. (2001) *Dry bones rattling: Community building to revitalize American democracy*, Princeton, NJ : Princeton University Press.

Winston, D. (2000) *Red-hot and righteous: The urban religion of The Salvation Army*, Cambridge, MA: Harvard University Press.

Wolch, J.R. (1990) *The shadow state: Government and voluntary sector in transition*, New York: The Foundation Center.

Working Group on Human Needs, Faith-Based and Community Initiatives (2002) *Finding common ground: 29 recommendations of the Working Group on Human Needs, Faith-Based and Community Initiatives*, Washington, Search for Common Ground.

Wright, E.O. (ed) (1995) *Associations and democracy* (The Real Utopias Project, Vol 1), London and New York: Verso.

Wright, E.O. (2006) 'Compass points: towards a socialist alternative', *New Left Review*, vol 41, September-October, pp 93-124.

Wright, E.O. (2010) *Envisioning real utopias*, London and New York: Verso.

Yeung, A.B. (ed) (with N. Edgardh Beckman and P. Pettersson) (2006a) *Churches in Europe as agents of welfare – Sweden, Norway and Finland*, Working Paper 2:1, from the project 'Welfare and religion in a European perspective', Diakonivetenskapliga instiutets skriftserie, nr 11, Uppsala: Pris.

Yeung, A.B. (ed) (with N. Edgardh Beckman and P. Pettersson) (2006b) *Churches in Europe as agents of welfare – England, Germany, France, Italy and Greece*, Working Paper 2:2, from the project 'Welfare and religion in a European perspective', Diakonivetenskapliga instiutets skriftserie, nr 12, Uppsala: Pris.

Part I
Defining relations of faith-based organisations

TWO

State–religion relations and welfare regimes in Europe

José Luis Romanillos, Justin Beaumont and Mustafa Şen

Introduction

One of the defining features of post-Second World War European economies has been the assumption that the state is responsible for alleviating social hardships produced by capitalist relations. Over the past 20 or 30 years this assumption has been challenged to differing degrees in various national, political and economic contexts. We have witnessed both structural shifts to the functioning of different national 'welfare regimes' (Esping-Andersen, 1990; Jessop, 1999), and a situation in which the very notion of 'welfare' is increasingly an important site of ideological contestation and political debate. These developments are bound up with a series of political shifts that include new forms of governance through which states exercise power as demonstrated by processes of decentralisation and devolution (Rose, 1996; Jones et al, 2005); the rise of public–private partnerships in the conception and delivery of local, regional and national policies (Peck and Theodore, 2001; Bode, 2006); and the increasing encroachment of neoliberal logics on arenas previously considered 'public' (Peck and Tickell, 2002). It is also in this horizon that the growing importance of non-governmental organisations (NGOs) can be charted, various kinds of voluntary agencies, grassroots citizenship groups and the faith-based organisations (FBOs) with which this volume as a whole is concerned.[1] Crucially, these organisations are often intervening in debates over progressive social justice, reappraising the ethics, politics and scope of 'welfare', as well as delivering forms of welfare traditionally considered to be the state's concern. The purpose of this volume is precisely to interrogate the nature of these interventions by religious organisations, and in particular by FBOs, into debates around European welfare and social exclusion. This chapter provides an introduction to the key terms and debates useful for the conceptualisation of the political work of FBO activity. In particular, it explores how the multiplicity of FBO activities signals a broader set of (re)configurations of state–religion relations across different European contexts. As the chapter demonstrates, researching the FBO phenomenon necessarily involves raising questions about the meanings and limits of secularism as the dominant ideological narrative for thinking about welfare practices. It also opens up interesting perspectives on the different ways in which social exclusions are identified and challenged by particular urban publics and forms of citizenship.

The structure of the chapter is as follows. In the first section, 'Secularism, the public sphere and the postsecular', some conceptual and historical frameworks are provided for thinking about the different manifestations of FBO activity across Europe in the context of state–religion relations more broadly. Here, an understanding of the sociological processes at work in secular*isation* and the ideological positions that inform secular*ism* is essential for making sense of the specific state–religious differences between European nations. It is also a necessary context for thinking about how, and in what ways, the notion of the 'postsecular' might act as a useful descriptor for contemporary state–religion relations. Drawing on the work of democratic theorist Jürgen Habermas, one of the key arguments is that a critical understanding of the *public sphere* offers an important way of exploring the contested notions of secularism and the postsecular, and for evaluating the political promise of specific FBO activities.

In the second section, 'Neoliberalism, welfare and the political', the growing strength of neoliberalist ideologies are explored in shaping assumptions about what welfare means and how it operates. While neoliberalism is most clearly associated with the 'liberal' UK welfare regime model and cannot simply be extrapolated across continental European or Nordic social democratic welfare models (Esping-Andersen, 1990; Bäckström et al, 2004; Edgardh Beckman, 2004), these latter welfare regimes are nonetheless also experiencing profound reconfigurations of their welfare systems in the form of cuts, increased public–private partnerships and shifts in how the causes of, and solutions to, social exclusion are understood (Bode, 2003). The critical argument made in this section revolves around the ways in which FBOs are challenging habitual neoliberal economic metrics through which welfare is conceived and articulated. In particular, there is an outline of how FBO activities both critically engage with government policies on social exclusion and help extend understandings and practices of 'welfare' in terms of the everyday forms of citizenship and sociality displayed in practices of care, generosity and hospitality taking place in urban contexts. In these ways, the chapter acts as a foundational piece for thinking about the political promise of FBOs explored across the volume as a whole.

Secularism, the public sphere and the postsecular

There has been growing interest in religion across the social sciences and the humanities (Casanova, 1994; Enyedi, 2003; Spohn, 2003; Gill, 2005; Brace et al, 2006; Lilla, 2007; Thomas, 2009). The continued presence of religions on political stages and in debates in the public sphere provides an empirical refutation of a longstanding sociological hypothesis concerning modernisation and secularisation, namely, that religious beliefs, practices and communities evaporate with economic growth, scientific education and the spread of democracy (see Thomas, 2001; Fox, 2006). Key canonical figures in the sociology of religion, such as Karl Marx, Emile

Durkheim or Max Weber, have shaped this understanding of religion in terms of wider historical narratives of progress and enlightenment. After these figures, secularisation appears as an inexorable historical development, one that necessitated the relinquishing of traditional, dogmatic value systems and communities. It is also this narrative of secularisation-as-modernisation that has perhaps contributed to the politicising of social science research on religion, for example, as necessarily conservative or reactionary. However, rather than categorising contemporary religious practices and beliefs as exceptions to a teleological narrative, there is instead a demand to respond to religious organisations and discourses as formations that might require us to think again about the sociological terms and frameworks of analysis and interpretation.

Indeed, the modernisation thesis has been challenged conceptually insofar as it presents a 'grand narrative' that fails to both (1) adequately address geo-historical difference and complexity, and (2) reflexively take on board the critiques of rationality found across contemporary social theory. Reflecting these arguments, perhaps the most important terrain of debate for social science analyses of religion is to be found in critical reappraisals and interpretations of 'secularism' that are attentive both to the specificities of place and the various ways in which different 'secular' public rationalities unfold (Habermas, 2002; Asad, 2003; Martin, 2005).

Rooted in the Enlightenment project and the values inscribed in the modernisation of states, the immediate sense of the 'secular' can be thought of as a political separation of church and state. The French Revolution of 1789 and the First Amendment to the US Constitution are often taken as the inaugural signs of secularism.[2] As the sociologist of religion José Casanova argues, the rise of scientific understandings of the world and the projects of nation building led to a context in which the role of religion in the public sphere diminished. However, as Casanova points out, the secular does not then simply refer to a clearly definable state of 'secularity'. Rather, the secular unfolds as a contested process in which key political debates revolve around how different states affirm secular principles, and the extent to which religion is subsequently separated, not just from the state, but from public life more broadly. It is precisely for this reason that we consider the *public sphere* to be such an important space for thinking through state–religion relations. An important contemporary example here is that of the French headscarf ban in 2001. Couched in terms of a struggle over the meaning of *laïcité*, or secularism, the 'debate' was less about religious relations with the state, and more about the everyday, public manifestations of religious practice in the public sphere. Thus, the headscarf 'debate' took place in the context of an increasingly pluralised set of public spaces, raising normative questions over how individual freedoms and identities interweave with those pluralities. For example, feminist and Republican arguments for the ban argued that the veil symbolised patriarchal power inscribed on female bodies, and that it contributed to forms of communitarianism. At the same time, these arguments were often articulated alongside a range of other political positions and ideologies including Islamophobia and anti-immigrationism (see Badiou, 2004; Kuru, 2009). This is just one recent example that demonstrates how, while the secular appears to be about separation, it is itself inseparable from the wider political, religious and ideological contexts with which it intersects.

Indeed, if we were to take the principle of separation as self-evident and absolute, how could one account for the public presence of FBO activity across Europe? To describe nations such as the UK, France, Belgium or the Netherlands as self-evidently 'secular' is to miss, among other things, the ways in which FBOs present themselves as complex sites of interaction and partnership between church, state and voluntary organisations (Dinham and Lowndes, 2008). In short, by exploring the empirical instances of social action by FBOs in secular states it is clear that the 'secular' does not simply describe a given national position on religion. States demonstrate historically varying and complex positions on secularism and should not be addressed as monolithic entities (Martin, 2005). In this vein, contemporary sociologists and anthropologists of religion such as Ahmet Kuru (2009) and Talal Asad (2003) have argued that 'secularism' should not be understood as a static historical stage reached by nations, but as a complex and plural *process*, a site of ongoing ideological contestation. For example, in his recent book, Kuru proposes to think about secularism in terms of a *continuum* precisely to help account for secularism's historical and geographical differentiations, its modification by specific ideological positions and how it is conditioned through particular path-dependent contingencies. Kuru's continuum spans archetypal positions from an anti-religious communist state such as Cuba, to a religious state such as the Vatican or Iran under Shia Islamism (see Figure 2.1).

Figure 2.1: Continuum of state-religion relations and secularism

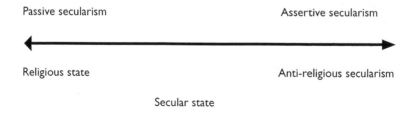

While any given secular nation will tend to occupy a space between these two extremes, Kuru stresses the importance of focusing on the assemblage of micro-political manifestations of state–religion relations in particular contexts (that is, specific policies, programmes and legal decisions in spheres such as education, immigration or citizenship). Likewise, Asad (2003) argues for an 'anthropology of secularism' that shuns macro-scale assertions about the virtues or vices of 'national' patterns of secularism in favour of critical attention on the different forms of political life in which religious activity manifests itself, as well as the specific historical contexts that act as the conditions of possibility for secular thought and action.

Similarly, Kuru also argues for the importance of examining the historical contexts and trajectories of state–religion relations because it forces critics to adopt a nuanced differentiation between *assertive* and *passive* forms of secularism. Once again the public sphere is crucial here because the key distinction between these two perspectives is the extent to which the state, respectively, 'pursues exclusionary or inclusionary policies towards religion in the public sphere' (Kuru, 2009, p 31; emphasis added). As intimated, for Kuru, one of the most important factors in explaining why a given nation displays assertively secular or anti-clerical positions is the historical presence (or absence) of an *ancien régime* (2009, pp 23-6). Attending, then, to specific historical path-dependencies is an important step in any diagnosis of the differing forms of state–religion relations across Europe. At the same time, however, part of the difficulty of thinking about religion–state relations, particularly in the context of progressive strands of social science research, is precisely the historical associations determined by the state–religion relations crystallised in the figure of the *ancien régime*. As Richard Wolin outlines, the French Enlightenment critique of the *ancien régime* inaugurated the political division of the left as the site of reason and public autonomy, from the right's ties with emotion, religious myth, the monarchy and hegemonic church authorities (Wolin, 2004; cf Harvey, 1979). In part it is because of the historical weight of these associations that faith and religion have tended to remain 'taboo' within human geography (Brace et al, 2006; Cloke, 2011), and the social sciences more broadly (see Casanova, 1994). Clearly, these political histories and associations between the right and religious institutions continue to find contemporary resonance. The US is an example often mobilised in this context, having witnessed a rise in the political power of Christian evangelism after Ronald Reagan's election in 1981 (see Kuru, 2009, pp 41-73), and more recently the unveiling of the Office of Faith-Based and Community Initiatives (www.dhs.gov) by George W. Bush in 2001 during his first month as President.

However, one of the conceptual principles that we want to stress here, and which the research has substantiated in a variety of denominational and social contexts, is that there is no transparent correlation between religion on the one hand, and political positions on the other. A corollary to this principle is the notion that religious practices and statements can be present in the public sphere without thereby being decried as acts of proselytisation, as if the mere presence of religion in the public sphere was *a priori* ideologically coercive. What this means is that secularism is not a zero-sum game between anti-clerical, assertive secularists and reactionary, conservative religious institutions. As Habermas has argued in his recent texts on the postsecular presence of religion within the public sphere, to maintain this political–religious separation between left and right, in which an atheist–scientific rationality lays sole claim over the capacity to decide on progressive politics, is to discount the longstanding religious basis to a huge variety of progressive political events and actions (Habermas, 2004, 2005). Further, it is to also write out the foundational role of Judaism and Christianity in shaping understandings of freedom, equality and democracy within the historical context of Europe:

> ... [u]niversalistic egalitarianism, from which sprang the ideals of freedom and a collective life in solidarity, the autonomous conduct of life and emancipation, the individual morality of conscience, human rights and democracy, is the direct legacy of the Judaic ethic of justice and the Christian ethic of love. (Habermas, 2002, p 149)

Following Habermas, then, the comparatively recent increase in interest in religion and faith can perhaps be described in terms of a postsecular space in which the inaugural moments of secularism are critically reconsidered. If, as Habermas argues, secularism describes both the separation of church and state and the affirmation of the constitutive role of reason and rationality in the public sphere, then the postsecular describes a political situation in which secularism abandons certain rationalist assumptions over the disappearance of religion from the public sphere, and over the political import of religion as such (cf Bedford-Strohm, 2007).

In this spirit of reflexivity, it also interesting to note how certain 'Western' assumptions about secularism and reason have been mobilised to upholster the insidious rise of Islamophobic public discourse. Tellingly, debates over the position of Islam within Europe are often inseparable from the resurgence in the 'politics' of immigration, asylum and national identity (Kuru, 2009, pp 103-35). A central element of this discourse takes Islam to be incompatible with democracy and secularism, a position grounded on an essentialist characterisation of (certain) religions as holding dogmatically to anti-secularist and 'non-rational' positions. Famously, and lamentably, this claim finds academic expression in the narratives about a 'clash of civilisations' between a Christian West and a Muslim 'Other' (see Huntington, 1993). As Derek Gregory argues in *The colonial present* (2004), the way in which Christianity and Islam are mobilised here provides a cultural forum for the (re)production of racist and Orientalist geographical imaginations. Importantly, as Gregory argues, these kinds of essentialisms are only possible when the complex, intertwining spatialities of different communities and cultures are ignored (see also Said, 1994). Further, as Habermas argues in terms of the demand for responsible forms of recognition and rational dialogue in the public sphere, these narratives are politically problematic because they often work to script and prefigure relations with 'the Other' in the public sphere. To draw on Habermas' language, these narratives act as a veil that stops people working through the 'cognitive demands' of rationally engaging in a democratic spirit of tolerance and recognition with 'Others' (Habermas, 1999).

Politics, secularism and the public sphere

Drawing on Kuru's typology, the infamous 2001 French headscarf ban can be described as an instance of *assertive secularism*, a policy that reflects an active excluding of religious presence from the public sphere. The headscarf ban also signalled an *asymmetry* in how assertive secularism is deployed and highlighted a broader set of political agendas. For example, while the primary target of the headscarf ban concerned approximately 1,500 Muslim girls, we nonetheless find that approximately half of French public secondary schools have Catholic chaplains, and that the state pays around 80 per cent of the budget of private Catholic schools (Kuru, 2009, p 110). In this context, the revealing arguments for the ban revolved around the belief that the hijab (head covering) was a contagious symbol of communitarianism, violence and ghettoisation (see Asad, 2003, pp 9-11; Dikeç, 2007). The ban on the veil is thus an example of how debates around secularism are inseparable from wider political and social geographies. As Frantz Fanon reminds us, the 'politics' of the veil in the French public sphere demands to be understood in the light of a colonial history that determines not only the terms of debate, but also the fact that there is a debate about scarves at all (Fanon, 1969; cf Badiou, 2004).

What is interesting about this example is that by raising questions about difference, disagreement and the demand for consensus in the public sphere, it actually speaks to the formative processes of democratic society. The work of Jürgen Habermas would perhaps have traditionally been mobilised in support of the kind of assertively secularist rationalities that found policy expression in the headscarf ban. The most obvious reason for this stems from Habermas' conception of the public sphere as a fundamentally secular space for rational discourse and communication. The key argument mobilised against religion in this context is that religion is based on a series of doctrinal beliefs and dogmatic convictions which, precisely because they are beliefs, are not equally available to all and thereby fail to affirm the democratic requirement of discourse in the public sphere to be open to contestation, debate and rational consensus. However, in his recent turn to the question of religion in the public sphere, Habermas has critically re-thought the nature of the rationality or *rationalities* at work in the public sphere, and thereby the scope and limits of how *consensus* operates within legitimate public democratic deliberation. In many ways this signals something of a radical, reflexive critique of his earlier work on mediation, communication and discourse, precisely insofar as it puts into question the possibility of a final rational reconciliation of value claims. Habermas' work on religion underlines how certain forms of disagreement and dissensus are non-eliminable aspects of contemporary democracies, statements that are perhaps more often associated with the radical democratic writings of Chantal Mouffe (1992) or the philosophy of Jacques Rancière (1999). For example, while Habermas upholds the Enlightenment rationality that allows one to 'reject the convictions of others', the demand for democratic tolerance supplements that rationality with another set of reasons 'to accept nevertheless common membership of essentially disagreeing people within the same political community' (Habermas, 2004, p 9).

Habermas works towards the notion that the democratic public sphere places *reciprocal* cognitive demands on both religious and non-religious elements. For instance, on the one hand the affirmation of the normative principles of a secular democratic order, Habermas argues, needs to be cognitively understood as arising from *within* religious worldviews.

> Thus, the cognitive demand we make of someone in expectation of tolerance is the following: he shall develop from his own worldview reasons that tell him why he may realise the ethos inscribed in that view only within the limits of what every one is allowed to do and to pursue. (Habermas, 2004, p 13)

On the other hand, Habermas argues that the possibility for accepting the 'truth content' of certain forms of religious discourse must be recognised by non-religious elements of the public sphere. Indeed, he claims that religion can play a role politically, even in the secular institutional spheres of decision making, as long as the language and rationality of that particular faith is *translated* into the secular language of the public sphere (Habermas, 2006, pp 9-11). Crucially, Habermas underlines that:

> ... [t]his requirement of translation must be conceived as a cooperative task in which the non-religious citizens must likewise participate, if their religious fellow citizens are not to be encumbered with an asymmetrical burden. (Habermas, 2006, p 11)

In short, the cognitive processes of tolerance and recognition within the public sphere are democratic to the extent that they work both ways:

> ... [t]he insight by secular citizens that they live in a post-secular society that is *epistemically adjusted* to the continued existence of religious communities first requires a change in mentality that is no less cognitively exacting than the adaptation of religious awareness to the challenges of an ever more secularized environment. (Habermas, 2006, p 15)

While rethinking his understanding of the public sphere in a postsecular situation, Habermas also conceptually underlines the political work of religion in the public sphere. Interestingly, in the context of debates over welfare and social exclusion, Habermas argues that this work can be thought of in terms of making claims for civic *inclusion*:

> The inclusion of religious minorities in the political community kindles and fosters sensitivity to the claims of other discriminated groups ... religious pluralism makes us aware in an exemplary fashion of the *claims of minorities to civic inclusion*. (Habermas, 2004, p 15)

To help explicate Habermas' argument we can turn here to Ingo Bode's examination of the Catholic charity Caritas in Germany. Bode points to the ways in which this FBO strove for 'new visibility in the public sphere' (2003, p 217) by engaging with contemporary media and advertising (2003, p 219). Bode describes how this attempt to reach new publics was bound up with forms of political campaigning, in particular, 'lobbying for the poor in the public sphere' (Bode, 2003, p 218). Similarly, to take an example from our own FACIT study, the Church of Sweden has recently proclaimed September 2010 as 'The Month of the Deacony' in order to raise awareness about persistent forms of vulnerability in Sweden, and by organising conferences on poverty and social exclusion with FBOs such as The Salvation Army and the Swedish Alliance Mission. What these examples help demonstrate is the value of FBO activity in making public demands for forms of social *inclusion*. In his progress reports on extant human geographical accounts of social exclusion and social justice, Angus Cameron has outlined how this notion of 'inclusion' has been distinctly under-explored and under-theorised (Cameron, 2005, 2006, 2007). Precisely because it has not been specifically addressed, 'inclusion' all too easily becomes a question of access to services, consumption practices and wealth. In short, inclusion is effectively understood as an *economic* condition, in which to be socially 'included' is to embody the norms of neoliberal subjectivity (Cameron, 2005, p 194).

As Casanova would argue, however, the demands for civic inclusion made by FBOs are nonetheless valuable interventions in the public sphere. Reflecting what Casanova considers to be the political promise of the 'de-privatisation of modern religion' (2001, p 1048), these interventions have the value of putting the notion of social inclusion into public debate. In so doing, the examples above also show the critical presence of FBOs in the public sphere as political actors that can disseminate issues of social exclusion and bring notions of ethical citizenship to public consciousness. In so doing, they challenge what could be described as a neoliberal gentrification of the public sphere in which issues such as homelessness, extreme poverty and other forms of exclusion are swept away as matters of 'private' concern.

As Habermas argues in his account of religion in the public sphere, the political work of FBOs draws on an *ethos* of social praxis and solidarity through which religious communities respond to forms of social hardship and foster forms of civic inclusion: 'Religious traditions have a special power to articulate moral intuitions, especially with regard to vulnerable forms of communal life' (Habermas, 2006, p 10; cf Cloke, 2011). Again, this is an argument also developed by Casanova (2001) who describes three ways in which religious traditions are helping to articulate moral positions and debates in the public sphere, first, through what Casanova describes as the religious defence of 'traditional lifeworlds' in the face of contemporary scientific orthodoxies. Explicating this, Casanova points to how religious organisations have put things such as bioethics, market norms and consumerism into public debate. Second, through a critical questioning of how the logics of states and markets operate without 'traditional moral norms'. An interesting contemporary example of this could perhaps be found in the critical report by the Church of England concerning the moral standards of bankers in the City of London. Finally, and drawing on the sociality of religious experience, Casanova underscores the importance of religion in affirming how moral decisions take place in a shared, intersubjective space (Casanova, 2001, pp 1048-50). What Casanova shares with Habermas here is the recognition of the possibilities for religious interventions in the public sphere to be charged and situated in the context of an ethos of shared citizenship. Recalling political events and activism across the 20th century, Habermas stresses the religious basis for the '*motivations* of most social and socialist movements in both the United States and European countries' (Habermas, 2006, p 7; emphasis added). As this volume also shows, the 'religious' dimension of FBO activity is not simply about church–institutional membership: 'true belief is not only a doctrine, believed content, but a source of energy that the person who has a faith taps performatively and thus nurtures his or her entire life' (Habermas, 2006, p 8). To draw briefly on a further example from our FACIT study – the hiding of refugees in West Sweden by parish priests (see Elander and Fridolfsson, 2010) – religious motivations for care are intimately connected with affirmations of individual political freedom. In this, and other cases, the provision of welfare, hospitality and support to vulnerable 'Others' unfolds irrespective of cultural, racial or religious differences.

For Habermas, the kinds of ethical praxis found with religious bodies provide a way of thinking that moves the notion of citizenship away from the bounded limits of a juridical and economic individual, and towards the shared, complex and relational basis of citizens' identities (Habermas, 2004). This also raises the issue of how to think about the welfare of the citizen-subject that is similarly expanded and situated within a broader ethics of citizenship. This is particularly important given how social science accounts of welfare have tended to ignore the *subjectivity* of the citizen-subject as a complex, relationally constituted being (Esping-Andersen, 1990). This expansion of the notion of 'welfare' is a topic we shall return to, particularly in terms of addressing the kind of ethical citizenship at work in FBO activity and the various forms of hospitality, care and generosity that they practice. At this point in the chapter, however, we want to return to the discussion of state–religion relations in the context of a transition from secularism to the postsecular.

Postsecularism and post-metaphysical thought

The postsecular is a term used by Habermas to describe a situation in which one finds debate and dialogue between religious and non-religious elements in a public sphere that is nonetheless 'secular'. In other words, and recalling Kuru's typology, the postsecular appears to be a form of *passive secularism* in which the state pursues inclusionary policies to religion in the public sphere. For Habermas, this position can be more broadly understood in terms of a critical thinking of the *nature of rationality* through which the state and public sphere are conceived.

In his recent work, Habermas' account of postsecular rationality is often bound up with his account of what he calls 'post-metaphysical' thought: 'The secular awareness that we live in a post-secular world is reflected philosophically in the form of post-metaphysical thought' (Habermas, 2006, p 14). Perhaps the most important aspect of post-metaphysical thinking is the way in which it challenges a singular, authentic rationality. While for Habermas post-metaphysical thought nevertheless draws a line between 'faith' and 'knowledge', it refrains from making the rationalist assumption that it can decide on the rational and irrational aspects of religion, or that it can authentically pass judgement on religious truths. In short, it rejects a scientifically limited conception of reason in terms of a naturalistic empiricism from which religion is simply excluded (cf McLennan, 2011).

One of the hallmarks of certain kinds of assertive secularist positions is the vehemence of claims for exclusionary policies towards religion in the public sphere. In short, while rallying against irrational convictions, convictions are nonetheless mobilised for the active separation and exclusion of religion. For Habermas this can be considered a metaphysical position that sets itself apart from more nuanced accounts of secularism that stress the state's *neutrality* towards religion. As Kuru argues in the French context of assertive secularism, certain critics such as Jean-Paul Willaime are arguing for a 'secularisation of secularism' precisely because secularism has itself become too *dogmatic* and not sufficiently *neutral* (Kuru, 2009, p 118). To summarise the above accounts, then, the postsecular can be grasped as a reflexive and critical space in which the principles of secular life are de-dogmatised and stripped of their metaphysical or transcendent status. Crucially, this allows the different geographical and historical manifestations of religion to be recognised as part of the public sphere rather than excluded *a priori*.

What the work of Habermas also demonstrates, alongside other careful interpretations over the sense of secularism (Asad, 2003; Martin, 2004), is the value of conceptualising debates over state–religion relations at a more concrete sociological and political level. In short, rather than talk of these relations in terms of the familiar modernist narratives that revolve around the national disappearance of traditional beliefs with the march of reason and economic development, they become ways into more specific ethical and political questions concerning contemporary forms of socialisation, civility and belonging. As this chapter argues below, one strand of this critical rethinking of secularism that stands out, particularly in the context of thinking about the place of welfare, is the political promise for an *ethics of citizenship* sketched out by the practices of certain kinds of FBO activities. We are particularly interested, for example, in those dispositions of *care*, *civility*, *hospitality* and *generosity*, practised across different urban spaces. Further, and as this volume as a whole also demonstrates, the ethico-political practices of FBOs demand to be addressed in the light of critical reflections over traditional social science understandings of welfare, sociality and publicness. In short, we argue that the practices of FBOs demand to be both (1) affirmed as legitimate and creative political forces within the public sphere, and (2) recognised by wider streams of social science to be providing critical interventions into the ways in which social exclusion and inclusion are conceptualised.

Neoliberalism, welfare and the political

How are we to conceptualise the emergence of religious actors in several secular European states as increasingly important agents of welfare? A powerful political-economic argument is to conceive of this shift, whereby the state in certain forms draws on religious organisations to help it meet its obligations for welfare, in terms of the historical development of neoliberal capitalism (see Harvey, 2006, pp 9-68). Interest in a relationship between FBOs and neoliberalism perhaps first arose in studies on international development. In this context, many critics point to the intimate relations between neoliberal structural adjustment programmes and the rise of NGOs and FBOs as deliverers of aid, health and education services (see Hoksbergen and Madrid, 1997; Clarke, 2006). However, neoliberalism is not solely the deregulation and rolling out of *laissez faire* stances towards markets and economies. It perhaps more importantly describes an ideological and governmental shift in which the logics of market-driven competition and its attendant normalised understandings of individuals as entrepreneurs and consumers come to shape conceptions of the citizen, subjectivity and the public more broadly (Rose, 1996; Peck and Tickell, 2002). The UK in particular is currently an important example here of the ways in which neoliberalist 'common sense' is playing a crucial role in scripting and reconfiguring contemporary understandings, analyses and responses to both welfare and social exclusion (Peck and Theodore, 2001; Cameron, 2005). Crucially, while the phenomenon of neoliberalism is critically understood by progressive academics as an economic system that is actively *producing* exclusion and expanding social inequality, neoliberal policies are increasingly being considered precisely as the *solutions* to these social problems. As Judith Goode describes in her study of FBO activity in Philadelphia:

> Neoliberal cultural beliefs focus on the efficacy of the unfettered market as a mechanism for solving social problems by reforming individuals into entrepreneurs and consumers. (Goode, 2006, p 205)

In the context of her own research into church-based organisations in Philadelphia, Goode found how FBOs, rather than reviving a progressive system of civic voluntarism, are instead much more conditioned by the imperatives of contemporary political and economic life. Goode outlines the processes by which faith-based interventions in matters of social justice undergo modifications in the light of hegemonic neoliberal ideologies:

> ... [t]hey have moved from making claims for social justice through public demonstrations (such as civil disobedience and vigils) to calling for the reform of individuals through market-oriented individual

> entrepreneurship and/or strong patriarchal values ... in which [the] analysis of social problems gives priority to moral redemption, rather than to recognizing inequality and making claims for social justice. (Goode, 2006, p 210)

It is important to be attentive to the ways in which FBOs can reproduce, and even support, reactionary and conservative political agendas. At the same time, however, it would be too simple – and unfaithful – to the range and specificity of research in our FACIT study to extrapolate from particular examples, particularly from outside of a European context. And such a reading would equally draw attention away from examples of radical and more progressive faith-based praxis from our research (see Cloke et al, Chapter Five in this volume). Recalling one of the principles noted earlier in this chapter, the danger associated with the power of the neoliberalist argument is that it can too easily specify and correlate particular religions to given political positions. To follow this path would be to take faith-based delivery of social welfare as little more than an *apology* for neoliberalism.

Welfare regimes

However, as Ingo Bode demonstrates, a simplified neoliberal narrative that revolves around the disappearance of the state as a public entity, its replacement with public–private partnerships and a correlated rise of NGOs and FBOs would also ignore much historical and geographical complexity to the ways in which welfare has been conceived and delivered throughout the 20th century:

> ... [w]hen addressing evolutionary logics, the crucial point is not the partnership between the state and the voluntary sector, or the participation of civil society in the social welfare sector as such [precisely because these were also present during the development of the welfare state], but the *transformation* of this partnership including the *form* of civic participation. (Bode, 2006, p 348)

In short, for Bode the history of European welfare has always been one of plural welfare mixes rather than of nationally distinctive welfare regimes that differ solely in their separation of public from private agencies. This is not to say that there are not national and regional specificities to state–religion relations corresponding to different welfare systems. As Esping-Andersen's path-breaking *The three worlds of welfare capitalism* (1990) argues, one can broadly position European welfare regimes within a tripartite structure: (1) the liberal Anglo-Saxon model that advocates market-based solutions and means-tested social assistance; (2) the conservative, familial regimes of social care characteristic of Germany or France; and (3) the social democratic regimes of Nordic nations in which welfare is conceived as a universal right. Current research on European welfare regimes in the context of church–state relations affirms the continued relevance of this typology for thinking about European welfare (Bäckström et al, 2004; Yeung et al, 2006; van Kersbergen and Manow, 2009). For example, there are broad geographical differences in the roles churches play in welfare delivery: 'In a Southern European context, the church becomes a significant actor [in a conservative, familial welfare regime] while in Northern Europe, it is considered as a complement to the state' (Bäckström et al, 2004, p 176). However, in our FACIT study we depart from the methodological framework outlined by Esping-Andersen because we are not seeking to explain, for example, the causes of European welfare differences by way of a macro-economic analysis. Rather, we aim to respond to how welfare differences are manifest as particular moments of ethical citizenship and social praxis. In so doing, our study addresses how 'welfare' is being reconfigured and practised in new ways in the different European contexts of specific FBO activities.

Indeed, for Bode the history of European welfare has to acknowledge the formative role of FBOs as political actors. From the 'social contract' in France in the early 20th century, allowing 'church related organizations to participate in the provision of welfare' (Bode, 2006, p 349), to the civil agencies of Germany where 'a major proportion of social service provision was, from the 1920s onwards, devolved upon voluntary organisations forming networks of so-called "welfare associations" (*Wohlfahrtsverbände*).' In both cases, these FBOs reflected partnerships that were 'based on a "concordat" between the state and the churches' (Bode, 2006, p 349). For Bode, however, the contemporary situation is one in which these plural and contingent partnerships between state institutions and FBOs are becoming disorganised and powerfully shaped by neoliberal metrics (cf Chapman and Lowndes, 2008). As he puts it in the context of French and German welfare systems:

> ... [i]f a public interest in social welfare persists today, this interest is increasingly defined in terms of a tangible, short-term output of service provision.... Under such circumstances a doctrine stressing unconditional solidarity with the needy has become less compelling. (Bode, 2003, p 214)

What Bode underlines here is the tension between affirmations of unconditional solidarity with the poor and needy and how these affirmations are realised – or disabled – in the context of civil society organisations that are increasingly reliant on unsteady resources and market logics that demand short-term, non-sustainable solutions.

> Many voluntary agencies now compete in "civil markets" where smart "just in time" projects are in much more demand than complex interventions with unknown or non-measurable outcomes. (Bode, 2006, p 354)

While the solutions to social exclusion are considered within a short-termist policy horizon, another of the distinctive aspects of neoliberal conceptions of social exclusion is the way in which it is geographically imagined as a product of particular localities. For example, in France the geographical imaginary of exclusion, and the discourses of welfare and 'dependency', are bound up with the *banlieues* (Dikeç, 2007). In the UK context, exclusion is often mapped onto housing and council estates. However, as Angus Cameron (2005) argues, it is important not to conceptualise poverty and the poor as singular manifestations of particular local places. Often, policy-driving studies of social exclusion and poverty rely on enumerations of particular locales, mapping those spaces suffering social exclusion. The critical point for Cameron is that, while this kind of mapping has the value of visualising the extent – and reality – of exclusion, it also lends itself to those kinds of understandings of exclusion that take it to be 'a feature of people in places' (Cameron, 2006, p 398). In other words, it can reproduce behavioural and individualistic logics of exclusion that *specify* poverty to particular people, groups and communities, rather than as a geographically extended and socially relational phenomenon. Importantly, if exclusion is conceived in this specified, local horizon, then the solutions for 'inclusion' are likewise assumed to be at the local and personal scales. In short, the assumptions about social exclusion as having causal roots in local sites and personal behaviours are also bound up with the notion that any effective solution to these problems should be deliverable within a short-termist, spatially bounded and simplistic policy framework.

Welfare and (un)conditionality

These assumptions, inherent to a neoliberal welfare shift, have recently been clearly articulated by another Cameron – David Cameron – in his first keynote speech as Prime Minister to the Conservative Conference in October 2010: 'Fairness means giving people what they deserve – and what people deserve depends on how they behave' (The Guardian, 2010). The state welfare system will be fair, then, when deployed in relation to the particular individuals who make demands on it. Recalling a strangely Victorian understanding of the poor as more or less deserving, and conceiving of the individual in terms of a behavioural psychology of the subject, welfare is pitched precisely in terms of a market logic in which the supply of fairness becomes conditional on a kind of behavioural credit-rating.

As the work of Nikolas Rose shows, this kind of political rhetoric can be thought of as a manifestation of much broader shifts in governmentality, particularly in relation to social welfare and assumptions about citizenship. For Rose, a key characteristic of neoliberal governmentality lies in the way that those who are to be governed are 'now conceived as individuals who are to be *active* in their own government' (Rose, 1996, p 330, emphasis in original). The causes of, and solutions to, unemployment, for example, are increasingly devolved onto the 'conduct of the unemployed person' (Rose, 1996, p 331), particularly in so far as their conduct deviates from a normalised entrepreneurial subjecthood. As Cameron argues in the context of New Labour's 'third way' policies towards social exclusion, 'recent years have seen a significant shift in the political rhetoric away from the construction of poverty as exclusion, to an emphasis on the responsibilities of the poor to become more "competitive"' (Cameron, 2005, p 198; cf Morrison, 2003). For Rose, this means that welfare and care for abjected people are no longer conceived within the discursive framework of the 'social' obligations of the state, but take place outside of the traditional spaces of state-led public governance:

> ... [a] new territory is emerging, after the welfare state ... traced out by a plethora of quasi-autonomous agencies working within the "savage spaces", in the "anti-communities" on the margins, or with those abjected by virtue of their lack of competence or capacity for responsible ethical self-management. (Rose, 1996, p 347)

The increasing presence of FBOs in these 'savage spaces' can be understood precisely in this context of the withdrawal of the welfare state, and the erosion of the traditional sense of the 'social' from public discourse across the political spectrum. It is also in this context that a variety of FBOs provide a sharp point of critique to the kinds of welfare shifts taking place in the UK and across Europe more broadly. A range of FBOs and individuals studied during our FACIT project conceived of welfare as an *unconditional gesture*, a social affirmation of civic solidarity. In certain contexts, such as in the Nordic welfare models, aspects of this unconditionality are concretised through the way in which welfare is conceived nationally as a rights-based system (Bäckström et al, 2004). However, as our FACIT study shows, unconditionality is perhaps more importantly an expression of an embodied, social relation, a relational moment of subjectivity manifested through instances of dialogue, the giving of time and the taking place of communal care without prescribed limits on who can and cannot be included. In his later work on democracy and hospitality, Jacques Derrida argues for a thinking of hospitality grounded on its being open to anyone at all (Derrida, 1996, 2003). The key conceptual argument for Derrida lies in the way in which hospitality cannot in fact claim to be hospitable if it is given solely to those who are already civically 'included' within a polity, and who therefore do not demand effort, care and time. Again, as the work of Habermas reminds us on religion and civic inclusion in the public sphere, an important example of the political work of FBOs is simply to raise the ethical question, 'Who counts?'

As Paul Cloke, Sarah Johnsen and Jon May (2005) argue in their analysis of discourses of charity in the provision of services for homeless people, this notion of unconditionality is a particularly useful way of distinguishing between different kinds of welfare agencies (cf Cloke et al, 2010). Interestingly, while their discourse analysis of UK emergency social services was compartmentalised between faith-based (Christian) organisations, and more secular, humanist agencies, a more important differentiator was the way in which the subject of welfare was moralised towards behaving in particular ways: 'The principle fault line evident from our surveys appears to reflect the divisive moralities which desire or expect particular behaviour on the part of homeless recipients of service' (Cloke et al, 2005, p 400). So, while certain religious organisations actively promoted evangelical conversion on account of the assumption that social problems derived from personal failings, certain secular agencies likewise held to the expectation that the recipient of welfare would subsequently 'raise their levels of self-endeavour and self-responsibility' and thereby reciprocate with 'deliverable changes in attitude and lifestyle' (Cloke et al, 2005, p 400). In contradistinction, the authors affirm alternative forms of care, drawing on *both* secular *and* faith-based traditions that lay 'no moral expectation on service clients' (Cloke et al, 2005, p 400). Perhaps this notion of unconditionality can be considered as a litmus test for progressive forms of social care and hospitality, precisely because it provides a critical challenge to the argument that recipients of care must 'normalise' themselves according to either spiritual doctrine or secular self-responsibility.

Conclusion

Throughout this chapter we have drawn on debates about neoliberalism as a way to think about the political promise of FBO activities in the context of European welfare. In concluding this introductory chapter, however, it is worth reflecting on this 'neoliberal narrative' to raise a series of questions about the value of political-economic critique. First, it should be stressed that despite attentiveness to the plurality of neoliberal logics, when 'welfare' is conceived from the perspective of neoliberal orthodoxies it tends to be couched within a narrowly defined economics that ignores and devalues the multiple forms of welfare based on political and ethically derived normative demands. For example, a range of authors interested in welfare–church relations across Europe stress how religion has expanded welfare beyond a macro-economics of wealth redistribution and historical class relations (Bäckström et al, 2004, pp 176-8; Grassman, 2004, pp 18-19). For these authors, welfare in the context of FBOs is necessarily bound up with a series of psychological, gendered, spiritual and emotional attributes that find expression in a variety of 'forms' of welfare through FBOs and their activities. Indeed, perhaps the very term 'welfare' might serve as a barrier to understanding the distributed and complex forms of care, responsibility, recognition and hospitality that transcend different kinds of welfare practices and organisations.

Finally, and perhaps most important, the neoliberal narrative reproduces a quite debilitating political framework for action in which 'politics' is often couched in terms of a zero-sum game of macro-economic structural upheaval (on the lack of 'hope' within neoliberal orthodoxies, see Davis, 2004; Cloke, 2011). In this vein, this neoliberal narrative misses the kinds of ethical and political action and activism to be found in FBOs that cannot be simply reduced to accounts of religion and religious life that focus on its reactionary and conservative aspects. As this chapter has outlined, and as substantiated by the following chapter, our FACIT study shows a multiplicity of FBOs engaged in energetic and progressive action: forging new kinds of alliances by exceeding the institutional frameworks of the church; critically engaging, challenging and even subverting particular state policies; and making social issues known through constructive kinds of dissemination.

Methodologically, this chapter has affirmed a thinking of state–religion relations that attends to their historical and geographical specificity. In this way we have sought to challenge abstract, monolithic pseudo-political accounts of religion in terms of civilisational clashes, or the familiar grand sociological and modernising accounts of secularisation. Given this, we have not sought to provide a detailed comparative analysis of European differences for the sake of asking after patterns of 'convergence' or 'divergence' of state–religion relations and the role of FBOs in welfare services (see Madeley, 2003; Bader, 2007, pp 61-2). Rather, we have provided an historical and conceptual overview of state–religion relations and FBO involvement in public welfare.

In the first section, we drew on the work of Jürgen Habermas and argued for a critical and reflexive account of the public sphere as a way of grasping the notion of the 'postsecular'. Habermas' democratic theory also helped to conceptually outline some of the political work carried out by FBO activity. Most importantly, this was in terms of a wider sensitivity to a shared ethics of citizenship whereby claims to civic inclusion can be raised more explicitly. Habermas also helped underscore the kinds of ethical and motivational energies that certain people derive from religious belief as crucial motors for the development of normative political and ethical action. In the second section, we explored welfare regimes in the context of neoliberal policies and ideological agendas, taking place in different ways and speeds in different European nations. However, one of the consequences of the critique of neoliberal forms of welfare manifested in FBO activity is that it also gets us to think about welfare in different ways, as constituted by a shared ethics of citizenship, a manifestation of a compassionate ethos of sociality and in relation to unconditional forms of care and hospitality.

Notes

[1] This chapter does not engage in any taxonomic categorisation of FBOs; this kind of typologisation can be found, for example, in Ebaugh et al (2003) and Sider and Unruh (2004).

[2] 'Congress shall make no law respecting an establishment of religion, or prohibiting the free exercise thereof; or abridging the freedom of speech, or of the press; or the right of the people peaceably to assemble, and to petition the Government for a redress of grievances' (www.usconstitution.net/const.html).

References

Asad, T. (2003) *Formations of the secular: Christianity, Islam, Modernity*, Stanford, CA: Stanford University Press.

Bäckström, A., Edgardh Beckman, N.E. and Pettersson, P. (2004) *Religious change in Northern Europe: The case of Sweden*, Stockholm: Verbum.

Bader, V. (2007) *Democracy or secularism? Associational governance of religious diversity*, Amsterdam: Amsterdam University Press.

Badiou, A. (2004) 'Behind the scarfed law, there is fear', *Islam Online.net*, 3 March (translated by Norman Madarasz) (www.lacan.com/islbad.htm).

Bedford-Strohm, H. (2007) 'Nurturing reason: the public role of religion in the liberal state', *Deel*, vol 48, pp 25-41.

Bode, I. (2003) 'A new agenda for European charity: Catholic welfare and organizational change in France and Germany', *Voluntas: International Journal of Voluntary and Nonprofit Organizations*, vol 14, no 2, pp 205-25.

Bode, I. (2006) 'Disorganized welfare mixes: voluntary agencies and new governance regimes in Western Europe', *Journal of European Social Policy*, vol 16, no 4, pp 346-59.

Brace, C., Bailey, A.R. and Harvey, D.C. (2006) 'Religion, place and space: a framework for investigating historical geographies of religious identities and communities', *Progress in Human Geography*, vol 30, no 1, pp 28-43.

Cameron, A. (2005) 'Geographies of welfare and exclusion: initial report', *Progress in Human Geography*, vol 29, no 2, pp 194-203.

Cameron, A. (2006) 'Geographies of welfare and exclusion: social inclusion and exception', *Progress in Human Geography*, vol 30, no 3, pp 396-404.

Cameron, A. (2007) 'Geographies of welfare and exclusion: reconstituting the "public"', *Progress in Human Geography*, vol 31, no 4, pp 519-26.

Casanova, J. (1994) *Public religions in the modern world*, Chicago, IL: University of Chicago Press.

Casanova, J. (2001) 'Civil society and religion: retrospective reflections on Catholicism and prospective reflections on Islam', *Social Research*, vol 68, no 4, pp 1041-80.

Chapman, R. and Lowndes, V. (2008) 'Faith in governance? The potential and pitfalls of involving faith groups in urban Governance', *Planning Practice and Research*, vol 23, no 1, pp 57-75.

Clarke, G. (2006) 'Faith matters: faith-based organisations, civil society and international development', *Journal of International Development*, vol 18, pp 835-48.

Cloke, P. (2011) 'Geography and invisible powers: social action and prophetic potential', in C. Brace et al, *Emerging geographies of belief*, Cambridge: Cambridge Scholars Publishing, pp 9-29.

Cloke, P., Johnsen, S. and May, J. (2005) 'Exploring ethos? Discourses of "charity" in the provision of emergency services for homeless people', *Environment and Planning A* vol 37, pp 385-402.

Cloke, P., May, J. and Johnsen, S. (2010) *Swept-up Lives? Re-envisioning the homeless city*, RGS-IBG Book Series, Oxford: Wiley-Blackwell.

Davis, M. (2004) 'Planet of slums: urban involution and the informal proletariat', *New Left Review*, vol 26, pp 5-34.

Derrida, J. (1996) *The gift of death*, Chicago, IL: University of Chicago Press.

Derrida, J. (2003) *On cosmopolitanism and forgiveness*, London: Routledge.

Dikeç, M. (2007) *Badlands of the republic: Space, politics and urban policy*, RGS-IBG Book Series, Oxford: Wiley-Blackwell.

Dinham, A. and Lowndes, V. (2008) 'Religion, resources, and representation: three narratives of faith engagement in British urban governance', *Urban Affairs Review*, vol 43, no 6, pp 817-45.

Ebaugh, H.R., Pipes, P.F., Chafetz, J.S. and Daniels, M. (2003) 'Where's the religion? Distinguishing faith-based from secular social service agencies', *Journal for the Scientific Study of Religion*, vol 42, no 3, pp 411-26.

Edgardh Beckman, N.E. (ed) (2004) *Welfare, church and gender in eight European countries*, Working Paper 1 from the project 'Welfare and religion in a European perspective', Uppsala: Uppsala Institute for Diaconal and Social Studies, Uppsala University.

Elander, I. and Fridolfsson, C. (2010) *Faith-based organizations and social exclusion in Sweden*, Leuven/Den Haag: Acco.

Enyedi, Z. (2003) 'Conclusion: emerging issues in the study of church-state relations in Europe', *West European Politics*, vol 26, no 1, pp 218-32.

Esping-Andersen G. (1990) *The three worlds of welfare capitalism*, Oxford: Polity Press.

Fanon, F. (1969) 'Algeria unveiled', in C. Oglesby (ed) *The new left reader*, New York: Grove Press.

Fox, J. (2006) 'World separation of religion and state into the 21st century', *Comparative Political Studies*, vol 39, no 5, pp 537-69.

Gill, A. (2005) 'The political origins of religious liberty: a theoretical outline', *Interdisciplinary Journal of Research on Religion*, vol 1, no 1, pp 1-33.

Goode, J. (2006) 'Faith-based organisations in Philadelphia: neoliberal ideology and the decline of political activism', *Urban Anthropology*, vol 35, nos 2-3, pp 203-36.

Grassman, E.J. (2004) 'Welfare in Europe: new trends and old regimes', in N.E. Edgardh Beckman (ed) *Welfare, church and gender in eight European countries*, Working Paper 1, from the project 'Welfare and religion in a European perspective', Uppsala, Uppsala Institute for Diaconal and Social Studies, Uppsala University, pp 11-25.

Gregory, D. (2004) *The colonial present: Afghanistan, Palestine, Iraq*, Oxford: Blackwell.

Habermas, J. (1999) *The inclusion of the other: Studies in political theory*, Cambridge, MA: The MIT Press.

Habermas, J. (2002) *Religion and rationality: Essays on reason, God and modernity*, E. Mendieta (ed), Cambridge, MA: The MIT Press.

Habermas, J. (2004) 'Religious tolerance – the pacemaker for cultural rights', *Philosophy*, vol 79, pp 5-18.

Habermas, J. (2005) 'Equal treatment of cultures and the limits of postmodern liberalism', *Journal of Political Philosophy*, vol 13, pp 1-28.

Habermas, J. (2006) 'Religion in the public sphere', *European Journal of Philosophy*, vol 14, no 1, pp 1-25.

Harvey, D. (1979) 'Monument and myth', *Annals of the Association of American Geographers*, vol 69, no 3, pp 362-81.

Harvey, D. (2006) *Spaces of global capitalism: Towards a theory of uneven geographical development*, London and New York: Verso.

Hoksbergen, R. and Madrid, N.E. (1997) 'The evangelical church and the development of neoliberal society: a study of the role of the evangelical church and its NGOs in Guatemala and Honduras', *The Journal of Developing Areas*, vol 32, pp 37-52.

Huntington, S.P. (1993) 'The clash of civilizations', *Foreign Affairs*, vol 72, no 3, pp 22-49.

Jessop, B. (1999) 'The changing governance of welfare: recent trends in its primary functions, scale and modes of coordination', *Social Policy & Administration*, vol 33, no 4, pp 348-59.

Jones, M., Goodwin, M. and Jones, R. (2005) 'State modernization, devolution and economic governance: an introduction and guide to debate', *Regional Studies*, vol 39, pp 397-403.

Kuru, A.T. (2009) *Secularism and state policies toward religion: The United States, France, and Turkey*, Cambridge Studies in Social Theory, Religion, and Politics, Cambridge: Cambridge University Press.

Lilla, M. (2007) *The stillborn god: Religion, politics and the modern west*, New York: Alfred A. Knopf.

McLennan, G. (2011) 'Postsecular cities and radical critique: a philosophical sea-change?', in J. Beaumont and C. Baker (eds) *Postsecular cities: Space, theory and practice*, London: Athlone Press.

Madeley, J.T.S. (2003) 'A framework for the comparative analysis of church–state relations in Europe', *West European Politics*, vol 26, no 1, pp 23-50.

Martin, D. (2005) *On secularization: Towards a revised general theory*, London: Ashgate Publishing.

Morrison D. 2003 'New Labour and the ideological fantasy of the good citizen', *Journal for the Psychoanalysis of Culture and Society*, vol 8, no 2, pp 273-8.

Mouffe, C. (ed) (1992) *Dimensions of radical democracy: Pluralism, citizenship, community*, London: Verso.

Peck, J. and Theodore, N. (2001) 'Exporting workfare/importing welfare-to-work: exploring the politics of Third Way policy transfer', *Political Geography*, vol 20, no pp 427-60.

Peck, J. and Tickell, A. (2002) 'Neoliberalizing space', *Antipode*, vol 34, no 3, pp 380-404.

Rancière, J. (1999) 'The rationality of disagreement', in *Disagreement: Politics and philosophy*, London and Minneapolis, MN: University of Minnesota Press, pp 43-60.

Rose, N. (1996) 'The death of the social? Re-figuring the territory of government', *Economy and Society*, vol 25, no 3, pp 327-56.

Said, E. (1994) *Culture and imperialism*, New York: Vintage Books.

Sider, R.J. and Unruh, H.R. (2004) 'Typology of religious characteristics of social service and educational organizational programs', *Nonprofit and Voluntary Sector Quarterly*, vol 33, no 1, pp 109-34.

Spohn, W. (2003) 'Multiple modernity, nationalism and religion: a global perspective', *Current Sociology*, vol 51, nos 3-4, pp 265-86.

Thomas, G.M. (2001) 'Religions in global civil society', *Sociology of Religion*, vol 62, no 4, pp 515-33.

Thomas, S.M. (2009) 'Taking religious and cultural pluralism seriously: the global resurgence of religion and the transformation of international society', *Millennium – Journal of International Studies*, vol 29, no 3, pp 815-41.

van Kersbergen, K. and Manow, P. (eds) (2009) *Religion, class coalitions and welfare state regimes*, Cambridge: Cambridge University Press.

Wolin R. (2004) *The seduction of unreason: The intellectual romance with fascism from Nietzsche to postmodernism*, Princeton, NJ: Princeton University Press.

Yeung, A.B., Edgardh Beckman, N.E. and Pettersson, P. (eds) (2006) *Churches in Europe as agents of welfare: England, Germany, France, Italy and Greece*, Working Paper 2:2, from the project 'Welfare and religion in a European perspective', Uppsala: Uppsala Institute for Diaconal and Social Studies, Uppsala University.

Websites

US Constitution online: www.usconstitution.net/const.html

DHS Center for Faith-based and Neighborhood Partnerships: www.dhs.gov/xabout/structure/editorial_0829.shtm

THREE

Spaces of postsecular engagement in cities

Agatha Herman, Justin Beaumont, Paul Cloke and Andrés Walliser

Introduction

Postsecularism presents an opportunity – for a space in which religious and secular worldviews can co-exist and enter into dialogue (Gorski and Altinordu, 2008), a 'rapprochement of ethical praxis' (Cloke, 2011, p 381). In this chapter, we engage with postsecularism through the spatial lens of the city because we consider that a postsecular approach provides a useful set of tools for conceptualising the rich and diverse ground-level engagements occurring between religious and secular groups within the intensive urban environment.

We start by establishing our understanding of postsecularism before moving on to consider existing literatures on the postsecular city. The multi-scalar role of faith-based organisations (FBOs) in urban spaces, their mobility and their performativity, is essential to our later discussion of what we call a *postsecular ethics*. A key contention of this section is that faith remains central despite the diversity in FBO responses to the challenges posed by neoliberal policies. We then consider some of these reactions from FBOs, which highlight the multiple and dynamic natures of *postsecular spaces of engagement*.

In the second half of the chapter, we introduce empirical examples that allow us to open up the political and ethical scope of postsecularism. The central aim of these sections is to develop the idea of a postsecular ethics, a highly contextual concept enacted through a dialogue, which ensures a performed virtue ethics based on a recognition of an intersubjective community. In order to construct our argument, we introduce this through reference to an oft-quoted example of postsecular engagement, London Citizens; this case establishes a certain lens, which offers a very particular way of interpreting other FBO cases. We found the vociferous discourse of an alternative to the neoliberal hegemony extremely useful in positioning postsecularism within the postpolitical, 'there is no alternative' (TINA) condition that we take as this current, neoliberal moment. Understanding postsecularism as offering a revival of debate grounds our conceptualisation of a postsecular ethics on collaboration, praxis and an intersubjective sense of identity. The other empirical examples – Exodus Amsterdam and the Christian Aid and Resources Foundation (CARF) – offer lived cases through which the preceding theoretical discussion is explored. In these ways the empirical material weaves through the chapter's exploration of the political and ethical promise of FBOs in urban spaces, through their creation of collaborative and connected communities.[1]

What is postsecularism?

We recognise that our conceptualisation of postsecularism is optimistic and that this is not uncontested. Despite the multiple nature of postsecularisms, or understandings of this term, in this chapter we agree with McLennan's (2007) positioning of postsecularism as a space of dynamic potential arising out of the gathering force of questioning and debate within academic and policy circles. This viewpoint highlights the capacity of postsecularism to act as a bridge, an intra- and interdisciplinary interface, which offers a fluid means of analysis trying to move beyond binaries (McLennan, 2010) that echoes movements towards a similarly postdisciplinary approach taken in geography, sociology and elsewhere.

Postsecularism is therefore understood as the renewed visibility and consciousness of religion in contemporary culture and politics (Knott, 2010), which presents a complex and dynamic relationship between diverse religious, humanist and secularist positionalities (Molendijk et al, 2010).[2] Postsecularism is explicitly not a new phenomenon because, following Habermas (2005, p 26), it is 'the vigorous continuation of religion in a continually secularizing environment.' This recognition of continuity is not to state that the relations between religion and the secular have been static nor that this marks a return to, as Eder (1996) considers, a presecular state of affairs. The spaces and engagements between the two have transformed with the continual developments occurring in the political, economic, social and cultural environment with religion gaining confidence and re-emerging into the public sphere (Eder, 1996). Postsecularism recognises that FBOs have long played a social role, particularly in urban areas (Cox, 1965; Molendijk, 2010), but it is only with the contemporary postsecular turn that their contribution to welfare, community and inclusion has been acknowledged and they have formally returned to debates of public importance.

Harvey (2003, p 939) states that 'the city has never been a harmonious place, free of confusions, conflicts, violence', which positions these spaces as potential receptors for the benefits of FBO contributions. The relational, lived spaces of cities offer an effective spatial lens through which to explore postsecular engagements. Their concentration of lives and experiences provides a wide and intensive range of opportunities for encountering the 'Other'; therefore, tensions between diverse identities are particularly virulent and efforts towards postsecular engagements most intensely observed (Beaumont, 2010). The heterogeneity and mobility within cities can act as a space for hope as well as misery (Molendijk, 2010), for a *rapprochement* between factions to overcome structural constraints on inclusive and healthy communities.[3] This chapter contributes to this optimism through its positioning of postsecular engagements as actively shared and mutual spaces within cities.

Postsecular cities

Cities are dynamic and multiple spaces in which the roles of religion and science are increasingly blurring, allowing new relations of possibility to emerge (Beaumont and Baker, 2010). Molendijk (2010) highlights the tension that exists between the perception of the city as a secular, even anti-religious, space and the actual, often strong, presence of religion. The postsecular recognition of values, ethics and spirituality, in a broad sense, as potentially useful building blocks in the creation of a city establishes what Baker (2008) terms an 'urbanism of hope'. This grants urban policy and planning the possibility for alternatives to the current neoliberal development of city spaces and a starting point for a more values-driven approach towards co-existence in shared space (Healey, 1997).

Many commentators have used Lefebvre's 'right to the city' as a way to build an inclusive shared space with recognition of the 'Other'. Amin (2006) notes that the 'being-togetherness' of urban life demands an attendance to the politics of living together and proposes 'the good city' as a way to build solidarity out of multiplicity and encourage a city that learns to value difference. This is based on an acceptance of 'relatedness' by inhabitants, a genuine participative parity and a re-enchanted everyday public space that encourages free associations between individuals.[4] This conceptualisation has been criticised for '"sustaining a certain ease with unassimilated difference" rather than forging an insurgent subject of justice' (McLennan, 2010, p 30). The danger of this emphasis on constitutive multiplicity to an overarching notion of human collectivity is clear, but Amin's reminder of the need to engage with mobility and performativity are, to us, essential to understanding postsecular engagements, a point that we shall return to later.

Mobility is central to urban dynamism and fragmentation, and the impact of globalisation has contributed to creating postcolonial cities; fluid, multiple and hybrid collections of ethnicities, cultures, practices and faiths. The interconnections that exist between migrants and their 'home' communities as well as the presence of global brands and corporations points to the fact that cities cannot be considered bounded spaces but are 'a node in a grid of cross-boundary processes' (Sassen, 2000, p 146), 'inflected by the overlaps of historical legacy and spatial contiguity' (Amin, 2007, p 112). The local remains important as a motivator for action (MacIntyre, 1999); however, the inequalities occurring at this scale are understood not as local problems requiring local solutions but as connected into an international nexus of policy and praxis.

FBOs have a distinctive ability to link the local scale to wider affiliations and mobilise across communities (Davey and Graham, 2010), offering a way to negotiate the complex local–global relations in urban issues. Their utility has increasingly been recognised by governments, drawing them into strategies of co-governance (Bode, 2006). The rise of neoliberal policies have created new opportunities for FBOs (Ley, 2008), which have been increasingly involved in the planning and delivery of urban regeneration and services in the UK (Davey and

Graham, 2010). FBOs are positioned as repositories of resources, potential tools for community cohesion and as adding diversity to community representation (Cloke, 2011), particularly within UK Prime Minister David Cameron's enthusiastic espousal of 'Big Society'. The latter reflects broader trends towards a mixed welfare state based on partnership, alongside 'growing concerns over polarisation and religious extremism and perceptions of "untapped" faith group resources and capabilities in building sustainable communities' (Chapman, 2009, p 204).[5] This discourse centres on empowering communities through opening up public services and promoting social action and is positioned as a great opportunity for the voluntary and community sector, which 'sits at the heart of the Government's ambitions' (Cabinet Office, 2010b) in this arena. However, the spending cuts to reduce the UK deficit are simultaneously increasing the demands placed on voluntary organisations and detrimentally affecting funding sources. The challenge this combination of pressures brings is recognised by the UK government, which has created a rhetoric of efficiency and effectiveness (Cabinet Office, 2010a) that has the potential to draw some organisations into the 'shadow state' (Cloke et al, 2007a) while excluding others who do not fit with the preferred delivery strategy.

This utilisation of organisations such as FBOs opens up the more reactionary understanding of postsecularism as a puppet of, and apology for, neoliberalism, allowing the state to maintain but devolve responsibility for social services. Jamie Peck notes the capacity of the 'new urban right' to 'frame' issues in ways that facilitate neoliberal ideological objectives, which have had a significant influence on urban and social policy in the US. This new urban vision relies on 'the compassionate conservatism of private charity, faith-based interventions, and voluntarism, in place of government-led approaches and entitlement programming' (Peck, 2006, p 686). The emphasis by many conservative think-tanks in the US on the need for moral renewal in urban strategies also points to the inclusion of faith-governed values in policy initiatives.

While it is argued that FBOs are not simply puppets because they offer a competitive rationale for partnerships through their particular strengths (Cloke, 2011), there is concern within FBOs over the ways they are being instrumentalised. The predominant paradigm of faith's public impact is as a deliverer of particular social outcomes (Davey and Graham, 2010) and a source of grassroots legitimacy, which policy makers can utilise without necessarily engaging with the values (Chapman and Hamalainen, 2010). There has been a move in some FBOs towards more secular language to secure relationships with funders, gaining 'insider' status in networks of power (Chapman, 2009; Chapman and Hamalainen, 2010; Cloke, 2011). De Witte (2010) highlights the unpredictability of state–religion relations, arguing that interactions are based on specific policy interests, which makes the position of FBOs more precarious and demands greater market orientation to compete for resources in this volatile environment (Bode, 2006). This specificity of state–religion path dependencies is discussed in more detail in Chapter Two, this volume.

Despite these issues, faith remains strong in *performative* terms with the activities of many FBOs more grounded in ethical praxis than dogma (Chapman and Hamalainen, 2010; Cloke, 2010).[6] This establishes a willingness to work with different people for different people (Cloke, 2011) and therefore offers a way to mobilise a variety of people to act collectively (Bretherton, 2010); involvement in FBO activities thus encompasses a variety of motivations and allows for a multiplicity of identities (Chapman and Hamalainen, 2010). The presence of FBOs in inner-city areas is long established, particularly in the UK context through the *Faith in the city: A call for action from church and nation* report of 1985, and their role in these areas continues. Wills et al (2009, p 447) comment that 'faith groups are now often the only credible institutions functioning in inner-city neighbourhoods, providing an obvious place from which to articulate the needs of those communities', a statement corroborated by Ramsay (1998) in the US context. Faith plays a role in the selection of these marginalised spaces for action as it contains 'a predisposition towards engaging socially excluded people or a speedy and proactive response to changing needs' (Chapman, 2009, p 211).

It is clear that the spaces in which FBOs operate are diverse, albeit within a welfare-oriented sector of action. They can work within or outside of state relationships, which belies a simple binary opposition between insider and outsider status. They contain a variety of motivations both at the organisational level and that of the individual participants. Additionally, they have specific strengths and capabilities due to their faith basis that are utilised differently according to the needs of a project. In the following section, we offer a selection of spaces of postsecular engagement that we have drawn from our readings of the literature. We show some of the common practices and aims within the highly disparate FBO sector, which grounds the following discussion of a postsecular ethics.

Spaces of postsecular engagement on the ground

Understanding the varied nature of spaces of postsecular engagement in cities presents a challenge, as a typology is fraught with the complications of arbitrary simplification and Weberian 'ideal types'. Elsewhere, typologies of faith-based service agencies are based on operational characteristics (see Ebaugh et al, 2003; Sider and Unruh, 2004), but here we focus on the style of interactions. We intend the following outline of at least six modes of engagement as an heuristic device, recognising that these are not exclusive or exhaustive, to show the continual interplay between religiosity and the secular. We are not aiming to 'impose system on an inherently untidy experience' (Douglas, 2002, p 5), and accept that our division is arbitrary since many of the spaces are strongly interconnected. However, we consider that highlighting some of the common motifs of postsecular engagements within the literature makes this complex terrain more accessible and offers an excellent grounding for the following discussion of ethics. These open up alternative strategies to the supposedly secular hegemony and make 'a space for the political by making a demand for genuine deliberation about what constitutes the common good' (Bretherton, 2010, p 211).

- *Spaces of community and participation* utilise FBOs' capabilities to mobilise across communities and act as a source of capacity building among people. These aim to negotiate potential and actual points of friction through establishing intercommunity encounters and thus develop understanding and relationships between otherwise disparate groups. One example of this is the 'Building Bridges in Burnley' programme, which emerged from discussions between Christian and Muslim community leaders following local social unrest in 2001. The aim of this inter-faith organisation is to make the uniting possibilities of faith visible and 'to create opportunities for people to discuss shared values and understand and celebrate differences' (Building Bridges in Burnley, 2010; Davey and Graham, 2010).
- *Space of care*, interrelated with this community-centric ethos, offer targeted service provision by FBOs, often staffed by volunteers, for those who have 'fallen through the net' of state welfare. These spaces are grounded in the role of faith in engendering a predisposition towards engaging socially excluded people and an active response to social needs (Chapman, 2009). One example are those FBOs that target the homeless, offering basic services to users in the form of food, shelter and advice and thus acting as spaces in which care is performed towards socially excluded individuals (May et al, 2005; Cloke et al, 2007a, 2007b).
- A *space of sanctuary* is 'of a completely different order to the profane, indefinite space that surrounds it' (Greve, 2010, p 221). It is ambiguous, receiving meaning from the meetings and exchanges performed within it; in this sense its essence is moulded to the needs of those using it. The Muslim study circles, discussed by Baker and Beaumont (2010), can be understood as an 'other' space in this sense, a space of retreat, to recharge away from the perceived hostility of their surroundings. A potential danger in this instance is of reinforcing differences based on religious and cultural identities, and restricting participation outside of this community.
- *Spaces of learning* can support more generic feelings of citizenship through encouraging individuals to learn about the surrounding culture and accessing local services. These can be an interface between local communities and are therefore connected with the aforementioned spaces of community and participation. By encouraging interaction and education about the 'Other', these spaces promote a 'mutual learning process' (Habermas, 2008) and work to break down fear of the unknown. Baker and Beaumont's (2010) study also included a Hindu community complex, which offered activities specifically for the local Hindu community as well as working in partnership with local secular agencies such as the council, National Health Service (NHS) and local schools.
- *Spaces of active faith* utilise a spectrum of implicit and more explicit practices to demonstrate faith-based ethics and beliefs. These are not arenas for

proselytisation since explicit missionary work is increasingly recognised as a barrier to the achievement of funding and hence successful outreach strategies (Chapman, 2009). There now exists a complex relationship between missionary and post-evangelical consciousness, with the latter based in a postmodern recognition that individuals need 'the freedom and space to think through their faith lives in dialogue with their experience' (Guest and Taylor, 2006, p 50). For example, Cityside Baptist Church in Auckland, New Zealand, encourages active participation among its congregation, establishing an open forum ('thinking aloud, thinking allowed') that is supportive of chosen identities and accepting of those who are not Christian (Cityside.org.nz 2011). This more open and creative ministry has attracted young, disillusioned members of other churches and established a vibrant and praxis-centred church.

• *Spaces of market interaction* recognise that faith extends into all aspects of a believer's life and include specific efforts to engage with existing economic systems and challenge their perceived injustices. One example of this is Islamic Banking and Finance (IBF), which represents one way for Muslims to negotiate the simultaneous repulsion and appeal of capitalism that is both ethically offensive and yet has clear transformative powers (Samers and Pollard, 2010). By prohibiting 'unearned or excessive profit' (Timewell and DiVanna, 2009, p 52), investment in 'socially or morally injurious' businesses and excessive risk and speculation, IBF brings the ethical principles of Islam into financial institutions. It is grounded on the idea of wealth creation through socially conscious means, where profit is allowed but must be directed towards improving the condition of others. Islamic banking has grown less in the retail sphere as it remains a relative unknown and there is scepticism relating to its 'Islamic-ness' and the history of Islamic bank failures. The postsecular space emerges from the necessary balance between the familiar, conventional banking products and *Shari'a* compliance.

This potential for dialogue and collaboration makes new 'spaces of hope' (Cloke, 2010) possible within cities, creating room for alternative practices and strategies to the status quo to develop. How can we conceptualise these engagements of disparate interests, of multiple subjectivities and varying motivations? We seek to explore these distinctive spaces through developing a *postsecular ethics*, in which ethics are understood as the habitual actions involved in constructing a particular life and identity (Barnett et al, 2005). We first present the case of London Citizens to provide an empirical grounding to the subsequent theoretical discussion. This offers an initial contextualisation for our thoughts on postsecular ethics through positioning postsecularism in relation to the contemporary postpolitical condition.

Empirical moment 1: London Citizens, UK

London Citizens is a broad-based community initiative that enacts a particular conceptualisation of the 'good city' and performance of the politics of living together. Founded in 1996, London Citizens is an alliance of 160 organisations including faith institutions, universities, schools, trade unions and community groups.[7] The aim to create a permanent and diverse alliance to effect social and economic change in the UK capital (Jamoul and Wills, 2008) establishes a means to connect these diverse groups through a focus on concrete local concerns. Emphasising the commonalities between the members allows for a shared sense of place and political interests to be recognised (Wills et al, 2009), with differences not explored unless absolutely necessary (Jamoul and Wills, 2008). London Citizens therefore offers an urban solidarity that engages with multiplicity through the collective basics of everyday urban life (Amin, 2006), and allows individual institutions to make a difference across a broader stage. 'We believe these strands, connections and alliances are vital for a healthy democracy and should be the building blocks of any vibrant civil society' (Citizens UK, 2010).

London Citizens is based on the work of Saul Alinksy, who, in his book *Rules for radicals: A pragmatic primer for realistic radicals*, offers advice to those who wish to learn from the broad-based community initiative he established in 1930s Chicago. Alinsky proposed a set of rules for successful civic engagement grounded in humour, irony and imagination that guide a 'creative engagement that must be fresh in each instance and particular to each context' (Alinksy, 1989, p 218). He emphasised the need to provoke conflict, within the bounds of the law, in order to open up a space for an alternative given that 'the price of a successful attack is a constructive alternative' (Alinsky, 1989, p 130). This perpetual challenge combined with the solidarity and mutuality of the community-based structure helps prevent the participant organisations from being co-opted or depoliticised by the state (Bretherton, 2010). This supports the establishment of a genuinely democratic space in which all member organisations have a voice and a chance to affect their wider community.

Religious institutions are in the majority within London Citizens (Wills et al, 2009), and this network grants them a broader impact than they would otherwise achieve. Faith is clearly an important factor in encouraging participation in such an initiative because London Citizens concentrates the power of the outward-facing ethic, which all the involved faith traditions have, and allows them to retain an explicit faith within a tolerant and diverse alliance. Religious belief entails a specific set of non-materialist values that are also often a lifestyle choice; operating through London Citizens as opposed to a direct relationship with the state allows faith a more active role in shaping and structuring local change. The combination of multiple FBOs and non-FBOs has created a genuinely postsecular space in which the religious, the secular and the postsecular enter into effective and democratic dialogue, releasing the potential of each component organisation through collaboration and recognition of commonality and rights. This multiplicity is to the benefit of London Citizens as a whole, for the variety of FBOs brings the capacity for contact with a wider community. Successes include the Living Wage Campaign, launched in 2001, and the consequent Strangers into Citizens initiative, launched in 2007 (Cordero, 2010), which bring discourses of care and community into spaces that were previously alienating and exploitative.[8]

We consider London Citizens, at present, to offer an engaging example of the potential that postsecular interactions can contain, although this is always tinged with the possibility of discord and breakdown, due to the personal, lived natures of the belief worlds brought into contact.

We suggest that the limitations to London Citizens are visible in its position as the oldest citizens' group in the UK because others, which started at a similar time, such as in Bristol, Sheffield and North Wales, 'had a brief and glorious start lasting roughly 3 years' (Citizens UK, 2010). The Citizens UK website explains this as a lack of committed organisers, so what makes London different? It is beyond the scope of this chapter to explore this further, but one key limitation to London Citizens may be its lack of transferability to other contexts. Something clearly came together in London and this makes it an interesting and unique example; we recognise that it offers only one lens, but London Citizens remains an engaging example of the political potential contained in spaces of postsecular engagement.

The sense of a revival of debate (Braidotti, 2008) presented in London Citizens is a good starting point in exploring a postsecular ethics, which we understand as a contextual and fluid dialogue that encourages the recognition of moments of common value. To position this, we first place the postsecular in contrast to the postpolitical constitution deemed by thinkers such as Rancière and Žižek to be constitutive of our contemporary condition.

Postsecularism and the postpolitical

Postsecularism, postpolitical ... as Ley (2005, p 3) comments, 'we live in an era of "posts" ... as theorists rush to be first ... in identifying a new economic break, political transition, or social transformation to warrant the creation of new conceptual and discursive space'. Ley returns to this point in the preface to *Postsecular cities: Space, theory and practice* (Beaumont and Baker, 2010) when he asks 'is the world indeed changing so rapidly across so many dimensions with such marked discontinuities that we can so confidently mark the end of one era and the start of another?... Could it be that what has changed is the focus of our gaze rather than the things themselves?' (Ley, 2010: xii). This is a cogent point when considering postsecularism as simply attention to an already existent phenomenon. We introduce the postpolitical into this chapter with a wry recognition that it is yet another post but one which we feel provides a critical contextualisation for postsecularism.

The postpolitical is a facet, and perhaps a consequence, of the rise and consolidation of neoliberal governmentality. This strong and currently hegemonic discourse is based on a TINA consensus built around 'neoliberal capitalism as an economic system, parliamentary democracy as the political ideal, humanitarianism and inclusive cosmopolitanism as a moral foundation' (Swyngedouw, 2010b, p 8). The emphasis on consensus nullifies the genuine democratic experience, which, to Swyngedouw, should always be disruptive and hence contain transformative potential. The discourse of post-politics encourages discussion and dispute as long as this remains inside of the general frame of elite consensus (Swyngedouw, 2010a); politics becomes policing and policy making, managing within the confines of the 'common sense of the day' (Bourdieu, 2000). This reactionary discourse enacts a self-fulfilling prophecy of its TINA basis because it 'forestalls the articulation of divergent, conflicting, and alternative trajectories of future urban possibilities and assemblages' (Swyngedouw, 2010b, p 10) and forecloses any real engagement, separating the city from its grassroots (Jamoul and Wills, 2008).

Neoliberalism is increasingly built on a stakeholder-based system of multi-scalar governance involving the state alongside experts, NGOs and other partners deemed 'responsible' (for example, in the UK with the 'Big Society'). However, this remains within the accepted neoliberal frame of reference, which makes its claims to being genuinely open and participatory questionable. Paddison (2009), however, suggests that the post-political undervalues the capacity of human agency to challenge consensus politics, and the cracks and exclusions that the latter contains allows the return of the genuinely political and creates a space for naming other futures (Swyngedouw, 2010a). The presence of the postsecular enacts a rupture with the consensus because post-politics explicitly rejects the ideological divisions (Swyngedouw, 2010b) contained within this concept.

The presence of religion forces modern society to reflect publicly and collectively on its own normative foundations (Casanova, 2001). The revival of the recognition of religion marks the creation of a space for the spiritual, which need not be religious, and the translation of the impulses of love, generosity, justice and equality into everyday practices (Cloke, 2010). In the literature, there is a clear emphasis on postsecular interactions with welfare, and so while FBOs may be drawn into the neoliberal consensus through strategies of 'governance-beyond-the-state' (Swyngedouw, 2010b), the presence of faith maintains their 'otherness' and this focus on the marginalised (Chapman, 2009). The increasing visibility of, and the social need for, FBOs make the cracks in the neoliberal, postpolitical condition apparent and demand 'the part for those who have no part' (Ranciére, 2001, p 6). While some FBOs have been drawn 'inside' the consensus through public–private partnership strategies, this systematic outsourcing affirming in part the neoliberal condition, they continue to offer a challenge because the future they offer, not grounded in an economic imperative, appeals to many who are seeking ways to alleviate neoliberalism's impacts on the marginalised. As Harvey (2003, p 939) comments, 'We can dream and wonder about alternative urban worlds. With enough perseverance and power we can even hope to build them'. The postsecular offers one possibility of an alternative urban space as can be seen in the creative and active conflict offered by London Citizens, which offers broad-based, independent, non-partisan strategies challenging the unequal status quo (Bretherton, 2010).

Conceptualising this rupture with the neoliberal consensus is aided by a relational understanding of space as 'disruptive, active and generative' (Massey, 1999, p 287) – which connects to Ranciére's notion of the political – and always in the process of becoming. This move away from a static modernist space helps break down the TINA orthodoxy of neoliberalism. There is clearly contestation and space as relational allows for a recognition that every discourse, including neoliberalism, already contains the potential for resistance, the possibility for change and subversion. Considering the six spaces of engagement outlined above and the example of London Citizens, it appears that the postsecular is grounded in specific place and time-based moments, although the relational nature extends these across scales. A postsecular ethics is therefore highly contextual as it emerges from the specific assemblages that construct a space, which frames an alternative as possible and allows normative values to connect with practice. Whether from a religious or secular starting point, the appeal of 'seemingly impossible hope' (Cloke, 2010, p 236) and explicit place for values attracts subjects who feel a need for action, to make the space other than it is. Practices may be motivated by religious and/ or secular values, such as love, faith, hope and charity/solidarity, equality and justice values, but in these spaces, the common, and indeed constituting, ground is recognised.[9]

Postsecular ethics

To us, postsecular ethics draw on the traditions of virtue and relational – or better dialogical – ethics, centred on interaction, which allows for a collaboration of strengths and encourages a positive engagement with 'Otherness'. There are also connections with theo-ethics, the values and virtues of faith, grace, love and hope, which bring an excess beyond material logic and provide a motivating factor for faith-based praxis in postsecular spaces. Postsecular ethics includes this while leaving room for those coming towards postsecularism from the secular. It recognises the contextuality and potentially fleeting nature of the moment in which a reconnection across difference can emerge. For Cloke, 'Otherness' is an expression of something that can be shared and acclaimed universally, which allows a position that envisages 'equality with difference'. If we understand the self as open and actively practised (Butler, 2005), it is never fully bounded or separate from the 'Other', which recognises the always present fractures within identity and creates space for alternative and multiple subjectivities (Jackson, 2004). Multiplicity within the unfinished, postsecular 'I' contributes to recognition of commonality between subjects and a productive rather than confrontational relationship with difference.

Recognising the constitutive self–other interface positions postsecular ethics in and among non-Western ethical systems such as African ethics and humanist philosophy. One example of the former is *ubuntu*, which has a strongly humanitarian and social core based on the values of interdependence, collective responsibility and mutuality (Rosei et al, 2008).[10] As among intersubjectivist philosophies, an individual exists only through their relationship with others; 'a person is incomplete unless he or she maintains an active connection with the society or culture of which he or she is part' (Libin, 2003, p 126). The potential of this space *between* individuals is articulated well by Martin Buber, who argues that 'through reciprocal relationships between individuals, new values ... are created that are not possible in isolated individuals' (quoted in Friedman, 1999, p 404). *Dialogue* is critical in this relational frame of reference in which the self emerges through its active interaction and communication with the other.

We have argued that postsecular ethics are emergent from specific places and *ubuntu* positions this as the negotiation of the subject's relationship with others through the nexus of contingencies in a place that enact an 'alternative-in-common' as possible and necessary. This strong community focus does have its negatives, as the emphasis on consensus can make decision-making cumbersome, conservative and closed to the voiceless – criticisms that have already been levelled at the postpolitical condition. However, philosophies and ethical systems such as *ubuntu* are theoretically useful in reminding us that the subject is connected within social and non-social networks and the need to ensure that no voice goes unheard (Nicolson, 2008).

In offering a *rapprochement* of religious and secular ethics, the spaces of postsecular engagement offer a specific alternative-centred discourse and praxis-focused arena for subjects to perform their chosen identities. This emphasises a flexible agent, which allows for the world being an open and fluid arena in which priorities change with context. This creative space is facilitated by the turn by many FBOs away from dogma and towards practice, which allows a focus on ethical sympathies rather than moral stances, which could prove divisive or even inflammatory (Cloke, 2011). Despite this focus, the potential for resistance and subversion remains and the postsecular moment remains conceivably fragile. The ethical practices it brings about could be positioned as 'an ethics of necessity', which recognises the inherent potential for transience and change; when the need has been met or new actors emerge, where does this leave the space of engagement?

Amin (2006), in his 'good city', recognises the temporary coalitions that arise to disrupt preceding ones, and this continual dynamism maintains the possibility for an alternative, especially given postsecularism's capacity for co-option. Postsecular spaces can be both long-term and fleeting, being grounded in specific place-based ethics. These draw individuals into partnerships based on an active performance of a chosen subjectivity, which recognises the connections between the self and other and the positive space for collaborative alternatives that this creates. But how does this play out in reality? We now move on to consider this within two empirical moments: Exodus Amsterdam and the Christian Aid and Resources Fellowship (CARF). These were chosen as they open our exploration of postsecular spaces and ethics into the European context. Exodus Amsterdam illuminates a faith-based space of partnership, learning, care and community within a currently effective, if shifting, relationship with the state. CARF highlights the highly contextual and adaptive responses of FBOs and their ability to link to, and mobilise across, wider communities.

Empirical moment 2: Exodus Amsterdam

Exodus Amsterdam is an FBO that has highlighted a particular social need and enacts a praxis-based strategy in response. It was established in 1997 and is a member of the national Vereniging Samenwerkingverband Exodus Nederland umbrella organisation. This collective started in 1981 in The Hague with a local initiative from a collaboration of Protestant pastors and Ministry of Justice volunteers. They identified ex-detainees as a group who were unsupported by the existing welfare regime and wanted to provide them with care in the form of daytime activities to reduce the chances of re-offending. The Exodus movement therefore started as a local programme responding to a specific crack in the welfare system; faith played a role in identifying the socially marginalised ex-detainees and the recognition of responsibility towards these people. The theo-ethics of love, hope and grace provide a powerful rationale for reaching out to the forgotten and ignored of society; as Frank Stam, manager of Exodus Amsterdam, argues "the way we have organised this society means that many people miss the boat … we, as society, have a responsibility to take care of those who do not make it."

Exodus Amsterdam offers an alternative in which the ex-detainees do not disappear from society but are successfully reintegrated into it. This aim is made possible through a praxis-based expression of hope and love by the volunteers and the participants in the form of four core principles: *housing, work, relationships* and *meaning*.[11] Of these, we find the emphasis on relationships and meaning most interesting as they demonstrate a drive to an active intersubjective identity that we consider representative of postsecular ethics. *Zingeving* or 'meaning giving' is considered "the cement for the building blocks of a new life" (Frank Stam) because it encourages a consideration of identity, a questioning of 'who I want to be?' and a recognition of the participant's *responsibility* both to their own life and to others. Participants are supported in building or repairing personal relationships and this active reflection on questions of virtue ethics and relation to others in society offers a route out of repeated, criminal behaviours.[12] It offers ex-detainees a choice and encourages a realisation that they do not have to accept the status quo that their life has been. In Exodus it is felt that this chosen performance of subjectivity and recognition of social duty gives a chance to build a new future. Although the phrase 'meaning giving' has religious connotations, Frank Stam was clear that Exodus Amsterdam does not require participants to find this within the Protestant church. The mission that this project represents is based on an active performance of faith by those volunteers and workers who are religious rather than proselytising. Stam did note that there are four religious celebrations a year, where the connections between faith and meaning are given greater prominence; participation is voluntary although residents are required to take part in the preparations. Exodus Amsterdam draws together 22 employees, around 20 volunteers and 25 ex-detainees into this space that aims to offer an alternative to overcome a perceived failing in the existent justice structure. Frank Stam commented that "in order to work in this branch you have to feel attracted to the target group and are convinced that you can mean something to them.'' The motivations of the employees and volunteers vary but while they are required to support the mission and goals of the organisation, these are not explicitly religious in foundation and Exodus remains open to all.

Although Exodus started as a local scheme, it has grown into a national programme in partnership with the state. At present, 70 per cent of the Amsterdam residents are involved in a judicial procedure, for which the organisation receives funding from the Ministry of Justice. The result has been the increasing professionalisation of Exodus Amsterdam as this involvement requires greater accountability and administration. The alternative space of care offered by Exodus has been changed by its relationship with the state; although the profile of its users has correspondingly altered, a space is retained for the original target group of ex-detainees who voluntarily apply for the programme with the express aim of bettering their lives.

This case highlights the relationships that can exist between state and FBO, with the state being attracted by the specific capabilities that Exodus utilises in its projects. The latter is not a puppet of the rollback or rollout neoliberal state although the change in aim does suggest a degree of co-option; however, by retaining a space for its original goals, Exodus maintains a space for an alternative to the hegemony. This relationship is now changing with the current right-wing political climate within Amsterdam affecting the approach the authorities are taking to projects such as Exodus Amsterdam and therefore the budget of the project. State–FBO relationships can be highly volatile as these are spaces in which postsecular ethics demonstrate their necessitarian nature; when the ideologies or priorities of the state change so too do the needs identified as important, which then disrupts relationships with FBOs. This situation is particularly significant when the FBO has been drawn into relations of financial dependence and can no longer operate without state assistance.

Empirical moment 3: Christian Aid and Resources Foundation

CARF is an Amsterdam-based FBO dedicated to the rescue and rehabilitation of female victims of the sex 'slave trade'. Mostly from Africa, these women have been brought to the Netherlands against their will by a trafficking syndicate and have suffered torture and abuse. The Reverend Tom Marfo established the organisation in 1990 in response to a recognition that, as he states, "there is no other group of people more excluded from basic fundamental human rights ... than the victims of the sex slave industry." Gender is a clear shaper of this space of care, with women both targeted recipients of care and among the volunteer providers. At first this appears to perpetuate traditional gender roles with the male reverend initiating and coordinating the rescue of women; however, the female victims need to be active participants in this process. While Marfo may be responsible for providing a route to escape, this is not an easy one for the women who must confront both their traffickers and, as many are illegal immigrants, the state. It was only in 2001 that the B9 rule was introduced in the Netherlands, which grants victims temporary rights of residence for the duration of the criminal proceedings as well a right to shelter, medical care and legal assistance. Although a step forward, the B9 rule has been criticised as providing only limited protection, with no right to work or access to education and with many victims being subsequently deported (BDRTHB, 2002). Tom Marfo participated in the documentary that contributed to this change in the law and this demonstrates the multi-scalar strategy taken by CARF to try and tackle this socially and politically sensitive issue.

Within Amsterdam, CARF provides five apartments/mission houses in secret locations across the city. The women are given food as well as social and spiritual support and are offered education and work opportunities. Training in IT, hairdressing, sewing and cooking offers a route to a different life, giving the transition away from prostitution more chance of being permanent. CARF is also involved in similar educational projects in the countries of origin, particularly Ghana and Nigeria, where it provides information about human trafficking to families and organises professional training opportunities. Being faith-based has helped CARF reach out to the victims, with Tom Marfo helping to break the spiritual bondage of girls through voodoo, which allows them to testify.

Although CARF is still grounded in physical and spiritual support and care, Marfo has shifted his role over time to one more of political advocacy. He considers this as the only way to achieve the international abolition of the modern slave trade and therefore has a highly collaborative and cooperative approach. CARF works with other Christian faith-based organisations and NGOs as well as the police and justice department. Despite some initial difficulties with the latter, Marfo has played an instrumental role in closing down several criminal networks in Amsterdam; he recognises that "the police cannot win the battle against crime unless they have local knowledge and local expertise." Therefore, despite receiving no public funding, Marfo works as a government expert, giving occasional training to the immigration service on the spiritual component of human trafficking and cooperating with a research unit on human trafficking within the Ministry of Justice.

CARF's motivations are strongly faith-based, with Marfo stating that, "it is not a project. It is a personal crusade…. I am a reverend and everything I do, I do it from the perspective of my faith. This [the sex slave trade] is evil and we have to fight against evil. So my motivation is 100 per cent faith-based." Six volunteers from the church community support CARF and all of the money to fund the projects is raised within this. To Marfo, the faith that grounds CARF's work is critical as it places the organisation in a better position to "help heal inner wounds … [as] the church is a healing place. The church is the family home that holds all the family members together."

Conclusion

The dynamism and mobility characteristic of urban areas, combined with the impact of neoliberalism and globalisation on inner-city welfare and communities, has created an array of spaces for postsecular engagement that have multiple and fluid characteristics. A selection of spaces of postsecular engagement were introduced that showed the interconnected and various characteristics of these arenas of dialogue and collaboration. The empirical moments of London Citizens, Exodus Amsterdam and CARF provided lived examples of postsecular spaces, which demonstrated the inherent complexity and dynamism within these highly contextual and place-based engagements. The postsecular may have an impact on the global scale but it comes from a local recognition of mutuality and need. London Citizens in particular shows the political capacity of postsecularism and the strong enactment of an alternative, which, we argued, grounds the development of a postsecular ethics based on solidarity, justice and hope. Through Exodus Amsterdam and CARF, the intersubjective nature of postsecular ethics was shown in the emphasis placed on relationships and meaning; we are all individuals within society and can perform a particular identity that recognises our self *in community* and hence our responsibilities to others. In addition, CARF highlights the necessity of a multi-scalar approach to tackling 'local' problems and the role that faith can play in connecting the complex local and global dimensions of urban issues. One aspect of both postsecular spaces and ethics that emerged through the cases was the potential transience of the postsecular moment, which can be a durable and sustainable dialogue but equally can break down once an identified need has been addressed.

The practices of postsecular engagements offer a two-fold challenge to the neoliberal consensus by exposing its limitations, while offering a concrete alternative. They create a space for those who seek something different to hegemony and offer a way for individuals to engage their everyday ethics into broader community arenas. Choice, tolerance and solidarity create a fragmented and complex postsecular space, in which the religious and the secular can co-exist, with excessive fervour tempered by the *between* space, the dialogue. Faith clearly remains a strong element within these arenas, both as a motivator for religious participation and as a more implicit creator of a space in which non-materialist and other values are permitted. Through faith and more humanist, communitarian routes, individuals enter into engagements based on postsecular ethics, which recognises the 'I' in the 'we' of us and the importance of the relational between space in constituting a socially responsible self.

The aim of this chapter was to provoke thought regarding the spaces in which postsecular interactions take place and the active ethics that make these dialogues possible. We have considered only three case studies, which present a snapshot of postsecularism in British and Dutch cities. These are not necessarily representative of the wider postsecular experience and we strongly encourage further research that considers the political and ethical promise of postsecularism in other spaces in the UK, the Netherlands and more widely. The study of postsecularism in relation to the ethical and political engagements in cities remains in development and we hope that our insights inspire further exploration into this useful and interesting lens on contemporary society.

Notes

[1] The empirical moments are based on research conducted in 2009 for the 'Faith-based organisations and exclusion in European cities' (FACIT) project funded by the European Commission's 7th Framework Programme.

[2] *Positionality* is the recognition that our understandings are shaped by our position in the world, which has a particular place, a particular history, particular experiences and cultures although we are not contained by this position.

[3] Cloke (2011) and Cloke and Beaumont (2012) develop the notion of *rapprochement*.

[4] 'Re-enchanted' refers to Jane Bennett's work in which she argues for the continued capacity for enchantment – an emotional openness to the strange, the wonderful and the disturbing in everyday life – and the crucial role this plays in motivating ethical behaviour.

[5] The current relationship between state and civil society is a process that started with the Thatcher government in 1979 and was enhanced with the election of New Labour in 1997.

[6] We refer here to the move away from dogma to praxis, in terms of the turn in many FBOs towards 'living out' values by bringing welfare and care to the ground level through 'no-strings-attached' interactions. By 'performative', we refer to an act that performs the action to which it refers, requiring continual, repetitive praxis.

[7] London Citizens is part of the Citizens Organising Foundation (COF), which is a national umbrella for broad-based community organising in the UK and was established in 1989. Its formation recognised the need to address the crisis facing inner-city communities, a result of successive Thatcher government's policies in the 1980s (Jamoul and Wills, 2008).

[8] The Living Wage Campaign aimed to secure a living wage for the low-waged, subcontracted, primarily immigrant workers in London. Many also needed support to secure legal rights and so Strangers into Citizens campaigns for access to citizenship to be given to those who can prove that they have been in the UK for at least four years and who can demonstrate 'character' through a lack of criminal record and employer references.

[9] Recent philosophical and theological reflection has called into question the distinction between alleged religious concepts of love, faith, hope and charity with so-called secular values of justice, solidarity and equality. Nicholas Wolterstorff (2007), in *Justice: Rights and wrongs*, provides a philosophical account of justice, while bridging the divide between religious discourse and human rights.

[10] As Desmond Tutu in Rosei et al (2008, p 4627) explains, 'Africans believe in something that is difficult to render in English. We call it *ubuntu* or *botho*. It means the essence of being human…. It speaks about humanness, gentleness, hospitality, putting yourself out on behalf of others, being vulnerable. It embraces compassion and roughness. It recognizes that my humanity is bound up in yours, for we can only be human together.' The concept was central in the 2004 John Boorman film *In My Country*, praised by Nelson Mandela as an account of South Africa's Truth and Reconciliation Commission.

[11] Programme participants are placed in supported communal housing and are aided in finding employment, which can include volunteering or training.

[12] Virtue ethics move beyond the traditional binary between 'ends' and 'means' in Western ethics to ensure that ethical choices connect with, and actively constitute, the subject and their practices.

References

Alinksy, S. (1989) *Rules for radicals: A pragmatic primer for realistic radicals*, New York: Vintage Books.

Amin, A. (2006) 'The good city', *Urban Studies*, vol 43, nos 5/6, pp 1009-23.

Amin, A. (2007) 'Re-thinking the urban social', *City*, vol 11, no 1, pp 100-14.

Baker, C. (2008) 'Seeking hope in the indifferent city – faith-based contributions to spaces of production and meaning making in the postsecular city', Association of American Geographers Annual Meeting, Boston.

Baker, C. and Beaumont, J. (2010) 'Postcolonialism and religion: new spaces of "belonging and becoming" in the postsecular city', in J. Beaumont and C. Baker (eds) *Postsecular cities: Religious space, theory and practice*, London: Continuum, pp 35-67.

Barnett, C., Cloke, P. et al. (2005) 'Consuming ethics: articulating the subjects and spaces of ethical consumption', *Antipode*, vol 37, no 1, pp 23-45.

BDRTHB (Bureau of the Dutch Rapporteur on Trafficking in Human Beings) (2002) 'Protection of victims and prosecution of perpetrators of THB – some information on the approach in the Netherlands', EU/STOP Conference on Preventing and Combating Trafficking in Human Beings, Brussels: BDRTHB.

Beaumont, J. (2010) 'Transcending the particular in postsecular cities', in A.L. Molendijk, J. Beaumont and C. Jedan (eds) *Exploring the postsecular: The religious, the political and the urban*, Leiden: Brill, pp 3-17.

Beaumont, J. and Baker, C. (2010) 'Introduction: the rise of the postsecular city', in J. Beaumont and C. Baker (eds) *Postsecular cities: Space, theory and practice*, London: Continuum, p 1-14.

Bode, I. (2006) 'Disorganized welfare mixes: voluntary agencies and new governance regimes in Western Europe', *Journal of European Social Policy*, vol 16, pp 346-59.

Bourdieu, P. (2000) *Pascalian meditations*, London: Polity Press.

Braidotti, R. (2008) 'In spite of the times: the postsecular turn in feminism', *Theory, Culture & Society*, vol 25, no 6, pp 1-24.

Bretherton, L. (2010) 'Religion and the salvation of urban politics: beyond co-option, competition and commodification', in A.L. Molendijk, J. Beaumont and C. Jedan (eds) *Exploring the postsecular: The religious, the political and the urban*, Leiden, Brill, pp 207-22.

Building Bridges in Burnley (2010) 'Home' (http://bbburnley.co.uk).

Butler, J. (2005) *Giving an account of oneself*, New York: Fordham University Press.

Cabinet Office (2010a) 'Big Society strategy for charities, voluntary groups and social enterprises', *Cabinet Office News*, CAB 171-10, 14 October (www.cabinetoffice.gov.uk/newsroom/news_releases/2010/101014-big-society-strategy.aspx).

Cabinet Office (2010b) *Building a stronger civil society: A strategy for voluntary and community groups, charities and social enterprises*, London: Cabinet Office.

Casanova, J. (2001) 'Civil society and religion: retrospective reflections on Catholicism and prospective reflections on Islam', *Social Research*, vol 68, no 4, pp 1041-80.

Chapman, R. (2009) 'Faith and the voluntary sector in urban governance: distinctive yet similar?', in A. Dinham, R. Furbey and V. Lowndes (eds) *Faith in the public realm: Controversies, policies and practices*, Bristol: The Policy Press, pp 203-22.

Chapman, R. and Hamalainen, L. (2010) 'Understanding faith-based engagement and volunteering in the postsecular society: motivations, rationales and translation', in J. Beaumont and C. Baker (eds) *Postsecular cities: Religious space, theory and practice*, London: Continuum, pp 289-319.

Citizens UK (2010) 'History happens only once' (www.citizensuk.org/about/history/).

Cityside.org.nz (2011) 'The Cityside Baptist Community Website' (www.cityside.org.nz/).

Cloke, P. (2010) 'Theo-ethics and radical faith-based praxis in the postsecular city', in A.L. Molendijk, J. Beaumont and C. Jedan (eds) *Exploring the postsecular: The religious, the political and the urban*, Leiden: Brill, pp 223-42.

Cloke, P. (2011) 'Emerging postsecular rapprochement in the contemporary city', in J. Beaumont and C. Baker (eds) *Postsecular cities: Religious space, theory and practice*, London: Continuum, pp 380-407.

Cloke, P., Johnsen, S. et al (2007a) 'Ethical citizenship? Volunteers and the ethics of providing services for homeless people', *Geoforum*, vol 38, no 6, pp 1089-101.

Cloke, P., Johnsen, S. et al (2007b) 'The periphery of care: emergency services for homeless people in rural areas', *Journal of Rural Studies*, vol 23, no 4, pp 387-401.

Cordero, J. (2010) 'TELCO takes stock of the past year's achievements', 18 November (www.citizensuk.org/2010/11/telco-takes-stock-of-the-past-year%e2%80%99s-achievements/).

Cox, H. (1965) *The secular city*, London: S.C.M. Press.

Davey, A. and Graham, E. (2010) 'Inhabiting the good city: the politics of hate and the urbanisms of hope', in J. Beaumont and C. Baker (eds) *Postsecular cities: Religious space, theory and practice*, London: Continuum, pp 181-207.

de Witte, N. (2010) 'Exploring the post-secular state: the case of Amsterdam', in J. Beaumont and C. Baker (eds) *Postsecular cities: Religious space, theory and practice*, London: Continuum, pp 320-54.

Douglas, M. (2002) *Purity and danger: An analysis of concept of pollution and taboo*, London: Routledge.

Ebaugh, H.R., Pipes, P.F. et al (2003) 'Where's the religion? Distinguishing faith-based from secular social service agencies', *Journal for the Scientific Study of Religion*, vol 42, no 3, pp 411-26.

Eder, K. (1996) 'Post-secularism: a return to the public sphere', *Eurozine*, 17 August.

Faith in the City (1985) *Faith in the City: A call for action by church and nation*, the Report of the Archbishop of Canterbury's Commission on Urban Priority Areas, London: Church House Publishing.

Friedman, M. (2001) 'The interhuman and what is common to all: Martin Buber and sociology', *Journal for the Theory of Social Behaviour*, vol 29, no 4, pp 403-17.

Gorski, P.S. and Altinordu, A. (2008) 'After secularization?', *Annual Review of Sociology*, vol 34, pp 55-85.

Greve, A. (2010) 'Sanctuaries of urban virtues: learning from Edo Tokyo', in J. Beaumont and C. Baker (eds) *Postsecular cities: Religious space, theory and practice*, London: Continuum, pp 208-35.

Guest, M. and Taylor, S. (2006) 'The post-evangelical emerging church: innovations in New Zealand and the UK', *International Journal for the Study of the Christian Church*, vol 6, no 1, pp 49-64.

Habermas, J. (2005) 'Equal treatment of cultures and the limits of postmodern liberalism', *Journal of Political Philosophy*, vol 13, no 1, pp 1-28.

Habermas, J. (2008) *Beyond naturalism and religion*, Cambridge: Polity Press.

Harvey, D. (2003) 'The right to the city', *International Journal of Urban and Regional Research*, vol 27, no 4, pp 939-41.

Healey, P. (1997) *Collaborative planning. Shaping places in fragmented societies*, London: Macmillan.

Jackson, A.Y. (2004) 'Performativity identified', *Qualitative Inquiry*, vol 10, no 5, pp 673-90.

Jamoul, L. and Wills, J. (2008) 'Faith in politics', *Urban Studies*, vol 45, no 10, pp 2035-56.

Knott, K. (2010) 'Cutting through the postsecular city: a spatial interrogation', in A.L. Molendijk, J. Beaumont and C. Jedan (eds) *Exploring the postsecular: The religious, the political and the urban*, Leiden: Brill, pp 19-38.

Ley, D. (2005) *Post-multiculturalism?*, UBC RIIM Working Paper 20. No. 05-18, Vancouver, RIIM [http://riim.metropolis.net/assets/uploads/files/wp/2005/WP05-18.pdf]

Ley, D. (2008) 'The immigrant church as an urban service hub', *Urban Studies*, vol 45, no 10, pp 2057-74.

Ley, D. (2010) 'Preface: towards the postsecular city', in J. Beaumont, and C. Baker (2010) *Postsecular cities: Space, theory and practice*, London: Continuum, pp xii–xiv.

Libin, M. (2003) 'Can the subaltern be heard? Response and responsibility in South Africa's human spirit', *Textual Practice*, vol 17, no 7, pp 119-40.

MacIntyre, A. (1999) *Dependent rational animals: Why human beings need the virtues*, London: Duckworth.

McLennan, G. (2007) 'Towards postsecular sociology?', *Sociology*, vol 41, no 5, pp 857-70.

McLennan, G. (2010) 'Postsecular cities and radical critique: a philosophical sea-change?', in J. Beaumont and C. Baker (eds) *Postsecular cities: Religious space, theory and practice*, London: Continuum, pp 7-34.

Massey, D. (1999) 'Spaces of politics', in D. Massey, J. Allen and P. Sarre (eds) *Human geography today*, Cambridge: Polity Press, pp 279-94.

May, J., Cloke, P. et al (2005) 'Re-phasing neoliberalism: New Labour and Britain's crisis of street homelessness', *Antipode*, vol 37, no 4, pp 703-30.

Molendijk, A.L. (2010) 'God made the country, and man made the town: some observations on the place of religion in the Western (post)secular city', in A.L. Molendijk, J. Beaumont and C. Jedan (eds) *Exploring the postsecular: The religious, the political and the urban*, Leiden: Brill, pp 147-62.

Molendijk, A.L., Beaumont, J. et al (2010) 'Preface', in A.L. Molendijk, J. Beaumont and C. Jedan (eds) *Exploring the postsecular: The religious, the political and the urban*, Leiden: Brill, pp ix-xii.

Nicolson, R. (2008) 'Introduction. Persons in community: *Ubuntu* in the global village', in R. Nicolson (ed) *Persons in community: African ethics in a global culture*, Scottsville: University of KwaZulu-Natal Press, pp 1-14.

Paddison, R. (2009) 'Some reflections on the limitations to public participation in the post-political city', *L'espace Politique*, vol 8, pp 2-15.

Peck, J. (2006) 'Liberating the city: between New York and New Orleans', *Urban Geography*, vol 27, no 8, pp 681-713.

Ramsay, M. (1998) 'Redeeming the city: exploring the relationship between church and metropolis', *Urban Affairs Review*, vol 33, no 5, pp 595-626.

Ranciére, J. (2001) 'Ten theses on politics', *Theory and Event*, vol 5, no 3, pp 1-10.

Rosei, F., Vayssieres, L. et al (2008) 'Materials science in the developing world: challenges and perspectives for Africa', *Advanced Materials*, vol 20, pp 4627-40.

Samers, M. and Pollard, J. (2010) 'Alterity's geographies: socio-territoriality and difference in Islamic banking and finance', in D. Fuller, A.E.G. Jonas and R. Lee (eds) *Interrogating alterity: Alternative economic and political spaces*, Farnham: Ashgate, pp 47-58.

Sassen, S. (2000) 'New frontiers facing urban sociology at the millennium', *The British Journal of Sociology*, vol 51, no 1, pp 143-59.

Sider, R.J. and Unruh, H.R. (2004) 'Typology of religious characteristics of social service and educational organizational programs', *Nonprofit and Voluntary Sector Quarterly*, vol 33, no 1, pp 109-34.

Swyngedouw, E. (2010a) 'Apocalypse forever? Post-political populism and the spectre of climate change', *Theory, Culture & Society*, vol 27, nos 2-3, pp 213-32.

Swyngedouw, E. (2010b) 'Post-democratic cities: for whom and for what?', Regional Studies Association Annual Conference, Pecs, Budapest.

Timewell, S. and DiVanna, J. (2009) 'More growth, more challenges', *The Banker Supplement: Top 500 Islamic Financial Institutions*, pp 3-8.

Wills, J., Datta, K. et al (2009) 'Religion at work: the role of faith-based organizations in the London living wage campaign', *Cambridge Journal of Regions, Economy and Society*, vol 2, no 3, pp 443-61.

Wolterstorff, N. (2007) *Justice: Rights and wrongs*, Princeton, NJ: Princeton University Press.

FOUR

Faith-based organisations, urban governance and welfare state retrenchment

Ingemar Elander, Maarten Davelaar and Andrés Walliser

Introduction

In the context of successive financial crises and diminishing welfare provision offered by European governments, new demands and market conditions open new opportunities for profit as well as non-profit providers of social services targeted at socially excluded people. This chapter provides an analysis of faith-based organisations (FBOs) and their relationship to central–local government and related changes in welfare provision aimed at combating social exclusion in the Netherlands, Spain and Sweden. The central questions addressed are:

- Why are FBOs of interest in times when financial and economic crises trigger governments at all levels to reconsider their responsibilities as providers and protectors of social welfare?
- How do FBOs in different welfare regimes operate at the local level in the context of welfare retrenchment and/or redesign?
- What are their (faith-motivated) interests and strategies?
- Are FBOs in a process of replacing public authorities as welfare providers, or are they, at best, capable and willing to give complementary support at the margin?

A substantial part of the current forms and practices of FBOs in Europe, especially the Christian ones, have a long history, mostly pre-dating the welfare state. Thus, to understand the current manifestations of FBO practices in different countries we also need to be aware of their historical roots and successive developments, thus following the methodological line of thinking stated by Romanillos, Beaumont and Sen in Chapter Two of this volume, that is, that state–religion relations should be grasped in 'their historical and geographical specificity.' The Swedish case was partly chosen because it is a country where local government has an outstanding tradition and position in terms of welfare provision, and partly because it is dominated by a longstanding Lutheran state church. In contrast, Spain has a Catholic heritage, and postwar development, where local government, after formal democratisation (1978) co-administers, or has gradually taken over, social responsibilities from FBOs and other non-governmental organisations (NGOs). The Netherlands, finally, is a hybrid between a social democratic and a liberal welfare state (in the language of Esping-Andersen), with a reformist tradition of quite extensive involvement by Protestant (Calvinist) and Catholic FBOs as well as other NGOs in social affairs, where central government has increasingly downloaded responsibilities to local governments while retaining fiscal centralism, and where the developments also 'have a clear leitmotif of a shift from collective to individual responsibility' (van Oorschot, 2009, p 365).[1]

The analysis proceeds within a framework considering the importance of the three different cultural, religious, political and institutional settings. In other words, we set the national framework within which urban welfare regimes, networks and policies manifest themselves. For each country we assess how FBOs operate at the local level in the context of welfare retrenchment and/or redesign, and which (faith-motivated) interests they have in engaging more extensively in the provision and protection of social welfare. We also consider the extent to which FBOs are using different strategies to cope with the new arrangements, that is, competition with other NGOs or with for-profit suppliers of services. Finally, we discuss whether FBOs are in a process of taking over social responsibilities from a withdrawing welfare state, or if they are capable and willing to give complementary support at the margin.

Experiences from the three countries are penetrated on the basis of documentary studies and interviews (2008-10) with professionals and volunteers undertaken within the framework of the FACIT project. The country-by-country analyses are based on in-depth studies reported in extensive publications (Dierckx et al, 2009; Davelaar et al, 2011; Elander and Fridolfsson, 2011; Walliser and Villanueva, 2011), and are followed by comparative reflections in the concluding section of the chapter. However, before diving into the three case studies there is a need for conceptually specifying the relationship between FBOs, government and governance.

Faith-based organisations in relation to government and governance

As demonstrated by Neil Brenner (2004) and others, contemporary state institutions are rescaled at once upwards, downwards and outwards. One consequence of this development is that cities and local governments are increasingly becoming crucial sites for exploring how the social needs of poor people are met or ignored in local politics. According to the European Union (EU) framework for urban policy, for example, 'the long-term integration of economic, social and environmental policies at the local level should counter social exclusion and enhance urban liveability and economic prosperity' (Kokx and van Kempen, 2010, p 357). But if local government *should* do this, what, then, happens in practice?

At first sight, the shift downwards of responsibilities to the local level of government may look like a process in favour of a more decentralist and participatory style of politics. But this process is more complicated as it is often accompanied by central state-governed, neoliberal practices, including decreasing central government grants and severe fiscal stress on local government budgets, thus making local governments dependent on cooperation with external partners such as private companies and voluntary organisations (Elander and Montin, 1990; Granberg, 2008; Kokx and van Kempen, 2010). Of course, outright privatisation is another option.

The social consequences of the downward policy shifts create space for FBOs and other NGOs to mobilise their resources and play a greater role than before as providers, and protectors, of social welfare. In some countries there have even been settled national agreements between the government and 'organised civil society' about a kind of division of labour in the field of social welfare provision (ECAS, 2010). Irrespective of such agreements, FBOs and other NGOs have mobilised their members and professional workers to complement social service welfare provision. Thus, when governments for financial and/or ideological reasons do not fulfil the expectations of meeting social needs and demands, the potential role of FBOs increases.

FBOs may then take on a role as alternative or complementary providers of social services. Roughly, three forms of FBO activities can be identified, that is, *service delivery* (including relational as well as infrastructural service provision); *capacity building* (including resourcing, networking and faith sector advocacy); and *political campaigning* (including representing marginalised groups, consultation, lobbying and protest) (Cloke et al, 2009, p 286). Most of the activities performed by FBOs are officially legitimised or at least not illegal, for example, sheltering homeless people, or helping drug addicts to get rid of their drug dependency, but FBOs may also cross the borderline to illegal action, for example, by helping undocumented immigrants, or supporting doctors giving healthcare to these people. Next, we show how the role of FBOs has developed in the three selected European countries.

Beyond pillarisation: the case of the Netherlands

Describing the relations between the government and religious organisations in the Netherlands is unthinkable without extensive reference to the history of pillarisation (*verzuiling*). The development of the Dutch welfare state is closely interwoven with group formation of orthodox Protestants, Roman Catholics, Socialists and, to a lesser extent, Liberals (Knippenberg, 2006). The institutionalisation of freedom of religion and education, as stated in the 1848 Constitution, gave rise to a struggle for equal treatment in terms of public funding for secular and faith-based schools. This development became the precursor of a struggle for full political rights of both Protestants and Catholics, one that encouraged institutionalisation along religious and ideological lines in all sectors of society (including social work, healthcare and housing) and led to the so-called pillarisation of Dutch society (Polderman, 2002). It also marked the beginning of what Lijphart (1975) has referred to as a 'consociational democracy', marked by pacification of religious and ideological diversity within the political system. The (confessional) 'pillars' developed into bulwarks of organisational power. Subcultures flourished, and while the elites cooperated intensively in political and socioeconomic institutions, platforms and other relevant consultation bodies, distrust of the 'others' and isolation, fuelled by the leadership, was common among group members. By financing a broad range of FBOs operating in the fields of education, care and welfare, the state was able to monitor and regulate the activities of religious groups (Kennedy and Valenta, 2006). The Catholic doctrine of subsidiarity and the parallel principle of 'sphere sovereignty', developed by the Calvinist leader Abraham Kuyper (1837-1920), were very influential in the inter-bellum and post-Second World War period (Monsma, 2006).

Gradual empowerment of local government

After the Second World War, the central state and its constitutive pillars gradually created a comprehensive welfare state. The strong influence of pillarisation and the centralist character of the Dutch state, in which organisations with a religious or social democratic background were primarily responsible for delivering services on the ground, rendered the municipalities relatively powerless in terms of welfare policies. However, from the 1980s onwards there was a shift in emphasis towards decentralisation. This process allowed the municipalities to gain influence in various areas, especially in the field of social assistance and social work as well as parts of direct, frontline care for older people, people with disabilities and the homeless. However, in spite of local taxation policy the municipalities still heavily depend on the central state for financial support through the municipal fund (*gemeente fonds*). The central state also decides the extent to which budgets are earmarked, or could be invested, according to local priorities. Important national frames include the Social Support Act 2007 and the recently created single 'participation budget', integrating budgets on activation, labour reintegration and sheltered labour. In addition, national programmes are important for local policies, hence the popularity of and disputes around the successive major cities policies and the adherent national district policies. These national programmes have increased consultation on urgent social urban problems between national and local authorities (Davelaar et al, 2003). To summarise, therefore, decentralisation is a dominant trend in the Netherlands, although national laws and programmes have not always granted local authorities the personnel and financial means needed to meet the growing list of tasks for which they are responsible (van Berkel and van der Aa, 2005).

Secularisation and depillarisation

In the 1960s, late in comparison with other 'modern' societies, a period of rapid secularisation started. This trend, both in terms of declining beliefs and practices, weakened the authority of the faith-based 'pillars' and heralded the beginning of a process of 'depillarisation'. Within Western Europe, the Netherlands is among those countries with the steepest decline in church attendance and belief in god over the last half a century (Norris and Inglehart, 2004). The new 1983 Constitution sealed the transformation of the Netherlands into a secular country. The financial ties between the state and churches – based on historically established rights – were dissolved, and the distinction between religious and non-religious worldviews disappeared. Although the Dutch Constitution does not contain formal articles on the separation of church and state non-interference in institutional matters is the rule.

While the scope of the welfare state increased considerably in the 1960s and 1970s, the delivery of public services largely remains in the hands of third sector organisations, including (former) FBOs. The government took over the lion's share of the financial responsibilities, while the denominational organisations opened their doors for the general public, regardless of their beliefs or memberships. As a result, many FBOs transformed into quasi-governmental organisations, characterised by corporatist forms, and supported by large sums of state subsidies. FBOs that did not adjust their activities witnessed a significant decline in their projects and were forced to abandon a large part of their work due to lack of sufficient funding. In the long run, only those *national* organisations with strong ties to ideological mother organisations succeeded in retaining their relative independence from the state, although they, too, asked for public funding such as the welfare and health division of The Salvation Army (de Boer and Duyvendak, 2004). *Local* faith-based services also survived, although commonly losing most of their share in the (semi-) institutionalised care and welfare provision. Instead, their activities shifted towards the most vulnerable and unreachable groups in society, and they became heavily dependent on volunteers (Davelaar et al, 2011).

Among FBO volunteers, as elsewhere in Europe (Edgardh, 2011), women are overrepresented, and especially active in 'caring'. In the main Protestant church, however, women are entitled to fulfil all positions, and are hence also able to chair diaconal bodies and lead faith-based services (Davelaar et al, 2011). Even in the Roman Catholic church, the diaconal activities of several local parishes are, at least de facto, supervised by women. In many urban platforms women are strongly represented and a growing number of local organisations, especially in the bigger cities like Amsterdam, Rotterdam and Tilburg, are led by female directors and managers. The largest service provider in the survey, The Salvation Army, welfare and healthcare organisation (about 5,000 employees in 2009) has a female commander in charge. In Christian services with a non-Western background and an evangelical signature, there are highly influential women in (stand-alone) services such as food banks, children's services and neighbourhood services. Christian orthodox and Muslim FBOs are still largely male dominated. Although the female contribution to social and political activities in Dutch Muslim FBOs is growing, this is still basically taking place in women's branches of Islamic organisations. At the local level, however, the influence of individual women as members of staff or executive bodies should not be under-estimated.

Faith-based organisations as supplementary providers of welfare

The trend toward decentralisation of services intensified during the 1990s. New tasks called for new responsibilities and more freedoms in terms of policy, and – until 2010 – expanding local budgets for vulnerable people, such as people with disabilities, people with socio-psychological problems, young people at risk and the homeless. By stressing the need to build new partnerships and involve local civil society in policy delivery, FBOs attracted attention:

> 'They have discovered us as a place where you can do something with social cohesion and citizenship.... For years they have not seen that we already did this for a very long time.' (de Kruijf, 2009)

The revival and revaluation of faith-based action for the socially excluded can be illustrated by the Social Support Act 2007, which links informal and professional care, preventing the use of 'expensive' individual services and developing new tailor-made approaches. The aim of the Act is to promote the empowerment of vulnerable groups including people with disabilities, long-term care patients, the homeless and young people at risk. The Act also strives to enhance volunteering in society and promote social cohesion in neighbourhoods and towns. Service delivery is partly privatised or at least market-driven, with NGOs and companies competing. Civil society organisations, including churches and mosques, are encouraged to assume the role of intermediary organisations between clients and social services agencies (Dautzenberg and van Westerlaak, 2007; Davelaar et al, 2009).

From a government perspective, FBO involvement within the framework of the Social Support Act has some advantages. First, churches, mosques, service providers with a religious background and inter-religious platforms are able to represent clients or citizens in formal consultation bodies appointed by law. This representation may benefit client participation and accountability in local communities. Second, FBO involvement provides public services with an additional or first entrance to vulnerable and unattainable groups within the local population, thus linking informal and family care to professional, specialised care. Subsequently, the involvement of religious communities forms an attractive gateway to recruit (new) volunteers for public purposes, and increases the number of potential (semi-) professional service providers for vulnerable groups.

Limitations of faith-based organisation involvement in welfare provision

FBOs are also committed to taking care of problems that are considered of low priority or are unrecognised by public authorities. Moreover, they are aware of the danger of being 'used' by public and private organisations, or being overloaded by tasks that are, in theory, the responsibility of government. In general, FBOs are driven by the importance of long-term involvement in supporting people in need, and offering good public services ('helping under protest'). They seem to be ready for doing whatever the government or others fail to do ('helping where there is no helper'), and lay emphasis on their own responsibility for working with people and for increasing social cohesion, although they have also criticised and attempted to influence policies. One example of conflict is the contracting out of public services of which the Netherlands is an early champion, especially in the fields of labour reintegration and domestic care for people with disabilities and older people. Although this habit has already reached its peak and is currently declining in significance, it opened new spaces for FBO involvement in service delivery, while also creating challenges to working methods. One example is the *Strategy plan for social relief* (2006), initiated by the national government, the four biggest cities and leading service providers, including The Salvation Army. As a result of this ambitious national action plan (from 2008 onwards, including 43 cities), the interviewees active in homeless services have witnessed an increase in available funding and state intervention, although this intervention also takes the form of increased centralisation in policy design and regulation, including restrictions on the choice of clients and on the support provided (Davelaar and van den Toorn, 2010a).

Faith-based organisations and governments – mutual dependence

Dutch authorities subsidise the activities and projects of FBOs, either within the context of official policies, or because they have an interest in FBOs who provide assistance to certain groups that the welfare state does not include. The government has also been keen on financing projects of faith-based self-organisations of migrants aimed at fostering the emancipation and participation of their members in society. Although there is much continuity in the relationship between state and religion, especially at the local level, there are also innovations. In national integration policies there is a development from stimulating the emancipation of minorities in society towards civic integration of newcomers. Religion – that is, Islam and to a lesser extent, African Christianity – is more than ever before perceived as an obstacle for integration. New tensions arise when society is no longer officially organised along the old socio-religious lines, whereas at the same time new religious groups claim their right to build capacity in their own communities. Many Dutch people fear the return of 'religiously-based practices [of] intolerance within structures of tolerance' through the support of minority communities (Kennedy and Valenta, 2006, p 348).

In addition, previously undisputed forms of state support for FBO activities in society are being met with more suspicion and are openly debated. Discussions concerning government subsidies to FBOs generally commence at the local level. The outcome often depends on the perceptions of the mayor and members of the municipal executive about whether social activities of FBOs can be defined in non-religious terms, and whether these are perceived as representative interlocutors or partners for implementation (see also Canatan et al, 2003). Overall, the discussion is increasingly concentrated on principal questions such as the separation of state and religion (Davelaar and Smits van Waesberghe, 2010).

Over the last decade, rather than withdrawing, the state took an unprecedented level of control over services for the homeless and other marginalised people, although FBOs remain responsible for a large proportion of service delivery. In other social welfare domains, however, secular services are dominant (Davelaar and van den Toorn, 2010b). The economic crisis and the trend towards greater responsibilities for individuals, their families and friends might alter that development, thus in the future putting more pressure on FBOs in providing care for the most excluded in society. It is unlikely that they will answer that call unconditionally, or on their own, without support and cooperation from the local state. They expect public authorities to be the providers of social welfare. Just as a Rotterdam-based 'Old Districts pastor' stated: "The state is still the biggest charity around" (quoted in Davelaar et al, 2011, p 93).

Retrenchment in a welfare state under construction: the case of Spain

The relations between FBOs and the welfare system in Spain are defined not only by the historical role of the Catholic Church in social action, but also by the fact that the welfare state as such grew and consolidated in a period of restructuring of European classic welfare state paradigms. This process was an outcome of the first democratic Constitution in 1976. In Spain, as compared to many other European countries, there has *not*, until recently, been a retrenchment of a welfare state. Rather, the country has witnessed the advent of a welfare regime that has been 'invented' in a period of accelerated secularisation of society, increasing social demands and the blossoming of democratic civil society.

Two transitions in government–civil society relations

There have been two big transitions in Spain in relation to the welfare state and FBOs. The first one came with the transition towards democracy and the subsequent years of state building and consolidation. In those years there was a primitive social security regime that integrated a number of the assistance and charitable services provided earlier by the Catholic Church, which was then hegemonic as a religious group by law and by membership. During the 1980s the centralist authoritarian rule structure gave way to a quasi-federal state with 21 autonomous regions divided into 8,114 municipalities.

The three institutional levels (regions, provinces and municipalities) have jurisdiction over welfare provision and provide services directly or fund other organisations to do so. Although the central state defines the general framework of the welfare regime, implementation is decentralised to the regions, provinces and municipalities, with regional and intra-regional variations. Big cities have the capacity to develop their own strategies, although the region also provides services in a more complementary sense. However, smaller municipalities are still dependent on the *diputaciónes provinciales* (supra local administrative realm) for complementary services. In this process, and despite the fact that liberty of creed was formally proclaimed in 1967, it was not until 1980 that non-Catholic FBOs were legally acknowledged and given the right to develop associations, foundations or other institutions. Once religious liberty was legalised, the role of the still largely Catholic FBOs varied from one place to another, mainly due to the capacity of the FBOs to adjust their mission to a context of secular or 'neutral' public policy implementation.

During the 1980s FBOs were affected by the transformation of the third sector, that is, the 'emancipation' of the Spanish Red Cross from its historical ties with the state, to the 13/1982 Law of Social Integration of the Handicapped. The statist character of the Law demands that the public sector provides non-profit organisations with technical assistance, coordination, planning and economic support. However, to be eligible, private organisations must strictly follow the criteria set up by public administration (Casado, 2008). Some FBOs came together and agreed on collaboration with the corresponding public bodies:

> 'In that sense we can say that there was a regularisation of the situation.
> This does not imply, however, that it took place without any tensions.
> That is another issue.' (Caritas España, 2009)

In those days there was still increasing support to the third sector given by central government, encouraging volunteering and social action. Catholic FBOs benefited because there was a new law passed in 1987 through which the state would give a share of the taxes (0.5 per cent) to the Catholic Church, although taxpayers could decide whether they wanted their taxes to go to the Catholic Church or to other social interest organisations. For many Catholic FBOs this implied a dual flow of financial support since they could receive money both as members of the church and as NGOs.

The second transition took place during the 1990s with the introduction of new public management strategies. Thus, Spanish society was now facing a welfare mix as a result of the evolution of the embryonic welfare regime that started 10 years before (Marban, 2008). As in other EU countries, these processes were spurred by the Directive 2004/18/EC, which opened transnational territorial competition for welfare service providers, both for profit and non-profit organisations, among them FBOs. For-profit organisations were now invited to a field traditionally dominated by the third sector, and by Catholic FBOs in particular. In spaces where civil society is stronger in the local realm, transition is slower, whereas transition is faster where civil society is weaker. NGOs in general, including FBOs, are now facing a big challenge: either to keep their relative independence and run the risk of losing new market opportunities, or becoming more sensitive to public sector demands, thus stimulating partnership relations and corporate growth (Marban, 2008). Most respondents claim that these changes might alter the essence of their secular action, that is, as providers of such social care that for-profit-making companies are not ready or willing to provide: "How can social services fight against loneliness? We defend human company" (Comunidad de San Egidio).

In terms of gender there has traditionally been an overrepresentation of women in Catholic FBOs, mainly nuns, who still do the bulk of face-to-face contact with clients. Women perform about 85 per cent of all church roles that do not require ordination (Stewart, 2008). Caritas Diocesana, depending directly on each parish, is a good example. Although men tend to be more active in voluntary work at an older age once they are retired, the secularisation process has caused a crisis of voluntary engagement in favour of the professionalisation of social work. As a consequence the skills required have opened certain positions to male workers. However, social work, education, nursery care and so on are still dominated by women. On the other hand, women have also become more represented at the higher ranks of some FBOs, especially those with a leftist orientation, and some organisations directly depending on the Catholic Church have women, usually highly qualified nuns, in leading positions.

Different local welfare regimes

The relations of FBOs with local administration are more intimate than with the strictly regulatory central state framework. The role of FBOs in the governance schemes of the local welfare regime has to do with the colour of the city government. Different local welfare regimes allow FBOs to participate more or less in the debate, design and implementation of policies, ranging from a very inclusive (with the whole third sector) Barcelona, to a much more market-led Madrid. The two cities show different degrees of externalisation of social service provision and decentralisation, also reflecting different ways of understanding social cohesion in the city. Madrid has had a conservative (right) government for the last 21 years while the left has governed Barcelona since 1979 (Walliser, 2003; Walliser et al, 2010). The situation has changed recently, however, as Barcelona is now (since 2011) governed by a nationalist conservative majority. The sharp economic crisis of city and regional government has led to massive cuts in expenditure, with a strong emphasis on subcontracting provision of social services to the profit sector and to civil society.

Welfare provision in Madrid is increasingly being privatised, with the consequence that bidding is putting FBOs and NGOs out of the market by big for-profit companies that often under-bid in order to win public contracts. Barcelona, on the other hand, has developed a social welfare policy based on broader action networks. FBOs are also facing the consequences of this process although they may keep their own resources and infrastructure, thus facing a less disadvantaged position. Still, they have to confront the dilemma of keeping quality and service efficiency in times when economic efficiency has become the main criterion for public procurement. There is a risk that the added value of the mission, and the commitment with the most vulnerable people, are substituted by the lower costs faced by the public administration, with quality sacrificed for financial reasons. The difference between Madrid and Barcelona is largely explained by the traditionally stronger role of civil society in Catalonia, where a diversity of social movements and civic organisations are embedded in the social fabric, providing services in education, leisure, popular culture and so on. Often children and young people engage in different kinds of associations, remaining, for most of their lives, linked to the associative world although shifting with age and personal interests.

In Barcelona the model implemented in the last decade regards social inclusion as a main priority of social policies. FBOs, as other NGOs, are integrated into a tight system of local social welfare. This system, contained in the *Municipal plan of social inclusion* (2005-10), regards the third sector not only as a strict service provider but also as a key actor in achieving social cohesion at the local level through action networks and community plans. In a city like Barcelona, with a leftist government and a strong secular tradition, FBOs have a protagonist role in the governance pattern of the local welfare regime, both as policy implementers and as advisers and key social agents. On the other hand, in Madrid, ruled by a conservative party, the access of FBOs to social policy is as service providers in competition with for-profit organisations.

Dominance of Catholic faith-based organisations

Another issue regarding the relation of FBOs with public administration is the availability of opportunities for different denominations. Catholic religion was the only one allowed in Spain between 1939 and 1967. The advent of democracy brought freedom of belief, including cooperation agreements with other denominations, mainly Protestant, Muslim and Jewish. The minority position of these three religions in relation to the Catholic Church in an increasingly secularised country has led to a de facto monopoly of this church as a service provider for public administration (Walliser and Villanueva, 2011, pp 47-51).

Today, talking about FBOs and welfare provision as public administrator contractors means talking about hegemonic Catholic FBOs with a significant absence of other denominations due to their own organisational structures and strategies. The main umbrella organisation of the Protestant church, Diaconia, is developing training schemes that increase the visbility of social action among churches. Although the Protestant churches are very active in fighting social exclusion and have developed some impressive programmes (such as Remar for treating drug addicts and Betel for integration), the heavy reliance of their methods on their religious mission, and the historical reluctance to Protestantism in Spain, often make them ineligible for public procurements.

In the Roma community (500,000 people), Roma-funded Protestant churches like the Church of Philadelphia have gradually managed to withdraw the majority of the community from the Catholic creed. The Catholic Church has not paid a great deal of attention to the community except for the FBOs working with integration and accessibility for the community into mainstream society:

> 'There has been an emergence of new leaders with "acquired power" rather than the old men with "ascribed power". The new type of leader, the pastor of the intermediate generations, know how to read and write. What is always wanted from a multicultural leader is to establish connections between both cultures. Therefore, pastors have fulfilled many functions that were not only religious, but social as well.' (Fresno, 2009)

Muslims, despite increasing in numbers with migration, have not yet developed big FBOs with a social assistance dimension as in some other EU countries. There is a latent conflict in some towns, especially in Catalonia, where the Muslim community is discriminated against and not allowed to open mosques in the city centres but in industrial areas or in the outskirts of towns. As a response to this negative stance on the part of the authorities, a growing number of informal 'cellar mosques' have been created, providing religious services and social aid to the Muslim community.

Continuity and innovation: the case of Sweden

The history of Swedish FBOs is very much the history of the Lutheran Church of Sweden and its relation to the state, although there has always been important, complementary welfare provision offered by other religious actors such as free churches (since the late 19th century), philanthropic societies and private foundations. The Church of Sweden originally had a demarcated mission to provide public welfare within the spiritual sphere, and was integrated into the country's welfare system during the 20th century, but lost this privileged status in 2000 when it, at least formally, became just one of many independent FBOs. The Church of Sweden expresses its social (diaconal) mission with the following words: 'The church should be a voice for the vulnerable and the weak – in Sweden and abroad' (Church of Sweden, 2010). As stated by an official spokesman, the church is "a complement to the public sector, an alternative and a critical voice"; in other words, diaconal work is all about standing on the side of the unfortunate, giving them a voice to target responsible actors, for example, local government officials. In line with this mission and without siding with any particular political party, the church should be critical towards deteriorating public health and well-being (Hjalmarsson, 2009).[2]

The diaconal mission of the Church of Sweden is largely provided by the approximately 1,200 employed and ordained deacons, the majority of whom are women, educated as social workers, nurses or psychologists. In 1958 women were allowed to become ordained priests, the first three female priests were inaugurated in 1960, and today, 45 per cent of the priests are women. Among priest students there is a majority of women. However, among vicars, 75 per cent are men, thus still indicating a patriarchal hierarchy (Berg, 2010). As noted by Ninna Edgardh on the basis of an eight-country comparative study on welfare and religion in the 21st century, these figures indicate 'a highly gendered area in the churches, with strictly divided roles for women and men; women are primarily located in relational caring work and men in more technical and organizational roles, as well as in the higher levels of decision-making' (Edgardh, 2011, p 95). Women are further 'much more frequently found in lay structures such as the sewing circle, a major movement through much of the twentieth century which has played an important role both for the women concerned and through the collection of money for local and international projects' (Edgardh, 2011, p 83). The study also found that 'men do not want to be seen doing caring work while women do not want to be visible in a "public" place' (Edgardh, 2011, p 79). The striking gender divide between men in leading and managing roles on the one hand, and women in social care on the other, also goes for most free churches in Sweden, with mostly male pastors by tradition, although with a stronger female representation in socially orientated activities. The Salvation Army, however, is the exception, with about 60 per cent female principals (*föreståndare*) and pastors (Dagen, 2009). Generally, voluntary work with a social orientation engages women more than men (Svedberg et al, 2010, p 22).

Lately, the Church of Sweden and other Swedish FBOs have been facing the challenges of increasing immigration. Although there has been fairly broad political and popular support for this development, the structural discrimination and anti-immigration protest, often with an islamophobian touch, are also common phenomena is well documented (Khakee and Johansson, 1999; Andersson and Molina, 2003; Dahlstedt, 2007). The entrance of the anti-immigration anti-Islamic party, the Sweden Democrats (*Sverigedemokraterna*) into the *Riksdag* (the parliament) as a result of the September 2010 elections has caused a debate in Swedish society, and will certainly do so for years to come (Elander and Fridolfsson, 2011). What about the Islamic congregations in this context?

The United Islamic Congregations in Sweden, founded in 1974, now organise 54 local FBOs with about 50,000 members. Beneficiaries are poor immigrants, asylum-seekers and visiting people from other countries passing through. The organisation plays an important role for Muslims residing in Sweden who hesitate to contact authorities due to fear or lack of language skills (FIFS, 2010). As stated by the president of the Islamic Association in Stockholm, Abdallah Salah, "Our vision is that Islam should be a natural part of Sweden. It should not be anything odd being a Swedish Muslim. Our task is to strengthen Muslims in Sweden and to give non-Muslims more knowledge about Islam" (Salah, 2009a). He also says: "We are part of society. Saving souls is not enough" (Salah, 2009b).

In line with Islamic tradition and practice, Muslim congregations are strongly male dominated in terms of leadership and management (Edgardh, 2006, pp 23-4), although Muslim women may be very active in everyday matters. This kind of 'invisible activity' was documented by historian Klara Folkesson in a study of Muslim women in a Swedish neighbourhood (Folkesson, 2011). In the local branch of Verdandi, a non-religious temperance movement with roots as far back as 1896, Muslim women's long-time unemployment was balanced by the opportunity to participate in certain activities such as sewing, baking and education in the Swedish language and knowledge about Swedish society. Within their local networks these women experienced a sense of belonging and identity, making themselves better equipped for life in the new country. Increasingly Swedish media are reporting on social activities undertaken by Muslim women, for example, when one woman engaged 120 girls in learning and training basketball in a multi-ethnic neighbourhood. As stated by the employed (male) manager of the neighbourhood centre:

> 'Malika mirrors the women here and is one of them. As Muslim and woman they have a special trust in her. She is a star in the neighbourhood.' (*Nerikes Allehanda*, 2010)[3]

Faith-based organisations as a complement

The central–local government system of Sweden is integrative with the 290 municipalities, having substantial financial, constitutional, legal, political and professional resources. During the last 20 years, however, the country has experienced a transformation process with great repercussions for the municipalities. 'Deregulation', 'privatisation', 'partnerships' and 'citizen participation' are catchwords symbolising the character of this transformation (Elander and Montin, 1990; Granberg, 2008), thus opening an arena for more intense communication and potential cooperation between local governments and FBOs.

There is also widespread support for the universal Swedish welfare system among FBOs. Consequently, FBOs have taken occasionally taken action, as they believe, as they believe that public authorities have a general responsibility for social welfare. Many of the informants whom we interviewed described the cuts in public welfare as being a problem, transferring the burden onto the FBOs, as shown in these two quotes below:[4]

> 'Social workers employed by the city are sometimes forced to tell people in need to turn to the church instead, because there is not

enough money in the budget to guarantee the basic rights anymore.' (Kyhlström, 2009)

'Beneficiaries have confidence in the mosque and therefore turn to the mosque for support. This confidence is good, but we would also like the public welfare institutions adapt to needs among new groups of citizens in order to safeguard also their constitutional rights.' (Salah, 2009a)

In brief, FBO money should not be spent on things that ought to be financed by taxes, goes the reasoning.

Faith-based or for-profit substitution of public welfare?

The most recent, and potentially most thorough, change involving FBOs in the social arena is an agreement (Agreement 2008) between the Swedish government, national non-profit organisations in the social sphere and the Swedish Association of Local Authorities and Regions (SALAR). According to the basic principles of the Agreement, democracy and welfare should be developed, state and local government should be sensitive to the experience of civil society organisations and SALAR should participate in all phases of the Agreement process, thus confirming the strong historical ties between the central state, the municipalities and civil society. Although the Agreement is mainly a statement of principle, its implications may be far-reaching depending on the outcomes of ongoing local dialogues.

The Agreement signifies a rhetorical shift of welfare provision in the direction of civil society, although in practice the move towards for-profit welfare provision has been much more substantial than the devolution of social responsibilities to FBOs and other NGOs so far, especially with the EU Directive 2004/18/EC which opened a larger geographical territory for competition. Thus, for-profit provision of social welfare takes a much bigger share than non-profit provision and the tendency is a further growing share of the former, although both forms are still small compared to the still dominant role of public welfare provision.

Despite the strong tendency towards for-profit provision of welfare, the Church of Sweden, through its diaconal work, remains an important provider of social welfare both in specific areas such as hospitals, prisons and armed forces as in various everyday social matters. FBOs, like city missions as well as The Salvation Army and other free churches, offer shelter to homeless people, help drug addicts and offer a number of other social services. For the many immigrants having entered Swedish society, the Stockholm Mosque and a growing number of mosques and cellar mosques in many cities offer welfare provision in a broad sense. In the case of asylum-seekers and undocumented people, a nation-wide engagement from the grassroots in the church parishes and other congregations around Easter time in 2005 ('the Easter Call') triggered the parliament and the government to decide on temporary asylum for 20,000 asylum-seekers, and to reconsider the whole issue of immigrants' rights. This protest campaign against tougher policies towards refugees was orchestrated by the Christian Council of Sweden, an ecumenical forum. In a short time a petition, also supported by Islamic congregations and a large number of non-religious NGOs, was signed by 157,000 people, and turned over to the Minister for Migration and Asylum Policy (Elander and Fridolfsson, 2011). Employees and volunteers in many parishes by their own initiatives began hiding refugees, normally giving arguments such as "I simply had to" or "It had to be done." One priest in a parish in West Sweden says:

> 'To me it is about preserving my freedom, my conscience and my belief. One must be able to act and make such choices that one gets adversaries and ends up in minority. I don't see any difference between hiding Kosovo Albanians today or hiding Jews during World War II.[…] People have always done like this. Just as they have always loved, given birth to children, and died, they have hidden others if necessary. Josef and Maria were offered a place in the stable.' (interview reported in Qviström, 2005, p 100)

Keeping in mind the broad support of 'the Easter Call' from religious as well as secular organisations and individuals, the citation indicates an unconditional hospitality that could be related to the ethics of citizenship mentioned in Chapter Two earlier, an ethics crossing between the secular and the religious.

Finally, although FBOs have a self-interest in engaging themselves in the provision and protection of social welfare, they also see a risk that professionalisation of their own organisations may dilute the motivations of their voluntary work, thus potentially weakening the faith core of their mission. On the one hand, they feel a pressure to develop business-like management structures; on the other, they fear that this might lead to betraying their basic value commitments for helping people in need. One citation from the principal manager of the City Mission in Stockholm illustrates well these worries:

> 'The private companies are way ahead of us, with submitting tenders, calculating the price and think efficiency. We are only starting to learn how to use our value-system to present a competitive alternative and to manage public sector outsourcing where we don't sell out our souls.' (Markovits, 2009)

In Sweden a tendency towards for-profit privatisation of social welfare provision is more probable than non-profit alternatives, although this is not to deny the importance of the latter as a much-needed complement.

Conclusion

Let us return to the questions raised at the start of this chapter.

Why are FBOs of interest in times when financial and economic crises trigger governments at all levels to reconsider their responsibilities as providers and protectors of social welfare? Our brief answer is that governments at central and local levels turn to FBOs and other NGOs for complementary support when financial, economic and social problems pile up and put pressure on regular public welfare provision. Thanks to their longstanding social tradition, many FBOs are motivated, competent and experienced (sometimes even pre-welfare state) to manage soup kitchens, homeless shelters, old people homes, walk-in centres in neighbourhoods and other social services. In the case of asylum-seekers and undocumented people there is very little, if any, support these people are able to get from government. In this case, there are numerous examples in which FBOs, or individuals affiliated to FBOs, circumvent the legal system, sheltering and supporting people in distress, as highlighted in the case of 'the Easter Call' in Sweden in 2005. Other FBOs concentrate on groups whose needs are recognised by official policies, but who fall outside the view and reach of the authorities. They assist people who are entitled to but make no use of debt-related advice, visit people who lead isolated lives and might be helped out with informal care, support clients of food banks, and so on. They are working for people who have, for very different reasons, lost faith in regular services, or who have made themselves 'untraceable' for the public authorities.

How do FBOs in different welfare regimes operate at the local level in the context of welfare retrenchment and/or redesign? What are their (faith-motivated) interests and strategies? Although public welfare provision has been increasingly handed over to profit-making companies (with this trend declining in significance in the Netherlands over the last few years), FBOs still have an important role in combating poverty and social exclusion. The strong historical heritage of the Catholic Church in Spain, the former Lutheran state church and the free churches in Sweden, and the diverse yet deeply rooted traditions of religious motivated social engagement in the Netherlands, means that there is, in all three countries, a strong presence of activities targeted at poor people in need. The Church of Sweden and the free churches offer a multitude of social services in Sweden as do various Protestant, Catholic and ecumenical FBOs in the Netherlands, whereas in Spain there is an overwhelming dominance of Catholic FBOs.

Muslim FBOs are developing at the local level, often facing an environment with strong anti-Islamic sentiments, especially in the Netherlands. Cellar mosques, independent Islamic organisations and a limited number of big mosques have become important centres serving Muslim immigrants with social support. Occasionally, Christian, Muslim, Jewish and other FBOs even cooperate around activities to combat social exclusion and help people in need, thus well illustrating Cloke's statement (2010, p 228), that FBOs 'represent some of the last islands of social capital as well as spiritual capital in some urban communities [...] and present potential resources (buildings, volunteers, social leadership and so on) as well as a sense of longstanding local presence and commitment to local areas.' Notably, women are generally more active than men in voluntary work at the face-to-face level of society, whereas the reverse goes for men in leading FBO positions.

Finally, *are FBOs in a process of replacing public authorities as welfare providers, or are they, at best, capable and willing to give complementary support at the margin?* The answer is that, despite a growing need for private, non-profit engagement in welfare provision and non-public activities to counter social exclusion, the development is far from one where FBOs (and other NGOs) are taking over a lot of social responsibilities from a withdrawing welfare state. Except for Spain, FBOs seem to have a general trust in public welfare provision, thus expecting and demanding central and local governments to take responsibility for poor families, vulnerable children, older people with disabilities, drug addicts, the homeless and other people in need. They deliberately concentrate on offering complementary care at the margin only when public provision of welfare wavers.

In post-Franco Spain, however, there has been a case of FBOs and other NGOs playing an active role in establishing a social welfare system based on a mix of government, market and civil society. Neither in the Netherlands nor in Sweden has there been a clear break with a largely public-led welfare system. Thus, although the welfare state is now, to an extent, withdrawing, or at least restructuring, in all three countries, FBOs are not the primary substitutes for providing a corresponding amount of services in areas such as healthcare, drug addict rehabilitation, vulnerable children and so on. Instead, it is rather a great opportunity for profit-seeking companies to invade a (partly) new market boosted by the EU Directive 2004/18/EC. In the Netherlands, however, where NGOs, including faith-based ones, are competing with private for-profit companies in tenders, the first seem to have a comparatively better position because of their non-profit status/identity. In all three countries the FBOs themselves are hesitantly noticing the opportunity to increase their responsibilities in welfare provision, partly because they lack the financial and professional muscles of the profit-seeking actors, and partly because they expect public authorities to be mainly responsible for the provision of social welfare.

To conclude, there is a fear among many FBOs in the three countries that the increasing habit of tendering in the social sector will primarily favour for-profit rather than non-profit provision of welfare, thus pressing FBOs to professionalise and become more profit-orientated themselves, to the potential detriment of the socially deprived and the excluded groups they want to support. This may also create a risk for diluting the deeper ethical motivations traditionally driving voluntary work. Or, to put it more bluntly, the prospects for FBOs to retain their legitimacy as helpers of people in need are challenged as they themselves face pressures to become more for-profit orientated without losing their faith-based engagement.

Notes

[1] Following recent welfare systems research, the Esping-Andersen typology has a limited power of discrimination. Thus, the editors of the new *Handbook of the European welfare systems*, in their introductory chapter, instead of using 'dubious generalisations' leading to 'systematic misinterpretations', recommend a considerable enlargement of comparative categories, deciding 'for each individual case which variables and political actors are relevant for a specific welfare system' (Schubert et al, 2009, pp 20-1).

[2] In March 2011 the Christian Council of Sweden (an umbrella organisation including the Church of Sweden and other Christian congregations in Sweden) sent an open letter to the government demanding revisions of the socially devastating rules in the health insurance system, 'because we have seen [...] how people are hit, how the social and economic platforms of many people are eroded. Our mission is to be an ethical voice in society following Jesus Christ, his words and deeds. But our churches are not political parties, we have no party programs, investigation committees or civil servants mandated to bring forward solutions. Solutions must be presented by politicians in government and parliament as well as by civil servants in the public administration' (Svenska Kyrkan, 2011).

[3] Malika Boulalla, born in Casablanca, was awarded the local sports journalists grant for 'Sports leader of the year'.

[4] Detailed references to all interviews with Swedish informants are given in Elander and Fridolfsson (2011, Appendix II).

References

Agreement (2008) *Agreement between the Swedish Government, national idea-based organisations in the social sphere and the Swedish Association of Local Authorities and Regions* (www.overenskommelsen.se/pdf/agreementsocialvolsector.pdf).

Andersson, R. and Molina, I. (2003) 'Racialization and migration in urban segregation processes. Key issues for critical geographers', in J. Öhman and K. Simonsen (eds) *Voices from the north: New trends in Nordic human geography*, Aldershot: Ashgate, pp 261–82.

Berg, J. (2010) *Varför präst? En studie om yrkesvalsprocess bland prästkandidater* [*Why priest? A study of vocation choice among priest students*] Uppsala: University of Uppsala. Department of Pedagogy [Bachelor thesis 2010: 23].

Brenner, N. (2004) *New state spaces. Urban governance and the rescaling of statehood*, Oxford: Oxford University Press.

Canatan, K., Oudijk, C.H. and Ljamai, A. (2003) *De maatschappelijke rol van de Rotterdamse moskeeën* [*The social role of mosques in Rotterdam*], Rotterdam: Centrum voor Onderzoek en statistiek.

Caritas España (2009) Victor Renes, interview by Andrés Walliser, Departamento de Estudios.

Casado, D. (2008) 'Regimen Institucional en España del sector voluntario y opciones de perfeccionamiento' [Institutional regime of the Spanish volunteer sector and perspectives for improvement] *Revista Española del Tercer Sector*, no10, pp 69-107, Septiembre-Diciembre.

Church of Sweden (2010) *Facts about the Church of Sweden* (www.svenskakyrkan.se).

Cloke, P. (2010) 'Theo-ethics and radical faith-based praxis in the postsecular city', in A.L. Molendijk, J. Beaumont and C. Jedan (eds) *Exploring the postsecular: The religious, the political and the urban*, Leiden and Boston, MA: Brill, pp 223-42.

Cloke, P., Williams, A. and Thomas, S. (2009) 'FBOs and social exclusion in the United Kingdom', in D. Dierckx, J. Vranken and W. Kerstens (eds) *Faith-based organisations and social exclusion in European cities*, Leuven/Den Haag: Acco, pp 283-42.

Comunidad de san Egidio (2009) Anonymous informant, interview with Sara Villanueva.

Dagen [daily newspaper presenting itself as ʹindependent newspaper on a Christian foundationʹ] (2009) 'Kvinnliga föreståndare i frikyrkan blir färre' [The number of female principals in the free church is decreasing] 27 October 2010.

Dahlstedt, M. (2007) *Utbildning, arbete, medborgarskap: strategier för social inkludering i den mångetniska staden* [*Education, work, citizenship: Strategies for social inclusion in the multiethnical city*], Umeå: Boréa.

Dautzenberg, M. and van Westerlaak, M. (2007) *Kerken en moskeeën onder de WMO: Een verkennend onderzoek naar kansen en bedreigingen* [*Churches and mosques under the Social Support Act. An explorative survey into challenges and threats*], Amsterdam: DSPGroep.

Davelaar, M. and Smits van Waesberghe, E. (2010). *Tussen principes en pragmatisme. Een onderzoek onder Nederlandse gemeenten naar subsidiëring van levensbeschouwelijke organisaties* [*Between principles and pragmatism. Research on financial relations between Dutch cities and organisations based on religion or world view*], Utrecht: FORUM.

Davelaar, M. and van den Toorn, J. (2010a) 'Faith-based solidarity marginalised? Homelessness, faith-based organisations and the national action plan for social relief in the Netherlands', Paper presented at the 5th Annual Research Conference on Homelessness in Europe, Budapest, 17 September.

Davelaar, M. and van den Toorn, J. (2010b) *Geloof aan het werk. De rol van levensbeschouwelijke organisaties bij het bestrijden van sociale uitsluiting in Rotterdam* [*Faith at work. The role of faith-based organisations in combating social exclusion in Rotterdam*], Utrecht: Verwey-Jonker Instituut.

Davelaar, M., Swinnen, H. and ter Woerds, S. (2003) *European cities and local social policy: Survey on developments and opinions in six European countries*, Bern: Federal Social Insurance Office.

Davelaar, M., de Witte, N., Swinnen, H. and Beaumont, J. (2009) 'FBOs and social exclusion in the Netherlands', in D. Dierckx, J. Vranken and W. Kerstens (eds) *Faith-based organisations and social exclusion in European cities: National context reports*, Leuven/Den Haag: Acco, pp 197–246.

Davelaar, M., van den Toorn, J., de Witte, N., Beaumont, J. and Kuiper, C. (2011) *Faith-based organisations and social exclusion in the Netherlands*, Leuven/Den Haag: Acco.

de Boer, N. and Duyvendak, J.-W. (2004) 'Welzijn', in H. Dijstelbloem, P.L. Meurs and E.K. Schrijvers (eds) *Maatschappelijke dienstverlening: Een onderzoek naar vijf sectoren* ['Welfare', in: H. Dijstelbloem, P.L. Meurs and E.K. Schrijvers (eds) *The provision of services: a survey into five sectors*], Amsterdam: Amsterdam University Press, pp 17–63.

de Kruijf, H. (2009) Interview by Maarten Davelaar and Jessica van den Toorn, Rotterdam: Society for Social work by the Churches, 20 February.

Dierckx, D., Vranken, J. and Kerstens, W. (2009) *Faith-based organisations and social exclusion in European cities. National context reports*, Leuven/Den Haag: Acco.

Dutch Government and four major cities (2006) *Strategy plan for social relief* (http://english.minvws.nl/en/Orders/dmo/2006/Strategy-Plan-for-Social-Relief.asp).

ECAS (European Citizen Action Service) (2010) 'Enabling your voice to be heard with EU' (www.ecas-citizens.eu/content/view/173/205).

Edgardh, N. (2006) *Welfare and Values in Europe (WaVE). State of the art. Part B. 1. Sweden: Overview of the national situation*, Uppsala: Uppsala universitet, Centrum för studier av religion och samhälle (CRS) [Centre for Research on Religion and Society].

Edgardh, N. (2011) 'A gendered perspective on welfare and religion in Europe', in A. Bäckström, G. Davie, N. Edgardh and P. Pettersson (eds) *Welfare and religion in 21st century Europe. Volume 2. Gendered, religious and social change*, Farnham: Ashgate, pp 61-106.

Elander, I. and Fridolfsson, C. (2011) *Faith-based organisations and social exclusion in European cities: The case of Sweden*, Leuven/Den Haag: Acco.

Elander, I. and Montin, S. (1990) 'Decentralization and control: central-local government relations in Sweden', *Policy & Politics*, vol 18, no 3, pp 165-80.

FIFS (Förenade Islamska Föreningar i Sverige) [Union of Islam Associations in Sweden] (2010) www.fifs.se

Folkesson, K. (2011) 'Invisible activity : the case of Muslim women immigrants in Fittja, Sweden', in F. Eckardt and J. Eade (eds) *The Ethnically Diverse City. Future Urban Research Series*, Vol 4. Berlin: Berliner Wissenschaftsverlag, pp 115–40.

Fresno, J.M. (expert in faith-based organisations) (2009) Interview with Andrés Walliser.

Granberg, M. (2008) 'Local governance "in Swedish"? Globalisation, local welfare government and beyond', *Local Government Studies*, vol 34, no 3, pp 363-77.

Hjalmarsson, E. (2009) Interview with Charlotte Fridolfsson, Uppsala: Central Church Office, 18 February.

Kennedy, J. and Valenta, M. (2006) 'Religious pluralism and the Dutch state: reflections on the future of Article 23', in W.B.H.J. van de Donk, A.P. Jonkers, G.J. Kronjee and R.J.J.M. Plum (eds) *Geloven in het publieke domein: Verkenningen van een dubbele transformatie* [*Faith in the public domain: An exploration of a double transformation*], Amsterdam: Amsterdam University Press, Wetenschappelijke Raad voor het Regeringsbeleid.

Khakee, A. and Johansson, M. (1999) 'Not on our doorstep: immigrants and "blackheads" in Sweden's urban development', in A. Khakee, P. Somma and H. Thomas (eds) *Urban renewal, ethnicity and social exclusion in Europe*, Aldershot: Ashgate, pp 10–39.

Kokx, A. and van Kempen, R. (2010) 'Dutch urban governance: multi-level or multi-scalar?', *European Urban and Regional Studies*, vol 17, no 4, pp 355-69.

Knippenberg, H. (2006) 'The changing relationship between state and church/religion in the Netherlands', *GeoJournal*, vol 67, pp 317-30.

Kyhlström, A. (2009) Interview with Charlotte Fridolfsson, The Whole Person/Heal the Man [*Hela Människan*], Stockholm, 20 March.

Lijphart, A. (1975) *The politics of accommodation: Pluralism and democracy in the Netherlands*, Berkeley, CA: University of California Press.

Marban, V. (2008) 'Panoramic view of the social third sector in Spain: environment, development, social research and challenges', Special Issue, *Revista Española del Tercer Sector*, no 9, pp 59–87.

Markovits, M. (2009) Interview with Charlotte Fridolfsson, Stockholm City Mission [*Stockholms stadsmission*], 15 April.

Monsma, S. (2006) 'The relevance of solidarity and subsidiarity to reformed social and political thought', Paper prepared for the International Society for the Study of Reformed Communities, 9-12 July, Princeton, NJ.

Nerikes Allehanda [Regional daily newspaper] (2010) 'Hon är årets idrottsledare' ['She is the sports' leader of the year'], 6 August.

Norris, P. and Inglehart, R. (2004) *Sacred and secular: Religion and politics worldwide*, Cambridge: Cambridge University Press.

Polderman, C.P. (2002) *De kerk gepasseerd: Van kerkelijke zorg naar Verzekeringscontract* [*The church passed by: From care by the churches to insurance contract*], Middelburg: Pro Regio.

Qviström, D. (ed) (2005) *Välgrundad fruktan. Om asyl, amnesti och rätten till trygghet.* [*Well motivated fear. On asylum, amnesty and the right to security*], Örebro: Cordia.

Salah, A. (2009a) Interview with Charlotte Fridolfsson, *The Islamic Association in Stockholm,* Stockholm Mosque, *12 March.*

Salah, A. (2009b) FACIT cross-evaluation interview, *The Islamic Association in Stockholm,* Stockholm Mosque, 14 September.

Schubert, K., Hegelich, S. and Bazant, U. (2009) 'European welfare systems: current state of research and some theoretical considerations', in K. Schubert, S. Hegelich and U. Bazant (eds) *The handbook of European welfare systems*, London and New York: Routledge, pp 3-28.

Stewart, C. (2008) *The Catholic Church: A brief popular history*, Winona, MS: Saint Mary's Press.

Svedberg, L., von Essen, J. and Jegermalm, M. (2010) *Svenskarnas engagemang är större än någonsin. Insatser i och utanför föreningslivet* [*The engagement of Swedes is bigger than ever. Contributions within and outside associational life*] Rapport till Regeringskansliet. Stockholm: Ersta Sköndal högskola [Ersta Sköndal University College].

Svenska Kyrkan (2011) 'Öppet brev till regeringen från Sveriges Kristna Råd' ['Open letter to the government from the Christian Council of Sweden'] (www.svenskakyrkan.se/default.aspx?id=758877).

van Berkel, R. and van der Aa, P. (2005) 'The marketisation of activation services: a modern panacea? Some lessons from the Dutch experience', *Journal of European Social Policy*, vol 15, no 4, pp 329-45.

van Oorschot, W. (2009) 'The Dutch welfare system: from collective solidarity towards individual responsibility', in K. Schubert, S. Hegelich and U. Bazant (eds) *The handbook of European welfare systems*, London and New York: Routledge, pp 363-77.

Walliser, A. (2003) *Ciudad y Participación* [Participation and the city], Madrid: Instituto Juan March.

Walliser, A. and Villanueva, S. (2011) *Faith-based organisations and social exclusion in Spain*, Leuven/Den Haag: Acco.

Walliser, A., Blanco, I. and Bonet, J. (2010) 'City centre regeneration policies and governance: the cases of Madrid and Barcelona', *Urban Research and Practice*, vol 4, no 3, pp 326-43.

FIVE

Radical faith praxis? Exploring the changing theological landscape of Christian faith motivation

Paul Cloke, Samuel Thomas and Andrew Williams

Introduction

The principal focus of this book is to chart the significance of faith-based organisations (FBOs) and individuals in tackling various forms of social injustice and exclusion in the city. Underlying this trend is a double-edged question stemming from the changing context of interconnectivity between politics and religion. First, how do we explain the increasing capacity of governance within society to embrace, or at least to tolerate, the involvement of faith groups in issues of justice, welfare and care? This part of the question is addressed in Chapter Four. Second, what factors help to explain the increasing propensity for some faith groups to become involved in this way? This part of the core question is addressed in this chapter through the specific lens of Christian faith motivation and involvement in the UK.

Clearly, the multicultural nature of the contemporary postsecular city dictates that any full discussion of faith-into-action should take account of a range of different religions, and of the multifarious ways in which theology and doctrine are practised in different contexts. However, for the purposes of this chapter, we focus on investigating issues relating to the Christian faith in the UK context that we know best, realising that our account provides but a partial answer to the wider question of religious involvement. Our basic argument is that while it is relatively straightforward to discuss how political, social and economic contexts shape the ways in which FBOs operate, it is more difficult to understand the changing nature of Christian agency in response to these contexts. Underlying these responses there is a significant move from faith simply as personal belief to faith-as-practice, but this shift is informed by a number of different theological perspectives, of which we discuss three: evangelicalism, radical orthodoxy (RO) and postmodern theology. The radical faith praxis we address here, then, is not the 'radicalisation' that has been associated with, for example, Islamic extremism, but a sometimes unruly mix of often rather ordinary faith-motivated people who have become determined to act on social issues, and in so doing discover something significant about their faith identity.

It is important to emphasise that religious commitment to social action has a long and varied history, and that at key points in that history – for example, the emergence of 19th-century social reformers such as Shaftesbury and Wilberforce in the UK (Prochaska, 2006) – social politics and religion have been inescapably entwined. In the UK context (and those like it), Christians have for many centuries expressed their politics in and around the Christendom politics of government. However, as Murray (2004) has argued, we are now in a 'post-Christendom' age in which Christian churches, and the narratives they preach, have become marginal to the practice of government and power, and in which previous privilege and control has collapsed into a minority witness among the social and political plurality. However, it can also be suggested that the post-Christendom era has provided the context for Christian *radicalisation* (Bartley, 2006; Bretherton, 2010), affording new opportunities for the political application of faith. Radicalisation has both theological and organisational components. Having been marginalised by Western secular modernity, theology has now 'returned with a vengeance' (Davis, 2009, p 3). Its influence on contemporary philosophy, political science and critical theory has come about in no small part because the hegemony of global capitalism has been accompanied by an overarching and dulling nihilism based on material consumption that begs new questions about forgotten mysteries and hopes and alternative relations that transcend the now seemingly flawed reliance on individual will-to-power. Although still hotly contested by contemporary atheists, theology offers new and fertile ground for radical social criticism, and accompanying alternative ethics and virtues (sometimes labelled 'theo-ethics'; see Cloke, 2010). Organisationally, too, religion has a contribution to make in this new environment. Despite declining patterns of formal religious adherence, in terms of ritual participation and regularised commitment (Davie, 1994, 2007), religious organisations possess and embody key attributes for the facilitation of activism. Smith (2006) recognises some of these as: *transcendent motivation* that legitimates protest, provides theo-ethical imperatives and prompts sacrificial altruism; *organisational resources* including leadership, finance, volunteers and channels of communication; and *social and geographic positioning and legitimacy* at local, regional, national and international scales.

It is one thing to identify discursive and practical contexts which appear to facilitate an upsurge in faith-motivated activity, but it is quite another to understand the changing nature of Christian agency that populates these spaces of possibility. Ekstrand (2011), for example, traces the involvement of the European majority churches in welfare issues by investigating the social doctrines recognisable in their 'operative ecclesiologies' – that is, the principles of what the church should be that are incorporated within particular ecclesial practices. In seeking to avoid any overarching or global explanations here, our approach is to suggest more broadly that a number of different kinds of response to post-Christendom have emerged which sponsor a propensity for Christians to act, albeit for rather different theological and practical reasons. In what follows, we trace three rather different theological pathways, each associated with the idea that theology has to be practised in order to be understood. In so doing we are aware of potential overlaps, but we are also keen to deconstruct any overly simple summaries of faith motivation. Too often, for example, it is assumed in secular literature that Christian action is motivated universally by a simple wish to proselytise. As is evident in the following discussion, the move towards faith-motivated praxis in the contemporary city involves more numerous and complex connections between theological discourse and political praxis.

The evangelicals: emerging agendas for social action

Although the Christian church is often subdivided in terms of basic distinctive traditions (protestant, catholic) or of denominations (Anglican, Roman Catholic, Methodist, Baptist, Pentecostal, supposedly anti-denominational 'house churches', and so on), one of the key foundational distinctions affecting Christian social action has been between evangelicals and liberals. Although complex and multifaceted, in outline liberal theology cuts across denominations, and accepts a less-than-dogmatic understanding of God through interpretation of scripture that is open to critical and literary analysis (see, for example, Bradley, 2010). In eschewing a unified set of doctrines and dogmatics, the liberal tradition applies human reason and tradition to biblical interpretation, and is open to discovering Christ in and through contemporary culture. Liberals emphasise corporate sin as equally evil and destructive as personal sin, and typically display a strong commitment to social justice, for example, by embracing contemporary identity politics as well as opposing poverty and social exclusion. It follows that liberal theology has invoked a longstanding passion among proponents for involvement in social action and care, both within and beyond the church communities concerned.

Liberal theology has also acted historically as a contradistinctive marker for evangelicals. Bebbington (1989) identifies four main priorities of the evangelical theological position: an acceptance of the necessity of personal conversion; a belief in the Bible as the inspired and infallible source of that message; the centrality of the cross at the heart of the salvation message; and the necessity for the active spreading of that message (evangelism). These attributes differ significantly from more liberal viewpoints, and despite the suggestion (for example, by Tomlinson, 1995) that evangelicalism has its cultural roots in modernity, there is a wider insistence (for example, by Cray et al, 1997) that the primary evangelical doctrinal convictions pre-date modernity and represent the indelible traditions of Bible-believing Christianity. As such the distinctions between liberal and evangelical approaches have often served to demarcate the borders of two very different Christian territories with rather different attitudes towards social action; keepers of evangelical theology have typically regarded their liberal counterparts as representing a 'social gospel' that is more interested in liberal social politics than in scriptural truths and moral positioning. Accordingly, theological liberalism has been presented as a 'blind alley' (Chester, 2004, p 12) and as having 'muzzled' the idea that Jesus was who he said he was (Edwards, 2008, p 28), even by evangelicals with a propensity towards social action. It can thus be argued that avoiding the perceived heresy of the social gospel has been a cultural imperative for many evangelicals until recent times.

Evangelical Christianity, however, cannot be regarded as a homogeneous block of opposition to the 'social gospel' (see Wells, 1993, 1994; Jones, 1997); expressions of evangelical Christianity have taken many different forms in many different contexts, from being positioned within traditional denominations to the remarkable growth of new (or 'emerging') churches (see Gibbs and Bolger, 2006), and of major national conferences, such as Spring Harvest in the UK. This increasingly tribal nature of the evangelical movement reflects a relationship between ecclesiology and new values associated with generational change (see Gerali, 1995), and is characterised by what Ward (1997, p 30) has called the 'entrepreneurial activity of a new generation of leaders', each building a particular subculture within the evangelical territory. And it was via these leaders and their subcultures that evangelicals began in earnest to question the heretofore culturally prohibitive connections between the social gospel and Christian social action. We should emphasise that the reconciliation of previous rifts between evangelism and social action was a long and multifaceted process with its own prehistory. For example, the International Congress on World Evangelisation, held in Lausanne in 1974, saw Christian leaders from around the globe assemble to address the longstanding divisions in the Christian church between those who saw the church's prime responsibility as evangelism, and those who saw it as taking action against social ills. In parallel to the impact of the Lausanne Congress, key theologians in North America and the UK (see, for example, Sider, 1977; Stott, 1984) charted the 'reversal of the great reversal' as evangelicals rediscovered their social conscience. There followed a degree of mixing of previously firm theological stances, as socially active evangelicals began to discover that some of their closest allies were to be found in other theological traditions. A key landmark recognised by social scientists in the UK was *Faith in the city* (1985), a report by the Archbishop of Canterbury's Commission on Urban Priority Areas, highlighting both the emerging inequalities in 1980s Britain and (crucially) the role of the church in responding to the needs of disadvantaged urban populations. The report was followed by another, entitled *Faithful cities* (Commission on Urban Life and Faith, 2006), in which the diversity in urban contexts of culture, ethnicity and faith was recognised (see Dinham, 2009; Dinham et al, 2009).

Perhaps relevant as an example, and significantly more indicative of the entrepreneurial activity of evangelical leaders, is the case of Steve Chalke, a Baptist minister who has become a prominent and vocal faith-based social activist in the UK. In 1985, he established the Oasis Trust, which initially provided a hostel for homeless young people, but has grown over the years into a major provider of educational, healthcare and housing services, both in the UK and overseas. He also pioneered the Faithworks Movement, which from 2001 has inspired and equipped a social action network consisting of local Christians developing service and caring roles in their communities. Faithworks has also been active in seeking to challenge and transform public attitudes towards Christian faith-based involvement in key social issues. Since 2006, Chalke has been integrally involved in Stop The Traffik, a global coalition against people trafficking. Both through these kinds of practical involvements, and in a series of books (see, for example, 1996, 2001, 2002, 2003, 2006, 2009) he has embodied the idea that evangelical Christians can and should practise their faith through involvement in practical matters of justice, service, care and protest. His challenge to the evangelic movement is to understand the world, to listen and to learn its language, but to retain a distinctive position from which to act:

> We have watched a some Christians, anxious to listen and respond to the world's agenda, have slowly surrendered to its standards and principles. We have seen the gospel not only compromised, but altogether lost as the distinctiveness of the Christian approach has vanished almost without trace. The big question is, therefore: how can we be orthodox in our theology and yet radical in our application of it? The answer can only be: to listen hard to our culture, and then reflect on it with equal commitment, analysing it through the lens of Scripture and allowing the Holy Spirit to revolutionise our understanding. (Chalke, 1996, p 16)

Addressing this 'big question' has produced a transforming upsurge in the degree to which evangelicals have been prepared to take their faith out into public arenas. Despite some lingering theological revulsion of the social gospel, and some continuing adherence to the idea that faith is private and personal, and therefore antithetical to social or political involvement, aspects of evangelical theology began to be commonly deployed in favour of faith praxis in social arenas (see, for example, Chester, 2004). Cray (2007) notes a transformation in the theological understanding of citizenship, in terms of the outworking of theological ideas about the kingdom of God. He contrasts earlier *quietist* approaches, in which escapist negative or conformist postures towards society draw on ideas about the kingdom of God being reserved for the eschatological future, with emergent *transformational* approaches, in which it is acknowledged that the outworking of the kingdom of God can transform society in the here and now. Transformational approaches encourage active social practice on the basis that knowing what is right should lead to doing what is right in contemporary social contexts; prayerful concern for the poor becomes accompanied by an openness to being part of the answer to the problems of the poor (Claiborne and Wilson-Hartgrove, 2008). These eschatological perspectives reflect a theological position from which to advance an engagement between evangelicals and the social and political (Oakley, 2007). Engagement in transformational service becomes part of the outworking of the here and now element of God's kingdom. In this way, proclamation evangelism of the poor in the context of loving action is extended to become loving care and service for the poor as part of the extension of kingdom values and practices in the present time. Whether such service can ever be 'without strings' in terms of evangelistic intent is highly debateable, but the exercise of loving, serving and caring certainly transcends intentional proselytisation (see Cloke et al, 2005, 2010; and Chapter Six in this volume).

In some contexts these newfound freedoms to take action in the practice of faith have remained firmly wedded to the core evangelical issues of sex, marriage and morality, resulting in highly conservative, and sometimes reactionary, political involvement, including attempts to establish political institutions (such as the Christian Party and the Christian Institute) with which to re-colonise the public arena. Some such initiatives can clearly be aligned with the idea that theology can be connected with a desire for political domination (see, for example, Bartley, 2006; Dittmer and Sturm, 2010; Hackworth, 2010; Hill, 2010). However, an integral element in the re-fashioning of evangelical social action has been to interrogate the biblical text in order to identify a wider, and far less conservative, slate of relevant social issues on which to act out faith. One very significant advocate for involvement by evangelicals in social transformation is Joel Edwards. His book, *An agenda for change* (2008), was written while he was general director of the Evangelical Alliance, UK, an organisation that had taken a leading role in the upholding of traditional evangelical values and their conservative political outworkings. However, Edwards seeks to revitalise evangelicalism with a vision for spiritual and social change. He acknowledges that traditional evangelical concerns have resulted in people hearing about 'a Jesus solely concerned with sex, abortion, marriage, gambling and the like' (2008, p 30), and while these issues remain important, he points instead to a Jesus who advocated freedom for captives, the opening of blind eyes and liberty for the oppressed. This Jesus, he concludes, is a Jesus for whom social action is a core part of the evangelical message.

As part of his agenda, Edwards identifies three loose evangelical categories with differing propensities for social action:

- *Evangelicals to the left*, who hold the key to evangelical theologies, and are likely to be sympathetic with charismatic and contemplative spiritualities. They hold onto Christian ethics, but are embarrassed by the perceived overemphasis on sexuality and abortion. They are committed to social engagement and political activism and to issues of global poverty and injustice. They often struggle with prescriptive forms of gathered church structure, and are more at home with fresh or emerging expressions of church.
- *Evangelicals to the right* are more likely to adhere to reformed theologies[1] and traditional worship practices and are comfortable with prescriptive forms of gathered church. They have a strident opposition to homosexuality and abortion, and support for family values. They are cautious about social and political activism which substitutes social action for gospel proclamation, although the current Conservative/Liberal Coalition government in the UK has certainly fostered opportunities for the involvement of some of these groups in debates and activities relating to social welfare.

- *Evangelicals to the centre*, who may or may not be theologically reformed, but who are likely to be mainstream charismatic and involved in prayer movements and spiritual warfare. They are attentive to traditional moral concerns, but they also accept that social engagement is important and are increasingly politically aware and active in the community. They may not be highly motivated by issues of global poverty and injustice.

Edwards accepts the crude nature of these categories, but in sketching them out he demonstrates the multifaceted character of evangelical Christianity. His own message is that it is in the evangelical centre – at the fulcrum of left and right – that 'twenty-first century evangelicals can be converted into active citizens who ... work through the complications of rights and equalities' (Edwards, 2008, p 90). In traditional churches, reformed or charismatic, and in all kinds of emerging expressions of church, gathered Christian community or incarnational mission, faith-motivated people are now being exposed to the idea that evangelical theology is utterly inaccessible without the core horizon of practices that constitute the church and realise its theology (Hutter, 1997). In other words, if Christians do not care about the poorest among them, locally and internationally, then 'they are not being true to their faith' (Dionne, Jr, 2008, p 14).

This remarkable (if partial) transformation from opponents of the social gospel to embracers of social action – albeit of very significantly different kinds – has brought evangelicals into a range of theological positions in which biblical truth is being transposed into ways of living out the Christian life in public as well as in private. And with this transformation has come a theological emphasis on two aspects of biblical/spiritual praxis that serve to connect faith motivation with action. The first is a focus on *Christian virtue ethics.* Christians are gently urged to develop character through a deep and habitual disposal to respond consistently and thereby to bring God's wisdom and glory to birth in the world. As Hauerwas and Pinches (1997) contend, character articulates the continuity of our lives, the recognition that our lives are not just the sum of what we have done, but rather are constituted by what God has done for us. And as Cray (2007) has argued, character is formed by practice, in the choices that we make and in the communities to which we belong. Such character is not forged in the conditioning of social arrangements, but rather in the fostering of social agents who are capable of creating just, caring, truthful and peaceful societies (Volf, 1996). Increasingly such fostering occurs through the device of living tactically by practising faith in social action and in so doing entering into contexts that allow lives to be permeated with learned attitudes of agape and caritas for the other that affects all that we do. Through the face of the impoverished or downtrodden other we are shown our own character and are brought closer to God (Kapuscinski, 2008). In this way, to belong to Christian communities that accentuate the building of virtuous character through social action is to embrace the radical theology of incarnation (Brewin, 2010). This focus on virtue, then, provides two crucial emphases for the understanding of faith-motivated social action. First, Christian belief increasingly belongs to Christian practice which enacts a narrative about how God speaks into the world in order to redeem it, and therefore enacts a counter-ethics which embodies a social ontology of duty and virtue (Milbank, 2006a). Second, in putting belief into practice, we see not a picture of self-serving moral heroes in the making, but of an ethics that conveys a wider God-reflecting vocation (Wright, 2010).

The second theological insight into the turn towards faith praxis involves the practice of *Christian hope*. The transformation from an almost pathological wariness of the liberal social gospel to an embrace (at least in principle) of a practising of faith in social contexts has been accompanied by a subtle but important attitude towards evangelism. The previous focus on 'seeing people get saved' has become toned down; through socially active faith, some will get to understand and follow the message of Jesus, but everyone will benefit from an expression of hope in wider society. Wallis (2005), in the North American context, has suggested that the confrontation between cynicism and hope is a key political and moral choice of the contemporary period. Evangelicals have embraced this theology of hope, and signified it in terms of famine relief in Africa, restorative action after an Asian tsunami, and – closer to home – in a night shelter for the homeless, a sanctuary for the asylum-seeker and a rehabilitation programme for the addict.

How, then, is hope practised by faith-motivated social activists? In part this concerns the sponsoring of prophetic utterances about, and responses to, the injustices and calamitous orthodoxies of the current order. As detailed elsewhere (see Cloke, 2011), although much of orthodox religion has tended to separate eschatological and political elements of hope, there has been a growing theological urgency for the conjoining of the eschatological and the political and the ethical (see, for example, Wright, 2007). An influential writer in this context is Walter Brueggemann (2001), who presents a powerful picture of the American church as being so encultured to the ethos of consumerism that it has little power to act on its faith traditions. He presents a powerful call for evangelical Christians to nurture, nourish and evoke an alternative and energising consciousness and perception that challenge the dominant surrounding culture, and in so doing he marks out new ground between traditional liberal and evangelical positions.

Such energising counteracts social despair with prophetic hope. It recognises that God is on the move among the darkness of contemporary inequality, exclusion and injustice; not the bloated comfortable God of the capitalist and consumerist empire, so made in the conservative political image as to be inattentive and neutral to injustice, but a God whose doxology cuts through the current ideology (see Heschel, 1965), allowing compassion and justice to emerge. Brueggemann urges the adoption of this prophetic imagination, not as simply a good idea, but rather as a concrete practice in the outworking of faith. In this way, the hope vested in the subversive power of spiritual belief can be recognised in three imaginative manoeuvres that are evident in parts of contemporary evangelical Christianity (see, Cloke, 2010):

- The possibility of the prophetic – the introduction of fresh, hopeful ideas and practices into the dominant culture. While the framework for the prophetic need not be spiritual, the combination of anchored belief and unfolding faith praxis provides a potentially significant platform for the prophetic.
- The possibility of engaging spiritual interiority (see Wink, 1984, 1986, 1992) – diagnosing the problems inherent in the current order in terms of its spiritual as well as materialist core. At the heart of systems and organisations of oppression lies a spiritual interiority, which needs to be addressed alongside more obvious outer material manifestations.
- The possibility of alternative discernment (see Myers, 2003; Wallis, 2005) – discerning the inner spiritual nature of the political, economic, cultural institutions of the day, with an attendant rise in alternative consciousness, perception and emotion, can permit a rupturing of the seemingly hegemonic spaces of the current order, producing new lines of flight and new spaces of hope.

This theological combination of virtue ethics and hope provides a significant platform for a shift of evangelical faith towards taking action. While the implementation of such action is certainly patchy, there does seem to be a significant shift in the propensity to align an evangelical understanding with a practical outworking of faith in ways that are not solely geared to evangelism. Acting on this propensity, the bringing together of a prophetic role with an embodied role (Oakley, 2007), forms one major strand of the increased involvement of faith-based organisations and individuals in tackling social injustice and exclusion in the city.

Radical orthodoxy and the theology of participation

If evangelical Christianity in general has been moving towards a rediscovery of faith virtues through praxis in the social arena, a more specific segment of theological and philosophical persuasion – radical orthodoxy (RO) – has provided an influential and sometimes controversial parallel dialogue on how a renewed emphasis on credal Christianity can offer a bold critique of contemporary society and politics. RO was pioneered by John Milbank along with Catherine Pickstock and Graham Ward (see 1999a) during the early 1990s, and to a significant extent it reflected their positionality as Anglo-Catholic Anglicans working at the time at the University of Cambridge. The basic argument underpinning RO is that new thinking about contemporary politics should 'include at its centre an openness to religion and to the question of whether a just politics must refer beyond itself to transcendent norms' (Milbank, 2006b). 'Orthodoxy' here reflects the acceptance of traditional Christian creeds as normative in such a way as to bypass and overcome the partisan failings of both liberal and evangelical theologies. 'Radical', on the other hand, signals the use of these rooted Christian traditions to oppose secularism, and to sit alongside postmodern philosophy in order to restore depth and worth to the materiality and embodiment of life (Milbank et al, 1999b, pp 2-3).

In essence RO argues that secularism has come to define the world, rendering religion and its attendant theologies as either discredited or as the harmless private commitments of the faithful. However, the society produced by secularism exhibits significant problems, three of which are highlighted by Blond (1998) in his analysis of the need to go beyond secularism (see Cloke, 2010; 2011). First, secularism has permitted religion to become dominated by fundamentalists, whose capacity to ostracise and condemn 'others' as somehow unworthy of moral consideration has been identified by Hedges (2006) as a dangerous form of fascism. Davie (2007) illustrates such fundamentalism both in terms of different forms of fundamentalist right-wing Christianities in the US, and in the rise of Islamic fundamentalism in many other areas of the world, although it should be emphasised that the levels of fundamentalist domination vary in different contexts. Second, secularism has been accompanied by a basic belief that the kinds of advances made in science can be replicated in political and ethical arenas, especially those relating to the politics and ethics of welfare. Shorn of any reference to transcendent norms, the self-referencing of secularism has tended to construct a scientific politics and an assertive political economy that are complicit with an ontology of violence that valorises selfish individualism and accepts the priority of force and counter-force. Milbank (2006b) has suggested that such secularism has led to a 'debased democratic politics' which not only tends toward tyranny, but also struggles for responses to 'non-civic philosophies which instil an uncompromising relativism' (p 338). Third, secularism has often resulted in a kind of hopeless vacuity, as serial acts of self-serving negation and denial become the new weak mysticism of the age. Overarching neoliberal narratives of the governmentalities of the market and the state have led to a society that is permeated with cynicism and a lack of hope. Secularism has implied a broad disavowal of any possibility that social melancholia and desperation might be attended to by a form and shape that could transform the circumstances of individuals and their worlds. The result is what Blond (1998) regards as a sense of contemporary nihilism, an indifference to the extinction of our own possibility and that of others. In summary:

> Today the logic of secularism is imploding. Speaking with a microphoned and digitally simulated voice, it proclaims – uneasily or else increasingly unashamedly – its own lack of values and lack of meaning. In its cyberspaces and theme-parks it promotes a materialism which is soulless, aggressive, nonchalant and nihilistic. (Milbank et al, 1999b, p 1)

The message from RO here is that the secular has been fashioned in order to serve human interests of conquest and domination rather than those of reason or tolerance (Smith, 2004). The secular episteme should not be viewed simply as a period in which the beliefs and institutions based on religious authority or faith tradition have been supplanted by a regime of scientific reason. Rather, the discourse of secularism is akin to an alternative religion, and one that by definition refuses to coexist peacefully with Christian religion because its worldview is diametrically opposed to the transcendental normativities that religion espouses. The RO project seeks to reclaim the world painted by secularism by situating its concerns and activities within a theological framework organised around the centrality of *participation*, which insists that there can be no territory independent of God and that every situation should be understood using theological perspectives. Although it might seem that a view of the social and political worlds as being independent of God would serve to safeguard the very worldliness of these worlds, RO suggests that by contrast such a view results in this worldliness dissolving away. Without recourse to eternal stability, any sense of security is reduced to immanence. As Milbank et al (1999b) put it:

> Whereas the former [eternal stability] allows temporality, the contingency of language and the fecundity of bodies to retain their ultimacy in the finite sphere, the latter [immanent security] abolishes these phenomena in favour of an immanent static schema or mathesis. Curiously, perhaps it is immanence that is dualistic and tends to remove the mysterious diversity of matter in assuming that appearances do not exceed themselves. (p 3)

By contrast RO's theology of participation recognises the significance of excess. The material cannot be separated from the spiritual; behind any material density lies an even greater density, and all there is always relates to more than all there is. For RO, no part of the world can therefore be empty of God, and separated discursively from God, the world becomes meaningless and prey to destructive empty ideologies. This concept of participation offers a way of dealing with the seeming social fragmentation of postmodern globalisation and cyberspatiality, promoting the interconnections between physical, social, political and ecclesial bodies rather than emphasising their separation and self-containment.

As well as asserting the universal participation of God, RO also seeks to re-connect some of the previous divisions between evangelicals and liberals. It sees evangelicals as often being hampered by a frequent theological distancing from the secular world, with a separatist disdain for its evil deviations from the certainties of an unchanging biblical narrative. Likewise it sees liberals as often being prone to validate secular ideas and processes, seeing them as inevitable settings for Christian praxis. RO's participatory theology offers a more ecumenical proposal, with a vision for reformed Catholicism that has been adapted by Baptists, Methodists, Mennonites, Nazarines and others (Ward, 2000a; Pickstock, 2001). As such its orthodoxy consists not of a singular biblical agenda, but of a certain spirit of belief, 'a hermeneutic disposition and a style of metaphysical vision' (Pickstock, 2000, p 63) that is unapologetically Christian in nature, and based on a critical retrieval of the pre-modern narrative roots of that Christianity. Naturally, the refusal to buy into evangelical certainties has led to controversy, and to a range of different accusations, from rootlessness to monism and ambiguity to imperialism (see Long, 2003; Shakespeare, 2007). Nevertheless, RO seems to have touched a nerve in contemporary Christian theology:

> The sensibility that is RO has something unique to say and to contribute not only to the contemporary theological scene but also to the shape of Christian practice in a post-secular world. Despite the fuzziness of its boundaries, the label Radical Orthodoxy is effective in naming a certain spirit of theologically driven cultural engagement. (Smith, 2004, p 67)

This contribution to postsecular faith practice can be traced to at least three main elements. First, it has interconnected in the discursive arena with those searching for critical theoretical insights into the future of materialist socialism. For example, Milbank's engagements with Deleuze, Badiou and Zizek (2005) have not only allowed RO to find its voice in the opening up of a continental-style cultural analysis, but have also used the deep theological resources of the Christian tradition to speak back to postmodernism – suggesting that the insights given by the Holy Spirit to the early church have plenty to say to the contemporary church and the society in which it is placed. Second, RO emphasises *both* God's revelation of himself in the material world, as in art and wider culture, *and* God's concern for the redemption and transformation of the world, as in the political economy. Critically, RO has been associated with a revitalisation of left-wing political perspectives. As Ward (2000b, p 103) has claimed, 'in the collapse of socialism as a secular political force I see RO as offering one means whereby socialism can be returned to its Christian roots.' RO, then, has played an assured role in emphasising the political nature of the church and the gospel, and the necessity to practice these politics as part of the practice of faith. This does not amount to a ceding of political validity to the secular, but rather the unfolding of a distinctly Christian politics of socialism by grace (Smith, 2004). This impression of RO as politically socialist needs, however, to be tempered by the more recent linking of RO with Red Toryism, forging connections between egalitarianism and the pursuit of objective values and virtues (see Newman, 2009). Third, Milbank (2006b) emphasises that the church does not *have* a social theory, but it *is* a social theory. In its practice it reflects the outcomes of socialism by grace. It follows that under the RO framework, the church cannot be seen as an organisation that simply fits in with the civil society of the nation-state or simply provides a convenient ethos for democracy or any other kind of social association (see Hauerwas, 2003). Rather, the church stands as a witness to the kind of social praxis that is possible for those who are formed by the narrative of Jesus. For example, RO points to the redeeming of community through the demonstration of both *polis* and *koinonia* constituted specifically through its animation by a *telos* of loving both God and neighbour. It follows that the wider norms of social life and ethical action are specified by this distinct telos, and that the theological perspectives of RO serve as a prompt to practice these norms rather than to guard them in some kind of theological vault that precludes their usage in everyday life.

RO, then, can be understood as part of a new theological mood at the outset of the 21st century. The mood is one that enables, at least in part, a stepping back of theology into the public domain, and a consideration of its contribution to both discourse and praxis. Although the mood runs parallel to, and perhaps on occasions overlaps, the wider move within evangelical traditions towards social action, it is not easily characterised in terms of evangelical–liberal dualisms. RO in some ways can be thought of as an uneasy marriage between theology, philosophy and politics, an ecumenical project that speaks to different Christian communities and traditions, and finds different practical expression in different contexts. However, what it does is to articulate a picture of the postmodern church as radically incarnational, acting in opposition to the practices of modernity's markets and empires (Smith, 2006). It is hard to say what its precise impact has been on the increased propensity for faith-motivated Christians to take action in social spheres, but the emergent 'mood' of RO does appear to have contributed significantly to the changing discursive and practical contexts for such action.

Poststructural religion: recovering the messages of agape and caritas

To some extent, both the opening out of evangelical practice to include social action and the project of RO to identify a distinctive Christian social ontology and counter-ethics of practice reflect institutional forms of faith praxis. We want to argue, however, that another fragment of understanding the radical deployment of faith in social arenas requires a focus on more anti-institutional and individualised forms of religion. As Christian faith has begun to wake up to its new cultural reality beyond Christendom, part of its journey has been to explore forms of faith that emphasised the love and suffering of God rather than the power and glory of God. As Robbins (2007) puts it, this was a journey from the being of God to the story of God's being, and especially of God being with the poor, the hungry and the outcast. To some extent this exploration formed part of a wider postmodern critique of the interconnections between modernism and organised religion, but it can also be recognised as part of a wider philosophical embrace of poststructural deconstruction in search of new forms of religion without religion, as represented in the writings of Gianni Vattimo (1999, 2002, 2004) and John D. Caputo (2001a, 2001b, 2006).

For Vattimo, living in a metaphysical age involves eschewing the idea of absolute truths and prioritising instead particular interpretations that are formed from the constitution of lived traditions through belief. As Smith (2006) puts it:

> We can't know that God was in Christ reconciling the world to himself. The best we can do is to *believe*. Why? Because to know would mean

being certain. We know that such certainty is an impossible dream; therefore, we actually lack knowledge. We don't know; we can only believe, and such faith will always be mysterious and ambiguous. (pp 118-19)

By this analysis, the lack of knowledge is seen to be liberating and just, as it is the expression of knowledge about God that led to the modernist habit of erecting boundaries and instituting discipline and control though religion. Postmodern religious faith, then, looks to a more transcendent and less pre-determined commitment to the essences of belief. For Vattimo, such essences relate to agape (love) and caritas (charity) that represent the scriptural limits to the de-sacralisation of society. It is not the case that postmodernity represents the point where there are no limits and we can simply do what we like. In the midst of interpretation, belief remains, and through a recovery of the message of charity, he looks for a new spirit of ecumenism to fill the church and to release it from its previous dogmatic burden:

> As I see it, Christianity is moving in a direction that cannot but lighten or weaken its moral load in favour of its practical-moral charity. And not only the weakening of its moral-metaphysical assumptions, but, by this transformation, charity will eventually replace truth.... The future of Christianity, and also of the Church, is to become a religion of pure love. (Vattimo, 2007, pp 44-5)

For Vattimo, then, faithful interpersonal relationships are more about charity than about truth, and the future of Christianity and its churches is about becoming a religion of agape and caritas. This is more than a humanist message of tolerance: religious truth establishes the limits of secularisation, and sets people free because it frees people to realise the true destiny of non-dogmatic loving of neighbours and enemies.

Caputo is similarly keen to engage in religion without religion, affirming faith but setting aside absolute or certain knowledge. His is a theology of weakness rather than power, a focus on an untranslatable and indecipherable God who is encountered in the event (what Zizek, 2001, calls the 'fragile absolute') of love and ethical service to the poor. In *On religion* (2001a) Caputo recognises the focus of religion as simply 'the love of God', a love that is beyond human understanding and that breaks free from human restrictions, a love that is unconditional and excessive, engaged and committed, passionate and radical. The secularisation of modernity forced religion into a defensive position, having to answer to reason, but postmodernity has opened out new forms of de-secularisation, or more precisely, a re-sacralisation, in which a sense of faith without knowledge is being recovered. In some ways this is a matter of the future prising open the present by offering the possibility of something new, something transformational, something unforeseen and unforeseeable – a future characterised by hope, faith and love. In this way Caputo charts the significance of the impossible and the invisible for a religious sense of life that stirs when we come up against something that is beyond our bearings, that exceeds our powers, something that renders us transformed into people of love, unhinged (as Caputo calls it, 2001a, p 13) and freed by exposure to radical uncertainty. The condition for this religious passion, then, is a not-knowing, an unwillingness to pigeon-hole God into the restricted spaces of our understanding. In turn, this passion exposes us to something impossible, and breaks us free from the hegemony of loving the self, prompting instead an impossible love for the other and desire to serve the other. This, then, is a religion that reflects what Caputo terms a 'hyper-real' (2001a, p 91), a reality beyond the visible and the possible, making available that which eluded the narrow-minded idea of what was possible within modernity. Faith in turn constitutes a leap of love into this hyper-reality. The love of God is witnessed in the contradiction and reversing of human and cultural drives, in the unhinging of human powers and the drawing on impossible and unseen powers.

Caputo's illustration of the enactment of these uncertain leaps of love into the hyper-real reflects the practical engagement of believing people in serving disadvantaged others, and in so doing opens out the potential contradictions in the enactment of becoming-faith within postsecular society:

> If, on any given day, you go into the worst neighbourhoods of the inner cities of most large urban centers, the people you will find there serving the poor and needy, expending their lives and considerable talents attending to the least of us, will almost certainly be religious people – evangelicals and Pentecostalists, social workers with deeply held religious convictions, Christian, Jewish, and Islamic, men and women, priests and nuns, black and white. They are the better angels of our nature. They are down in the trenches, out on the streets, serving the widow, the orphan and the stranger.... That is because religious people are lovers; they love God, with whom all things are possible. They are hyper-realists, in love with the impossible, and they will not rest until the impossible happens, which is impossible so they get very little rest. (Caputo, 2001a, p 92)

This religious loving of the impossible is in constant tension with its alter ego, the impossibility of religious people when they start to assume knowledge of God and use that knowledge to be judgemental, and to create 'others' out of those who disagree with them. Caputo regards this as a creative tension, not to be swept under the carpet, but to be encouraged for its productivity. The meaning of God is therefore enacted with an openness to the possibilities in future events and circumstances that are neither known nor predictable. It is an enactment that is characterised when human drives are challenged and reversed, when people are drawn out of self-prioritising strategies by event experiences of the love of God, when human strengths and potentials become 'unhinged' and people are 'left hanging on a prayer for the impossible' (Caputo, 2001a, p 139). Human powers are surpassed, as people are drawn to the limits of the possible, which draw them out to God. And this drawing out is to be found in events, including those of agape and caritas, which seem or feel sacred, 'where the sparks we experience in words and things are sacred sparks, divine promptings, or holy intensities' (Caputo, 2007, p 49). Caputo's postmodern religion, then, involves the gardening of sacred events, a move beyond the rational visible frameworks of secularism in order to uncover new senses, and events, of the sacred within the postsecular. The emphasis here is on the:

> Anarchic effects produced by re-sacralizing the settled secular order, disturbing and disordering the disenchanted world, producing an anarchic cosmos of odd brilliant disturbances, of gifts that spring up like magic in the midst of scrambled economies. (Caputo, 2006, p 291)

A poststructural appreciation of the changing nature of religion does not necessarily point the way towards new forms of Christian organisation or strategy. Rather, it alerts us to new lines of flight both within and beyond existing registers of organisation and concern – lines of flight that reflect a non-violent and peaceable anarchy arising from a context in which the church no longer holds power and therefore in which Christian people are exploring new and different ways of enacting agape and caritas. Both within the church and beyond it, new movements for a re-sacralising anarchy are emerging, drawing on the event experiences of marginal and contrary Christian communities that have dared subversively to imagine a faith and belief beyond Christendom (Murray, 2004). As Bartley (2006) has argued, part of such anarchy involves the re-imagining of the church's political perspective, especially in its relationship with government that has come to be regarded as one of the key sites for the struggles with principalities and powers. Anarchy, therefore, often involves 'a suspicion of top-down notions of political engagement and a confidence in the subversive and creative potential of prophetic truth-telling and grass-roots action' (Murray, 2004, p 10), and as such can be thought of as entering somewhat similar territory to that which is tentatively being approached by some evangelicals via their emphasis on prophecy and the message of hope. So, anarchistic lines of flight will probably involve leaving behind traditional patterns of left and right politics, and the so-called third way that often simply trades on a combination of these attributes, preferring instead to explore new event spaces and event experiences that witness to the power of God, without ruling in the name of that power (see Wright, 2000).

Conclusion

Faith-motivated social involvement is certainly not a new phenomenon; at different times and in different ways some Christians have been involved in loving, caring and being charitable towards their fellow women and men since the earthly ministry of Jesus from whom they adopt their identity. Part of the landscape of care exhibited by FBOs in the 21st century certainly represents a continuation of longstanding historical activity by organisations such as The Salvation Army. However, even for these long-present FBOs, the theological underpinnings of their work seem to be changing with the times, reflecting perhaps the twin demands of post-Christendom and postmodernism. Historically, the divide between evangelical and liberal theology was paramount in terms of any propensity towards social action. In the words of Tony Campolo:

> To most evangelicals, "social action" as a theological tenet once had liberal, suspicious, and unbiblical connotations. Such "social gospelers" were considered politically left, semi-Christians who had forsaken a biblically based salvation message for a diluted gospel of mere social ethics. And because it was largely the theological liberals who embraced social action, evangelicals reacted by making both liberals and social action their adversaries. (quoted in McLaren and Campolo, 2003, p 113)

Now, however, this dualistic model of theological reflection is being reconsidered from a number of different directions. Although there remains some adherence to the evangelical diehard position of opposition to social action, increasing numbers of evangelical Christians are allowing themselves, and being allowed by their spiritual leaders, to acknowledge what their uneasy consciences had long been prompting them – that caring for the poor, and standing up for justice for the oppressed, are entirely compatible with the biblical narrative. We have suggested in this chapter that one underlying trend in faith-motivating theology has therefore been the increasing take-up of transformational approaches by evangelical Christians. This is certainly not to suggest any homogeneous shift, nor that re-prioritisation of theology has led to any wholesale participation in socially active praxis. Indeed, we have emphasised Joel Edwards' analysis that attitudes towards social action vary considerably between those who lean to the left, middle and right of the political spectrum, evident in the disparate issues that are mobilised under its banner. However, there does seem to be a significant movement beyond the traditional conservative and moralist political battlegrounds and towards an acceptance that social engagement is an important part of faith practice. Some evangelicals are increasingly subscribing to the virtue ethics of their gospel, and are beginning to find practical means of enacting expressions of hope among the poor and marginalised of contemporary society.

As evangelicals transmogrify their biblical truths into an acceptance of a Christian imperative to act on behalf of the poor and needy, they have begun to enter the public domain of the secular world and to claim the relevance of Christian faith to the ethics required for social change. The RO movement has similarly enabled theology to step back into the public domain and to reconsider its contribution to both discourse and practice. Without buying into the biblical truth certainties of the evangelicals, RO has nevertheless asserted the universal participation of God throughout society, and provided a new ecumenical theological mood that has sponsored the practice of counter-ethics that embody a Christian social ontology. To some extent, RO has delivered a form of 'socialism by grace', both reconnecting postmodern Christianity with the critical theoretical insights of materialist socialism, and returning socialism to its Christian roots. According to this new theological mood, a politics of justice must refer beyond itself to transcendent norms based on traditional Christian creeds. This theological basis for political activism has been widely adopted in different areas of the Christian church, although it is difficult to assess the degree to which such acceptance has translated into faith-motivated activism.

The theo-ethics of both evangelicalism and RO have accentuated the Christian virtues of love and charity, and the practice of these ethics also lies at the heart of poststructural religion without religion. Here, the questioning of, and in many cases abandonment of, absolute certainties about God has led to a falling back on *belief*, which is best understood in the particular event spaces and encounter experiences associated with the practice of agape and caritas. Here, then, are strange bedfellows gathering around the core Christian beliefs. Alongside the biblical certainty of evangelicals and the assertion of universal God participation under RO stands the radical setting aside of certain knowledges of God prompted by poststructural religion. But what is interesting and important is that these fascinatingly different theological positionings each draw adherents into the significance of social action. For those seeking a religion without religion, belief in God is associated with leaps of love into situations that seem impossible. Solutions to poverty and injustice cannot be comprehended or envisaged in the current social order, but to participate in events of love and charity is to practice the love of God, and gardening these events can often result in anarchistic lines of flight which serve to re-sacralise the impossible existing order.

In suggesting these three themes of theological transformation, we are not proposing a precise and specific three-pronged attack on social injustice, with three different groupings each informed by different theologies. Indeed it would be foolish to assume any straightforward relationship between theological discourse and Christian practice, not least because we are convinced that theologies of participation are just as likely to arise from bottom-up grounded encounters that inform discourse as from ontological discourse directing praxis. Rather, we suspect that there is often a muddying of the divisions between these theological approaches. Faith-praxis happens within different kinds of organisations; elsewhere (see Cloke, 2010) we have traced how socially active praxis can be seen in churches from traditional denominations, in 'emergent churches' (see Gibbs and Bolger, 2006) formed in critical response to traditional denominations and in more neo-anarchic movements, often embracing a communitarian style of activity. We would contend that the different theological strands discussed in this chapter can be found spread across each of these three organisational categories. Indeed, it is entirely feasible that faith-motivated individuals involved in social action may, knowingly or unknowingly, draw on and inform a range of different theological perspectives. Thus someone whose faith has been nurtured in an evangelical context might well also subscribe to the socialism by grace, or Red Toryism, of RO, and in the very practice of loving and serving the poor and oppressed might pose themselves fundamental questions about the supposed certainties of God's character and the role of the church. In this way, it is possible to envisage these three theological strands each being relevant in the faith-by-praxis of particular individuals who become involved in the flickering local performances of 'a politics of becoming' (Connolly, 1999) that transcends left–right, evangelical–liberal, radical–orthodox and religious–non-religious distinctions. Faith motivation, then, turns out to be a muddy, yet potentially very potent brew of theology and praxis.

Note
[1] A broad set of theologies established during the 16th-century Protestant Reformation, which are best known for Calvinist doctrines of predestination and total depravity, emphasising the absolute sovereignty of God.

References

Archbishop of Canterbury's Commission on Urban Priority Areas (1985) *Faith in the city*, London: The Commission.

Bartley, J. (2006) *Faith and politics after Christendom: The church as a movement for anarchy*, Milton Keynes: Paternoster.

Bebbington, D. (1989) *Evangelicals in modern Britain*, London: Unwin Hyman.

Blond, P. (1998) 'Introduction: theology before philosophy', in P. Blond (ed) *Post-secular philosophy: Between philosophy and theology*, London: Routledge, pp 1–66.

Bradley, I. (2010) *Grace, order, openness and diversity: Reclaiming liberal theology*, London: Continuum.

Bretherton, L. (2010) *Christianity and contemporary politics*, Chichester: Wiley-Blackwell.

Brewin, K. (2010) *Other*, London: Hodder & Stoughton.

Brueggemann, W. (2001) *The prophetic imagination* (2nd edn), Minneapolis, MA: Fortress Press.

Caputo, J. (2001a) *On religion*, London: Routledge.

Caputo, J. (2001b) 'What do I love when I love my God?', in J. Caputo, M. Scanlon and M. Dooley (eds) *Questioning god*, Bloomington, IN: Indiana University Press.

Caputo, J. (2006) *The weakness of god: A theology of the event*, Bloomington, IN: Indiana University Press.

Caputo, J. (2007) 'Spectral hermeneutics: on the weakness of God and the theology of the event', in J. Caputo and G. Vattimo (eds) *After the death of god*, New York: Columbia University Press, pp 47–88.

Chalke, S. (1996) *I believe in taking action*, London: Hodder & Stoughton.

Chalke, S. (2001) *Faithworks: Stories of hope*, Eastbourne: Kingsway.

Chalke, S. (2002) *Faithworks unpacked*, Eastbourne: Kingsway.

Chalke, S. (2003) *Faithworks: Intimacy and involvement*, Eastbourne: Kingsway.

Chalke, S. (2006) *Intelligent church: A journey towards Christ-centred community*, Grand Rapids, MI: Zondervan.

Chalke, S. (2009) *Stop The Traffik*, Oxford: Lion.

Chester, T. (2004) *Good news to the poor*, London: InterVarsity Press.

Claiborne, S. and Wilson-Hartgrove, J. (2008) *Becoming the answer to our prayers*, Downers Grove, IL: InterVarsity Press.

Cloke, P. (2010) 'Theo-ethics and radical faith praxis in the postsecular city', in A.L. Molendijk, J. Beaumont and C. Jedan (eds) *Exploring the postsecular: The religious, the political and the urban*, Amsterdam: Brill.

Cloke, P. (2011) 'Geography and invisible powers: philosophy, social action and prophetic potential', in C. Brace et al (eds) *Emerging geographies of belief*, London: Cambridge Scholars, pp 9–29.

Cloke, P., Johnsen, S. and May, J. (2005) 'Exploring ethos? The provision of emergency services for homeless people', *Environment and Planning A*, vol 37, pp 385-402.

Cloke, P., Johnsen, S. and May, J. (2010) *Swept-up lives? Re-envisioning the 'homeless city'*, Oxford: Wiley-Blackwell.

Commission on Urban Life and Faith (2006) *Faithful cities*, London: The Commission.

Connolly, W. (1999) *Why I am not a secularlist*, Minneapolis, MN: University of Minnesota Press.

Cray, G. (2007) *Disciples and citizens: A vision for distinctive living*, Nottingham: InterVarsity Press.

Cray, G., Dawn, M., Mercer, N., Saward, M., Ward, P. and Wright, N. (1997) *The post-evangelical debate*, London: Triangle.

Davie, G. (1994) *Religion in Britain: Believing without belonging*, Oxford: Blackwell.

Davie, G. (2007) *The sociology of religion*, London: Sage Publications.

Davis, C. (2009) 'Editorial introduction: Holy Saturday or Resurrection Sunday? Staging an unlikely debate', in S. Zizek and J. Milbank (eds) *The monstrosity of Christ: Paradox or dialectic*, Cambridge, MA: The MIT Press, pp 2-23.

Dinham, A. (2009) *Faiths, public policy and civil society*, Basingstoke: Palgrave-Macmillan.

Dinham, A., Furbey, R. and Lowndes, V. (eds) (2009) *Faith in the public realm*, Bristol: The Policy Press.

Dionne, E. Jr (2008) *Souled out: Reclaiming faith and politics after the religious right*, Princeton, NJ: Princeton University Press.

Dittmer, J. and Sturm, T. (2010) *Mapping the end times*, Aldershot: Ashgate.

Edwards, J. (2008) *An agenda for change: A global call for spiritual and social transformation*, Grand Rapids, MI: Zondervan.

Ekstrand, T. (2011) 'Thinking theologically about welfare and religion', in A. Bäckström, G. Davie, N. Edgardh and P. Pettersson (eds) *Welfare and religion in 21st century Europe. Volume 2: Gendered, religious and social change*, Aldershot: Ashgate, pp 107-50.

Gerali, S. (1995) 'Paradigms in contemporary church which reflect generational values', in P. Ward (ed) *The church and youth ministry*, Oxford: Lynx.

Gibbs, E. and Bolger, R. (2006) *Emergent churches: Creating Christian community in postmodern cultures*, London: SPCK.

Hackworth, J. (2010) 'Neoliberalism for God's sake: sectarian justifications for secular policy transformation', in A. Molendijk, J. Beaumont and C. Jedan (eds) *Exploring the postsecular: The religious, the political and the urban*, Amsterdam: Brill, pp 357–80.

Hauerwas, S. (2003) *The peaceable kingdom: A primer in Christian ethics* (2nd edn), London: SCM Press.

Hauerwas, S. and Pinches, C. (1997) *Christians among the virtues*, Notre Dame, IN: Notre Dame University Press.

Hedges, C. (2006) *American fascists*, New York: Free Press.

Heschel, A. (1965) *Who is man?*, Stanford, CA: Stanford University Press.

Hill, S. (2010) 'Why I'm not voting for the Christian Party', *Ekklesia*, 6 May.

Hutter, R. (1997) *Suffering divine things: Theology as church practice*, Grand Rapids, MI: Eerdmans.

Jones, H. (1997) 'The Protestant ethic: Weber's model and the empirical literature', *Human Relations*, vol 50, pp 757–78.

Kapuscinski, R. (2008) *The other*, London: Verso.

Long, S. (2003) 'Radical orthodoxy', in K. Vanhoozer (ed) *The Cambridge companion to postmodern theology*, Cambridge: Cambridge University Press.

McLaren, B. and Campolo, T. (2003) *Adventures in missing the point*, Grand Rapids, MI: Zondervan.

Milbank, J. (2005) 'Materialism and transcendence', in C. Davis, J. Milbank and S. Zizek (eds) *Theology and the political: New debates*, Durham, NC: Duke University Press, pp 393–42.

Milbank, J. (2006a) 'Liberty versus liberalism', *Telos*, vol 134, pp 6–21.

Milbank, J. (2006b) *Theology and social theory* (2nd edn), Oxford: Blackwell.

Milbank, J., Pickstock, C. and Ward, G. (eds) (1999a) *Radical orthodoxy*, London: Routledge.

Milbank, J., Pickstock, C. and Ward, G. (1999b) 'Introduction: suspending the material: the turn of radical orthodoxy', in J. Milbank, C. Pickstock and G. Ward (eds) *Radical orthodoxy*, London: Routledge, pp 1–37.

Murray, B. (2004) *Post-Christendom: Church and mission in a strange new world*, Carlisle: Paternoster.

Myers, C. (2003) *Binding the strongman*, Maryknoll, NY: Orbis.

Newman, M. (2009) 'Lazarus-style comeback', *Times Higher Education*, 16 April.

Oakley, N. (2007) *Engaging politics: The tensions of Christian political involvement*, Milton Keynes: Paternoster.

Pickstock, C. (2000) 'Radical orthodoxy and the meditations of time', in L. Hemming (ed) *Radical orthodoxy? A Catholic enquiry*, Aldershot: Ashgate, pp 63–75.

Pickstock, C. (2001) 'Reply to David Ford and Guy Collins', *Scottish Journal of Theology*, vol 54, p 407.

Prochaska, F. (2006) *Christianity and social service in modern Britain*, Oxford: Oxford University Press.

Robbins, J. (2007) 'Editor's introduction: after the death of God', in J. Caputo and G. Vattimo (eds) *After the death of god*, New York: Columbia University Press.

Shakespeare, S. (2007) *Radical orthodoxy: A critical introduction*, London: SPCK.

Sider, R. (1977) *Rich Christians in a world of hunger*, Nashville, TN: Nelson.

Smith, C. (1996) 'Correcting a curious neglect, or bringing religion back in', in C. Smith (ed) *Disruptive religion: The force of faith in social movement activism*, London: Routledge, pp 1-28.

Smith, J. (2004) *Introducing radical orthodoxy*, Grand Rapids, MI: Baker Academic.

Smith, J. (2006) *Who's afraid of postmodernism? Taking Derrida, Lyotard and Foucault to church*, Grand Rapids, MI: Baker Academic.

Stott, J. (1984) *Issues facing Christians today*, Grand Rapids, MI: Zondervan.

Tomlinson, D. (1995) *The post-evangelical*, London: Triangle.

Vattimo, G. (1999) *Belief*, New York: Columbia University Press.

Vattimo, G. (2002) *After Christianity*, New York: Columbia University Press.

Vattimo, G. (2004) *Nihilism and emancipation*, New York: Columbia University Press.

Vattimo, G. (2007) 'Towards a nonreligious Christianity', in J. Caputo and G. Vattimo (eds) *After the death of god*, New York: Columbia University Press, pp 27-46.

Volf, M. (1996) *Exclusion and embrace: A theological exploration of identity, otherness and reconciliation*, Nashville, TN: Abingdon Press.

Wallis, J. (2005) *God's politics*, New York: HarperCollins.

Ward, G. (2000a) *Cities of god*, London: Routledge.

Ward, G. (2000b) 'Radical orthodoxy and/as cultural politics', in L. Hemming (ed) *Radical orthodoxy? A catholic enquiry*, Aldershot: Ashgate, pp 97-111.

Ward, P. (1997) 'The tribes of evangelicalism', in G. Cray et al (eds) *The post-evangelical debate*, London: Triangle, pp 19-34.

Wells, D. (1993) *No place for truth*, Leicester: InterVarsity Press.

Wells, D. (1994) 'On being evangelical: some theological differences and similarities', in M. Noll, D. Bebbington and G. Rawlyk (eds) *Evangelicalism*, Oxford: Oxford University Press.

Wink, W. (1984) *Naming the powers*, Minneapolis, MN: Fortress Press.

Wink, W. (1986) *Unmasking the powers*, Minneapolis, MN: Fortress Press.

Wink, W. (1992) *Engaging the powers*, Minneapolis, MN: Fortress Press.

Wright, N. (2000) *Disavowing Constantine: Mission, church and the social order in the theologies of John Howard Yoder and Jurgen Moltmann*, Carlisle: Paternoster Press.

Wright, T. (2007) *Surprised by hope*, London: SPCK.

Wright, T. (2010) *Virtue reborn*, London: SPCK.

Zizek, S. (2001) *The fragile absolute*, London: Routledge.

SIX

Ethical citizenship? Faith-based volunteers and the ethics of providing services for homeless people[1]

Paul Cloke, Sarah Johnsen and Jon May

Introduction: organisations, volunteers and ethics

One of the key questions underlying the work of faith-based organisations (FBOs) is about the precise role of 'faith' in the working and achievement of non-governmental organisations (NGOs). In other words, what is the significance of the 'f' in FBOs? In this chapter, we introduce some research in the field of homelessness in order to explore some aspects of this question. To some extent the emergence of FBOs as an appropriate subject of investigation hangs on this question. The significant empirical trend of increased faith-based activity in particular social settings, serving particular groups of excluded people, has caused academic researchers to sit up and take notice regardless of the near-hegemonic assumption that religious 'faith' is a difficult concept in a secular academy. What role, then, does such faith play? We have to be very careful here in extrapolating impact from activity. Recent research by Sarah Johnsen (see Johnsen with Fitzpatrick, 2009; Johnsen, 2012, pp 295-98), for example, argues that many clients of services for homeless people do not differentiate between faith-based and secular services in their understanding of how they are served by particular organisations. This finding at least seems to challenge the idea that religious service providers are engaged in overt proselytisation (or at least if they are, their clients are not noticing it), but if marginalised social clients are not recognising the role of faith in these services, then how and why is it important? This chapter seeks to address this question in terms of the way in which paid workers and volunteers in services for homeless people represent some kind of faith-inspired citizenship and ethos that motivates their activity and their care for marginalised people. It suggests, then, that the significance of faith may be most evident in the motivational underpinning and performance of staff and volunteers in faith-based services.

This chapter draws on a wider-scale research project that has sought to investigate and explain the uneven spatialities of emergency services for homeless people in England.[2] As part of this research we focused especially on the provision of shelters/hostels, drop-in centres and soup runs, seeking to understand both the co-constitutive relations by which services are initiated and sustained in particular places (see Johnsen et al, 2005a, 2005b; May et al, 2006) and their role in the wider performativities of the homeless city (Cloke et al, 2008). While it is important to emphasise that these relations are complex and multifaceted, we were particularly interested in exploring the reasons why organisations and individuals engage with the task of caring for homeless people. Accordingly, our research included extensive surveys of service providers, and intensive research in seven English cities and towns involving both interviews with professionals and volunteers engaged in serving homeless people and periods of participant observation in spaces of emergency service provision in those places.

In a previous paper (Cloke et al, 2005), we examined the ways in which overarching organisational ethos represents a significant waymarker in the moral landscapes of caring for homeless people. Deploying Romand Coles' (1997) ideal types of ethos in charitable organisations – Christian 'caritas', secular humanism and postsecular charity – we suggested that many organisations serving homeless people were not only undergirded by strong and deliberate discourses of 'mission' or 'values' but that these discourses presented significant ethical bases for involvement and action. However, our accounts of organisational ethos in this context called into question any neat ethical distinction between faith-based and secular ethics of generosity and service. Service provision for homeless people in England involves Christian organisations functioning in a secular humanist world often engaging in partnership projects involving Christian and non-Christian organisations and individuals. Equally, secular organisations seemed often to be drawing implicitly on ethical principles that were equivalent to those which provided the foundation for faith-based service organisations. This seeming muddle of ethos was compounded by the variations within different categories of organisations in terms of professionalism, rule regimes and the expectations of social responsibility on behalf of clients. The principle fault-line of organisational ethos reflected divisive moralities in terms of the expectations imposed on service users. Some organisations unashamedly desired some kind of conversion of the homeless other, elevating spiritual needs alongside the more commonly recognised physical and emotional needs. Other organisations expected homeless people to raise their own levels of self-responsibility, reflecting an ethos of care in return for deliverable changes in lifestyle and attitude. Yet other organisations espoused something closer to postsecular charity, eschewing both evangelism and any expectation of the changing self of homeless people.

Our research on organisational ethos in the context of serving homeless people recognised at least two limitations of understanding ethos in terms of organisations. First, any organisational discourse of ethos is likely to attract widely varying levels of allegiance from the staff and volunteers who represent the organisation to homeless people, and will therefore not necessarily be carried through into the spaces of care concerned. Second, Coles' idea of postsecular charity implies a receptive generosity – an ability to accept the other on their own terms and to be generous to them on those terms rather than in ways dictated by self-fulfilment. Recognition of such receptive generosity is most likely at the level of day-to-day performance and interrelations between the organisation's staff and volunteers and the homeless people whose otherness is being served and responded to.

In this chapter, then, we investigate the ethos claimed and performed by volunteers working in emergency services for homeless people. Accepting that voluntary and community sector non-statutory organisations are of crucial importance in the landscape of services for homeless people in England, we question how the ethics of these service spaces are influenced by the varying forms of ethos introduced by the volunteers on which so many services depend. In what ways are the spaces of care that are established to respond to the emergency needs of homeless people co-constituted by the ethical frames, attitudes and performances introduced by people who volunteer their time and embodied presence into these spaces? We draw on interviews with volunteers who worked in a range of different emergency services for homeless people in different places to ask questions about their motivation, their identification with homeless people and the ways in which organisational and individual ethics interconnected to produce discourses and practices of ethical volunteering. We also draw on our participant observation in some of these services to question how these interconnections were acted out in particular circumstances.

Again, it is important to recognise the limitations of this approach. Although, as Jenkins (1996) puts it, 'institutions are emergent products of what people do as much as they are constitutive of what people do' (p 128), the role of individual agency within organisations has been hotly disputed. Early accounts in the field of non-profit organisations allocated a core role for the agency of individuals (Zucker, 1977; DiMaggio and Powell, 1983, 1991; Tolbert and Zucker, 1996), but subsequent development of organisational theory has inserted a degree of determinism into neo-institutional accounts (Scott and Meyer, 1994; McDonald and Warburton, 2003). Only recently has the importance of individual agency been reasserted in these contexts (Barley and Tolbert, 1997; Hirsch and Loundsbury, 1997). While recognising the potential strength of institutional discourse, and the potential institutionalising of habitual practice within organisations, we nevertheless argue, following McDonald and Warburton (2003), that volunteers contribute to the discursive construction, and perhaps deconstruction, of the institutional order of the field in which they work.

A second potential limitation of our approach comes with the recognition that not only are organisational ethics stretched and transformed by individual ethics, but also that organisational spaces are performatively brought into being. An emerging body of literature (Philo, 1989, 1997; Crang, 1994; Knowles; 2000; Parr, 2000; Conradson, 2003b) has emphasised the importance of interconnections between organisations, space, discourse and practice. Conradson's (2003a) account of the organisational space of a drop-in centre, for example, discusses how a recognisable faith-based ethic of social care among volunteers is somehow 'woven through' with personal and collective forms of Christian belief which imbues the organisational environment with a particular sociability and experiential texture. Far from being able to 'read off' the impact of volunteers from their ethical standpoint, the ethical in such situations will always at least in part be implicated in and emergent from the diverse sensibilities of embodied co-presences (McCormack, 2003), suggesting performative moves rather than codified rules or representable ethical positioning. We believe that understanding of spaces of care should pay heed to ways in which these 'emotionally heightened spaces' (Anderson and Smith, 2001, p 7) are processually enacted, and we deployed participant observation methods in our research to investigate aspects of these performativities.

In the first part of the chapter we explore the contemporary context of volunteering, suggesting significant shifts in the motive and character of voluntary organisations and of the voluntary sector more generally. We also trace attempts to conceptualise the motivation of volunteers in terms of altruism, egoism and the potential inseparability of giving and receiving in this context. These discussions frame the second part of the chapter where we draw on interview and participant observation research to discuss what motivated volunteers to identify with and to help serve homeless people. Here we interpret the discourses, practices and performances of volunteering in services for homeless people in order to understand how volunteers were implicated in the co-construction of spaces of care.

Volunteering in context

It is important to emphasise that there is a long history of involvement by religious networks in volunteering of one kind or another (Park and Smith, 2000; Edgell Becker and Dhingra, 2001). However, contemporary accounts of the voluntary sector emphasise its growing size, scale and impact (Dollery and Wallis, 2003; Kendall, 2003; Salamon, 2003; Evers and Laville, 2004), yet characterise its complex and under-researched nature – Kendall and Knapp (1995) call it 'a loose and baggy monster' and Salamon et al (2000) regard it as the 'lost continent' in the cartography of the social fabric of modern society. For some, the global explosion of volunteering represents a positive means of fostering citizenship, participation and community (Anheier and Salamon, 1999). However, the rise of voluntarism also reflects changing state ideologies about the apparatus of welfare and the positioning of responsibility for providing social services (May et al, 2005). Over the last 20 years or so a 'shadow state' of voluntarism (Wolch, 1989, 1990) has emerged as Western nations have embraced neoliberal strategies which have denuded the welfare state, privatised social services and resulted in an increased reliance on voluntarism and the non-profit sector (O'Connor et al 1999; Peck, 2001; Brodie, 2002; Larner, 2002). In the UK, responsibilities for social services have been devolved to voluntary organisations under successive governments (Deakin, 1995; Powell, 1999) as part of programmes of neoliberal welfare reform (Clarke et al, 2000). Along with these political reforms have come associated moral envisionings of the voluntary landscape. As we have suggested elsewhere (May et al, 2012: forthcoming), the Thatcher regime reduced welfare to voluntarism, but characterised volunteering as very much a matter of individual choice, while under Blair's 'third way' discourses, volunteering and providing for others is seen as a duty of public citizenship, and voluntary organisations are saluted as ideal vehicles through which to express the values, responsibilities and duties of the 'Giving Age' (see also Fairclough, 2000; Morison, 2000).

In a recent series of timely interventions to these debates, Fyfe and Milligan (2003a, 2003b; Milligan and Fyfe, 2004) have emphasised two significant aspects of the contemporary geographies of voluntarism. First, the distribution of urban voluntary welfare resources is geographically uneven. The poorest communities often lack voluntary resources, community income and institutional cultures of voluntarism. As a result, 'voluntarism may reinforce rather than alleviate social and spatial welfare inequalities' (Fyfe and Milligan, 2003b, p 400). Second, the local impact of voluntarism, for both volunteers and service clients, is highly dependent on the kind of service organisation that emerges in a particular locality. The difference between grassroots voluntarism and the new breed of highly professionalised service delivery organisations has destabilised the kinds of local citizenship expressed through volunteering in particular places. On the one hand, voluntary associations can be viewed as spaces of democratic politics, active citizenship and well-focused welfare service (Brown et al, 2000). On the other hand, such services now lie outside the sphere of traditional democratic politics yet remain tied to the state through funding and contractual obligation (Fyfe and Milligan, 2003a). Here, then, is one major shift occurring in contemporary landscapes of voluntarism – the shift from traditional to corporatist organisational structure. As organisations grow, and become increasingly enmeshed in shadow state regulation, they become professionalised (Parsons and Broadbridge, 2004) and bureaucratised (Morison, 2000), leading to the production and consumption of standardised welfare programmes and spaces. According to Berger (2002), corporatist organisational structures are also likely to be linked with a secularisation of the organisation concerned. And this shift has clearly been evident in the provision of emergency services for homeless people (see May et al, 2005). Spurred on by government programmes such as the Rough Sleepers Initiative and the Supporting People programme, the homelessness sector is being increasingly populated by large corporatist organisations that represent a voluntary sector that is significantly tied into government approaches and agendas, largely through reliance on government funding. Alongside this growing corporatism there remains a significant number of traditional organisations providing services such as night shelters, drop-in centres and soup runs which increasingly find themselves outside of the government's favoured approach to dealing with homelessness, and outside of the funding regime which frames that approach.

On the surface, this shift appears to limit the choices available to volunteers, who might be viewed either as increasingly squeezed into corporatist agendas and hierarchies or as marooned in remnant traditional organisations, struggling with the amateurism of under-funding and 'outsider' status in the new corporatised world. However, there seems to be another major shift occurring in contemporary landscapes of voluntarism – the shift from collective to individualised and reflexive volunteering (Beck, 2001; Eckstein, 2001; Meijs and Hoogstad, 2001). Collective voluntarism suggests a way of volunteering which is initiated, stipulated and supervised by groups (often faith-based or centred on some ideological alignment). Here, the intentions or preferences of individual group members are subjugated to the 'we' of group membership. As Hustinx and Lammertyn (2003) suggest, reflexive voluntarism recognises the volunteer as an individual actor, deciding where and how to volunteer on the basis of highly individualised situations and experiences, which are self-induced and self-monitored. Whereas collective volunteering relies on the ethics of religious traditions of benevolence and altruism or on the coordinating ideologies of humanist care, individualised volunteering mixes compassion and duty with more personalised objectives such as dealing with personal experiences of biographical discontinuity and opening out possibilities for self-realisation. The volunteer can thus become a consumer of volunteering opportunities, choosing their field of activity. Although it is arguable whether the past was quite as 'collective' as is painted here, any such shift tempers the previous characterisation of volunteers as squeezed into corporate agendas, suggesting rather the consumer volunteer with less affiliation to a particular organisation and a heightened sense of how the volunteering opportunity suits their sense of belonging and need. Equally, it seems likely that in the mixed environment of voluntarist organisations there will be some degree of niched provision of opportunities for different kinds of volunteers (McDonald and Warbuton, 2003).

Ethics and volunteer motivation

These shifts in the landscape of voluntarism signal potentially significant changes in the likely motivations for volunteering, and in the complexity of ethos that accompanies volunteers as they enter spaces of care such as emergency services for homeless people. Much of the discussion of the ethical values and objectives carried by volunteers has typically turned to polarities of altruism and egoism (van Til, 1988; Clary, 1996; Nylund, 2001). The pure selflessness of altruism, often thought to be framed by faith-based, political or associational discourses, is set against the pragmatic self-interest of the needy volunteer seeking fulfilment through helping others. The shift from collective to individualised reflexive voluntarism would suggest a swing from selflessness to self-interest according to this register. A sophisticated reading of the egoism argument is presented by Allahyari (2000), who recognised in her study of volunteers in Sacramento, California a process of 'moral selving', the work of creating oneself into a more virtuous, and often more spiritual, person.

We argue, with others (see, for example, Bloom and Kilgore, 2003; Yeung, 2004), that the processes of giving and receiving are inseparable for volunteers. Indeed, Levinas (1986, 1989) identifies the incalculable alterity of the other as the source of an ethical sentiment:

Responsibility for the Other, for the naked face of the first individual to come along. A responsibility that goes beyond what I may or may not have done to the Other or whatever acts I may or may not have committed, as if I were devoted to the other man before being devoted to myself....A responsibility for my neighbour, for the other man, for the stranger or sojourner, to which nothing in the rigorously autological order binds me. (1989, pp 83-4)

Here, we can begin to suggest a sense of an 'ordinary' ethics which presents a foundation on which more specific impulses to volunteer are developed. Ordinary responsibilities for others – neighbours, strangers or sojourners – are the platform for more specific acts of ethical practice. Ethics does not supplant a preceding existential base, but rather the very core of the subject is bathed in an ethics understood as responsibility (Campbell, 1999). Therefore, ordinary ethical responsibilities are already there to be shaped and enrolled. Instead of the human subject being some kind of blank canvass onto which appropriate ethics need to be painted, we can suggest that this sense of 'ordinary' ethics prefigures the precise impulse of voluntarism. Naturally, we also have to account for the rise of negative ethical responses to others, seen, for example, in racism. As Zylinska (2005) insists, otherness can evoke different reactions in the self, including ignoring and scorning as well as giving. So we need to understand how the call of the other evokes an active response for the other in volunteers – a response which cannot be dismissed in terms or mere guilt, noblesse oblige or even generalised reciprocity.

A useful reflection on this evocation of active response for the other is suggested by Schervish and Havens' (2002) formulation of how volunteers recognise a process of *identification* with the needs of others that generates a philanthropic sense of responsibility. In their empirical studies of wealth and philanthropy, they found that respondents did not frame motivation in terms of mere altruism or mere self-interest, but rather they could recall a moment or time when identification with an other was a significant, sometime life-changing, event, motivating a caring response. In this way, a caring response to others can be understood as an engagement of the self rather than as self-sacrifice (Toner, 1968). We would propose two additional emphases here. First, the sense of 'ordinary' ethics arising from nascent responsibility for the other seems likely to be more often expressed in the less visible (Herd and Harrington Meyer, 2002) routine activities of care (in the home, for the family, in the neighbourhood) than in the more visible irregular forays of care in more formal voluntary spaces. Second, the development of these 'ordinary' ethics into extraordinary spaces of care seems likely to be prompted by an accessible or appealing 'device' (see Barnett et al, 2005) which presents a bridge between the governing of the ethical self and the broader governing of welfare. The opportunity to volunteer represents a significant device of this nature, and constitutes a potential bridge between ordinary ethics and a more deliberate performance of 'ethical citizenship'[3] through volunteering. Equally, where no such device exists, ethical citizenship through volunteering can sometimes bubble up to fill the gap. Many small-scale day centre or soup run services have begun with just such a sense of a gap in the meeting of local needs. In these ways ethical citizenship differs radically from politicised citizenship, being wrapped around self-recognition in and self-identification with the needs of the other. We therefore argue that volunteers will be people who use some kind of identification with the other to bridge over from their lifescape of ordinary ethics into some form of extraordinary ethical citizenship.

In undertaking research on the ethos reflexively narrated and performed by volunteers working in organisations providing emergency services for homeless people, we have thus become interested in a series of claims about the dynamic nature of the voluntary sector and about volunteering. The expectation is that the organisational and institutional settings within which volunteering takes place will reflect the twin shifts from traditionalism to corporatism in organisations and from collective to reflexive individualism in volunteering. Binary explanations attributing motive to volunteering in terms of altruism or egoism seem likely to require a deconstructed understanding of how giving and receiving are inseparable in the self–other relations performed by volunteers. The specific prompts to individual volunteering may involve some kind of personal identification with particular others, whether this be a dramatic experience of conversion to the other, or a more gradual transformation. Either way, these prompts to the discursive construction of ethical citizenship seem likely to be accompanied by ethical freight associated with alignment or non-alignment with institutional ethics and order and with presuppositions about service clients – in this case about homeless people and homelessness. Such discursive constructions all in turn co-constitute the ways in which spaces of care are brought into being.

In what follows we draw on qualitative research with 10 different organisations in a range of UK cities and towns in Avon, Cornwall, Oxfordshire and North Yorkshire, designed to gain insight into the practice of volunteering with organisations providing emergency services for homeless people. The names of places, organisations and volunteers are anonymised so that particular information cannot be traced to specific individuals or situations. This specific part of our research involved interviews and focus groups with a total of 24 volunteers (whose ages and volunteering roles are given where quoted, alongside extensive periods of participant observation in many of the service outlets). The shift from traditional to corporatist organisational structure is immediately evident in this research design in that professionalised and well funded services such as hostels offer far fewer opportunities for volunteering compared with other types of service – day centres, night shelters and soup runs – which operate outside of the professionalised core. It is these more marginal services, then, which represent the nexus for volunteers in the places concerned, and as a result the volunteering experience is less likely to represent being squeezed into corporatist agendas than a struggle with the under-funding and 'outsider' status of marginalised traditionalist services.

Motivation and identification in volunteering

Although by no means a representative sample, the volunteers we interviewed suggested two specific vectors of motivation that prompted their participation in providing services for homeless people. First, the majority of volunteers highlighted a faith commitment (in this case almost exclusively Christian) to involvement with needy others. We do not suggest here that more secular motivation is unimportant. Several of our interviewees expressed their motivation to participate in terms of "putting something back into society" (Rob, night shelter volunteer) and of a "community responsibility to all work together" (Kath, night shelter volunteer), terms which were unmarked by faith involvement. Predominantly, however, volunteering was viewed in the context of a Christian response to the needs of others.

> 'I have been a Christian now for two years, my main perception of life has changed.... I just want to be involved with helping people.' (Don, 28, detox outreach volunteer)

> 'I can only say it was God sent me, personally, being a Christian.' (Dick, 61, night shelter volunteer)

> 'I think being a Christian now, it's so different, you know there's a purpose for living.' (Kate, 63, host for Nightstop, a scheme where homeless people are given temporary accommodation in the houses of volunteers)

This significant presence of Christian-motivated volunteers immediately prompts a questioning of the seemingly hegemonic shifts in the nature of the voluntary sector discussed above. For example, any overall suggestion of a shift from collective to individualised and/or reflexive volunteering needs to be tempered by recognition that collective networks of volunteers remain a key feature in the voluntary landscape. Our research suggests clear evidence not only that churches remain a fertile recruiting ground for volunteers, but also that such networks continue to initiate, encourage, valorise and even organise individual and group involvement in the provision of services for homeless people. Indeed, a symbiotic flow continues to exist between the volunteer pools represented by churches, and the role of homelessness services as devices for the fulfilment of active Christian service.

This recognition and continuing collective volunteering needs to be further questioned, however, by a clear indication from our research that Christian motivation can in reality represent rather different ethical approaches and practices of volunteering. Although none of our interviewees (unsurprisingly) admitted to being a 'holier-than-thou Christian do-gooder', they did recognise some of these qualities in other volunteers, although this was by no means the norm. There were, however, distinct differences in the degree to which voluntary practices involved overt 'witnessing' and evangelism rather than quiet service which made little or no demands of the homeless other. Kate's voluntary work as a night shelter host, for example, was part of her self-perceived role as 'a warrior for God' with 'evangelistic tendencies', and Lianne's work as a day centre volunteer could involve pulling people off the street and into the centre so that she could fulfil what was seemingly to share her religious convictions with them, although she was clear in her refusal to "force religion down their throat". By contrast Rose (54, support service volunteer), Harry (80, night shelter volunteer) and Anna (70, night shelter volunteer) only referred to their Christian faith in terms of how they began volunteering rather than as immediately integral to their day-to-day practices as volunteers. So although Christian church networks suggest continuing collective forms of volunteering, the expression of Christian faith in volunteering practices is likely to vary significantly.

The second vector of motivation for participation as volunteers in this arena is the previous experience of being a service user. Several of the respondents linked their volunteering with motivation drawn from such experiences:

> 'I got involved 'cos of Meg, she's the founder.... I know what it's like to sleep rough.... Meg was good to me.... If she met you on the streets ... she'd get you a cup of tea or sandwich. That means a lot when you're down. I know what it's like to be there, and it's nice to show that we have respect for them [homeless people]. They're humans like the rest of us.' (Edward, night shelter volunteer)

> 'Up until two years ago I was a heroin addict ... and I went into a drug rehabilitation centre and cleaned up.... I could see the real problem there was with homeless people on the streets and my heart felt for them.... I just felt that I wanted to put something back.' (Don, 28, detox outreach volunteer)

These connections with previous roles as service users offered complex motivational inducements for contemporary volunteering. Alongside the wish to 'give something back' there was a sense from these interviews that the transition from service user to volunteer could be part of a continuing 'getting back in', a re-establishment of social and work norms, or a meeting of needs for engagement in familiar, safe and even socially 'comfortable' places. There was also an expectation that such experience would be valuable in empathising with current service users, and for the individual volunteers themselves there might be an evangelistic fervour (Christian or otherwise) to pass on their life-changing experiences to others. Such experience and fervour could also, however, be less valuable when it took the form of seeking to 'control' situations that were previously 'out of control' for the individual concerned. Each of these possibilities could be significant in terms of the ethical freight carried by the volunteer into their practices and performances.

Whatever the strength of these particular vectors of self–other experience and ethics, volunteering is evidently cross-cut by myriad personal circumstances and consequent motivational traits. Thus Barbara (70, drop-in volunteer) began volunteering when her husband died, Ryan when his marriage broke up, Lianne when she received full-time sickness benefit and Rose when she retired. In cases such as these it seems reasonable to interpret volunteering as both a self-oriented 'filling of the gap' and an 'other-oriented' making good use of unanticipated available time. This pointer towards a didactic relationship between selflessness and self-fulfilment is supported by seemingly oppositional discourses of camaraderie and difficulty that punctuate accounts of volunteering in practice. Many respondents confirmed that their volunteering brought them positive benefits. Granville and Ryan, for example, had been volunteering on a soup run for 7 and 15 years respectively. Their work was clearly sustained by a desire to support each other (and other close colleagues on the team) as well as a broad desire to 'give something back' to society.

Although they found it difficult to admit that they enjoyed their volunteering, perhaps because they didn't want to be seen as do-gooders, their enjoyment came from an obvious camaraderie with other volunteers which compensated for the stress of working with such vulnerable people in often distressing circumstances.

These varied and complex motivations for volunteering are thought to be underpinned by a process of identification (Schervish and Havens, 2002) with particular others that prompt their desire to engage in a caring response. Notwithstanding the fact that many of the interviewees were 'serial volunteers' – engaging in a number of different voluntary projects through their lives, often contemporaneously – there was a strong sense of identification with homeless people in particular. For example, Alice (50, hostel volunteer) had given a beggar a can of food for his dog, and was then unable to direct another homeless man to the nearest homelessness service, so she asked a *Big Issue* seller for directions to the nearest hostel and promptly telephoned them and offered to volunteer. Dick heard a television bulletin that Caring for Christmas was desperate for volunteers, and his initial experience of homeless people motivated him to volunteer in a night shelter over the longer term. Richard began volunteering as a Nightstop host after a young homeless man came into the church where he was preaching, and sat at the back, thus transforming an abstract issue into a concrete person. Responding to the man's request for help led to the more formal commitment. In many cases, then, there does seem to have been a specific incident or circumstance that led volunteers to identify with homeless people and seek out a device through which they could participate in service provision. On other occasions the availability of the device itself, when valorised in particular social/ethical networks such as churches, was sufficient to attract those wishing to practice what they preached (or what was preached to them). Volunteering could therefore be seen both as a device which channelled initial identification into action and as a means by which deeper and more complex forms of identification were opened out 'on the job'. Indeed initial identification could undergo complex changes – both towards a greater compassion for the other, and towards a greater ambivalence or mistrust of the other – as participation in volunteering continued. As time passed, the power of identification might even gradually be replaced by less reflexive routine in which the focus of volunteering became a more complex and didactic negotiation between the self-fulfilling camaraderie and supportiveness provided by loyalty to the organisation, and a self-giving practice of stressful engagement with vulnerable people in often distressing circumstances.

Discursive constructions of ethical citizenship

The volunteers interviewed in this research conveyed little of the New Labour idea that providing for needy others was a *duty* of the contemporary citizen. Julie's (30, night shelter volunteer) declaration that "I don't like being told by Tony Blair that I should go and volunteer" signals a wider rejection of the rhetoric of volunteering as civic duty and good citizenship. Indeed, interviewees regularly distinguished between volunteering because they *wanted to* rather than because they felt *obliged to*. The latter sense of obligation tended to be linked with discourses about 'do-gooders' – a term which interviewees used to convey a segment of volunteers whose sense of duty left them ill-equipped for any lasting or useful work with homeless people. These distinctions complicate Allahyari's idea of moral selving (2000), in that there seems to be clear evidence that they themselves tend to differentiate between levels of dutifulness and heartfelt motivation in the way in which volunteers use their volunteering to create a more virtuous identity.

Rather than dutiful citizenship, volunteering seems to be constructed discursively as a bringing of ordinary ethics into extraordinary situations. Volunteers chose to express ethical traits of giving (time, money, emotional energy) and connecting (to the otherness of others as well as of the limitations of themselves) through the opportunity to serve homeless people in different ways. Given the faith-based motivation of many volunteers, this sometimes also involved more specific Christian ethical freight being transported in serving the homeless. Thus Don carried with him a desire to show society's outcasts that they were loved and accepted:

> 'They really don't think that they are part of society ... because people separate them out, and now that I have learned that I am loved, by God especially, and that there is nothing wrong with me, I want them to know that as well.'

Lianne felt "led directly into wanting to help others, and show them God's love". For Sally, her faith helped her "not to judge people because you really don't know where they've come from and what their circumstances are" and for Richard and Molly, volunteering as Nightstop hosts resulted in them "confronting our value systems" which had previously been based on a strong moral framework, including the 'undeserving' nature seemingly represented by many homeless people. So while volunteers carried with them their ordinary ethical frames, these frames were in turn questioned and confronted in the didactic practice of serving homeless people.

Within this bringing of ordinary ethics into extraordinary situations there were a range of differences that marked out different volunteers as having different characteristics. One very significant distinction lay in the choice between 'front' and 'back' tasks within the services concerned (Goffman, 1968). Take, for example, the night shelter which was a key site of participant observation in the research. It attracted a 'morning shift' of volunteers who worked behind the scenes cleaning and setting up, getting ready for the evening intake. We spoke to Carol (64), Daisy (60), Emma (70) and Bill (80) who were volunteers in the morning shift, undertaking work which did not involve encounters with homeless people, and was invisible to members of the public:

Carol :   'Well we're not looking for glory! If we were, we'd become a JP [Justice of the Peace] or such like.'

Daisy: 'It's just that there was a shortage of cleaners.'

Emma: 'Before I retired, it had to be evening work ... after I retired I slid into this.'

Bill: 'When folks come in, it's nice to see places clean and show that we have respect for them.'

Carol: 'Yes, that's right, and they're not clients they're guests.'

Interviewer: 'I guess if you're not necessarily involved in evening shifts, you might not get to see their appreciation of that ... and yet you still do it.'

Daisy: 'Yes but we've all done evenings, haven't we and been spat at.'

Emma: 'If you're looking for appreciation, you're in the wrong place!'

This morning shift, then, was able to express care and respect in a context where no direct encounter (appreciative or otherwise) with homeless people was possible or necessary. Interestingly, each had previously done evening shifts where encounter was integral, but had gravitated to the morning shift in search of continued service but in a less stressful setting where companionship and fun were inherent parts of the experience.

The evening shift at the night shelter also offered 'back room tasks' as well as more 'out front' work. The shelter's space is architecturally divided between the kitchen and serving area (out back) and the dining and sleeping areas (out front). The roles of volunteers tended to be shaped by these back and front areas, with some hardly venturing beyond the grilled serving hatch that connects the kitchen to the rest of the shelter, while others were unphased and even eager at the prospect of working 'out front' where homeless guests were to be found. As Kath told us:

> 'Some people don't like going out front because they find it intimidating. Other people just perhaps aren't confident enough to go out front, whereas I find out the front is … well it used to be a lot more interesting that it is now. They used to talk to you a lot more, whereas now they're much more doing their own thing. We used to have a lot more trouble as well.'

The discourses and practices of volunteering at the night shelter, then, were framed to some extent by these front/back distinctions. For some a form of service remote from contact with homeless people was desired, while others sought the interest of conversation and maybe even the challenge of dealing with 'trouble'. Both 'out front' and 'out back', regular volunteering in these circumstances of being nervous and scared, as well as often stressfully busy preparing meals with limited resources on a tight schedule, suggests motivation beyond simply the creation of a virtuous self. Although connections and relations with homeless people differ in terms of front and back roles, the overarching desire to be involved in a response to these people's needs was a key factor. So while the ethical citizenship involved in bringing ordinary ethics into extraordinary service spaces reflects different performative roles, emotions and expectations, the availability of different serving niches brings together potentially disparate volunteers around a common cause.

Just as volunteers gravitate between back and front roles, so other credentials are also flexible and dynamic. For example, we were told many tales of 'rookie' volunteers, fresh-faced, gullible and uninitiated in the practical interactions involved in serving homeless people. In particular, rookies being unfamiliar with rule regimes left themselves open to exploitation by worldly-wise service users, a situation which was informally policed by more experienced volunteers – Kath told us "I tell them that they're new and that's not how they're to be spoken to and not to try it on" – and by other service users. Some of the protectiveness of rookie volunteers represented a self-interested preservation of the overall volunteer workforce – as Rob told us "they may not ever volunteer again, and if that happens and we're short of volunteers then unfortunately we have to close". Experienced volunteers, then, nurture rookies, who in time could quickly become experienced. Although turnover of volunteers was considerable, the persistence of individuals through the rookie stage and beyond was testimony both to them wanting to be there (as opposed to some of kind of conscience-salving duty) and to the ordinary ethics of care being practised between volunteers as well as directed at homeless service users.

These different ways in which volunteers bring their ordinary ethics into service provision are reflected in the various and often ambiguous senses of the homeless other that co-constructed therein. Some volunteers, often ex-service users but also those who were long-serving and experienced, developed very detailed and deep knowledges of homeless lives, mixing a sharp realism with a refusal to blame the victim:

> 'A lot of them have given up on life and a lot of them are just out there waiting to die really. And it is pretty sad when they are really special people. When you chat to them some of the history of some of these guys – they really have lived amazing lives and just one tragic incident in their life and they are out on the streets and it can happen to anyone.' (Don)

Others recognised how volunteering had induced a sharp change in their perceptions as they had encountered and then 'got to know' homeless people. Dick told us how a broad identification with the problem of homelessness had become a more personalised appreciation of particular homeless people:

> 'I've never had any sympathy for them [homeless people] before.... But the more you get to know these people, and particularly the drug addicts you see they have to mix with the criminal classes to support their very unfortunate habit.'

More generally, however, volunteers often carried somewhat ambiguous attitudes towards homeless people. Granville and Ryan – the soup run volunteers – for example, were used to meeting homeless people as groups as well as individuals, and their grasp of homeless people's lives was a somewhat vague notion of how they were 'victims', alongside a sharper perception of the change from the old groups to 'gentlemen on the road' to more recent larger, younger more threatening groups of homeless people dealing with addiction and dependency. Indeed, there is evidence that they felt uncomfortable about the waning nature of their sympathy, which was only occasionally jogged by meetings with particular homeless individuals (in particular, 'deserving' cases such as vulnerable young women). By contrast, Richard and Molly – the Nightstop hosts – were used to meeting with individuals, and struggled with ambiguities between moral undeservedness and victimisation in the personal circumstances of such individuals:

> '... this Simon lad represented one end of the problem, which is the long-term homeless ... it's clear that he's had difficulty holding a job down ... but there's the question that he came from a home where father remarried....'

'... the young lady, I suppose she was 16 ... she was pregnant.
Obviously for me there's conflict ... whether she's left home or she's
been thrown out because she's pregnant. It's not our job to find out....'

Once again it can be argued that the ordinary ethics of volunteers frame and are
framed by their encounters with homeless people, which differ according to the
type of service and the role played within that service.

It is clear from the above that volunteering in the homelessness service sector
is less of an expression of some kind of duty to political citizenship and more
of a basic desire for an ethical citizenship by which the volunteers' ordinary
concerns and ethical codes are brought into identification with the needs of
homeless people and are transported into the extraordinary situation of emergency
service. Motivations varied, as did the seeking out of particular front or back
niches in service spaces. Perceptions and knowledges of the lives and issues of
homeless people also varied, although ambiguity between constructs of victim
and culpability were often present. These various trajectories of difference suggest
that any institutional ethics of the service organisations concerned are unlikely
to be applied or practised without significant filtering through the individual
volunteers who often embody the sharp end of service provision outside the
funded and professionalised sector. How, then, do institutional ethics interconnect
with the ethical frames and practices of volunteers? Our research suggests three
points of interconnection.

First, organisations can seek alignment of their overall goals and ethical proclivities
through selective recruitment of volunteers. For example, some Christian-based
services for homeless people will, by design or by routine practice, only recruit
from church-based networks, the assumption being that key shared values will
form the core of the enterprise. Certainly such recruitment may enable greater
awareness of the organisation's ethos among volunteers, particularly in close-knit
service forms such as a soup run operated by a single church. Nevertheless, many
Christian organisations recruit from a number of churches, and our interviews
clearly showed significant diversity among faith-based volunteers, particularly over
the issue of whether service should include overt forms of evangelism.

Second, organisations can align volunteers to their ethical positioning
through training. Our research suggests that the training of volunteers to work
in emergency services for homeless people was highly context-specific. The
Nightstop scheme, for example, involved introductory sessions, a training day, a
manual with significant rules about what should and should not be done and a
24-hour helpline to provide urgent advice. Understandably, given that volunteers
served homeless people in their own homes rather than in a centralised service,
the organisation found it necessary to provide a framework for practice. Even so,
the Nightstop hosts we interviewed routinely reported incidences where they
had broken these rules, exclusively to the benefit of their guests rather than to
benefit themselves. More generally, however, volunteers in services such as night
shelters, drop-in centres and soup runs received little formal training, and so any

institutional ethics had to be discerned through the day-to-day regulation and culture of the operation. Volunteers appeared to enjoy the potential flexibility that the lack of formal training enabled, although there are serious concerns in the wider context about the quality of care provided by untrained volunteers (May et al, 2006). Overwhelmingly, however, volunteers feared that training would be associated with over-regimentation, professionalisation and the loss of an ability to make a unique personal contribution through the exercise of ethics and personality. The strength of these feelings poses significant questions about the power of institutional discourse in these cases.

Third, volunteers can be aligned to organisational ethos through the rules imposed on how services are provided. Rules for the giving out of food and allocation of beds may appear to be relatively straightforward, but we heard consistent stories of how rules were interpreted differently by different volunteers, sometimes causing uncertainty and conflict over the continuity of service funding. Kath gives an example of this from the night shelter:

> 'The last thing we had was about extra beds and putting mattresses down ... that they had done it on other nights, which is where sometimes if falls down if it's not consistent. And I will say to them, "Health and Safety will only allow 15 beds" when actually we are allowed more. But that's the Health and Safety for the number of volunteers we had that night.'

Exercise of compassion or sympathy by bending such rules creates precedents from which other volunteers suffer. In the aggro that can ensure, institutional ethics of fairness and justice become complicated by individual acts of kindness. As with recruitment and training, then, there is scope for considerable slippage of organisation ethos as volunteers seek the flexibility to pursue their particular brand of ethical and personal connection with homeless people.

Performing care

The organisational spaces of emergency care for homeless people can be expected to be partially constructed from the ways in which organisational ethics are variously represented in, or transformed by, the ways in which volunteers bring their particular ordinary ethics to bear in their work. Yet although offering an understanding of how such ordinary ethics influence why volunteers present themselves in such spaces and what they are aiming to achieve through that presence, there can be no automatic assumption that the resultant space of care will be imbued by particular ethical characteristics. Indeed, it is clear that organisational spaces of care are performatively brought into being, not simply in terms of performing to impress or performing routines, but also in acting out care unreflexively and through improvisation during eruptions of non-routine events and practices (Conradson, 2003a; McCormack, 2003). Our account thus far has been punctuated by performances of various kinds, but here we draw on three examples to draw out more specific aspects of how volunteers performed their role.

Despite the fact that interviews are in many ways an inappropriate medium through which to record and understand these performances, the accounts given by some of the volunteers about their interactions with homeless people did point to the significance of performing spaces of care. An interesting example can be seen in the way in which Kate – a Nightstop host – tried to make a new guest feel 'at home'.

> 'They always come with a [organisation] member, and they're introduced, and I try and break the ice straightaway by saying "I'll put the kettle on, what do you want?" and "while that's on shall we go round the house" … so when we go round the house I sort of make jokes and laugh with them – try and make them feel at home, and by the time you've got down again (because it's a three-storey house) the person who brought them has usually got on with making the tea and … they go off and then I find they relax. Cos I just say "Do you wanna bath? Do you wanna have something to eat first? Tell me your plans – and then they open up and they're very shy in the beginning but it doesn't take them long. And I say "If you wanna put your feet up, put your feet up" and I tell them the rules about smoking. I'm a non-smoker … but I say "the veranda's free and if you really must smoke in the bedrooms, fine but can you sit near the window…?" Once they know that you're not going to be hard on them, they relax. And we laugh about the shower, the fact that they have to press the button down and put the knob on, and unless you do that it's too hot or cold, and we laugh about that.'

Kate's routines and improvisations performatively brought her home into being as a space of care. The tour of the house not only afforded one-to-one conversation with the homeless guest (the organisation 'official' was immediately sidelined) but also acted out the house as a place of opportunity. Rules were conveyed, but the conversational emphasis was on what could be done, what the young person wanted. Kate interspersed the introduction with humour and fun. She was self-deprecating and sought out ways for her guest to relax. Later she described her act as treating the guest just like she would treat "pals" of her son. There was the caring mother here, but without the fussiness that could sometimes arise between mother and children. Kate wove an acceptance and an ethic of (in her case Christian) care through the experience. As a result she offered her guest 'home space' if only for the brief stopover, and she empowered her guest to treat the experience as something more than just a bed for the night. It was not surprising that Kate kept in contact with many of her previous 'guests' as a result of this kind of relational care. Although some of her actions might reflect the organisational training given to Nightstop hosts, Kate brought particular capacities and affects to her caring.

The performance of care is perhaps more easily witnessed using participant observation. Our work as volunteers in a night shelter, for example, allowed us to record many instances of how spaces of care were performatively brought into being. For example, Sarah noted the stand-out qualities that accompanied Jilly's work as volunteer coordinator in the shelter:

> 'Jilly worked out back until opening and then oversaw proceedings out front. When watching her "in action" one would almost think that she found the drunken blithers of some service users endearing – laughing with and teasing them patting them on the arm etc.... Jilly seems to have a way of getting service users to do anything – even leave the premises – without upsetting/aggravating them. "She had one guy hugging her a lot tonight. Rather her than me" [this a comment from another volunteer]. One of the other volunteers laughed and said that she thought Jilly was a bit of a "mother figure" to some of the service users.' (Sarah, participant observation, 13 February 2002)

Although these kinds of performative relations were by no means dependent on the maternal role, and the gender relations attendant to that role, this example again illustrates the performance a mother figure serves bringing the space of care into being. Jilly's passion for homeless people shone through in terms of her interactions with individuals that involved strong elements of embodiment along with laughter and teasing. Jilly performed endearment and as a result could carry that performed relationship into more difficult disciplinary areas involving the behaviour of service users. Jill's personal ethos was expressed in terms of Christian faith, but her ability to be charismatically endearing came through her performance of endearment, perhaps embodying organisational and personal ethos, but by no means circumscribed by them. Our research thus suggests that spaces of care can usefully be understood as performatively brought into being, and that performativity represents yet further stretching of the scope provided by organisational and personal ethos. Coping is, however, an essential element in caring in the environment of emergency service provision for homeless people.

Conclusion

Voluntary sector organisations are integrally implicated in the provision of emergency services for homeless people in the UK, yet mainstream service provision increasingly involves highly professionalised corporatist organisations in which there are less and less opportunities for volunteers to participate in meeting homeless people's needs (Clarke et al, 2000). However, alongside these corporatist organisations there remain myriad smaller and more traditional organisations whose vision relies on continuing images of on-street homelessness, and whose provision of services for these homeless people continues to rely on the resources of volunteers for their operation. These more traditional organisations tend to be poorly resourced, and outside of the formal joined-up governance of homelessness enabled by state organisation and funding (McDonald and Warburton, 2003; May et al, 2005). Indeed, the services provided by traditional organisations – usually involving the meeting of basic needs for food and a place to sleep – are those which have increasingly been stigmatised for keeping homeless people 'on the street'. It is interesting, then, that it is these marginalised and 'outsider' organisations that are the principal sources of opportunity for volunteers wishing to do something to help meet the needs of homeless people. That part of the voluntary sector which has been embraced by the state as part of its third way discourse is becoming closed off to individuals whose propensity to volunteer seems to match the state's valorisation of volunteering as civic duty and good citizenship. Instead volunteers are most able to contribute to that part of the voluntary sector that is out of state favour. Interestingly, whereas staff and management of marginalised services have a clear understanding of their disadvantageous place in the homeless service sector (May et al, 2005), there is little evidence that volunteers had knowledge of, or reflected on, the marginalised status of the organisations through which their volunteering occurred. This suggests that their self-evaluation of volunteering did not reflect or appreciate that the volunteer experience could potentially be easier and more professionalised and in less marginalised service settings.

Volunteers can be branded socially as self-righteous do-gooders (van Til, 1988; Clay, 1996), and in the academic context their activities have often been interpreted in terms of moral selving – the creation of a more virtuous and even spiritual self (Allahyari, 2000). Our research suggests that the motivation of volunteers is far more complex than these stereotypes convey, and that volunteering usually involves elements of giving and receiving (Bloom and Kilgore, 2003). There is certainly evidence from our interviews with volunteers that they derive benefit from their volunteering, which provides companionship, camaraderie, sociability, a boost for self-esteem and for some forms part of a process of personal rehabilitation. It is also clear that volunteering can become unreflexively habitual and that its focus can shift away from homeless people per se becoming instead a matter of loyalty to fellow volunteers and/or to the organisation concerned. Certainly volunteers will often hold ambivalent views about homeless people, acknowledging both their status as victim and as culpable individual. However, our research suggests that these self-serving motivations are almost always intertwined with some form of identification (Schervish and Havens, 2002) with the plight of homeless people, and that the participation of volunteers reflects that identification, not in terms of guilt, but in terms of giving something of themselves to others. Motivation, then, is didactically worked out as volunteers bring themselves into contact with homeless others.

We argue, therefore, that volunteering can be interpreted as a way of bringing ordinary ethics into extraordinary circumstances. By ordinary ethics we refer to the complex everyday caring and relations with others that are widespread through society. Accordingly volunteering is not reducible to faith or political belief (although such factors can be important) but may be seen rather as a connection between ordinary ethics and an organised space of care, whereby individuals variously identify with the needs of particular others and respond to particular devices which enable volunteer involvement. Despite the current political culture which seeks to promote volunteering as an integral part of what citizenship should entail, people volunteer because they want to, not because of any sense of obligation or civic duty, reflecting a form of ethical citizenship rather than political citizenship. We also suggest that volunteers will be reflexive in choosing particular suitable devices for volunteering (Hustinx and Lammertyn, 2003) – they will niche themselves in particular organisations and particular back/front roles (Goffman, 1968). This is not to say, however, that collective volunteering is unimportant. These reflexive choices will often be influenced by social networks, such as churches.

A further finding from this research is that volunteers seek out flexibility. Far from being squeezed in marginalised organisations and roles, volunteers suggested that these organisations offered them opportunities to express their ethical citizenship without the perceived fettering of professionalisation, over-training and standardisation in service provision. There are potential disparities here between quality control for services, and favoured conditions for volunteers. Equally, the flexibility enjoyed by volunteers suggests that any enactment of overriding organisational ethos will be stretched significantly because volunteers often embody the organisation and represent it to users. While the organisation provides a device for volunteering, there is little evidence to suggest that this device is loaded ethically. Indeed, volunteer discourses are relatively silent on the matter of organisation ethics. In addition, from the point of view of the organisations concerned, the very pragmatics of operating a marginal voluntary organisation – unselective recruitment, little opportunity for training and potential inconsistency in the interpretation of rules – create inherent problems for implementing organisational, rather than personal, ethics. Our research adds weight to the idea that spaces of care are performatively brought into being and that individuals, in this case volunteers, play a formative role in routinely or spontaneously performing care which characterises the service as a whole with far greater intensity than any organisational set of ethos ever could.

Notes

[1] Apart from a new introduction, this chapter was previously published as: Cloke, P., Johnsen, S. and May, J. (2007) 'Ethical citizenship? Volunteers and the ethics of providing services for homeless people', *Geoforum*, vol 38, pp 1089-101. The chapter is reproduced with permission from Elsevier Publishing.

[2] The authors gratefully acknowledge the financial support of the Economic and Social Research Council (ESRC) for this research (R000238996: Homeless places: the uneven geographies of emergency provision for single homeless people). We would especially

like to thank the volunteers and service users who shared their experiences of emergency services and homelessness with us. The research is published in full in: Cloke, P., Johnsen, S. and May, J. (2010) *Swept-up lives? Re-envisioning the 'homeless city'*, Oxford: Wiley-Blackwell.

³ Schervish and Havens (2002) refer to a similar concept as 'moral citizenship' in which the moral comprises value-motivated associations that help forge social bonds.

References

Allahyari, R. (2000) *Visions of charity: Volunteer workers and moral community*, Berkeley, CA: University of California Press.

Anderson, K. and Smith, S. (2001) 'Emotional geographies', *Transactions of the Institute of British Geographers*, 26, 7–10.

Anheier, H. and Salamon, L. (1999) 'Volunteering in cross-national perspective: initial comparisons', *Law and Contemporary Problems*, vol 62, pp 43-65.

Barley, S. and Tolbert, P. (1977) 'Institutionalisation and structuration: studying the links between action and structure', *Organisation Studies*, vol 18, pp 93-117.

Barnett, C., Cloke, P., Clarke, N. and Malpass, A. (2005) 'Consuming ethics: articulating the subjects and spaces of ethical consumption', *Antipode*, vol 37, pp 23-46.

Beck, U. (2002) *The brave new world of work*, Cambridge: Polity Press.

Berger, P. (2002) 'Secularization and de-secularization', in L. Woodhead et al (ed) *Religions in the modern world*, London: Routledge.

Bloom, L. and Kilgore, D. (2003) 'The volunteer citizen after welfare reform in the United States: an ethnographic study of volunteerism in action', *Voluntas*, vol 14, pp 431-54.

Brodie, J. (2002) 'The great undoing: state formation, gender politics, and social policy in Canada', in C. Kingfisher (ed) *Western welfare in decline*, Philadelphia, PA: University of Pennsylvania, pp 90-110.

Brown, K., Kenny, S., Turner, B. and Prince, J. (2000) *Rhetorics of welfare: Uncertainty, choice and voluntary associations*, London: Macmillan.

Campbell, D. (1999) 'The deterritorialization of responsibility: Levines, Derrida and ethics after the end of philosophy?', in D. Campbell and M. Shapiro (eds) *Moral spaces*, Minneapolis, MN: University of Minnesota Press.

Clarke, J., Gewirtz, S. and McLaughlin, E. (eds) (2000) *New manageralism, new welfare?*, London: Sage Publications.

Clary, E. (1996) 'Volunteers' motivation: findings from a national survey', *Nonprofits and Voluntary Sector Quarterly*, vol 25, pp 485-505.

Cloke, P., Johnsen, S. and May, J. (2005) 'Exploring ethos? Discourses of "charity" in the provision of emergency services for homeless people', *Environment and Planning A*, vol 37, pp 385-402.

Cloke, P., Johnsen, S. and May, J. (2008) 'Performativity and affect in the homeless city', *Environment and Planning D: Society and Space*, vol 26, pp 241-63.

Cloke, P., Johnsen, S. and May, J. (2010) *Swept-up lives? Re-envisioning the 'homeless city'*, Oxford: Wiley-Blackwell.

Coles, R. (1997) *Rethinking generosity*, Ithaca, NY: Cornell University Press.

Conradson, D. (2003a) 'Doing organisational space: practices of voluntary welfare in the city', *Environment and Planning A*, vol 35, pp 1975-92.

Conradson, D. (2003b) 'Spaces of care in the city: the place of a community drop-in centre', *Social and Cultural Geography*, vol 4, pp 507-25.

Crang, P. (1994) 'It's showtime: on the workplace geographies of display in a restaurant in England', *Environment and Planning D: Society and Space*, vol 12, pp 675-704.

Deakin, N. (1995) 'The perils of partnership: the voluntary sector and the state 1945-1992', in J. Smith, C. Rochester and R. Hedley (eds) *An introduction to the voluntary sector*, London: Routledge, pp 40-63.

DiMaggio, P. and Powell, W. (1983) 'The iron cage revisited: institutional isomorphism and collective rationality in organisation fields', *American Sociological Review*, vol 48, pp 147-60.

DiMaggio, P. and Powell, W. (1991) 'Introduction', in W. Powell and P. DiMaggio (eds) *The new institutionalism and organisational analysis*, Chicago, IL: University of Chicago Press.

Dollery, B. and Wallis, J. (2003) *The political economy of the voluntary sector*, Cheltenham: Edward Elgar.

Eckstein, S. (2001) 'Community as gift-giving: collectivistic roots of volunteerism', *American Sociological Review*, vol 66, pp 829-51.

Edgell Becker, P. and Dhingra, P. (2001) 'Religious involvement and volunteering: implications for civil society', *Sociology of Religion*, vol 62, pp 315-35.

Evers, A. and Laville, J.-L. (eds) (2004) *The third sector in Europe*, Cheltenham: Edward Elgar.

Fairclough, N. (2002) *New Labour, new language?*, London: Routledge.

Fyfe, N. and Milligan, C. (2003a) 'Space, citizenship and voluntarism: critical reflections on the voluntary welfare sector in Glasgow', *Environment and Planning A*, vol 35, pp 2069-86.

Fyfe, N. and Milligan, C. (2003b) 'Out of the shadows: exploring contemporary geographies of voluntarism', *Progress in Human Geography*, vol 27, pp 397-413.

Goffman, E. (1968) *Asylums: Essays on the social situation of mental patients and other inmates*, Harmondsworth: Penguin.

Herd, P. and Harrington Meyer, M. (2002) 'Care work: invisible civic engagement', *Gender and Society*, vol 16, pp 665-88.

Hirsch, P. and Loundsbury, M. (1997) 'Ending the family quarrel: towards a reconciliation of "old" and "new" institutionalism', *American Behavioural Science*, vol 40, pp 406-19.

Hustinx, L. and Lammertyn, F. (2003) 'Collective and relfexive styles of volunteering: a sociological modernisation perspective', *Voluntas*, vol 14, pp 167-87.

Jenkins, R. (1996) *Social identity*, London: Routledge.

Johnsen, S. (2012) 'The difference that faith makes: the role of faith-based organisations in service provision for homeless people', in L. Woodhead and R. Catto (eds) *Religion and change in modern Britain*, London: Routledge, pp 295–98.

Johnsen, S. with Fitzpatrick, S. (2009) *Faith-based organisations and the provision of services for homeless people*, York: Centre for Housing Policy, University of York.

Johnsen, S., Cloke, P. and May, J. (2005a) 'Day centres for homeless people: spaces of care or fear?', *Social and Cultural Geography*, vol 6, pp 787–811.

Johnsen, S., Cloke, P. and May, J. (2005b) 'Transitory spaces of care: serving homeless people on the street', *Health and Place*, vol 11, pp 323-36.

Kendall, J. (2003) *The voluntary sector: Comparative perspectives in the UK*, London: Routledge.

Kendall, J. and Knapp, M. (1995) 'A loose and baggy monster: boundaries, definitions and hypologies', in J. Smith, R. Rochester and R. Hedley (eds) *An introduction to the voluntary sector*, London: Routledge, pp 66-95.

Knowles, C. (2000) 'Burger King, Dunkin Donuts and community mental health care', *Health and Place*, vol 6, pp 213-24.

Larner, W. (2005) 'Neoliberalism and Tino Rangatiratanga: welfare state restructuring in Aotearoa/New Zealand', in C. Kingfisher (ed) *Western welfare in decline*, Philadelphia, PA: University of Pennsylvania Press, pp 147-63.

Levinas, E. (1986) 'The trace of the other' (translated by A. Lingis), in M. Taylor (ed) *Deconstruction in context*, Chicago, IL: University of Chicago Press.

Levinas, E. (1989) 'Ethics as first philosophy', in S. Hand (ed) *The Levinas reader*, Oxford: Blackwell.

McCormack, D. (2003) 'An event of geographical ethics in spaces of affect', *Transactions, Institute of Bristol Geographers*, vol NS28, pp 488-507.

McDonald, C. and Warburton, J. (2003) 'Stability and change in non-profit organisations: the volunteer contribution', *Voluntas*, vol 14, pp 381-99.

May, J., Cloke, P. and Johnsen, S. (2005) 'Re-phasing neo-liberalism: New Labour and Britain's crisis of street homelessness', *Antipode*, vol 37, pp 703-30.

May, J., Cloke, P. and Johnsen, S. (2006) 'Shelter at the margins: New labour and the changing state of Britain's emergency accommodation sector', *Policy & Politics*, vol 34, pp 711-30.

May, J., Cloke, P. and Johnsen, S. (2012: forthcoming) *Reading for difference: Alternative grammars of homelessness*. Antipode.

Meijs, L. and Hoogstad, E. (2001) 'New ways of managing volunteers: combining membership management with programme management', *Voluntary Action*, vol 3, pp 41-61.

Milligan, C. and Fyfe, N. (2004) 'Putting the voluntary sector in its place: geographical perspectives on voluntary activity and social welfare in Glasgow', *Journal of Social Policy*, vol 33, pp 73-93.

Morison, J. (2000) 'The government-voluntary sector compacts: governance, governmentability and civil society', *Journal of Law and Society*, vol 27, pp 98-132.

Nyland, M. (2001) 'Mixed motives of young Nordic volunteers', in H. Helve and C. Wallace (eds) *Youth citizenship and empowerment*, Aldershot: Ashgate, pp 99-109.

O'Connor, J., Orloff, A. and Shaver, S. (1999) *States, markets, families: Gender, liberalism and social policy in Australia, Canada, Great Britain and the United States*, Cambridge: Cambridge University Press.

Park, J. and Smith, C. (2000) "'To whom much has been given…': religious capital and community volunteerism among churchgoing protestants', *Journal for the Scientific Study of Religion*, vol 39, pp 272-86.

Parr, H. (2000) 'Interpreting the hidden social geographies of mental health: ethnographies of inclusion and exclusion in semi-institutional places', *Health and Place*, vol 6, pp 225-37.

Parsons, E. and Broadbridge, A. (2004) 'Managing change in non-profit organisations: insights from the UK charity retail sector', *Voluntas*, vol 15, pp 227-42.

Peck, J. (2001) *Workfare states*, New York: Guilford Press.

Philo, C. (1989) 'Enough to drive one mad: the organisation of space in nineteenth century lunatic asylums', in J. Wolch and M. Dear (eds) *The power of geography: How territory shapes social life*, London: Unwin Hyman, pp 258-90.

Philo, C. (1997) 'Across the water: reviewing geographical studies od asylums and other mental health facilities', *Health and Place*, vol 3, pp 73-89.

Powell, M. (ed) (2003) *New Labour, new welfare state?*, Bristol: The Policy Press.

Salamon, L. (2003) *The resilient sector: The state of non-profit America*, Washington, DC: Brookings Institution Press.

Salamon, L., Sokolowski, S. and Anheiser, K. (2000) *Social origins of civil society: An overview*, Working Paper, Baltimore, MD: Center for Civil Society Studies, Johns Hopkins University.

Schervish, P. and Havens, J. (2002) 'The Boston Area Diary Study and the moral citizenship of care', *Voluntas*, vol 13, pp 47-71.

Scott, W. and Meyer, J. (1994) *Institutional environments and organisations: Structural complexity and individualism*, Thousand Oaks, CA: Sage Publications.

Tolbert, P. and Zucker, L. (1996) 'The Institutionalisation of institutional theory', in S. Clegg, C. Hardy and W. Nord (eds) *Handbook of organisational studies*, London: Sage Publications, pp 175-90.

Toner, J. (1968) *The experience of love*, Washington, DC: Corpus Books.

van Til, J. (1988) *Mapping the third sector: Voluntarism in a changing social economy*, New York: The Foundation Center.

Wolch, J. (1989) 'The shadow state: transformations in the voluntary sector', in J. Wolch and M. Dear (eds) *The power of geography*, Boston, MA: Unwin Hyman, pp 197-221.

Wolch, J. (1990) *The shadow state: Government and the voluntary sector*, New York: The Foundation Center.

Yeung, A. (2004) 'The Octagon model of volunteer motivation: results of a phenomenological analysis', *Voluntas*, vol 15, pp 21-46.

Zucker, L. (1977) 'The role of institutionalisation in cultural persistence', *American Sociological Review*, vol 42, pp 726-43.

Zylinska, J. (2005) *The ethics of cultural studies*, London: Continuum.

Part II
Sectoral studies

Changing policies: how faith-based organisations participate in poverty policies

Danielle Dierckx, Jan Vranken and Ingemar Elander

Introduction

Promoting participation in decision making is seen as a cure against many problems of policy making in modern societies, with the expectation that participation would ensure better quality of decisions, and close the gap between politicians and citizens. However, shortcomings in participatory processes have also been identified, such as the relation between decision making outside and within the political structure as a result of the formal electoral system. There is furthermore a middle-class bias in decision-making processes, which has led to the (in)voluntary exclusion of groups such as single mothers/parents, minority ethnic groups and the less educated in general.

The introduction of a faith dimension complicates the picture of participation even further. On the one hand, if faith-based organisations (FBOs) are close to the population (especially those groups who are excluded), then they improve their chances of participation. On the other hand, particular value systems may sometimes lead to the exclusion of certain groups from participating in FBOs, and strong cohesion within groups may lead to a closing off of people vis-à-vis society at large. In this chapter we present evidence from our fieldwork on FBOs in Belgium and Sweden to address these issues.

In this chapter we look at the participation of FBOs in larger networks, but also touch on the participation of members and clients in those organisations. Indeed, the power and/or authority of any organisation also depends on the characteristics of its clientele and on the different forms of capital that members – professionals as well as volunteers – bring with them into the organisation. We start with the almost classic statement that different degrees of participation exist, and not necessarily in the form of a 'ladder of participation', meaning that they are to be ranked hierarchically (Arnstein, 1969). While participation may have a horizontal as well as a vertical dimension, the 'steps' of the ladder are relevant to identify different forms of participation.

We begin looking at what FBOs are and why their participation is a relevant problem in present society and welfare states. One of the principles guiding this chapter is that we use concepts such as faith-based non-governmental organisation (NGO), FBO or NGO (some of which are faith-based) more or less interchangeably. We are interested in the position and role of FBOs in the current context of more horizontal power relations and an increased interconnectedness of different governmental and non-governmental actors. We are also interested in how the participation of FBOs in policy networks differs from other non-faith-based NGOs. We explore the main conditions and challenges for FBOs that want to increase or optimise their participation or that merely wish to remain outside any form of participation in existing structures.

Following Brown and Moore (2001), NGOs more generally embrace a combination of service delivery, capacity building and political participation. One of our findings was that service delivery among FBOs in Belgium and Sweden tended to predominate over capacity building and more overt political activities. However, language training, and related kinds of civic education, were quite common ways of improving the capacity of immigrants and other people in need, and sometimes FBOs might have got together and mobilised citizens on a broad scale, for example, in support of immigrants under threat of deportation. In the concluding section of this chapter we relate this finding to the potential shift towards a stronger involvement of FBOs in capacity building and political action as a consequence of deeper financial/economic crisis and the associated reduction of public provision of social welfare. This chapter does not analyse or explain, however, the reasons for the differences between the case studies of Belgium and Sweden.

Faith-based organisations

We define FBOs as *any organisation that refers directly or indirectly to religion or religious values, which functions as a welfare provider or as a political actor* (see Chapter One, this volume). FBOs are birds of many feathers, and because they may also be termed faith-based NGOs, the typology developed by Brown and Moore (2001) in comparing the accountabilities of three kinds of (international) NGOs is useful to understand the diversity within FBOs. Consequently, faith-based NGOs may also be classified under one of the following headings: service delivery FBOs, capacity buildingFBOs and policy influence FBOs.

It should be clear from the start that some combination of service delivery, capacity building and policy influence can be found in most and perhaps even in all FBOs. Particularly with respect to poverty, this integration of several functions is important, as we discovered ourselves when researching poverty organisations in Belgium – 'associations where the poor take the floor'. Indeed, these organisations defined poverty as a multidimensional problem that needed interventions on several levels. Service delivery and capacity building aim to empower people experiencing poverty. Service delivery supports them to get a better grip on their daily life; capacity building is a means to strengthen these people and to provide them with the necessary skills. In order to improve the living conditions of people experiencing poverty, policy initiatives are needed, and these are fostered through advocacy, lobbying and participation – with individual policy makers, in advisory boards, and so on.

The central hypothesis that we follow is that FBOs – as other NGOs – tend to fill the gap left after the supposed withdrawal of the welfare state, particularly in social welfare and social protection. Harris et al (2005) also identified this trend towards an increasing role for FBOs in this field. 'In both the United States and the United Kingdom, policy makers and politicians have shown increasing interest recently in faith-based organisations [FBOs] – religious congregations as well as those voluntary and non-profit organisations that are to some extent grounded in a faith tradition. The contribution that FBOs can and might make to providing welfare and other public services has been of particular interest (Smith and Sosin, 2001; Farnell et al, 2003).

FBOs seem to have a more direct entrance to the 'poor side' of cities because of their activities in deprived urban neighbourhoods and among excluded groups, and because their members often belong to these deprived and excluded groups themselves. At first sight, this looks like a return to the charity of former times, when such associations occupied the fore of social help. But we are also witnessing the beginning of a new type of welfare regime with a stronger focus on local policies and strategies and a new interplay between local authorities and civil society organisations.

We now look at the three different functions of faith-based NGOs, in the knowledge that some are mono-functional, and most possess two or even all three, albeit in varying degrees and proportions (see Table 7.1). The three functions are: service delivery ('deliver goods and services to under-served beneficiaries'), capacity building ('empower and build capacity of clients for self-help') and political participation ('foster political voice of under-represented constituencies').

Service delivery

Many FBOs have service delivery as their main practical activity. In some cases, service delivery is used to serve a 'higher' goal, which is, in some cases, a weaker or stronger form of proselytising, and in other cases, stimulating social cohesion within the (religious) community.

A study among all mosques in the Dutch city of Rotterdam (Canatan et al, 2003) revealed that their social role far exceeded that of religious centres. Next to religious and related educational activities (for example, Koranic and Arabic lessons), mosques – although widely differing with respect to the nature and number of their social activities – provide information, provision for older people, school selection for children, employment (laws and regulations, how to find or apply for jobs), education (information and communications technology [ICT], Dutch language, health, psychology, child rearing), homework guidance, emancipatory activities for girls and for women (for example, skills raising), inter-cultural and inter-faith activities, leisure activities and individual help (for example, advising

Table 7.1: Comparisons of accountabilities for different kinds of FBOs

	Service delivery FBOs	Capacity building FBOs	Policy influence FBOs
Mission focus	Deliver goods and services to under-served beneficiaries	Empower and build capacity of clients for self-help	Foster political voice of under-represented constituencies
Accountability to stakeholders in value creation	Beneficiaries have moral claim to services but may be passive recipients	Clients' participation essential to define and build capacities	Credibility with targets via values, information or representation; constituents' voices key to representation
Accountability to support and authorisation of stakeholders	Donor resources are vital to delivery; technical bodies assess service quality	Donor resources are important; regulators have legal sanctions	Donor resources from many stakeholders and member; legitimacy grounded in values, information or member voice
Accountability to operational co-producers	Staff and partners are means to service delivery goals	Staff and partners support capacity; capacity co-produced with clients	Staff and allies critical to influence campaigns; memberships co-produce influence

Source: Adapted from Brown and Moore (2001)

about regular social services or bridging the gap with them). Research has also shown that mosques succeed in reaching minority groups (usually characterised by low income and low educational levels) for which the threshold to regular services is too high (see also de Gruijter et al, 2006). Most mosques, moreover, function as informal meeting places for mutual aid organisations in case of financial or other need; financial support for a funeral or in case of chronic illness of a child; and/or fundraising in case of natural disasters such as the earthquakes in Turkey and Morocco. They also often function as informal centres to coordinate labour market supply and demand.

Our own research results confirm most of these findings. The interviewed key people had worked with people experiencing some form of social exclusion, ranging from vulnerability in a variety of forms to severe deprivation: legal migrants, young people in a difficult situation, isolated people (mainly older people), those with mental ill health and undocumented migrants. Some initiatives were more focused on one (smaller) population group, while others offered their services to a broader constituency of beneficiaries; some were very restrictive in terms of their clients' faiths, while others opened up to everyone at risk, irrespective of the person's religion or degree of religiosity.

As for their activities, the FBOs covered almost every domain of economic, social, political and cultural (including religious) life. They provided a range of services ranging from supported housing, to advice, work schemes and health clinics. Some were active in political campaigning and advocacy; some provided spiritual tools; some used proselytisation and conversion as a means for people to escape or lessen exclusion. Some simply provided shelter and basic support and advocacy for poor people, while others collected money for other projects and organised activities to increase public awareness.

Capacity building

Usually, capacity building refers to the 'empowerment' of clients or members rather than to the strengthening of the FBO itself as an organisation. Empowerment provides individuals (or groups) with the skills, confidence, self-respect and information needed to develop into agents of change. Both dimensions of capacity building are, however, very much connected, especially with respect to people living in poverty; they are, indeed, first and foremost deprived in terms of capacities (or forms of capital), which implies that increasing their capacities would probably lead to stronger organisations. The other sequence is also present: improving the social status of organisations that represent people in poverty, defending their interests or just providing services for them would certainly have a similar impact on their members or clients.

Organisational capacity building is about leadership, adaptability, management, technology, organisational culture, advocacy, accountability and human resources (CORE, 2005). That most FBOs are usually small, under- or non-funded is partly explained by the context in which they work. They provide basic services to small and poor communities without much voice and are driven more by their passion to help those in need than by a formal mission or structure. Giving those communities a voice means that their associations will be heard and listened to more attentively.

Indeed, whether a given FBO prioritises empowerment of its members or its clients depends very much on its mission, values and attitudes. Do they hold individuals responsible for their fate because of their behaviour? Do they explain poverty by various kinds of accidents, such as physical accidents or divorce or becoming unemployed? Or do they see poverty as resulting from the upward and downward turns of the economic cycle or of rapid and sudden social changes? Does poverty persist because of social structures, 'the organisation of society'? If people are blamed for their poverty, clearing society from any guilt, empowerment cannot work.

Because of the faith dimension of FBOs, we expect a much more outspoken presence of one of those perspectives than would be the case in 'secular' NGOs. The guiding perspective will be present in their overall mission, and/or in their organisational processes and/or in their day-to-day activities. Helping the poor, saving one life to save the world, teaching people to help themselves, or the concept of 'tzedakah' (the Old Testament obligation to perform acts of charity) are dictates that are remarkably similar across faiths and often permeate FBO providers' approaches to service delivery (Kramer et al, 2005).

The common mission of FBOs to 'help people' may be differently interpreted, however; it may be organised in a strongly paternalistic way, which keeps people in a dependent, disempowering relation, while 'teaching people to help themselves' suggests the preferable opposite (see also Cloke, 2005). Or, as Nieman (2005) says: 'Social development programmes can help people regain their dignity. This is because empowerment can be seen as one of the most valuable by-products of social development for individuals, groups and communities. Without empowerment, any successes in social development processes may be considered suspect.' Kunz and Kalil (1999) showed that the long-term implications of receiving material aid had a negative effect on decisions regarding education, work, marriage and childcare. Over a period of time, the so-called welfare stigma broke down self-esteem and self-efficacy because of the humiliation of being receivers of welfare and 'hand-outs'.

Another indicator for measuring empowerment is whether receiving social support is conditional on being or becoming 'a follower'. Conditionality in this case means that individual preferences of not being or becoming a follower are neglected. This disturbs the process towards empowerment in the sense of more self-control and independency of social support providers. Until now, research has not paid much attention to this (dis)empowering dimension of FBOs' activities.

Political participation

A third function of NGOs in general and of FBOs in particular is to gain or increase their political influence in order to promote their ideas and to realise their objectives. Harris et al (2005) state that some research on FBOs discusses the contribution that FBOs can and do make to public policy formulation and implementation, with or without dedicated governmental funding. Cnaan (1999) and Wineburg (2001) provide overviews of the issues arising from the involvement of religious organisations in public policy.

Most available studies, however, focus on the implications of FBOs as executors of national policies. This focus has been particularly promoted by the Charity Choice regulation of the former Bush administration in the US, which implied the devolution of service delivery to the local level and gave an important role to FBOs as service providers. Studies (Chaves, 2001; Chaves et al, 1999, in Stanziola and Schmidtz, 2003) reveal that 'race', political affiliation, budget size and geographical settings play a significant role in how faith-based agencies view devolution. For instance, Catholic and more liberal Protestant congregations are significantly more likely to indicate interest in applying for government funds to support their social services activities than conservative or evangelical congregations. Black congregations are, studies reveal, five times more likely than other congregations to seek public funds. Different views on the desirability of provision of social services by FBOs thus exist between them, resulting not only from the secular or faith-based character of the organisations.

Whereas some research has been conducted on how FBOs' service delivery is part of public policy, less research is available on political participation through deliberation, advocacy or civil dialogue. At present, the issue has been raised in Europe because social movements are trying to put it on the agenda of the debate on poverty eradication. One of these movements is the European Anti-Poverty Network (EAPN), which holds a position next to other advocacy organisations at the supranational level. Their members are a mix of faith-based and other NGOs.

A first conclusion thus is that the activities of FBOs concerning poverty matters are mainly developed in the field of service delivery and less in capacity building and political participation. In order to further explore the role of FBOs in poverty eradication, we need to contextualise those organisations and their activities, and an important part of that context is the policy context in which FBOs develop their activities.

Relations between FBOs and others

FBOs develop their activities in a context that is defined in terms of networks, of a policy arena (government or governance). In a climate of governance (interactive policy making) replacing government – at least at the discursive level – non-governmental actors are gaining access to policy-making circles and sometimes even taking the lead in initiatives, as has become clear from practical experiences with forms of public–private partnerships in various countries.

How are relations between FBOs and public authorities in general and the state in particular in the field of poverty and social exclusion? They are characterised by a kind of mutual dependency. Initiatives for which governments rarely take responsibility, due to legal or practical restrictions, are facilitated or established by FBOs, such as providing social services to undocumented people, helping people to navigate through complex administrative systems, providing shelter for women and for children who are under threat of violence or appealing government decisions. Another explanation is more pragmatic: initiatives that are not lucrative enough for other private partners are left to FBOs. However, by acknowledging the voice of FBOs, hidden risk groups are able to be identified and new needs met. Activities such as food banks or clothes donations can even be considered in terms of challenging the adequacy of current social policy.

Links between FBOs and public authorities often seem to be rather limited, because of visible and invisible thresholds or because an explicit will of some FBOs not to integrate into the state structure, such as the acceptance of public money which, for some, might imply accepting its legislation (for an alternative view, however, see Chapter Eight, this volume). From our perspective, FBOs do not want state authorities to interfere with their activities, whereas others (such as some evangelical churches) do not want to be subjected to legislation on discrimination (refusing homosexuals as clients) or equal opportunities (refusing women in paid positions).

Links with public initiatives are significantly stronger for large and institutionalised FBOs; for them the tension between incorporation into the government's financial framework and the will to remain (relatively) autonomous in order to pursue their own agenda is central, the main reason being that permanent and good access to the decision-making centres – to represent and defend their clients' interests – is their raison d'être. Diversification of financial resources then becomes important, as is the case for the Dutch Mara (independent Catholic organization): its programmes are primarily state-funded (50-90 per cent), while the core foundation is financed by the Catholic church, congregations, large philanthropic organisations and non-religious funds. Large and medium-sized FBOs need such organisational modernisation because they also want to attract both believers and non-believers as funders and volunteers or professionals, 'to demonstrate transparency, good management and accountability. Writing reports and meeting standards of partners is imperative to growth' (Davelaar et al, 2011, p 73).

Belgian and Swedish cases

Since Belgian FBOs are fairly absent in the existing formal political structures, their role as political actors in Belgium seems rather small or less visible than the role of other NGOs. Although the Belgian government has been opening up to non-governmental actors since the 1980s (Dierckx, 2007), the explicit political representation and visibility of FBOs is still relatively weak. In Sweden, more visibility for FBOs is generated through their explicit role in the universalistic Swedish welfare arrangements. Their roles and actions regarding poverty and social exclusion are foremost as providers of non-material welfare, non-partisan advocates and opinion builders, mediators representing people in relation to public authorities, deliverers of services that no one else provides, that is, being complementary to public authorities, and carrying out tendered programmes for reimbursement. Policies and programmes tackling poverty within Belgium and Sweden have largely been carried out at the local level.

Political activities

What kinds of activities do FBOs develop to contribute to combating poverty and social exclusion? In Sweden the actions of FBOs are direct or indirect, as illustrated in Figure 7.1.

Figure 7.1: Modes of FBO actions – examples running from direct to indirect measures

Cash support, homeless shelter, support programmes, education, sports, choirs, friendship

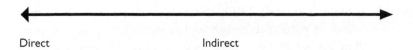

Direct   Indirect

Direct methods are carried out with a pronounced purpose to assist individual people or groups of individuals that need support; they include the homeless, older people, young people at risk and people with mental illness or addiction.

> 'Our mission is to promote the groups with severest problems and often to operate on arenas where no others want to operate, that is, if we identify a need perhaps also others see this need and act upon that, helping these people.' (Wäst, 2009, interview with a representative of Malmö City Mission)

The measures taken are running homeless shelters, rehabilitation and treatment centres, advice and support centres, legal aid receptions, debt remedy solutions, soup kitchen-type charities offering food, showers and a comfortable place to be during the daytime, job training programmes or helping ex-convicts to adjust to life outside prison.

More common, however, are the *indirect* measures of targeting poverty and social exclusion identified by the FBOs. They range from family counselling sessions and choir singing to Swedish language training workshops. These are sometimes pronounced as preventive measures, directed at young people at risk or people with poor language skills. Other indirect but still pronounced aspects of FBOs' preventive measures are a focus on healthy lifestyles with education around issues of abstinence from alcohol, tobacco, coffee or illegal drugs. Addressing the structural levels of economic inequality and racism are two more indirect ways of getting at poverty and social exclusion, mentioned by many FBOs.

> The perhaps most important achievement by the Islamic Centre in society is our external function to fight prejudice. Man's worst enemy is ignorance and the Centre counters this partly by helping authorities and companies with information and interpretation, and partly by the many field trips received. Every year 70,000 visits the Mosque; school classes as well as multinational companies and pensioner associations. Pupils often turn to the mosque for help with school work in education about religion. (Islamic Center, 2011 [www.mosken.se/]; our translation from Swedish)

This distinction in modes of FBOs' action is also applicable for the situation in Belgium and the kind of activities are similar. An additional observation, however, shows that FBOs fill the gap left by government where multidimensional problems are concerned. Government acts particularly on separate life domains, such as work, education and housing. FBOs seem to focus more on the complexity of life conditions of particular groups like refugees and people experiencing severe poverty. Looking at the kinds of activities that are provided, we make a distinction between emergency care (such as the distribution of food packages by the Protestant Social Centre in Antwerp) and moral and non-material support (listening, giving a voice, information delivery, as happens during meetings with 'needy' people at the Society of Saint Vincent de Paul).

The Swedish case confirms the challenge of providing illegal services – the activities may be illegal, but more often they are just incompatible with government responsibilities. FBOs in Sweden are increasingly voicing concerns about poverty and social exclusion to the media and the public – usually opposing local government welfare cutbacks. They are concerned that local government is not taking full responsibility.

> 'It [the church] should be salt, and salt may sting occasionally, but salt can also enhance the flavour and it can hurt sometimes. And I believe it has to be there because otherwise we lose it. And when we lose what we are we are nothing, we could just as well become any other organisation.' (Lidgren, 2009, interview with a representative of the Church of Sweden, Malmö)

To appeal for more governmental responsibility, FBOs are sometimes able to develop informal ways to influence government. Belgian FBOs often organise campaigns and other sensitising projects (for example, annual campaigns of welfare care, *Welzijnszorg*) and they regularly take up a signalling function (for example, Welfare Links, *Welzijnsschakels*). In many cases, this sensitising aspect is integrated as an organisational goal. Catholic FBOs are more dominant in developing these activities in Belgium; Islamic FBOs in Belgium are rather more occupied with interest maintenance, integration and emancipation.

In Sweden attention is also paid to addressing structural inequalities, as the example of the Stockholm City Mission illustrates:

> 'Our mission is also to challenge society as a whole, not just the public realm, but also as citizens when it comes to identifying and trying to resolve existing vulnerability, and change mechanisms and cultures that create vulnerability in society.' (Markovits, 2009, interview with a representative of the Stockholm City Mission)

Relation with government and policy influence

In most Belgian cases, cooperation between FBOs and government is not strong. While some FBOs have contacts with government, in most cases the relations of FBOs with government are rare and, especially in the case of Brussels, less developed than those with FBOs/NGOs. Albeit rare, the collaboration of FBOs with government is relatively good. Hence we see some indications of discontent as well, mainly relating to questions of interest and influence.

As far as the position of FBOs in policy making is concerned, some FBOs point to having (had) influence on national policies regarding poverty eradication. Under these FBOs fall mainly Christian associations. When we take a closer look at this 'influence', it becomes clear that it is often equated with participation in the policy-making process itself. The degree to which a FBO has influence on and participates in policies furthermore depends on its operational level. Compared to the local level, FBOs operating at the national level have slightly more impact on social policies and on legislation. The difference is modest, however, and mainly lies in the fact that national-level FBOs more often take an active stance and approach public administrations and politicians themselves.

Faith-based actors at the local level, however, respond to impulses initiated by the authorities. They are invited to comment on social policies and to cooperate around specific themes. This is not to say that there are many differences in the degree of political participation of FBOs, even within the same operational level. But participation can have tangible results. The main results mentioned by national FBOs is advice that has been taken into account and resulting changes in legislation concerning poverty. Whereas these 'influential' FBOs also feel stimulated by government to participate in policy making, the incentives for participation are often restricted. On the whole, FBOs take up a consultation and advice function. Some are consulted within the framework of Flemish local social policy, while others are established in advice councils at the federal level.

The Belgian case shows that some elements seem to increase the political influence and participation of FBOs. One of the most important factors is the network of FBOs: organisations operating in networks have more pull in reaching and influencing government than other, more independent ones. In order to attract the attention of government to poverty or social exclusion, moreover, it is important to have good connections with individual politicians. Another element relates to obtaining results.

The most recent, and potentially most thorough, change involving the work of FBOs in the social arena in Sweden is an agreement made between the Swedish government, voluntary organisations in the social sphere and the Swedish Association of Local Authorities and Regions (SALAR) (see Chapter Four, this volume). Although the Agreement is still mainly rhetorical, its implications may be far-reaching depending on the outcome of the local dialogues. Taken to its extreme it may signify the erosion of a welfare state based on universal rights in the direction of a 'patchwork' welfare society based on a mixture of interventions by state/local state, market and charitable/philanthropic actions.

The mediating role of FBOs, and their advocacy in relation to local government, include messages on how there are new groups exposed to poverty, and generally also a message for the local authorities to take responsibility, either by developing their own programmes, or by funding FBO initiatives supporting poor and socially excluded groups of people. Most FBOs, at least based on our findings, seem to interpret poverty in structural terms; with reference to problems with uneven distribution of wealth, however, they do not want to engage in party politics.

Local governments and FBOs in Sweden contribute to inter-religious cooperation: through cultural and social integration; inter-religious integration of social service provision (for example, FBOs serving target groups of other faiths); and inter-religious conflict resolution (for example, city governments bringing together religious leaders of all beliefs to solve particular problems in the city).

Hiding refugees by organising country-wide networks, organising study circles for various immigrant groups, language and civic courses at high schools and homework support for immigrant children are only a few of the activities undertaken by local branches of FBOs and ecumenical networks. It goes without saying that knowledge about some of these activities is not readily available. Nevertheless the background of 'the Easter Call' (*Påskuppropet*) is quite well documented, and displays an interesting process of intervention in nation-wide politics through building up inter-religious and secular support for undocumented and hidden asylum-seekers in Sweden. Although 'the Call' as such was a broad national appeal to harsh government policies towards asylum-seekers, it was anticipated by local initiatives, mainly within local parishes (see Chapter Four, this volume).[1]

Around Easter time in 2005 the Christian Council of Sweden (*Sveriges Kristna Råd*), an ecumenical forum of churches in Sweden, came together in a joint protest against tougher policies making it more difficult for refugees to get a residence permit. 'The Easter Call' used the following watchwords:

> WE MOURN that the rights of the child is not given priority in decisions made about resident permits in our country.

> WE WELCOME a court procedure that grants asylum seekers legal security.

> WE URGE the Swedish Government to grant amnesty to all previously denied asylum.

> WE DEMAND that the right to asylum is restored and broadens in a way worthy [of] a humane society founded on the rule of law.

In total, 157,251 people heard the call and signed the petition that was later turned over to the Minister for Migration and Asylum Policy. The result was that 20,000 asylum-seekers were granted residence permits in a second trial. Although 'the Easter Call' was organisationally initiated by the ecumenical Christian Council of Sweden, it not only gained support from most of the Christian congregations, but also from the Islamic Council of Sweden (*Sveriges Muslimska Råd*), and more than 60 non-religious NGOs and other political and civil organisations, for example, the Green Party, the Young Left, the Centre Party Women, the Male Network, Reporters without Borders, the Borås Students, the Iran Music and Cultural Association, the National Association of Somalian People and so on. Notably, several organisations that do not normally join manifestations like this one actively supported 'the Easter Call'. For example, the coordinator of the 13 orthodox churches in the Christian Council of Sweden said that, 'the support was never questioned. The orthodox churches live close to the asylum seekers and the statement was self-evident' (quoted in Qviström, 2005, p 208). The Islamic Council of Sweden supported 'the Call', although renaming it 'the Refugee Call' (Qviström, 2005, p 209).[2]

Notably, what may in retrospect look like an initiative from above, addressing the Swedish government and parliament with an outright demand for policy change by the Church of Sweden, and its Archbishop Karl Gunnar Hammar, had a pre-history of local engagement and strong criticism of the Church of Sweden for not acting on behalf of asylum-seekers. The people supporting 'the Easter Call' did not themselves generally dress their action in political terms, but rather as an act of religious and/or humanitarian inclination whereby it had an obvious political load.

Political role of FBOs

Considering the Belgian case, we now turn to the opinions of FBOs regarding the aim of influencing and participating in policies: how do they perceive their political role? Again, there is some variation between FBOs, although most appear quite satisfied concerning this issue. Some faith-based actors stress that they want to stay out of politics – they are not stimulated by public authorities to participate in public policies, but do not want to participate either. These associations prefer spending time helping others and they point to other organisations with more expertise in meeting techniques and the like to engage in political activities. On the other hand, some FBOs would even favour more involvement in the political process. For them, it would be good if the government heard the associations that are occupied with voluntary work in order to take particular policy decisions. Some of the issues and debates around the post-political (Rancière, 2001; Mouffe, 2005; Swyngedouw, 2010) in the context of neoliberal governmentality would appear relevant for situating FBOs and their political role (see Chapters Three and Eight, this volume). The growing visibility and social requirement of FBOs reveals the cracks in the neoliberal consensus, with certain FBOs brought into the rationalities and technologies of governance while simultaneously offering alternative discourses and futures.

Good practice

In Belgium, civil society actors are strongly involved in policy making and policy implementation. One could say that a political osmosis has developed between private non-profit institutions and the public sector. With respect to the issue of poverty and social exclusion, participation of civil society actors is rooted in the framework of the poverty decree and the federal follow-up of the *General report on poverty* (Koning Boudewijnstichting, 1995). The fact that during the last two decades a tradition was established of more involvement of NGOs in policy making concerning poverty eradication contrasts with the under-representation of FBOs in the formal interactive structures. An important reason is the high degree of volunteers in these organisations. Practical issues such as limited time available or the skills to use professional language in the debate with policy makers are thresholds for policy participation. Different from the other NGOs, some FBOs succeed in establishing personal contacts with people in power, and these contacts are used to express the needs of their clientele and to lobby for funding, apart from the formal funding regulations.

As good practice from Sweden we refer to the multi-actor agreement. Although the earlier mentioned Agreement (*Överenskommelsen*) between the government, civil society organisations and SALAR was basically a national process, it now continues at the local level. Several agreements at the municipal level are hence underway. In 2007 in one city, Örebro, with 120,000 inhabitants, the local government launched an inter-religious advisory board comprising representatives from the local branches of the Church of Sweden, the free churches, different Islamic groups, the Syrian Orthodox Church and people representing the municipality. Among the latter was the chair of the City Council, a Christian Democrat, who also became chair of the board. The stated aims of the board were to increase citizens' knowledge about different cultures and religions, stimulate inter-religious/inter-cultural dialogue, support civil society in developing complementary social services and support civil society work for creating an 'integrated Örebro' (Örebro kommun, 2009).[3] However, except for one of the municipal representatives, the inter-religious board was totally male-dominated, something that was critically noticed by some women who decided to initiate a women's inter-cultural network. The network, established within the United Nations (UN) UNIFEM framework, with some financial support from central government, promptly started 10 working groups around specific topics such as women's health, violence against women in the family and safety in the street. Notably, the women's network was explicitly inter-cultural and not inter-religious (ETC Örebro, 2010).

The Agreement between the Swedish government, the municipalities and civil society signifies a rhetorical re-shift of welfare provision in the direction of civil society, although on the part of the non-socialist governing coalition the move towards privatisation has been much more substantial than the devolution of social responsibilities to FBOs and other NGOs so far (see Chapter Four, this volume). However, this is not to deny the current and potential importance of FBOs as providers of social welfare. The Church of Sweden, through its diaconal work, is still an important provider of social services, both in specific areas such as hospitals, prisons and armed forces as in everyday social matters more generally. FBOs, like the city missions as well as The Salvation Army and other free churches in Sweden, offer shelter to homeless people, help drug addicts and offer a number of other social services. For the many immigrants having entered Swedish society, especially since the beginning of the 1990s, the big mosque in central Stockholm and a growing number of mosques and cellar mosques in many cities offer social services in a broad sense. In the case of legal immigrants as well as asylum-seekers and undocumented people nation-wide, engagement from religious and non-religious grassroots organisations may bring these issues to the top of the policy agenda and become a strong counter-voice to xenophobic and racist tendencies fostered by, for example, the Sweden Democrats (a political party gaining 5.7 per cent of the votes in the 2010 parliamentary election and 20 seats in the Swedish parliament).

Conclusion

Based on an extensive review of research on citizen participation, Amnå (2010) identifies a number of more or less co-existing dynamic motives for an individual to shift from latent (potential) to manifest (active) participation in politics and civic matters broadly: obligation ('one ought to'), importance ('I have to'), ability ('I can'), demand ('I am needed'), effectiveness ('it works') and meaningfulness ('it gives'). This list of possible motives for participation indicates that under particular circumstances anyone may be willing to participate, that is, potential active citizens are 'stand-by citizens' (Amnå, 2010). Although these motivations may well be deduced from a secular value basis, they can also be expressions of a faith-based creed, thus inducing action by FBOs as well as other NGOs. As illustrated in this chapter people volunteering in FBOs as well as many FBOs themselves as collective actors (including their employed staff) may take action under circumstances when people in need are under severe stress as a consequence of welfare cuts, harsh policies towards immigrants or other predicaments. Although this potential for action may seem marginal in relation to the bulk of service delivery still produced by the relatively well developed public welfare systems in Europe, this situation may quickly change in the current situation of financial and economic crisis. Considering their mostly limited capacity for service delivery (largely as a supplement to public welfare provision) this might strongly motivate FBOs to increase their efforts in capacity building and political action as a way to counteract the neoliberal drive towards reduction of public spending on social welfare.

Notes

[1] *Välgrundad fruktan. Om asyl, amnesti och rätten till trygghet* [*Well-founded fear. On asylum, amnesty and the right to security*] is the title of a book published in 2005, based on articles and interviews under and in the wake of 'the Easter Call' process in spring 2005 (QvistrÖm, 2005). These texts are the empirical platform for the story briefly told here. See also Elander and Fridolfsson (2011, pp 45-6).

[2] 'The Easter Call' that was delivered to the government on 16 May 2005, signed by 157,251 people, 64 organisations and the 25 member churches of the Christian Council of Sweden (Christian Council of Sweden, 2005).

[3] Similar boards have been established or are on their way in GÖteborg, LinkÖping, MalmÖ, and probably other cities as well.

References

Amnå, E. (2010) 'Active, passive, or stand-by citizens? Latent and manifest political participation', in E. Amnå (ed) *New forms of citizen participation*, Baden-Baden: Nomos, pp 191-203.

Arnstein, S.R. (1969) 'A ladder of citizen participation', *Journal of the American Institute of Planning*, vol 35, no 4, pp 216-24.

Brown, L.D. and Moore, M.H. (2001) *Accountability, strategy, and international non-governmental organizations*, Working Paper No 7, Cambridge, MA: The Hauser Center for Nonprofit Organizations, The Kennedy School of Government, Harvard University.

Canatan, K., Oudijk, C. and Lkamai, A. (2003) *De maatschappelijke rol van de Rotterdamse moskeeën* [*The social role of the Rotterdam mosques*], Rotterdam: COS.

Christian Council of Sweden (2005) *Påskuppropet* [*The Easter Call*] (www.skr. org/temp_paskupprop05_intro.htm).

Cloke, P. (2005) 'Exploring ethos? Discourses of "charity" in the provision of emergency services for homeless people', *Environment and Planning*, vol 37, pp 385-402.

Cnaan, R.A. (1999) *The newer deal: Social work and religion in partnership*, New York: Columbia University Press.

CORE (Communities Responding to the HIV/AIDS Epidemic) (2005) *CBO/FBO capacity analysis: A tool for assessing and building capacities for high quality responses to HIV/AIDS*, US Agency for International Development.

Davelaar, M., van den Toorn, J., de Witte, N., Beaumont, J. and Kuiper, C. (2011) *Faith-based organisations and social exclusion in the Netherlands*, Leuven: Acco.

de Gruijter, M., Dogan, G. and Rijkschroeff, R. (2006) *Stichting Ayasofya: Lokale schakel voor maatschappelijke participatie* [*Foundation Ayasofya: Local link for participation in society*], Utrecht: Verwey-Jonker Instituut.

Dierckx, D. (2007) 'Between poverty policy and policy poverty. A retrospective and intervention oriented analysis of the Flemish policy practice', Doctoral thesis, University of Antwerp, March, Leuven: Acco. [Published in Flemish]

Elander, I. and Fridolfsson, C. (2011) *Faith-based organisations and social exclusion in Sweden*, Leuven/Den Haag: Acco.

ETC Örebro [Weekly newspaper] (2010) 'Mer makt till kvinnor i Örebro' ['More power to women in Örebro'], no 6, p 7.

Farnell, R., Furbey, R., Al-Hagg Hills, S.S., Macey, M. and Smith, G. (2003) *'Faith' in urban regeneration: Engaging faith communities in urban regeneration*, Bristol and York: The Policy Press and Joseph Rowntree Foundation.

Koning Boudewijnstichting (1995) *Algemeen Verslag over de Armoede (General report on poverty)*, Brussels: Koning Boudewijnstichting.

Harris, M., Hutchison, R. and Cairns, B. (2005) 'Community-wide planning for faith-based service provision: practical, policy, and conceptual challenges', *Nonprofit and Voluntary Sector Quarterly*, vol 34, p 88.

Kramer, F.D. et al (2005) *Federal policy on the ground: Faith-based organizations delivering local services*, Washington, DC: The Urban Institute.

Kunz, J. and Kalil, A. (1999) 'Self-esteem, self-efficacy and welfare use', *Social Work Research*, vol 23, no 2, pp 119-26.

Mouffe, C. (2005) *On the political*, Abingdon: Routledge.

Nieman, A. (2005) 'Churches and social development. A South African perspective', *International Social Work*, vol 49, no 5, pp 595-604.

Örebro kommun (2009) *Örebro Kommuns interreligiösa/interkulturella råd [Örebro municipality's inter-religious/inter-cultural committee]*, 18 June.

Qviström, D. (ed) (2005) *Välgrundad fruktan. Om asyl, amnesti och rätten till trygghet. [Well motivated fear. On asylum, amnesty and the right to security]*, Örebro: Cordia.

Rancière, J. (2001) 'Ten theses on politics', *Theory and Event*, vol 5, no 3, p 21.

Smith, S.R. and Sosin, M.R. (2001) 'The varieties of faith-related agencies', *Public Administration Review*, vol 61, no 6, pp 651-70.

Stanziola, J. and Schmitz, T. (2003) 'The impact of devolution on organizational effectiveness: an exploratory case study of faith-based childcare', *The Qualitative Report*, vol 8, no 4, pp 655-75 (www.nova.edu/ssss/QR/QR8-4/stanziola.pdf).

Swyngedouw, E. (2010) 'Apocalypse forever', *Theory, Culture & Society*, vol 27, nos 2-3, pp 213-32.

Wineburg, B. (2001) *A limited partnership: The politics of religion, welfare, and social service*, New York: Columbia University Press.

EIGHT

Moralising the poor? Faith-based organisations, the Big Society and contemporary workfare policy

Andrew Williams[1]

Introduction

The aim of this chapter is to examine welfare-to-work 'ethics' in the UK in the context of the current policy regime of the 'Big Society' and the ways that faith-based organisations (FBOs) challenge those ethics towards more progressive conceptions of social justice. In this way the chapter contributes to the volume at large by showing from a broadly defined governmentality perspective how, in certain instances, FBOs work in and with government policy in order to simultaneously subvert those regimes to tackle social injustices in European cities.

Since the Coalition government in the UK came to power in May 2010, David Cameron has embarked on the most radical overhaul of the welfare state since its postwar establishment. The new austerity measures prompted by the financial crisis of 2008-09 have taken as their prime target the public sector, resulting in large-scale redundancies and unemployment (Coote, 2011), while helping legitimatise US-style workfare approaches to unemployment that further restricts eligibility to welfare entitlements and withdraws Jobseeker's Allowance for those who decline a job offer (Helm et al, 2010; DWP, 2011a). On the backdrop of this culture of austerity sails Cameron's plan for a Big Society that claims to remove the bureaucracies of big government and give people the power to control their public services.[2] Faith-based groups are said to play an integral role if the Big Society is to be a success, both as community anchors and representatives, and as service providers (Stunell, 2010; Warsi, 2011).[3]

This revalorisation of faith groups by politicians has led some commentators to view faith-based welfare efforts as willing or unwilling servants of neoliberalism, whose collusion in the logics of the Big Society and workfare functions to discipline the poor and legitimise political-economic restructuring (see Peck and Tickell, 2002; Goode, 2006; Lyon-Callo, 2008; Trudeau and Veronis, 2009). Yet little is known about how FBOs have responded to the Big Society and the arrival of 'pure' workfare policies in the UK. The details of these policy changes are still developing and thus it is too early to analyse how such programmes have shaped the practices of faith-based and voluntary organisations.[4] However, much can be learned about the role FBOs play in implementing workfare and the Big Society by examining how FBOs delivered contractual welfare-to-work programmes under the New Labour government.

By highlighting what I define as the 'ethics of engagement' – *both* the complex reasons and motivations why particular FBOs came to work as agents of government policy, *and* the ways in which the 'ethical agency' of staff and clients acts to modify, disrupt or negate the intended processes and outcomes of official public policy – it becomes clearer that faith-based and voluntary organisations working within the trappings of neoliberal government should not be dismissed outright. Rather a much more complicated picture arises, where FBOs can potentially be sites of resistance and subversion to the political-economy of neoliberalism.

This chapter is structured as follows. The first section introduces the concept of 'governmentality' used to elucidate the 'ethics' of the welfare-to-work policy and how policies are enacted and/or subverted by front-line welfare actors.[5] I then stake out my conceptualisation of resistance, performativity and ethical agency, drawing on the work of Barnes and Prior (2009) and recent formulations of theo-ethics (Cloke, 2010; see also Cloke et al Chapter Five in this volume) to frame empirical discussion of the subversive potential of faith-motivated actors working in neoliberal frameworks. The second section examines the 'ethics' of welfare-to-work in the current context of austerity measures and the Big Society, and outlines some of the shortcomings of this policy approach. The third section develops the case study of Pathways Ltd, an organisation that has delivered a number of welfare-to-work contracts over the last 20 years.[6] Here I illustrate the argument that the ethical agency of staff bringing alternative rationalities and technologies into these programmes carves out a *space for resistance* against neoliberal formulations of welfare-to-work. The fourth section illustrates alternative ways faith-based groups have engaged politically in various forms of resistance to the ascendant neoliberalisation of social policy. The chapter concludes by outlining the implications of this argument in debates concerning the role of FBOs within the proposed Big Society and workfare programmes in the UK.

Governmentality, subversion and theo-ethical performance

The concept of governmentality centres on the formation of *governing imaginations* and how these mentalities are materialised in a particular set of practices (Le Heron, 2007). As an analytic, governmentality attends to the (1) governing imaginations that have rationalities that justify and legitimate claims and actions; (2) intelligibility to others that attracts attention and commitment; (3) their direct or indirect relation to spaces that become potentially governable because they are identified; (4) the enrolment of governable subjects; (5) the translation of key ideas into immediate circumstances and practices; and (6) the help of technologies that facilitate action and assist with knowing the world in relatively unproblematic terms (see Le Heron, 2007, p 30). Governmentality is now an established analytical perspective in studies of the neoliberalisation of welfare provision, social exclusion and state governance of non-state actors (Jenkins, 2005; Larner and Butler, 2005; MacLeavy, 2008; Trudeau and Veronis, 2009). It has brought important insights concerning the intensification of central government power to regulate and discipline street-level organisations (see Bondi and Laurie, 2005; Fyfe, 2005; Larner and Butler, 2005; May et al, 2005; Camel and Harlock, 2008; Buckingham, 2009).

Analytically, however, commentators have recently expressed concern that governmentality is insufficient in understanding the ways that rationalities and technologies connect with the subjectivities of those it seeks to govern (see Barnett, 2009). According to McKee (2009), analytics of governmentality have tended to be overly discursive and have focused primarily on what the authorities wanted to happen at the expense of how such rationalities materialise and connect with dispersed entities on the ground. This disregard to messiness of the empirical, she argues, leads to totalising accounts of the way rationalities and technologies are automatically realised and normalised in practices and subjects of welfare organisations. She asserts that there is still a temptation to 'read off' consequences from governmental ambitions (Clarke et al, 2007, p 22), despite repeated warnings that it cannot be assumed that reproduction happens and power always realises its effects (see O'Malley et al, 1997).

In their book, *Subversive citizens: Power, agency and resistance in public services*, Barnes and Prior (2009) argue that presuming rationalities and technologies of government immutably brings about their governable intentions serves to underwrites resistance among actors working within these neoliberal governmentalities. They argue that in some accounts of governmentality, governmental processes are posited as always and necessarily operating as intended and are successful in meeting their objectives. Resistance is understood in terms of those who keep their distance from such governmental trappings and challenge neoliberalism from the outside more directly. This presents a dichotomy of resistance whereby actors are either successfully 'got at' and made into neoliberal subjects, or escape the rapture of subjectification in an act of glorified resistance. However, as Prior (2009) argues, resistance takes multiple forms, and oppositional/counter-agency is only one form of subversion. In a similar vein to Lipsky's (1980) influential work on street-level bureaucrats, Barnes and Prior (2009) challenge governmentality perspectives by providing a more sophisticated account of how government policy is subverted by the agency of insiders – of staff and clients. While governmental rationalities and technologies may reduce space for autonomy and discretion by encoding certain behaviours, they cannot be assumed to dictate what happens in particular contexts. However robust or definitive specific strategies and technologies may be, what actually happens on the ground is contingent on the interaction of rationalities and technologies on the one hand, and the agency of both practitioners and clients on the other. Agency, here, refers to the ways staff, service users and volunteers in public service organisations 'interpret and reinterpret policy; negotiate their own values, identities and commitments in relation to the way in which they are encouraged and exhorted to act; determine what they consider is the right thing to do in particular circumstances; and challenge or resist identities that are offered to or imposed on them by government' (Barnes and Prior, 2009, p 3). Prior (2009, p 29) identifies three separate forms of this subversion. The first can be understood as *revision*, whereby practitioners adopt alternative strategies and technologies that modify or 'bend' official policy and practice towards different outcomes. This could be said of a FBO fulfilling a government contract but doing so in a different way or bringing additional values and practices in so far as it changes intended policy outcomes. The second is *resistance*, whereby clients develop alternative strategies or technologies in response to specific situations, in order to achieve outcomes other than those prescribed in official policy. The third is *refusal*, and refers to a more passive mode of response to the official prescriptions of government policy, whereby organisations, staff or clients disengage with official rationalities and technologies of government. This can take the form of refusing the terms of engagement, identities and obligations imposed by government.

If the assemblage of neoliberalism is contingent on the inculcation of governmental rationalities and technologies on the ethical agency of practitioner and client, whose performance is inextricably a space of deliberation, interpretation and potential subversion of the intended processes and outcomes of government policy, then we must consider the values, identities and commitments that constitute ethical agency – religious and secular. For many faith-motivated practitioners' theologically derived values and virtues of compassion, hope and faith served as ethical precepts that encourage and exhorted one to act in particular directions. Often these theo-ethical proclivities were narrated with reference to scriptural parables such as the Good Samaritan, the sheep and the goats, the prodigal son and others, which were understood to prompt explicitly counter-cultural praxis: showing compassion, loving mercy and forgiveness, even loving your enemies (Caputo, 2001). Faith-motivated practitioners professed an obstinate hope that permeated into their ethical practice, a belief in transformation in someone's life or a situation where there are so little signs of it. This impassioned 'hope against hope', as St Paul says (Romans 4:18), was often rooted in eschatological belief[7] for religious believers. In FBOs, theo-ethical precepts are often shared across the staff group and embedded in the organisational ethos and decision making. This can be clearly seen in The Salvation Army Employment Plus services in the context of the Job Network in Australia. Here the Australian government social security department, Centrelink, gives contracted non-governmental welfare-to-work service providers the power to 'breach a client', that is, indirectly reducing, and in some cases withholding, income support for clients who do not meet the requirements devised by government to enable an unemployed person to receive welfare benefit. Garland and Darcy (2009) illustrate how the values, beliefs and organisational raison d'être of The Salvation Army Employment Plus ran antithetical to the philosophy of 'breaching' a client. They cite, despite having '13% of the market the Army was responsible for only 2% of all the "breaches" notified to Centrelink' (Garland and Darcy, 2009, p 767). The values and ethics held by The Salvation Army prompted an internal policy not to breach jobseekers if it was possible to find an alternative. Similarly I argue that the theo-ethics performed by staff and volunteers in welfare-to-work contexts in the UK serve as a bulwark to the more disciplinary 'ethics' of workfare, and in doing so subversively bring about more progressive conceptions of justice.

Ethics of workfare in the Big Society

This section examines the gradual emergence of 'pure' workfare in the UK, and traces its (dis)continuities with New Labour's welfare-to-work. It is well established that social protectionist ethics have given way to an ethic of self-responsibility in Western welfare states (Bauman, 1993; Rose, 1999), and there are different ethical foundations of 'welfare-to-work' or 'workfare' (Dean, 2007). This chapter focuses on the shifting ethics entailed in New Labour's 'welfare-to-work' and the Conservative's 'workfare' programmes, paying particular attention to the shifting *problematisations* – what is thought to be the problem of, and solution for, unemployment. The chapter details the role voluntary and faith-based groups are designated to play amid changing political and institutional contexts, illustrating the shifting rationalities and technologies of government set to bring about particular practices, objectives and subjectivities among both unemployed clients and service-providers, including non-statutory as well as statutory providers.

New Labour, neoliberalisation and welfare-to-work

New Labour made welfare-to-work a central theme in the mid-1990s in response to high unemployment, particularly youth unemployment, and high welfare dependency under the Conservatives (Fraser, 2004).[8] Tough new measures were posited as necessary to combat the twin evils of 'welfare dependency' and 'worklessness' (Theodore, 2007). The influence of President Clinton's workfare policies in the US and the neoconservative imaginaries propagated by writers such as Charles Murray, Lawrence Mead, Marvin Olasky and Frank Field,[9] have been accredited with developing the British welfare-to-work programmes (Heron and Dwyer, 1999). These imaginaries, most clearly articulated in the New Labour discourse of 'no rights without responsibilities', pronounced the deleterious nature of state welfare, arguing that means-tested benefits reward claimants for being inactive or deceitful, and undermine the morals of the poor and their motivation to become economically self-sufficient. New Labour's New Deal for the Unemployed was premised on the idea that benefits should not be simply handed out as a right to those in a condition of dependency on the state, and claim the problem of the unemployed was primarily related to the willingness, behaviours and attitudes of the individual – their readiness to accept responsibility to help themselves and contribute to society through paid work (Dean, 2002).

Yet these neoconservative imaginaries were combined with 'supply-side socialism', equality of opportunities and the promotion of human capital development (education, training and skills) in order to compete in a globalised market economy. Thus, Hartley Dean (2007) characterises the ethic of New Labour's welfare-to-work as broadly competitive/egalitarian. However, it is well documented that during New Labour's reign this ethic quickly subsumed into populist paranoia concerning welfare dependency, 'fraudulent' claimants and anti-social behaviour which led to the adoption of more punitive measures to tackle the perceived debilitating effects of long-term unemployment. It was claimed that welfare dependency had created a demoralised idle and work-shy sub-population or 'underclass' (see Lister, 2004). Increasingly, what was thought to be the problem of unemployment was the moral character of the individual, their (lack of) motivation and deficient attitudes towards work (Bryson, 2003; Crisp, 2008).

Welfare-to-work programmes were organised to 'moralise' the poor, inculcating 'good' behaviour through strict behavioural requirements and motivational engineering (Dwyer, 2004). Methods included mandatory training sessions to demonstrate claimants' willingness and ability to work, increased surveillance through case managers and mentoring and sanctions or withdrawal of benefits for those not meeting obligations or accepting any job. These contractual relationships between state and citizen embed a particular morality wherein 'social citizenship becomes conditional on individuals adopting an active disposition, narrowly defined in terms of economic participation' (McDonald and Marsten, 2005, p 379). Non-compliance and failure to perform the ethical citizen of welfare-to-work programmes resulted in the punitive withdrawal of assistance, practices of zero tolerance and paternalist impulses to use coercion on individuals who could not exercise their own autonomy or act in their best interest (see Dean, 2002; McDonald and Marsten, 2005).

The neoconservative critique of welfare dependency and its moral rationalities of the poor are closely tethered to the neoliberal rationalities of the facilitative state (Beaumont, 2004).[10] The retraction of welfarist modes of provision (legitimatised through appeal to managerial and fiscal pressures to ensure cost-efficiency) led to contracting out the responsibility and risk for welfare service delivery to voluntary, non-profit and private organisations (while in some domains of welfare the state excised some services from the palette of public activity altogether). This has created opportunities for FBOs to re-enter the public realm as service providers in areas of education, housing, healthcare and employment training, through both voluntary and increasingly professionalised service organisations. This embodies a faith-based re-colonisation of welfare services that were first established by faith-based philanthropic organisations of the 19th century and have since been absorbed by the state through the development of the welfare state in the 1940s (Prochaska, 2006).

Since 1997 New Labour's welfare reforms have resulted in new and more complex relationships between central and local government and their non-statutory partners. New Labour's 'compact' with the voluntary sector was an unparalleled act of repositioning the voluntary and community sector (now valorised as the third sector; see Camel and Harlock, 2008) in public policy in the

UK. This move changed the rationale of state welfare. The Conservatives under Margaret Thatcher turned to the non-statutory sector as a means of offloading the responsibilities of welfare provision from the state onto voluntary and other groups, whereas New Labour's rationale for partnership with the third sector involved both a recognition of the strengths of that sector (local awareness, creativity, expertise and so on), and a recognition of the need for the state to act strongly to ensure issues of quality control and policy direction.

This compact-reliant rationale for welfare required new technologies of delivery that allowed greater control over how partnering third sector agencies actually delivered services. Thus tendering procedures have increasingly spelt out exactly how agencies should fulfil their contract – and along with strictly enforced performance targets, these technologies were designed to ensure that non-statutory partners were 'fit' for a role in state-orchestrated programmes. This fitness included the requirement that the ethos and approach of partner agencies should be broadly aligned with the aims of central government policy, and in so doing, it is suggested (Newman, 2001; Wolch, 2006, p xiii) that government controlled the voice of potential critics by inducing a fear that critical agencies might lose their place at the table of government. In turn, these technologies have induced a process of self-regulation within agencies wishing to maintain their partnership status, or putting it another way, it was in the FBOs' interests to stick to a realpolitik of compliance.

Within such governmental frameworks FBOs are thereby subject to *new* forms and processes of state control, albeit through subtle mechanisms of performance targets and other 'technologies' that elicit self-regulation strategies among FBOs, to ensure state ends are met through clearly defined means (Bondi and Laurie, 2005; Fyfe, 2005; Larner and Butler, 2005; May et al, 2005). New Labour, through competitive tendering, accentuated existing trends of professionalisation and bureaucratisation by drawing providers into increasingly competitive local quasi-markets (Buckingham, 2009). It is through the intensification of government monitoring and contracting procedures that FBOs have found their organisational autonomy eroded through the imposition of economic rationalities and technologies of government, largely embedded in the frameworks of best practice, best value and tethered to funding stipulations (Deakin, 2001; Osborne and McLaughlin, 2004; Cairns et al, 2005).

Ethics of workfare in the Big Society

The Coalition's radical welfare reforms have implemented a much tougher approach to unemployment than their New Labour predecessors. The most striking development in the 'Work Programme' is the compulsion of claimants to undertake work placements in return for only their benefits. They are not given any choice as to where they work or the sort of work they do. If the benefit claimant refuses to take a particular work placement, or fails to turn up on time, they are threatened with a sanction of loss of three months' benefits. For their second 'offence' the sanction becomes six months, and then anything up to three years – a crude and cruel method of manipulating job figures. The programme is designed to 'give [long-term unemployed] people that extra push to make sure they are really keeping active and focused on what it takes to get into work' (DWP, 2011b). As part of the Big Society institutional set-up a total of 514 businesses (such as Tesco, Poundland and the London Underground) and charities (including The Salvation Army) have signed up to take on unpaid volunteers and give them the 'experience of the habits and routines of working life' (DWP, 2011c). While these organisations benefit from free labour, the biggest winners are much larger for-profit companies as they contract out placements to these smaller charities and businesses. Firms such as Action for Employment (A4e) are alleged to make up to £14,000 per long-term unemployed secured into a sustainable job (Timmins, 2011).[11] According to Employment Minister, Chris Grayling, the payment-by-results funding is intended to free up organisations to find 'innovative means of finding people work and making sure they stay there because if people do not stay in work the contractor loses payment' (BBC Newsnight, 2011). Since writing this chapter, a number of scandals surrounding the fiscal conduct of A4E, combined in part with the mobilising of public support against the Work Programme by protest groups, has meant a number of big companies and charities withdrawing from the scheme.

In a context of economic hardship, worsened by ideologically made redundancies in the public sector, the UK government threatens to treat unemployed people like criminals – people who have wronged the taxpayer – and they are sentenced to undertake community service, for instance, picking up litter, maintenance work for housing residents, furniture restoration or gardening. While the legality of forced labour has been raised in the media by unions (Petek, 2010), what is more significant is that this policy is likely to increase unemployment and drive down wages, as evidence is surfacing that people on workfare schemes have been used to replace full-time staff and reduce the paid hours of existing staff (see www.boycottworkfare.org). Furthermore, the policy fails to consider the discrepancies between an unemployment figure of 3.5 million and total number of job vacancies of 500,000. It fails to tackle systemic socioeconomic inequalities, regional employment disparities and neglects demand-side concerns of job availability and job quality (Theodore, 2007).

What is possibly new about these reforms is the greater emphasis placed on *punishment – sanctions that result in destitution if the claimant does not undertake forced unpaid labour.* The culture of austerity has made possible a more revanchist backlash against 'dependents', where work is held up as a moral obligation, not a choice.

The case of Pathways Ltd

This section substantiates these arguments through the case of Pathways Ltd, an organisation that delivered New Deal for the Unemployed programmes under the New Labour government. Methodologically, the chapter draws on interviews with several current and previous members of staff and ethnographic material from day-long site visits, as well as archival, internal documentation and media reports.

Background

Founded in London in 1989, Pathways was inspired by the vision of a few local Christian church leaders who recognised that serving their community needed to transcend traditional ideas of 'getting people into church'. Accordingly the social and religious capital inherent in these local churches began to be mobilised in an attempt to address issues of unemployment (and related crime and social exclusion) in their locality. By 1990 several of the churches located in the 'sink estates' had made their buildings available, and Pathways began running employment preparation courses that offered local people individual advice and guidance on how to succeed in the job market. Initially these courses were operated on a charitable basis, with volunteers going door-to-door in local estates to offer a free service to local people who were not reached by, or disillusioned with, public sector employment services.

By the early 1990s, Pathways had significantly extended the scope of its services, not only by running adult literacy and computer competency courses for local residents, but also by providing language teaching and personal counselling services to other groups, including undocumented migrants and asylum-seekers and people recovering from mental illness. These operations remained reliant on charitable funding, in part because of the aversion of left-wing local government to any formal involvement by Christian groups in local welfare, and what they perceived to be a move to privatise public services under Thatcher. To secure government grants, Pathways had to work hard to earn its rapport with local government, and became more inter-denominational in its support network as a strategy to avert possible critiques of sectarianism.

However, with the increasing opportunities opened up by central government during the 1990s for funded partnerships with FBOs, and the significant devolution of welfare tasks to non-governmental agencies over this period, Pathways found itself increasingly considering the possibility of accepting state funding for its work. The crunch came in 1997, when the Labour government's New Deal for the Unemployed started to scoop up the clients that Pathways was working with; either the rationale and scope of the organisation had to change significantly, or it would have to continue its work as a formal partner of government. After considerable internal debate – focusing at least in part on the question of whether the distinctive faith motivation of the organisation could be maintained when accepting government funding – Pathways submitted a successful bid for a voluntary sector option contract under the New Deal that enabled them to work with around 500 people per annum providing employment training and placements with local charities and voluntary organisations in the area. For a decade or so, Pathways became a large-scale local service provider, attracting other New Deal contracts such as the Environment Task Force (ETF) that ran on the same principles as the voluntary sector option, but the placements were based with environmental or socially oriented organisations (city farms, woodland management and recycling outfits). Furthermore, Pathways had secured large grants from the European Social Fund, the Single Regeneration Budget and the Further Education Funding Council for its different activities. However, by 2007 its New Deal contracts had been discontinued due to a strategy change in the Department for Work and Pensions (DWP), and replacement bids under the new Pathways to Work and Big Lottery schemes were unsuccessful. As a consequence, several of its services had to be closed and some 60 staff were lost, although it currently retains around 40 staff and a similar number of volunteers in 2012. In some ways, Pathways has once again shrunk down to its core foci – preparing young people and new immigrants for employment, and meeting the needs of the hard-to-reach long-term unemployed – although it has also become involved in new specialist services for ex-offenders and providing food bank services.[12]

It would be all too easy to regard Pathways as a typical case of how an FBO becomes incorporated into neoliberal governance, coopted into the ideology and practice of workfare in such a way as to lose its faith-motivated identity, and then spat out by that same governmental machine when fiscal restrictions led to public sector spending cuts, not only in major welfare programmes but also in smaller-scale local authority support for third sector activity. However, paying closer analytical attention to why and how Pathways became involved in delivering government welfare-to-work programmes presents a more complicated picture of FBOs working inside the trappings of government, one which underlines the emergent spaces of subversion and resistance that are carved out through the ethical performances of front-line workers.

Ethics of engagement

Over the first decade of its activity, Pathways delivered programmes that were detached from formal labour market activation policies. Effectively, the founders of Pathways set up an 'outsider' organisation as a direct response to what were perceived as the perniciously unjust socioeconomic and political policies of government. As one of the founding members of Pathways put it: "how the state could simply abandon people … we set up [Pathways] because something needed to be done … we wanted to bring hope into often hopeless situations where people are visibly suffering" (interview with one of the founding members of Pathways, 2 October 2010). The employment preparation courses established during this period differed significantly from the governmental norms encapsulated within labour market activation and welfare-to-work policies. For example, the Pathways courses made no use of sanctions to ensure client compliance, and there were no repercussions if clients failed to 'work the programme', compared to the likelihood within state-based systems of benefits being stopped as punishment for failure to fulfil various behavioural and motivational requirements.

The decision by Pathways to bid for New Deal contracts was one of necessity. Many members of staff and of support churches were critical of the philosophy and methods of New Deal's welfare-to-work programme, and fearful that government money would jeopardise their person-centred ethos and religious independence. Their service had been established in opposition to mainstream programmes which were perceived as operating in a contractual and impersonal manner; as one interviewee put it, "as if people were 'numbers' on an excel spreadsheet" (interview with a current member of staff at Pathways, 9 July 2010). There was concern that the New Deal technologies of strict time limits, targeted outcomes and the threat of sanctions to elicit compliance were completely 'out of sync' with Pathways' ethic of voluntary participation and unconditionality. The decision to deliver New Deal programmes thereby arose from a critical pragmatism. It was *critical* in the sense that they were aware of the likely tensions that would arise between Pathways' ways of doing things and that of the government; it was *pragmatic* because members wanted to continue working with their existing clients, and if they were to continue this work anyway they might as well receive financial support from the government to do so and expand the scope of their services.

However, this critical pragmatism was implemented according to a significant organisational ethos and performed in alignment with a strong ethical commitment between staff and clients, such that Pathways staff could be seen as subverting the ethical rationalities of welfare-to-work in their delivery of the programme. For example, the organisational ethos of Pathways was founded on the precept that unemployed clients were not idle or feckless but rather circumstantially disadvantaged from lack of education or training which has had consequences on their job opportunities and motivation. Pathways was therefore set up to address the "whole person to give them the fullness of life" (interview with a previous manager of Pathways, 2 October 2010). The founding churches never intended this approach to be directly evangelistic or proselytising; rather they designed Pathways to be a vehicle for local churches to help reduce unemployment as part of their expression of 'faith in practice'. The dominant theo-ethical vision that narrates the organisation's social action is that they are 'building the Kingdom of God predominantly by helping people overcome the barriers to employment and have a more abundant life' (extract from Pathways website). This approach involves 'freeing people from oppression in all its forms (social, economic, physical and spiritual)', 'healing any damaged sense of self-worth, security and feelings of significance' and coming into a 'living relationship with Jesus' (extract from Pathways website). In fact the organisation was critical of overt displays of proselytisation, instead hoping clients would develop an understanding of the Christian faith by seeing faith-in-action through the attitudes and performances of staff. Great emphasis is laid by the organisation on staff behaviour and values to ensure no one is discriminated against: 'all people we serve are to receive respect, value, love, care, patience, positive feedback, encouragement, integrity, individual attention' (extract from Pathways website).

Subverting the 'ethics' of welfare-to-work

These theologically inspired ethical approaches have challenged the dominant rationalities that otherwise characterise welfare-to-work. The conception of caritas, God's love for all people, in the context of welfare provision questions the distinctions made in modern society about the 'deserving' and 'undeserving', and the pursuit of unconditionality led the staff at Pathways to subvert the restrictive eligibility criteria on New Deal programme, for example, pooling funds from donations and other funding streams in order to offer 'ineligible' clients the same opportunities as those considered eligible by government targets. In this way people from whom the state had withdrawn statutory support (asylum-seekers, single homeless people and so on) came to benefit from government-funded programmes. Indeed, neoliberal welfare-to-work programmes are often criticised as 'cherry picking' or 'creaming' the most qualified unemployed into jobs while marginalising the long-term unemployed who are hardest to help. In contrast, many of the clients Pathways worked with were considered 'chaotic' and 'hard-to-help' by mainstream services:

> 'One of the challenges the government faces is flexibility, and that's very hard on a national level, but is it where local organisations can be, responsive to local needs, and that's what is ultimately everyone needs are different, particularly when you are working with people with complex backgrounds, environments and needs [people who] – have a number of barriers to integration to mainstream society. For someone who has just been made redundant from the banks – they've got their stuff in order – all they need is another job. They can be easily processed and find something. Compare that to someone who has never worked – third or fourth generation unemployed – has a whole load of other things going on. You need to get alongside that person over time and build trust, build relationship – the person will say ok I'm going to try and do something different here. And it's that group of people who government are trying to reach but can't. I've heard ministers say the focus is on those who have just lost job back into employment, so the hardest to reach are just pushed further away from the labour market. The quick turnaround of getting people back into work shouldn't be at the exclusion of others otherwise you're just storing up problems for yourself 15 years down the line.' (interview with a current Pathways manager, 9 July 2009)

Counter to the workfare philosophy that champions work as a categorical imperative – an enforceable individual obligation – and puts the onus on service providers to get the unemployed into a job: any job, never mind how low paid, uncongenial or inappropriate; Pathways pursued what Dean (2007, p 586) calls a 'life-first' approach to unemployment that prioritised a person's life needs, including their need to work, before their duty or obligation to take paid employment. Supposedly neoliberal technologies of workfare – characterised by compulsion, sanctions, strict monitoring of targets and putting the onus on recipients to find jobs – were also subverted within the operations of Pathways. Although interviewees were keen to position themselves legally as fulfilling the necessary requirements and target criteria of contracts, they were adamant that in its everyday practices and performances the organisation reworked the expected values and practices of welfare-to-work in order to provide a far more person-centred experience for clients compared to the job centre. As a previous manager explains:

> 'Outcomes became really important in those particular funding regimes, when we did accept contracts we worked very hard to both achieve the outcomes but also be very frank about who we were and how we presented ourselves in applying for those contracts, but also working with people on the coalface as it were, we still remained a very strong Christian ethos. So even though we might have changed the way we did things on the ground as it were, we worked, I suppose, possibly in slightly subversive way in the sense of, not being dishonest, but saying, we'll take the money but we put in quite a lot of extra work which wasn't required of us from the contracts we took, so with a large number of volunteers involved and staff doing more than what they really needed to. We managed to maintain an ethos on the ground that is person-centred but at the same time reached the level of outcomes required by our funding regimes.' (interview with a previous manager of Pathways, 2 October 2010)

The ethos and approach of Pathways begs to differ from the stark 'us' and 'them' mentality that tends to be institutionalised in job centres and reinforced through fixed appointments with case workers, and the threat of sanctions and surveillance. Indeed, this is an emergent space of resistance, where the apparent incorporation into the rationalities and technologies of workfare can more accurately be regarded as a deliberate co-constitution of alternative ethical performances within the overall framework that are capable of subverting the regressive nature of that framework. The revision that takes place occurs through the theo-ethical prompting of extraordinary performances of care that involves a going-beyond-the-call-of-duty by staff and volunteers:

> 'There's something about staff going beyond the call of duty, going around on the weekends and evenings to people's homes, just to support them, you know, going shopping for an outfit for a job interview – actually going to the job interview with them, sitting outside, giving them confidence and reassuring them there is someone there and they can ask questions if they need to. Other things like

that we are not paid to do but staff are doing it and are trying to find ways of working that in, so there is also a real sense as a faith-based organisation, or Christian organisation, I passionately don't believe that this world is it – that is one of the principles in which we operate, we have clients from all sorts of backgrounds, religions, faiths, whatever leaning, we respect everyone for their own independent choices and positions that is central to how we operate, we operate in a multicultural multi-faith environment with our clients and respecting that is central otherwise they wouldn't come back.' (interview with a current Pathways manager, 9 July 2009)

Other interviewees recounted stories of 'going-beyond-the-self' that included sharing meals together, remembering birthdays, babysitting, giving informal advice and support, taking people to interviews, buying a travel pass, going around their house on the weekend and helping them with DIY. Although this theo-ethical praxis is played out within the contractual environment of the New Deal, the enactment of such ethics brings a considerable "challenge to the capitalist version of economics that reduce people to units" and the sociality that developed reciprocal ethical commitments between staff and clients "gave people [clients] a real sense of hope that life could be different.... I know that [personal relationships] makes a difference and I know that is understood and appreciated by our clients. The environment in which people come into here is often commented on by clients – they see something different here, they want to come back. The fact that we get the majority of referrals here from friends and family members of past clients is testimony to the fact they are appreciating what they get when they come here" (interview with a current Pathways manager, 9 July 2009).

In Pathways, then, the performance of organisational and individual theo-ethical approaches by staff and volunteers stood between unemployed clients and the technologies designed to govern them according to particular political rationalities. This approach was formed when Pathways was established outside of any contractual partnership with government, and it was continued within the machinery of collaboration, where spaces of resistance were opened up even within contracted workfare environments. The approach continues at a smaller scale now that state funding has diminished. This journey of outsider/insider/outsider status has by no means defined the rationalities concerned; indeed this illustration indicates the futility of any sharp distinction between insider and outsider organisations in terms of their capacity to shape, as well as be shaped by, the wider neoliberal political environment. This illustration does not suggest that contractual partnership imposes no restrictions on agency, or indeed that the participation of FBOs can be counted on to bring about normative or even consistent performances of care. It does, however, indicate that locally situated activities and agencies do co-constitute grander scale rationalities, and that the technologies deployed in pursuit of these rationalities can be subverted by the practice of particular ethical precepts and affects, thus confirming that the performative assemblage of neoliberalism can be reshaped locally in such a way as to inculcate resistance and subversion.

This chapter now turns to explore more direct forms of resistance and considers the opportunities for postsecular alliances between progressive FBOs and other groups that assert structural interpretations of poverty and class inequality as a challenge to the political-economy of neoliberalism.

Neoliberalism and faith-based engagement in progressive politics

Here I present examples of more direct contestation between FBOs and neoliberal social policy. Although it can be argued (see Dinham, 2008; also see Goode, 2006) that prominent FBOs have abandoned a neo-Marxist critique of individuation, and become content with approaches that emphasise active citizenship at the local level, there remains an obdurate streak of prophetic radicalism among some campaigning FBOs that have successfully placed structural interpretations of international poverty and debt on the public agenda. The socially and geographically uneven effects of the austerity measures and arrival of workfare has heightened the involvement of all faith groups in progressive welfare politics in the UK. The most recent example is the whirlpool of debate created by the Archbishop of Canterbury's guest editorial in the *New Statesman* in June 2011. Dr Rowan Williams questioned the Coalition government's democratic mandate for the radical policies that have been sped through Westminster over the last year, particularly the reforms to welfare that have unjustly attacked the poor and have left issues of inequality untouched. Here I highlight two examples of faith-based activism against Conservative welfare reforms, and consider the possibility for collaboration between progressive FBOs and other activists.

Church Action on Poverty (CAP) is a national ecumenical Christian social justice charity, committed to tackling poverty in the UK. Drawing on a reformed strand of liberation theology CAP partners with those in poverty, churches, unions, anti-poverty campaigners and political organisations over a number of key social issues such as income inequality, the destitution of asylum-seekers, compulsory work for benefits, 'working poverty', living wages and debt. As a campaigning body CAP also has a number of grassroots community projects that aim to give a voice to the poor.[13] CAP has been prominent in mobilising *counter-hegemonic discourses of work and welfare*, contextualising and popularising alternatives to New Labour's welfare-to-work and the Conservative workfare approach to unemployment. For example, in 2009, CAP published grassroots research in association with Oxfam that helped produce a counter-hegemonic discourse challenging the criminalisation of 'welfare fraudsters, an imaginary popularised by New Labour media campaigns (McIntyre et al, 2009). CAP condemned New Labour's proposed policy that would have allowed people who inform on benefit 'cheats' to be given a share of the resulting savings. Contending the likely divisive effects this policy would have on communities and families, CAP sought to remind policy makers that those who commit benefit fraud are largely dependent on working cash-in-hand to support their families because under the benefit system and the shortage of work conventional employment is often not a viable route out of poverty. Furthermore, CAP tried to show the implicit class bias in the government crackdown on welfare fraud, citing estimates from the Trades Union Congress (TUC) that £25 billion is lost annually to the UK in tax avoidance: £13 billion from tax avoidance by individuals and £12 billion from avoidance by corporations. This is 25 times higher than the amount lost due to benefit 'fraud' (McIntyre et al, 2009).

Since the arrival of workfare, CAP has joined other groups in sharp criticism of benefit cuts and forced labour, deconstructing the discourse of 'worklessness' and 'intergenerational poverty' that posits that the problem of poverty is predominantly the morals and motivation of the poor passed down generation to generation as a clear misrecognition of inequality that serves to stigmatise the individual and obscure from view the misdistribution of wealth and income (see also Mooney, 2010). CAP have joined with trade union marches across the country and have met with politicians to reverse the Work Programme, demonstrating that the long-term unemployed want to work but are struggling to find work in a market where there is increasing pressure on both the public and private sectors, living on the wages offered, and meeting caring responsibilities in difficult circumstances. Alison Gelder, Director of Housing Justice, a partner of CAP, added that, "some [long-term unemployed] need help to develop the skills to find and keep a regular job. What they do not need are punitive measures such as the proposed cut in housing benefit by 10 per cent after a year out of work. Most of all, they should not be forced to do manual labour in return for their benefits for just £1.73 an hour – £4.20 below the current adult minimum wage."

CAP have also helped mobilise the cross-denominational group Common Wealth comprised of activists, ministers and theologians to call on Christians to join coalitions of resistance to the government's cuts in public spending and welfare provision. The group discourages FBOs to accommodate themselves in the Big Society ideology and rather to prophetically speak against the inequality systemic in the current economic system and discern whose interests are served by notions of 'fairness':

> Why are the jobless forced to work for nothing whilst bonuses are doled out to those in the banks whose greed and neglect threw people out of work in the first place? Why else, but that the current agenda of cuts and reforms have nothing to do with 'fairness' and everything to do with ensuring that a system founded on inequality stays in place. (Common Wealth declaration, 2010, pp 5-6)

> Again, Christians need a more radical perspective, not conforming to the world as though its current state were inevitable, natural or divinely sanctioned; but being conformed to Christ, who speaks a

word of judgement upon our systems of violence and exclusion. The Christian claim is that the earth and all that is in it belong to God. It is not ours by right of possession, to do with what we will. We cannot own the earth or any aspect of the ecology of which we are a part. Property is never an absolute right, only a relative one, a means to the end of universal human flourishing. As Anthony Reddie (2008) argues, 'fairness' simply leads to the reification of the status quo. Instead, the God revealed in the Judeo-Christian Tradition is one of Equity – which doesn't treat people all the same, but treats them according to their need. (Common Wealth declaration, 2010, p 6)

God did not create people to be the pawns and slaves of economic powers, shifted around by the political arbiters of 'fairness'. Nor did God make the earth to be the spoilheap and raw material for ever-increasing consumption. So we don't start from the assumption that people are naturally unequal and we have to iron things out a bit with a dose of philanthropy; we start from the conviction that creation is gift, to be stewarded in common. (Common Wealth declaration, 2010, pp 6-7)

In the battle lines that are being drawn some progressive FBOs are finding rather unusual partners in left-wing activists, community groups and trade unions. Yet it would be wrong to suggest this has been a wholesale transformation; rather, as Herman et al (Chapter Three, this volume) suggest, such forms of postsecular partnership is best thought of as an emergent phenomena occurring in specific spatialities. Yet the visible blind spots of current government policy has undeniably been a catalyst for postsecular rapprochement between religious, Marxist and secular humanist activists who find themselves on the same side in the fight for a more egalitarian future.

Conclusion

This chapter has traced the changing 'ethics' of New Labour's welfare-to-work and Conservative workfare approach, and has shown FBOs to occupy an ambiguous and fragmented space within and against the logics of neoliberalism. Here I draw out three implications that follow from this argument concerning the role of FBOs within the proposed Big Society and workfare programmes in the UK.

First, FBOs (such as the Pathways example relayed above) often tend to suspend the growing moralisation between deserving and undeserving recipients, and rather affirm a more unconditional gesture of social welfare premised on an ethic of universality and sociality with the other (see Chapter Two, this volume). The reworking of the neoliberal ethics of welfare is not just something that occurs outside the trappings of joined-up governance. Individuals within these insider organisations are less bound to the technologies and ideologies of these governmentalities than is often made out in the narrative of incorporation (Buckingham, 2009), and front-line actions of staff are incremental sites of subverting the intended processes and outcome of government policy (Barnes and Prior, 2009). Rather than a simple dismissal of FBOs as pawns in the hollowing out of the welfare state, we need to attend to these subtle intermediatory practices of subversion within the system that often enact more progressive conceptions of justice.

Second, in the punitive context of workfare, austerity and the Big Society, spaces for critical pragmatism may appear to be shrinking. The funding cuts to the voluntary sector outweigh the funding made available through the Big Society programme. This amounts to a total net disinvestment in the voluntary sector (Coote, 2011). This policy contradiction is forcing voluntary groups and FBOs who wish to maintain the same level of service provision to either reorganise as social enterprises in the hope of attaining a degree of financial self-sufficiency, and/or making even more pragmatic decisions to take whatever money comes available – government, private business, philanthropy or mergers with bigger voluntary organisations. Speculatively, one could suggest this will fundamentally change not only the compact between the state and the voluntary sector, but the structure and interests of the voluntary sector itself. Despite the rise of coerced pragmatism, and the associated risks of corporatisation and depoliticisation, the ethical agency of organisations and individuals involved in the FBO sector cannot simply be circumscribed by the structures and technologies of neoliberal government. Indeed, the theo-ethics of grace, mercy and caritas are in contradistinction to the 'ethics' of forced unpaid labour and sanctions for non-compliance that characterise workfare regimes. FBOs that deliver workfare programmes should not be straightforwardly characterised as incorporated into the regulatory and ethical frameworks of workfare, because, as illustrated in the subversive practices of Pathways Ltd, the manner in which an organisation performs its contractual obligations can directly challenge the 'ethics' of workfare to produce a more egalitarian approach to unemployment. It should again be emphasised that I am not arguing here that FBO involvement will necessarily produce progressive outcomes. We need little reminder of fundamentalist practices and theologies that serve to reinforce neoliberal ideologies (Hackworth, 2010). More modestly, I suggest that theo-ethics, and religious belief more generally, can delineate and sustain an ethical citizenship which deviates from, and speaks truth to, the powers that be. Yet while recognising the subversive potential theo-ethics can bring in systems of government, we need to retain a critical understanding of the inherent ambiguities concerning faith and politics, namely the porous and variegated connections between what is considered conservative and progressive expressions of belief.

Third, in addition to these subtle intermediatory practices of subversion, there is still an obdurate streak of prophetic radicalism among FBOs active in campaigning and political protest. The current political context has expanded opportunities for progressive FBOs entering into broad-based coalitions of resistance alongside anti-cuts activists. In our postpolitical times (see Chapter Three, this volume), where the parameters of public policy are predetermined to accept the inevitably of the technocratic governance of neoliberal capitalism, radical/alternative perspectives that challenge this 'consensus' are reprimanded as illegitimate, unrealistic or insignificant in the public realm. Ideological acquiesce seems to be a growing fault-line by which secular and religious voices are equally included or excluded in public debates. When faith is deemed a private apolitical affair and/or the prophetic voice of religious groups falls silent against the pernicious and unjust social-economic and political policies of neoliberal government, religious groups can be seen as upholding and even *sacralising* the dominant order rather than challenging it. As such, faith groups need to be wary of the Coalition's commendation of FBOs as exemplifiers of the Big Society and active citizenship, and critically unmask it as an attempt to marshal FBO activity as legitimacy for its conservative communitarian vision. Yet there has been a resurgence of prophetic faith praxis in many FBOs, speaking truth to power and standing with the poor, vulnerable and marginalised, especially those most disadvantaged by the welfare reforms. The hopeful imaginations derived from these beliefs-in-action can provide a groundswell of alternative ethical citizenship through which the logics of neoliberal government and its smokescreens can be contested and transformed. The symbolic act of care and solidarity with the poor can form a counter-narrative that transcends religious, ideological and social-economic differences, one that cannot be dismissed outright as partisan but that achieves cultural creditability through the passions of caritas and agape.

This chapter has shown, even within the contractual arena of neoliberal governance, that the front-line performance of care can often be understood as a site of subversion. In co-producing neoliberal structures of welfare governance, the ethical performance of staff and volunteers in FBOs rework and reinterpret the values and judgements supposedly normalised in the regulatory frameworks of government policy, bringing alternative philosophies of care into the fray. Here there are two direct possibilities for further research. First is the implication that the interconnections between faith, secularism and neoliberalism are much more fragmented and variegated than has been argued elsewhere, and there is a need to unravel the specific points of *resonance* where neoliberalism and faith converge to co-produce neoliberal forms, and *dissonance* where faith and neoliberalism diverge. The second area of research that requires attention is the formulation of theo-ethics, particularly the 'crossing over' of theological precepts among religious and non-religious actors. Further research on the subversive role of ethical agency is needed in the contexts of inter-faith and faith–secular partnerships. This will go far in understanding how postsecular rapprochement comes about and is sustained through shared ethical concerns and virtues of faith, hope and love.

Notes

[1] Department of Geography, College of Life and Environmental Sciences, Exeter. Thanks to Justin Beaumont for his help in the editing process and to Paul Cloke, Sam Thomas and Nick Gill for their comments on an earlier version of this chapter.

[2] David Cameron, Nick Clegg and others have adopted some of the ideas of the Red Tory, Philip Blond, who has also been influential in debates about the postsecular and the rise of a so-called postsecular society. Blond's ideas have influenced the direction of the Big Society. Curiously, in response, the leader of the opposition Labour Party Ed Miliband has looked to the political theorist Maurice Glasman (London Metropolitan University) and Marc Stears (University of Oxford) among others. Glasman was elevated to the House of Lords at the request of Miliband, to become Baron Glasman of Stoke Newington and Stamford Hill in the London Borough of Hackney. He has also worked with London Citizens for over a decade (see Chapter Three, this volume).

[3] The Big Society has attracted a great deal of attention in policy, political and academic circles. The Lincoln Theological Institute at the University of Manchester organised an international conference in October 2011, 'Big Society – Bigger Nature?', exploring the current renewal of interest in civil society from the perspectives of the environment, common good and human sociability. Speakers included John Milbank (University of Nottingham), Maurice Glasman (London Metropolitan University) and Luke Bretherton (King's College London).

[4] The Big Society proposals cannot be detached from a wider austerity drive which has seen a huge net reduction in the funding available to many third sector and FBOs (Coote, 2011). It is clear that charities and voluntary groups have been hardest hit in local government funding cuts (Toynbee, 2010), and many are turning to social enterprise to sustain the level and scope of service provision.

[5] Here I refer to Michel Foucault's analysis of how rule is exercised and precariously (re) produced in contemporary society through *rationalities* and *technologies* of government (Foucault, 1991). The chapter builds on recent debates that focus on the insufficient attention to the contestation of government policies in the delivery of public services (McKee, 2009; Prior, 2009).

[6] Pathways Ltd is a pseudonym that this chapter adopts in order to respect the anonymity of the organisation in question and the work of the individuals there.

[7] By *eschatological hope*, I refer to a strand of Christian theology that believes the establishment of God's kingdom, or God's reign, is 'now' and 'not yet', by which I mean God's kingdom is already here but it has yet to be consummated. This leads to a hopeful expectation to see God actively working in the present, sometimes even miraculously. The believer and the church are to manifest the kingdom of God on the earth, incorporating personal evangelism and social/prophetic action as to embody the new heaven and the new earth.

Kingdom theology should not be confused with kingdom now theology, which is a variant of dominion theology, and its political expression in the US (Hackworth, 2010).

[8] From 1979-97 the Conservative Party in the UK was in power under the premiership of Prime Ministers Margret Thatcher (1979-90) and John Major (1991-97). The socioeconomic policies implemented during this period followed a stark ideology of the free market. This involved the destruction of 'anti-competitive' institutions like trade unions, the reform of social welfare programmes and interventionist arms of government and the discreditation of Keynesian welfarist and social collectivist ideologies. Instead, market principles were normalised within welfare through so-called new public management (NPM) which entailed programmes of deregulation, privatisation and managerialism in which for-profit management techniques – value for money, the bottom line, and performance rating – were embedded into public services in the provision of welfare services.

[9] In 1997 Frank Field, MP for Birkenhead in Merseyside at the time, was commissioned by former Primer Minister Tony Blair to 'think the unthinkable' to revolutionise the welfare state. He is accredited as one of the key players in the development of welfare-to-work in the UK, although his original proposals never quite came to fruition. That is, until now. He was appointed 'poverty tsar' under the Conservative government and has been influential in the design of the Work Programme – which is more in keeping with his social conservative conception of unemployment.

[10] Beaumont (2004) notes that Jamie Peck discerns two sets of contested meanings of workfare that developed in the US at this time (Peck, 2001). First, there is a 'hard' conception referring to the New Right era under Ronald Reagan, illustrated by the 'Work First' model in Riverside, California, as well as other examples in Massachusetts, New York and Wisconsin. Central to Beaumont's argument there, the individualist, non-structural and moral underpinnings of workfare, where issues of personal (ir)responsibility lie at the heart of the so-called welfare crisis, the Christian community at large in the US played a role in the discussion over its design, conceptualisation and implementation. The argument in this chapter takes a step further to show how certain FBOs can *subvert* processes of neoliberalisation.

[11] A4e is a 'social purpose' company that has made huge profits from the contracting out of public services in the UK over the last 20 years. It has grown into an international contracted provider of employment, enterprise and training service and subcontracts to smaller businesses.

[12] Foodbank is a network established by The Trussell Trust in Salisbury. It is a store where food donated by community groups and supermarkets is banked, and can be drawn on by people in crisis. It is designed to provide emergency food for three days, which is the period assessed as the minimum time it takes for the appropriate agencies to be in a position to assist. This period can be extended if necessary. They usually run on a referral

system established with front-line agencies, for example, social services, health visitors, probation officers, community groups, schools and churches. Individuals and families eligible for the food package receive a voucher from their referral agent.

[13] Changemakers is a network of grassroots organisations in the UK working with local people to enable them to bring about change in their local communities and their city regions. They work with people of all ages, faiths and backgrounds to take action, engage with power holders and inspire others to become involved. Drawing on concepts from international development, Changemakers states that people living in poverty are the real poverty 'experts' and have the right to shape the decisions that affect their lives. It aims to enable the poorest and most marginalised communities to have a voice at the table of power by claiming their own political spaces (www.changemakersmanchester. org.uk/?page_id=296).

References

Barnes, M. and Prior, D. (eds) (2009) *Subversive citizens: Power, agency and resistance in public services*, Bristol: The Policy Press.

Barnett, C. (2009) 'Publics and markets: what's wrong with neoliberalism?', in S. Smith, S. Marston, R. Pain and J.P. Jones III (eds) *The handbook of social geography*, London and New York: Sage Publications, 269–96.

Bauman, Z. (1993) *Postmodern ethics*, Oxford: Blackwell.

Beaumont, J.R. (2004) 'Workfare, associationism and the "underclass" in the United States: contrasting faith-based action on urban poverty in a liberal welfare regime', in H. Noordegraaf and R. Volz (eds) *European churches confronting poverty: Social actions against social exclusion*, Bochum: SWI Press, pp.249–78.

Bondi, L. and Laurie, N. (2005) 'Working the spaces of neoliberalism: activism, professionalisation and incorporation', *Antipode*, vol 37, no 3, pp 394-401.

BBC Newsnight (2011) 'UK needs to adopt tough US stance on earning welfare', BBC2, 15 February (http://news.bbc.co.uk/1/hi/programmes/newsnight/9397570.stm).

Bryson, A. (2003) 'Permanent revolution: the case of Britain's welfare-to-work regime', *Benefits: The Journal of Poverty and Social Justice*, vol 11, no 1, pp 11-17.

Buckingham, H. (2009) 'Competition and contracts in the voluntary sector: exploring the implications for homelessness service providers in Southampton', *Policy & Politics*, vol 37, no 2, pp 235-54.

Cairns, B., Harris, M. and Young, P. (2005) 'Building the capacity of the voluntary nonprofit sector: challenges of theory and practice', *International Journal of Public Administration*, vol 28, nos 9/10, pp 869-85.

Camel, E. and Harlock, J. (2008) 'Instituting the "third sector" as a governable terrain: partnership, procurement and performance in the UK', *Policy & Politics*, vol 36, no 2, pp 155-71.

Caputo, J. (2001) *On religion*, London: Routledge.

Clarke, J., Newman, J., Smith, N., Vidler, E. and Westmarland, L. (2007) *Creating citizen-consumers: Changing publics and changing public services*, London: Sage Publications.

Cloke, P. (2010) 'Theo-ethics and faith praxis in the postsecular city', in A. Molendijk, J. Beaumont and C. Jedan (eds) *Exploring the postsecular: The religious, the political and the urban*, Amsterdam: Brill, pp 223-43.

Common Wealth (2010) 'Common Wealth: Christians for economic and social justice' (http://commonwealthnetwork2010.blogspot.com/).

Coote, A. (2011) 'Big Society and the new austerity', in M. Stott (ed) *The Big Society challenge*, Cardiff: Keystone Development Trust Publications, pp 82-94.

Crisp, R. (2008) 'Motivation, morals and justice: discourses of worklessness in the welfare reform green paper', *People, Place & Policy Online*, vol 2, no 3, pp 172-85.

Deakin, N. (2001) 'Public policy, social policy and voluntary organisations', in M. Harris and C. Rochester (eds) *Voluntary organisations and social policy in Britain: Perspectives on change and choice*, London: Palgrave, pp 21-36.

Dean, H. (2007) 'The ethics of welfare-to-work', *Policy & Politics*, vol 35, no 4, pp 573-90.

Dean, M. (2002) 'Liberal government and authoritarianism', *Economy and Society*, vol 31, pp 37-61.

Dinham, A. (2008) 'From "Faith in the city" to "Faithful cities": the "third way", the Church of England and urban regeneration', *Urban Studies*, vol 45, pp 2163-74.

DWP (Department for Work and Pensions) (2011a) *The Welfare Reform Bill* (www.publications.parliament.uk/pa/bills/lbill/2010-2012/0075/lbill_2010-20120075_en_2.htm).

DWP (2011b) 'Grayling: new welfare rules will give jobseekers the opportunity to gain valuable experience of the workplace', Press release, 14 March (www.dwp.gov.uk/newsroom/press-releases/2011/mar-2011/dwp027-11.shtml).

DWP (2011c) 'Extra push for jobseekers as mandatory work activity placements come on-stream for those who need more focus', Press release, 17 May (www.dwp.gov.uk/newsroom/press-releases/2011/may-2011/dwp049-11.shtml).

Dwyer, P. (2004) 'Creeping conditionality in the UK: from welfare rights to conditional entitlements?', *Canadian Journal of Sociology*, vol 29, no 2, pp 265-87.

Foucault, M. (2003) 'Governmentality', in P. Rabinow and N. Rose (eds) *The essential Foucault: Selections from Essential Works of Foucault 1954-1984*. London: The New Press, pp 229-45.

Fraser, N. (2004) 'Introduction: Britain's new deals', *International Journal of Manpower*, vol 25, no 5, pp 387-91.

Fyfe, N.R. (2005) 'Making space for "neo-communitarianism"? The third sector, state and civil society in the UK', *Antipode*, vol 37, no 3, pp 536-57.

Garland, D. and Darcy, M. (2009) 'Working together? The Salvation Army and the Job Network', *Organization*, vol 16, p 755.

Goode, J. (2006) 'Faith-based organisations in Philadelphia: neoliberal ideology and the decline of political activism', *Urban Anthropology*, vol 35, nos 2-3, pp 203-36.

Hackworth, J. (2010) 'Neoliberalism for God's sake: sectarian justifications for secular policy transformation in the United States', in A. Molendijk, J. Beaumont and C. Jedan (eds) *Exploring the postsecular: The religious, the political and the urban*, Amsterdam: Brill, pp 357-80.

Helm, T., Asthana, A. and Harris, P. (2010) 'How Britain's new welfare state was born in the USA', *The Observer*, 7 November, pp 32-3.

Heron, E. and Dwyer, P. (1999) 'Doing the right thing: Labour's attempt to forge a new welfare deal between the individual and the state', *Social Policy & Administration*, vol 33, no 1, pp 91-104.

Jenkins, K. (2005) 'No way out? Incorporating and restructuring the voluntary sector within spaces of neoliberalism', *Antipode*, vol 37, no 3, pp 613-18.

Larner, W. and Butler, M. (2005) 'Governmentalities of local partnerships: the rise of a "partnering state" in New Zealand', *Studies in Political Economy*, vol 75, pp 85-108.

Le Heron, R. (2007) 'Globalisation, governance and post-structural political economy: perspectives from Australasia', *Asia Pacific Viewpoint*, vol 48, no 1, pp 26-40.

Lipsky, M. (1980) *Street-level bureaucracy: Dilemmas of the individual in public services*, New York: Russell Sage Foundation.

Lister, R. (2004) *Poverty*, Cambridge: Polity Press.

Lyon-Callo, V. (2008) 'Cool cities or class analysis: exploring popular consent (?) to neoliberal domination and exploitation', *Rethinking Marxism*, vol 20, no 1, pp 28-41.

MacLeavy, J. (2008) 'Neoliberalising subjects: the legacy of New Labour's construction of social exclusion in local governance', *Geoforum*, vol 39, pp 1657-66.

McDonald, C. and Marsten, G. (2005) 'Workfare as welfare: governing unemployment in the advanced liberal state', *Critical Social Policy*, vol 25, pp 374-400.

McIntyre, D., Stewart, A., Brill. L. and Jarman, J. (2009) *Invisible workers: The informal economy*, Manchester: Community Pride Initiative/Oxfam UK Poverty.

McKee, K. (2009) 'Post-Foucauldian governmentality: what does it offer critical social policy?', *Critical Social Policy*, vol 29, p 465–86.

May, J., Johnsen, S. and Cloke, P. (2005) 'Re-phasing neo-liberalism: New Labour and Britain's crisis of street homelessness', *Antipode*, vol 37, no 4, pp 703-30.

Mooney, G. (2010) 'The disadvantaged working class as "problem" population: the "Broken Society" and class misrecognition', *Concept: The Journal of Contemporary Community Education Practice Theory*, vol 1, no 3, pp 2–6.

Newman, J. (2001) *Modernising governance: New Labour, policy and society*, London: Sage Publications.

O'Malley, P., Weir, L. and Shearing, C. (1997) 'Governmentality, criticism, politics', *Economy and Society*, vol 26, no 4, pp 501-17.

Osborne, S. and McLaughlin, K. (2004) 'The cross-cutting review of the voluntary sector: where next for local government voluntary sector relationships?', *Regional Studies*, vol 38, no 5, pp 573-82.

Peck, J. (2001) *Workfare states*, New York: Guilford Press.

Peck, J. and Tickell, A. (2002) 'Neoliberalising space', *Antipode*, vol 34, pp 380-404.

Petek, M. (2010) *Work-for-benefit schemes unlawful as forced or compulsory labour contrary to ECHR Article 4*, Boycott Workfare/Brighton Unemployed Workers Centre (www.boycottworkfare.org/wp-content/uploads/2011/06/workfareillegal.pdf).

Prior, D. (2009) 'Policy, power and the potential for counter-agency', in M. Barnes and D. Prior (eds) *Subversive citizens: Power, agency and resistance in public services*, Bristol: The Policy Press, pp 17-32.

Prochaska, F. (2006) *Christianity and social service in modern Britain*, Oxford: Oxford University Press.

Reddie, A. (2008) 'People matter too: the politics and method of doing Black liberation theology', *Practical Theology*, vol 1, no 1, pp 43-64.

Rose, N. (1999) *Powers of freedom: Reframing political thought*, Cambridge: Cambridge University Press.

Stunell, A. (2010) 'Keeping faith in the Big Society', CLG press release, 12 July (www.communities.gov.uk/newsstories/communities/1637515).

Theodore, N. (2007) 'New Labour at work: long-term unemployment and the geography of opportunity', *Cambridge Journal of Economics*, vol 31, pp 927-39.

Timmins, N. (2011) 'Finance threat to work scheme, says minister', *Financial Times*, 6 June (www.ft.com/cms/s/0/70f0b2c0-906d-11e0-9227-00144feab49a.html#axzz1URKRhl85).

Toynbee P (2010) 'The "big society" is a big fat lie – just follow the money', *The Guardian*, 6 August (www.guardian.co.uk/commentisfree/2010/aug/06/big-society-is-big-fat-lie).

Trudeau, D. and Veronis, L. (2009) 'Enacting state restructuring: NGOs as "translation mechanisms"', *Environment and Planning D: Society and Space*, vol 27, no 6, pp 1117-34.

Warsi, S. (2011) 'Have you found or lost faith in the Big Society?', Speech to the Blackburn Diocese Board for Social Responsibility (www.cabinetoffice.gov.uk/content/baroness-warsi-speech-blackburn-diocese-board-social-responsibility).

Williams, A., Cloke, P. and Thomas, S. (2012: forthcoming) 'Contesting co-option: faith-based organisations and neoliberal governmentality' (submitted to *Environment and Planning A*).

Williams, R. (2011) 'Leader: The government needs to know how afraid people are', *New Statesman*, 9 June (www.newstatesman.com/uk-politics/2011/06/long-term-government-democracy).

Wolch, J. (2006) 'Foreword: beyond the shadow state?', in C. Milligan and D. Conradson (eds) *Landscapes of voluntarism: New spaces of health, welfare and governance*, Bristol: The Policy Press, pp xii-xv.

NINE

A shelter from the storm: faith-based organisations and providing relief for the homeless

Maarten Davelaar and Wendy Kerstens

Introduction[1]

In this chapter we address one of the most significant areas of faith-based organisation (FBO) activity in many European cities – that of caring for homeless people. As has been made clear in a wide range of international research (see, for example, Jencks, 1995; Takahashi, 1998; Edgar and Doherty, 2001; Hopper, 2003; Edgar et al, 2004; Levinson, 2004; Cloke et al, 2010), homelessness is not a new phenomenon, but due to the increasing on-street visibility of homeless people it has emerged as a major social issue in most developed countries over the last 30 or so years (Toro, 2007). Simultaneously, homelessness has been rediscovered as an area of significant concern for faith-motivated individuals and organisations, and we suggest that there has been a particular affinity between the plight of homeless people and the targeting of faith-motivated social action in many European contexts. This chapter explores the role played by FBOs in the wider welfare landscape of care for the homeless.

The emergence of homelessness as a visible and multifaceted social issue has typically attracted a two-pronged response from central and local states (albeit with important local variations in different countries). The first phase of response has been to respond humanely to the crisis of (street) homelessness. Early service provision has typically been put in place by voluntary organisations, including FBOs. Some of these providers have had longstanding involvement in caring for excluded people (Protestant and Catholic organisations in cities, The Salvation Army), while others sprang up as a direct response to the visibility of, and encounters with, homeless people. In some cases, the state has often been prompted by third sector pressure groups (such as Shelter and Crisis in the UK) to become involved by making some specific provision for the welfare of homeless people. Taking the UK as an example, this provision has included programmes such as the Rough Sleepers Initiative and the Housing Action Programme (see May et al, 2005) that included the delivery of emergency accommodation for homeless people. Here, central state funding was used to enable service delivery by non-statutory providers, and this opened up opportunities for formal involvement by some FBOs in addition to the informal and non-funded service provision that was already taking place. Elsewhere in Europe, it was the *local* state that became responsible for funded programmes to various extents. Anderson (2010) and Benjaminsen et al (2009) have pointed to new ways of steering service provision and the difficulties in capturing 'increasingly complex structures of interaction between public and non-governmental stakeholders' (Anderson, 2010, p 48). Most notably, differences in local–central interdependency should be kept in mind here. The case of the Netherlands, shows, for example, how national responsibilities for homeless policies have been decentralised to 43 cities, whereas the central state still provides the lion's share of local expenditure in this field.

The second phase of public sector response showed a reclamation of city streets by invoking a range of regulatory measures to control begging, rough sleeping, drinking and drug using in public spaces or simply hanging around, and to 'contain' homeless people in the newly prescribed spaces of welfare services. Especially, but not only in the US and the UK, homeless people became 'swept up' (Cloke et al, 2010) and located in city spaces where they would not be visible to citizens going about their everyday commercial and retail business. In the Netherlands, a clear increase in repression has been combined with large investments in care and supported housing. This dual strategy was launched in 2004 and called 'captured in care' (Davelaar et al, 2005). Although perhaps less outspoken, this approach can be found elsewhere in Europe, for example, in Germany and Belgium.

If the first policy response (to respond humanely) has created a legitimated role for FBO involvement in city government, the second response (to reclaim the streets) has placed some FBOs at odds with the formal governance of homelessness, particularly those initiatives that rely on charitable finance and volunteer labour to address the immediate needs of homeless people via the establishment of small-scale services such as night shelters, day centres and soup runs (Cloke et al, 2005). This aid and comfort can be represented as perpetuating the 'on-street' nature of homelessness, although those involved tend to regard themselves as ethical actors resisting or complementing government policy by providing care to those who fall below the formal welfare safety net. In this way, FBO involvement in providing services for homeless people can be narrated *both* as incorporated into and complicit with wider state activity *and* as resisting that activity. As a result there has been considerable uncertainty and confusion about what exactly FBOs contribute to this sector.

Recent academic research has provided rather different pictures of the services for homeless people operated by NGOs in general, and FBOs in particular. On the one hand, Smith's (1996) thesis of the revanchist city portrays the city as a space in which overpowering coalitions of local businesses, developers and city managers do battle with homeless people to prevent the invasion of 'unacceptable' behaviours associated with homelessness into prime city spaces. Here, the city is described as *post-justice* (Mitchell, 2001), and those organisations such as FBOs involved in the servicing of homeless people in marginal spaces are chastised as merely an incorporated element of neoliberal governmentality. On the other hand, although the general trend is undeniable towards controlling and punishing deviant behaviour, it would probably be more precise to speak of revanchist episodes, or revanchist regulations, because repressive tendencies sometimes alternate or coincide with strategies that focus on the care and inclusion of homeless people and in which FBOs play an all but passive role. In addition, Lees (1998) and Ruddick (1996), for example, have presented an alternative view of homeless people as social subjects, capable of tactical agency and with an affective power to prompt ethical responses of care and charity as well as more revanchist tendencies. And Cloke et al (2010) argue that any reasonable exploration of the why and how of professionals and volunteers is likely to uncover alternative motivations to those suggested by urban revanchism:

> We do not seek here to present a romanticized version of these service environments, many of which lack adequate standards of security and comfort. Neither do we ignore the possibilities that serving homeless people provides for helping to build self-interested or self-absorbed charitable identities and subjectivities. But we do argue that it is a very considerable, and inaccurate, reductive leap to assume that providing welfare services for homeless people can only be understood in these terms. Instead we recognise these service spaces as demonstrative of deep-seated and powerful forces of charity and care ... in which there is a genuine ethical expression of going-beyond-the-self, or caring about and caring for the victims of neoliberal excess. (Cloke et al, 2010, p 10)

It follows that those FBOs involved in providing services for homeless people can get trapped in a crossfire of arguments. They are potentially represented as puppets of the state, innovative entrepreneurs on the welfare market, self-absorbed do-gooders, providers of services merely as a means of proselytisation, or caring agents of resistance against policies leading to social exclusion.

It is against this discursive background that this chapter assesses the importance of third sector involvement, and especially that of FBOs, with respect to service provision for the homeless. Our empirical data comprise case studies of the countries involved in the FACIT project (for summaries of these studies, see Cloke et al, 2011; Davelaar et al, 2011; Dierckx et al, 2011; Elander and Fridolfsson, 2011; Friedrichs and Klöckner, 2011; Sen, 2011; Walliser and Villanueva, 2011). These case studies are not presented in any detail here, but taken together they form the basis of our line of argument; some examples are given to substantiate the discussion. We start with a description of the diversification of definitions of homelessness both in the areas of research and politics. Then we discuss the framework of actors concerned with the homeless in European countries, and consider the role of FBOs in organising help for the homeless, analysing their characteristics and the services they provide. This is followed by an in-depth discussion of the strategies that FBOs use to guarantee access to different types of services. Across this canvas we argue that FBOs have become significant actors in the care of homeless people, and that as well as being cost-effective, they also provide accessible and often trusted services that contribute more generally to the development of an inclusive city.

The end of homelessness as we knew it

From an historical point of view, homelessness is a longstanding phenomenon (Sibley, 1995; Kusmer, 2003). What is more recent is an understanding of the extent of the phenomenon and its visibility (Forrest, 1999). Despite the existence of well-developed welfare systems in most European countries, homelessness still persists – and is even on the increase in many countries. For the general public, the perception of homelessness does not often extend beyond the highly visible but simplistic concept of rough sleeping, yet Minnery and Greenhalgh (2007) emphasise a growing awareness of the diverse nature of homelessness. However, the inability to robustly define homelessness seriously has an impact on the quality and quantity of statistical evidence relating to homeless people. Many of the statistics are based on those who are accepted as being homeless by a service provider. Many counts of homeless people are only a snapshot, and are limited in coverage (Minnery and Greenhalgh, 2007). Some progress has been made at European level; there is a broad overview of people who are homeless or at risk of homelessness in the European Union (EU) as a whole (Avramov, 1999), and FEANTSA (2005), the European Federation of National Organisations working with the Homeless, issued a European typology of homelessness and housing exclusion (ETHOS), including categories such as rooflessness (sleeping rough), houselessness (with a place to sleep but temporary in institutions or shelters, including women's shelters and temporary accommodation for immigrants), living in insecure housing (threatened with severe exclusion due to insecure tenancies, eviction, domestic violence) and living in inadequate housing (on illegal campsites, in extreme overcrowding). Still, at least in part because of the widely recognised difficulties in measurement (Doherty et al, 2002), only a minority of EU countries have developed a comprehensive homelessness information strategy (Edgar et al, 2007; Busch-Geertsema, 2010).

The homeless within the European framework of multiple welfare systems

Addressing these debates at a European scale is far from straightforward, not only because of the multiple welfare systems involved, but also because of the relative paucity of research that differentiates between non-governmental organisations (NGOs) and FBOs as service providers. In other words, there has been little attempt to ask the question of 'what difference faith makes' in non-governmental responses to homeless people. To some extent, then, the specific discussions of 'faith' motivation in other chapters of this book need to be read across into this more specific discussion of how FBOs present homeless people with access to different levels of services.

What is clear, however, is that local public authorities and non-profit organisations are typically the major service providers for homeless people in European cities, and that FBOs have a recognisable, and in some cases increasingly prominent, presence in the landscape of NGO activity. Research in the Netherlands (Davelaar et al, 2005) reveals the presence of many organisations with either a faith background or a clearly expressed faith identity working closely together with public agencies and secular NGOs in activation and work reintegration programmes targeted at homeless people and drug addicts. And research in the UK (Cloke et al, 2005, 2007) suggests that the majority of NGOs providing emergency services for homeless people include faith or religious affiliation in their statements of ethos. Moreover, this research also provides evidence that staff and volunteers in services for homeless people are often content to work together regardless of religious or non-religious affiliation. Thus, FBO services will often involve participation from people with no faith motivation, and NGO services are likely to be staffed by at least some faith-motivated people. Such 'fusions' could be viewed in the light of the emergence of different forms of postsecular activity (Beaumont and Baker, 2011), although 'economic reasoning', aimed at safeguarding organisational continuity, also has to be taken into consideration: for example, FBOs open their doors for non-believers to respond to secularisation within their communities and secular organisations try to reach out to new client or volunteer groups characterised by religious ties. These fusions render considerable complexity to the task of differentiating between FBOs and NGOs, however.

Equally, the distinction between the activities of public authorities and non-profit organisations in providing services for homeless people is often blurred. Research illustrates the difficulty in distinguishing between public and private services, given that some (faith-based) NGOs will be at least partially funded by public sector programmes, and that homeless people will often be the recipients of governmental measures to provide income support or health insurance (Helvie and Kunstmann, 1999). Despite these complexities, it is instructive to consider the provision of services for homeless people in terms of the multiple welfare systems in operation. Following Olsson and Nordfeldt (2008), we recognise that each lower level of these systems functions as an additional safety net. These authors differentiate between a primary, secondary and tertiary welfare system, referring to the national state, the local public authorities and non-profit organisations respectively.

Although the balance of provision varies across Europe, the state sector remains the weakest in all countries (Edgar et al, 2004). With the exception of the UK the national state does not *directly* target the homeless population and it generally places responsibility for the homeless with regional and local authorities. National welfare provision is usually embedded in the system of social security, which entails general programmes based on general allowances. The exception here, in terms of the case study countries covered by the FACIT project, is Turkey, that has not yet developed a formal state system of welfare. As Olsson and Nordfeldt (2008) put it, the *primary welfare system* – which is organised by public and governmental authorities with national responsibility and a national programme – mainly deals with long-term structural social issues such as unemployment and sickness. Since this welfare system is based on income-related, non-means-tested allowances, it is strongly connected to employment and earned income; benefits are based on previous earned income. As a result, a marginal position on the labour market or exclusion from the labour market means exclusion from the primary welfare system. The homeless, therefore, are almost by definition excluded from social allowances of this welfare system and assigned to the secondary one.

Local authorities administer the *secondary welfare system* and its allowances are usually means-tested. This system provides assistance and deals with local, individual social problems, and in contrast to the national service system, the homeless can rely on it for help in many countries. Across Europe, responsibility for the support of homeless people mainly lies with the local social services authorities at the provincial or municipal level. In Belgium, for instance, the Public Centres for Social Welfare (PCSWs) operate on the municipal level to guarantee basic rights, and homeless people are entitled to aid from these bodies, which can help in different ways. If homeless people satisfy legal conditions, they are entitled to financial support (subsistence income). But if that is not the case, the PCSWs will always look at what they can do to help. They can provide homeless people with urgent medical help, societal service provision, debt management aid and other forms of support (POD Maatschappelijke Integratie, 2007). In Sweden, the municipal authorities have been given responsibility to provide material support and housing for people not able to acquire this for themselves. Part of the secondary welfare system in Sweden is therefore the 'secondary housing market', which consists of a variety of transitional dwellings (Olsson and Nordfeldt, 2008).

Beyond these general public services, a multitude of non-statutory agencies and actors provide services to marginalised people at all levels. They do so in close cooperation with, and under the responsibility of, public authorities, or they act according to their own goals and judgements. This *tertiary system* recognises people who fall through the official safety net and are excluded from both the primary and secondary systems. As a complement to national and local public welfare systems, the tertiary system deals with the more acute, individual social problems of the most marginalised or excluded. Among other groups, this third system targets homeless people, and non-profit organisations including FBOs play a substantial role in the provision of homeless services. The issue of homelessness has rarely been a core element in struggles of social mass movements, or been included in the development of social legislation. So in a significant way, people experiencing homelessness always had to rely on this third system. Since the (late) 19th century, the care for the homeless has been the domain of third sector organisations such as The Salvation Army, specialised bodies of the 'leading' Catholic or Protestant churches in cities, and, to a lesser extent, charitable initiatives, from liberal-conservatist circles and socialist foundations aiming at the 'lumpenproletariat' living in overcrowded slums and those vulnerable to homelessness and alcoholism. Services for homeless people have largely emerged from third sector charitable initiatives prompted by the recognition of social need and exclusion that has not been dealt with by state welfare systems. The plight of the homeless has historically been, and still is, a niche occupied by non-profit organisations and charities, a system in existence long before European modern welfare began to take shape around the Second World War. By tradition, non-profit organisations working with the homeless are often related to religion or religious values. In Germany, Belgium and the Netherlands, the history of 'pillarisation' is illustrative in this respect. In Sweden, homeless organisations often relate to the Church of Sweden or are organised by the Christian free churches (Olsson and Nordfeldt, 2008).

It cannot be emphasised enough that the balance of provision varies across countries. As a result of differences in the scope of the welfare state, the range of the non-profit sector also diverges between countries. From our research it is clear that, when compared to the state, the position of non-profit organisations is much stronger in Spain – with more than 70 per cent of the social action in this field delivered by NGOs (and with 70 per cent of these NGOs services having a faith-based identity) – than it is in Sweden, for instance (see Elander and Fridolfsson, 2011; Walliser and Villanueva, 2011). But NGOs are operating at a greater distance from the state in Spain, while collaborating more with public services in Sweden (which may have an impact on their effectiveness). In Turkey, these organisations are the main providers of social services in general (Sen, 2011). A second conclusion must be that, despite variations in the balance of service provision for the homeless, there is evidence of a shift towards an increasing role on the *local* level for NGO and FBO agencies (Belgium, Sweden and the UK) or a continuation of their importance (Spain, Germany and the Netherlands). In addition, a third point to highlight is that local cooperation between public services and the (faith-based) NGO sector has increased over the last decade, leading to new networks and new interdependencies. Nowadays, the tertiary system in the field of homelessness consists mainly of non-profit organisations working beyond the public sphere but at the same time very much dependent on financing from the local public authorities, while concerned citizens, philanthropists and some private companies also give support to this system (Olsson and Nordfeldt, 2008).

In comparison, the central state sector remains weak with respect to homeless services provision, either because it has only recently developed a role (Spain) or because it is relinquishing that – albeit rather limited – role to the NGO sector (the UK) (see also Edgar et al, 2004). There are, nevertheless, clear indications of homelessness climbing in the ranking of social problems in most European countries. In some cases this leads to new national programmes or strategies aiming to boost local approaches with new legislation, or providing additional funding for local services. A profound example of this is the Dutch national *Strategy plan for social relief* (2006) designed by the government and the four biggest cities. This plan, with translations to other, smaller cities and including vast financial investments in care, support and housing, runs from 2006-14. Central to the strategy is the creation of central coordination ('one entrance') points in cities and 'personalised treatment' with 'phased programmes' that are obligatory for the target group and service providers (Davelaar et al, 2007; Davelaar and van den Toorn, 2010).

Faith-based organisations and homeless service provision

In general, the role of third sector organisations in providing services for homeless people has shifted over the last 15 years from emergency services focused on street homelessness to services aimed at resettlement and prevention and targeted on an individual basis or on groups of homeless people with specific support needs. That shift is also evident in an increasing diversity in the actors involved and in the roles they perform in service provision (Edgar et al, 2003; Anderson, 2010). What are, in that light, the characteristics of FBOs involved in service provision for the homeless? What services do they provide? Do FBOs still 'prefer' to offer basic services or are they widening their scope of activities?

Characteristics of faith-based organisations

The analysis of FBOs that service homeless people across Europe reveals that there is no single type of FBO caring for the homeless. Instead, we observe a rich variety in *organisational characteristics*. Whereas most FBOs in this field have a local or sometimes national basis, international organisations also cater for the homeless. The most prominent example is The Salvation Army. This Protestant movement is the main actor in homeless service provision in Germany where it is primarily responsible for transition houses for homeless men. In the Netherlands its large Welfare and Healthcare division is the 'market leader' in homelessness services. As one of the most diverse providers of social services in the UK, The Salvation Army provides food and shelter to homeless people in 57 centres. Our data reveal that its role in Belgium is rather small, however.

Since FBOs are structurally diverse, their *funding arrangements* are likewise highly variable. FBOs that provide basic food, shelter, clothing and/or hospitality usually tend to be small, staffed by volunteers, and resourced almost exclusively by charitable sources. An example is the Innercity Project, Rotterdam, a small initiative started by some friends from various churches, and cooperating with a missionary, evangelical centre. Under the slogan 'Company and Compassion', the group engages in outreach activities – conversations with people on the streets, distributing coffee – in a small walk-in centre and a discussion group. The group does not want public funding, acts as a voice for people on the street and as a gateway to the professional (faith-based) organisations.

High support hostels and day centres offering specialist services, on the other hand, are provided by larger agencies. These offer a wide range of services, typically employ staff (sometimes supported by volunteers) and derive a significant proportion of their funding from statutory sources. Examples are the services of the Lutheran (Diakonie) and Catholic (Caritas) churches in Germany. A local example in this category is the ecumenical organisation The Rainbow in Amsterdam. In this group a greater mix of faith-based and secular agencies can be found. Moreover, specialist projects with professional staff are dominated by older Christian organisations (with many different denominational affiliations), while a wider range of religious groups, including evangelical groups and Christian 'migrant' churches is represented in projects such as soup runs, food banks, social restaurants and walk-in centres. Some of the latter are generic community services regularly used by homeless people. According to our evidence from the FACIT countries, except for Turkey, Islamic foundations and mosques are not very active in this field, despite the growing attention for poverty, homelessness and related issues in Muslim communities and the substantial number of people with a Muslim background in homeless shelters.

It is not possible to quantify accurately what proportion of all homelessness provision is offered by FBOs as it is not always clear as to whether projects have a religious affiliation. Some have evolved in such a way that they are now faith-based 'in name only', and a few are 'rebranding' to disassociate themselves from former links with religious groups. New religious groups, for instance, representing African or Western evangelism, often aiming at specific groups within the homeless population, such as homeless drug addicts or young migrant youth, tend to be more outspoken of their faith identity and also tend to have a greater faith content in their activities. It is also important to note that FBOs, and some secular projects which grew from faith initiatives, regularly emphasise or de-emphasise their project's faith affiliation depending on their audience, 'playing it up' when seeking support from faith communities, and 'playing it down' when applying for public funding.

Services

In examining the range of services provided by FBOs to homeless people, we concentrate on the most common service categories, but take into account the trend in differentiation of services that can be observed in most countries under survey (see also Edgar, 2009; Anderson, 2010; Busch-Geertsema et al, 2010). Beside the basic services (emergency help, bed, bath, bread, healthcare) that can roughly be divided into accommodation and non-residential services, there are relatively new activities centring on reaching out and prevention on the one hand, and on the other, reintegration and rehabilitation: transitional and supported housing, activation to work, specialised counselling aimed at empowerment and regaining independence.

With respect to *accommodation*, we find that the focus of many FBOs is still on emergency accommodation, mainly night shelters. Examples of FBOs offering this type of accommodation are The Salvation Army in various countries and Home Triest – Tabor Community House in Ghent, Belgium. While shelters usually operate on a day-to-day basis, in some cases they are only available for a short period of time. Homeless people can stay there for a couple of weeks or a limited number of days per month. Despite the traditional focus of FBOs on emergency shelters, services aiming at resettlement appear to play an increasing role. More and more temporary accommodation serves as the first stage of accommodation in a 'staircase model' of resettlement (Anderson, 2010). The transition houses of The Salvation Army in Germany, for instance, offer temporary accommodation to homeless men to guide them towards living independently. The Christian orthodox organisation Meeting (*Ontmoeting*) provides 'time-out' facilities and supported housing, mainly for homeless men and drug addicts from Rotterdam.

In most countries, FBOs also provide a range of *non-residential* services, such as: distribution of food, clothes and furniture, daytime shelter, healthcare services, practical services and advice. The provision of food, clothes and furniture is perhaps the most visible practice of FBOs catering for the homeless in Europe, but day centres are also common. The supply of healthcare services by FBOs is less widespread. Day centres, for instance, sometimes make basic healthcare services available by offering daily or weekly medical consultations by a doctor. Likewise, FBOs can also take up additional practical services, like luggage stores, laundry and washing facilities. Advice is given in many FBOs as a means to inform the homeless about their rights and to refer them to the adequate places to seek help. The majority of FBOs are also combining direct help with political advocacy. Large FBOs are involved in developing and influencing policies at the national level, like The Salvation Army and large Catholic service providers in Spain, Belgium and Germany and their Protestant counterparts in Germany and Sweden. Others raise their voice on behalf of the homeless at the local scale, including local diaconal organisations and inner-city or homeless pastors active in many European cities. The diaconal centre Paulus Church in the centre of Rotterdam is an outspoken example, combining direct care for marginalised people with campaigning for progressive change.

In addition, various FBOs offer services with a strong faith component like religious counselling, prayer sessions or bible study. In most cases, clients are not obliged to join religious activities. Although proselytising is rare in this sector, a few FBOs, however, envision surrendering to Jesus Christ as a *conditio sine qua non* for a successful 'therapy'. Victory Outreach, an international evangelical church working in the Netherlands, for instance, wants to bring the Gospel to the most vulnerable, an important component of which is to inspire people and to support them to fulfil their potential in life. Drug addicts can stay in unsubsidised Victory Homes, 'Christian rehabilitation homes', where people live under (limited) supervision. The church offers a spiritual framework to people that is so overwhelming it might inspire and help some, while scaring off others.

Local division of labour and shifts in governance

There has been a change in the division of labour between local public services and third sector services. The huge and growing diversity within the homeless population – with people suffering from alcohol or drug addiction, people with mental health problems, ex-prisoners, runaway youth, homeless families and victims of domestic and sexual abuse – and the range of problems individuals are trying to cope with, has led to a growing demand for specialised services. Yet the supply of public sector care does not appear to be sufficiently directed to the needs of specific target groups. Our results indicate that specialised care is increasingly offered by (faith-based) NGOs. Today, FBOs regularly offer programmes that are specifically targeted at sub-groups within the homeless population. Some FBOs, for instance, offer rehabilitation programmes to homeless people suffering from alcohol or drug addiction. Others might invest in (medical) care for people with mental health problems or in labour training programmes for homeless ex-prisoners. As a result, FBOs offer particular services that go beyond the scope of the more general public social services for the homeless. In this way, FBOs are specialising on rehabilitation for 'difficult' groups. In a remarkable way, however, they are also specialising on their old domain of low threshold, easy accessible, social relief, as discussed in the next section.

It is essential to mention that we are not only witnessing changes in the division of labour between public and third sector services, but also shifts in *governance* of the sector. These shifts can be illustrated through cases where the (faith-based) NGO sector has *always* been responsible for delivering services on the ground and close cooperation between local authorities and NGOs has been the rule. Recently, in the Netherlands, for example, local public authorities did not set up new services themselves, or allow (faith-based) NGOs to specialise autonomously, but strengthened their control over these organisations: the selection of clients was made through central points of entrance and the organisations were obliged to cooperate closely in 'chains of care' with the obligation to get all clients in a trajectory. Public authorities and the bigger service providers established goals and indicators to which all subsidised providers – including FBOs – had to adhere. Another example is that of local authorities in the UK, who have been attempting to prevent FBOs continuing their soup runs because that activity obstructed the authorities in ending rough sleeping and getting people off the streets and into newly erected facilities. This points to the fact that there is often a strong element of regulation attached to local approaches towards the homeless, reflecting dual strategic purposes aimed at both guiding the homeless to better care and making a 'housing career' possible, and at 'reclaiming the public realm' by sweeping up beggars, drug addicts and homeless people into prescribed spaces of welfare or containment. This form of exclusion is either covert or openly aimed at fighting 'anti-social behaviour' (Minton, 2009; see also Hayward, 2004; Johnsen and Fitzpatrick, 2007).

The duality in strategic purposes is also highlighted in discussions on the relevance of the concept of 'revanchist urbanism' (Smith, 1996) for understanding populist policies in Rotterdam (2002-06). Uitermark and Duyvendak (2008) conclude that both revanchist and (social democratic) reformist government strategies nowadays aim at 'civilizing the city' and 'centre on the *management* of urban marginality' (2008, p 1499). The main difference lies in the wish to discipline people or to exclude them. Snel and Engbersen (2009) stress the differences of the 'social reconquest' strategy in Rotterdam and urban revanchism, one of them being that 'repressive policies in Rotterdam go hand-in-hand with social care' (2009, p 165). 'The largest policy success is that Rotterdam has hardly any homeless people sleeping rough any more. This is not because the homeless have been driven out of the city, as Smith would assume, but because Rotterdam – like several other Dutch cities – has invested in shelters for the homeless in several parts of the city' (2009, p 165).

The Issue of accessibility

There are several circumstances that can hinder homeless people from obtaining appropriate assistance. When appealing for help, homeless people can only rely on limited resources in terms of financial and social capital. Other factors, such as a feeling of shame about their situation and a reduced ability to assess and prioritise their needs – because of severe psychological issues and/or the day-to-day struggle to find shelter, food and money – could further weaken their position. In almost all cases, homeless people are not well organised, nor are they represented by powerful client associations or lobby groups.

It is apparent across different European countries that homeless people predominantly look for help among third sector organisations. It appears that the homeless cannot easily find their way to public services, which are typically characterised by a high level of professionalisation and specialisation. In this respect, Kal (2001) refers to the 'paradox of assistance', meaning that it is difficult for the most needy in society to reach professional help, and there are several reasons for this problem. Van Doorn (2004) distinguishes between four *institutional* and three *cultural* thresholds.

The first institutional threshold is the categorisation of the supply, meaning that separate services are responsible for each sub-problem – people with multiple problems are disadvantaged by this way of organising care. The second threshold is the rationalisation and fragmentation of the supply. Social workers have to be 'productive' and are looking for the most efficient *modus operandus* by routine actions and specialisation. The third institutional threshold is the lack of continuity, especially in the coordination between youth and adult care services. The guidance of young people might stop when they become adults, increasing their chances to social vulnerability. The final institutional threshold refers to the de-institutionalisation of care, which emphasises living an 'ordinary life' and being independent as much as possible. Institutional care is replaced by 'care in the community'. While many clients benefit from this change, others cannot cope with it easily (van Doorn, 2004).

According to van Doorn, the *cultural* thresholds act on contradictory conceptions of reality by homeless people and social workers. A first threshold is on the weighing of costs and benefits when searching for help. Disappointing personal experiences or stories of other people might hinder people in looking for assistance, and the fear of rendering control to social workers or other professionals is sometimes noticeable. The second threshold relates to the distance between professionals and homeless people sometimes resulting in difficulties building up a sufficient level of mutual trust. The third cultural threshold refers to the unwritten rules of assistance. For example, it is assumed that people in need have to take up and maintain contact themselves. They have to be able to formulate a request for help and this request needs to fit in the supply of care, otherwise people are referred to other services – not seldom too often and too quickly (van Doorn, 2004).

How faith-based organisations try to be accessible

While public services tend to focus on people who can be 'treated', many homeless people look for help elsewhere. Non-profit organisations are not immune from the above-mentioned processes leading to the erection of barriers to potential clients, but generally speaking their thresholds seem to be lower. FBOs in particular have an important potential to attract homeless clients who fall outside regular assistance. The accessibility of specific projects for these groups is guaranteed by different factors. First, there are no strings attached to making use of the services offered – the help is given unconditionally. Second, projects work with a minimum of house rules. Third, these initiatives try to work 'presence oriented' (Baart, 2001), that is, they reach out to people, connect with their environment, work on the rhythm of clients and have an open agenda that clients may fill in freely and try to avoid intervening too quickly ('sitting on your hands'). Rather than solving problems, they aim to establish a more satisfying relation between clients in a crisis situation and their lives. Various FBOs in the Netherlands and Flanders try to work with the presence-orientated methodology. While their secular counterparts might also invest in accessibility, FBOs more strongly appear to provide low threshold services. By and large, they try to avoid any barrier that might impede access to their services.

We now look in more detail at the accessibility of services related to space, practical accessibility and guidance and support. Accessibility *in terms of space* is related to the geographical distance between homeless people and FBOs. In general, FBOs providing homeless services are often located near their target group. This means that there is a relatively low physical threshold for people to access these FBOs. Our research demonstrates the variety of spaces in which FBOs catering for the homeless have developed a service presence in different European cities. In Bristol in the UK, for example, faith-based providers for the homeless are located in different urban zones. Similar to research by May et al (2006), our evidence suggests a presence of FBOs in prime but mainly marginal urban city spaces. The main night shelter for homeless people in Bristol is located in a converted industrial building in a distinctly marginal space close to the city centre. On the edges of this space are also found a series of hostels and drop-in centres run by FBOs, in one case using a church building. In and around this marginal space, but also closer to the city centre where homeless people go about their lives 'on-the-street', a regular soup run has built up a regular clientele, while in the red light district close to the night shelter, a yellow van provides a mobile service run by an FBO to support homeless sex workers (May et al, 2006). These mobile and outreach services are threshold lowering because care workers look for needy people who might otherwise not seek help. In the Netherlands, initiatives such as day centres and food banks often make use of the existing geography of religious buildings, using churches as places to 'reach out'.

One particular manifestation of how FBOs choose to establish a dwelling place in marginal areas of the city is the incarnational approach to mission (see Chapter Twelve, this book). Incarnational schemes are based on a desire to act sacrificially in order to live and work in an area, supporting and serving local people. Particular organisations, such as Eden and Urban Expressions in the UK, are now facilitating the placement of individuals or groups of people into socially deprived housing estates for the specific purpose of serving the people of these estates from within rather than as an external welfare agency. These incarnational approaches are not just located on housing estates. For example, the Oudezijds 100 ecumenical 'living community' is located in the red light district in Amsterdam and is involved in community outreach activities, supported housing and health services for undocumented people. The Emmaus movement, with its 'groups of idealists', living and working together with people in need, operates in various countries in the countryside and inner cities alike.

A second dimension of accessibility relates to *practical barriers* for seeking help. Most FBOs catering for the homeless apply an open door policy – they do not ask questions and people are free to come and go. As in many walk-in centres, people can just come and talk. Accessibility is also realised by being available to clients for a sufficient number of hours, based on the demands of homeless people. Another practical obstacle concerns the affordability of services. Since homeless people have to manage with very limited financial resources, many FBOs offer their services for free. Others charge a small amount of money. FBOs that prepare meals, for instance, often ask a contribution from their clients, inspired by the idea that by doing so a normal financial transaction takes place – people do not have to beg for food, but pay for a good meal.

The accessibility in terms of *guidance and support*, however, is perhaps the most important component of an accessible service provision, filling in missing links in the requested support, being able to refer people correctly, being able to 'get to the question behind the question'. If social workers are determined to offer tailor-made care to clients, services targeting all areas of life should be available. Our results suggest that FBOs indeed try to cooperate with other welfare and care organisations. In addition, FBOs seem keen to offer services where gaps in the (local) welfare system occur and support is not sufficiently supplied. In this way they complete welfare services and try to detect and cover new or less visible needs. A useful illustration can be found in the functioning of Welfare Links in Belgium, which have local branches in all municipalities. The local organisations try to establish a way of working that contributes to the local welfare network in each municipality by looking for missing links. Since most FBOs have a broad picture of the existing welfare services in the neighbourhood, they can also easily refer people to others. This referral process is valued by the majority of FBOs as an important strength.

Conclusion

This chapter has focused on the role of FBOs with respect to service provision for the homeless. To this end, we have analysed the 'division of labour' between the different systems of welfare provision, and conclude that care for the homeless has always been somewhat out of the picture of the main builders of the welfare state. In addition, in most countries the homeless very soon tumble through the safety net of the *primary welfare system* – which is organised by public and governmental authorities with national responsibility and deals mainly with long-term structural social issues such as unemployment and sickness – if they succeed in clinging to it at all. The last decades have seen growing cooperation between the *secondary* (local public) and *tertiary* (NGO) systems. In this cooperation (faith-based) NGOs in general mostly function as providers of complementary services to the 'regular' local services. In some countries (Spain, the UK, Germany and the Netherlands) they deliver almost all services (in the last two countries largely funded by public authorities); in other countries (Belgium and Sweden) public centres are also running accommodation and other services.

Within the third sector, the precise role of FBOs is complex. In many cities they are highly rewarded partners or contractors of local authorities and engaged in co-production 'concentrating on what each does best' (Daly, 1997, p 172). Local governments often prefer to contract out homeless services to non-profit organisations rather than supplying 'in-house services', because (faith-based) NGOs have longstanding experience in dealing with marginalised groups and may deliver cheaper services. Within the service provision of FBOs both a tendency towards specialisation on 'difficult' groups and rehabilitation *and* attempts to reinvent and transform the classic FBO domain of basic care ('presence-approach') can be noticed. FBOs are willing to engage in broad local coalitions with secular NGOs and public services to prevent and fight homelessness.

Elsewhere, they seem to fill a vacuum created out of the lack of political will and financial investment by public authorities. Here, FBOs can be seen as merely coopted by governments seeking to exploit the charitable and voluntary resources available through FBOs in order to provide cost-effective service provision. However, there is now a range of evidence that FBOs often defy description as mere agents of cooption, providing instead theo-ethical and performative resources that strive to provide holistic and attentive, lasting care for marginal individuals. Such resources may be increasingly significant when homeless people are facing revanchist-style clearance from city streets in some countries. However, although FBOs seem well regarded when they offer 'no-strings' services, they evoke far greater suspicion when their activities seem to be geared more towards overt evangelism than to charitable service.

We regard questions of access to be significant in reaching such evaluations. When it comes to the accessibility of services, the key axis eventually differentiating the homelessness projects of faith-based and secular providers is their stance on expectations of service users and the conditionality of service receipt. Stances on this generally fall somewhere along a spectrum, ranging from firmly 'non-interventionist' to highly 'interventionist' approaches. The interventionist end of the spectrum is dominated by secular organisations, and while both secular and faith-based organisations can be found throughout, the latter are more clustered toward the non-interventionist end. The interventionist agencies hold rather strong expectations with respect to service users. They often assertively encourage them to desist from damaging behaviours, make service receipt conditional on commitment to defined support plans and are less willing to welcome back notorious offenders of house rules or people (intentionally) frustrating reintegration trajectories. FBOs providing homeless services appear to be less demanding of service users and more willing to apply 'second chance' policies.

Unconditional support offered by FBOs is still widespread. Support is given unconditionally, that is, nothing has to be done or given in return. This contrasts with the major public policy trend of more emphasis on conditional support within the device 'no rights without duties'. However, FBOs do not stay unaffected by this trend. Due to changes in political goals (more emphasis on public safety and reduction of nuisance caused by rough sleepers, drug addicts and beggars) and (local) governments stressing the need for uniformity and (short-term) results, FBOs have lost room for manoeuvre, especially those organisations depending on public funding. Evidence from the UK, Germany and the Netherlands suggests that the possibilities to help out who ever they want (an open door policy) have reduced. Moreover, FBOs might have to abandon part of their more 'holistic' approach, that is, no strict boundaries between voluntary and professional care, the combination of professional care, direct material help, political advocacy and the opportunity to engage in reflection and contemplation (see Davelaar et al, 2011). This is not to say that FBOs are helpless in regard to these developments. FBOs are often influential and indispensable partners of governments in local welfare networks and able to face competition and pressure. And public authorities seldom have a clear interest in (informal) services for marginalised groups they cannot or do not want to cater themselves for. FBOs are willing – sometimes 'under protest' – to provide those services, supported by volunteers and religious funds or to cooperate for this sake with other, 'standalone' FBOs who operate outside local policy networks.

Another key feature distinguishing faith-based from secular services is related to the faith dimension of FBOs. As opposed to secular organisations, FBOs have a 'missionary zeal with which they approach their missions' (Martin, 2003, p 57). Many FBOs offer a 'spiritual' element. Sometimes this comprises a formal part of the programme – by means of the provision of chaplaincy services, prayer or opportunities for scriptural study, for example – but often it is delivered more informally. Some service users may not engage with this aspect of the service, but it is greatly valued by others.

Although many FBOs hold no expectations in this regard, faith can also be a key contributory factor motivating homeless people to make positive lifestyle changes. The willingness of professionals and volunteers to give company to people for a longer period of time, the open approach towards people's strengths and weaknesses and a sensibility for questions regarding 'the meaning of life' are important in that respect. Combining social service provision with proselytising is rare, although there are few examples of organisations that use proselytising as part of their 'therapy'.

While the peculiarities of the strength of faith-based homeless projects lie in a combination of their relatively non-interventionist approach, generally higher levels of involvement of volunteers and a working philosophy based on offering homeless people – in addition to professional support – 'Company and Compassion', it is also important to stress that in some ways the services provided by FBOs are not perceived as particularly different from those provided by NGOs (see Johnsen with Fitzpatrick, 2009). This perhaps indicates that despite fears to the contrary, many FBOs are succeeding in their attempts to provide open-access and non-proselytising facilities that are as much to do with caring humanity as with religious structure. In this sense, then, FBOs may not significantly differ from NGOs. Faith-based and secular providers may share more similarities than they hold differences in their fight against homelessness.

Note
[1] The authors would like to thank Paul Cloke for his valuable contributions to an earlier version of this chapter.

References
Anderson, I. (2010) 'Services for homeless people in Europe: supporting pathways out of homelessness?', in E. O'Sullivan, V. Busch-Geertsema, D. Quilgars and N. Pleace (eds) *Homelessness research in Europe*, Brussels: FEANTSA.

Avramov, D. (1999) *Coping with homelessness: Issues to be tackled and best practices in Europe*, Aldershot: Ashgate.

Baart, A. (2001) *Een theorie van de presentie* [*A theory of presence*], Utrecht: Lemma.

Beaumont, J. and Baker, C. (2011) 'Introduction: the rise of the postsecular city', in J. Beaumont and C. Baker (eds) *Postsecular cities: Space, theory and practice*, London: Continuum, pp 1-15.

Benjaminsen, L., Dyb, E. and O'Sullivan, E. (2009) 'The governance of homelessness in liberal and social democratic welfare regimes: strategies, structural conditions and models of intervention', *European Journal of Homelessness*, vol 3, December, pp 23-51.

Busch-Geertsema, V. (2010) 'Defining and measuring homelessness', in E. O'Sullivan, V. Busch-Geertsema, D. Quilgars and N. Pleace (eds) *Homelessness research in Europe*, Brussels: FEANTSA, pp 19-39.

Busch-Geertsema, V., Edgar, W., O'Sullivan, E. and Pleace, N. (2010) 'Homelessness and homeless policies in Europe: lessons from Research', European Consensus Conference on Homelessness, 9-10 December, Brussels: FEANTSA.

Cloke, P., May, J. and Johnsen, S. (2005) 'Exploring ethos? Discourses of charity in the provision of emergency services for homeless people', *Environment and Planning A*, vol 37, pp 385-402.

Cloke, P., May, J. and Johnsen, S. (2007) 'Ethical citizenship? Volunteers and the ethics of providing services for homeless people', *Geoforum*, vol 38, pp 1089-101.

Cloke, P., May, J. and Johnsen, S. (2010) *Swept-up lives? Re-envisioning the homeless city*, London: Wiley-Blackwell.

Cloke, P., Williams, A. and Thomas, S. (2011) *Faith-based organisations and social exclusion in the United Kingdom*, Leuven: Acco.

Daly, G. (1997) 'Charity begins at home: a cross-national view of the voluntary sector in Britain, Canada, and the United States', in M.J. Huth and T. Wright (eds) *International critical perspectives on homelessness*, Westport, CT: Praeger.

Davelaar, M. and van den Toorn, J. (2010) *Geloof aan het werk. De rol van levensbeschouwelijke organisaties bij het bestrijden van sociale uitsluiting in Rotterdam*, [*Faith at work. The role of faith-based organisations in combating social exclusion in Rotterdam*] Utrecht: Verwey-Jonker Instituut.

Davelaar, M., Nederland, T., Wentink, M. and Ter Woerds, S. (2005) *Aan de slag in de rafelrand. Werk en activering voor daklozen en verslaafden*, [*Getting started in the frayed fringes. Work and activation for homeless people and drug addicts*] Assen: Van Gorcum.

Davelaar, M., van Dongen, M., Rijkschroeff, R. and Flikweert, M. (2007) *Van de straat aan het werk. Dagbesteding en activering voor dak- en thuislozen in Rotterdam*, [*From the street to work. Daytime activity and activation for the homeless in Rotterdam*] Utrecht: Verwey-Jonker Instituut.

Davelaar, M., van den Toorn, J., de Witte, N., Beaumont, J. and Kuiper, C. (2011) *Faith-based organisations and social exclusion in the Netherlands*, Leuven: Acco.

Dierckx, D., Kerstens, W. and Vranken, J. (2011) *Faith-based organisations and social exclusion in Belgium*, Leuven: Acco.

Doherty, J., Edgar, B. and Meert, H. (2002) *European observatory on homelessness: Homelessness research in the EU – A summary*, Brussels: FEANTSA.

Edgar, W. (2009) *European review statistics on homelessness*, Brussels: FEANTSA.

Edgar, W. and Doherty, J. (eds) (2001) *Woman and homelessness in Europe*, Bristol: The Policy Press.

Edgar, W., Harrison, M., Watson, P. and Busch-Geertsema, V. (2007) *Measurement of homelessness at European Union level*, Brussels: European Commission.

Edgar, B., Anderson, I., Baptista, I., Kärkkäinen, S.-L., Schoibl, H. and Sapounakis, A. (2003) *Service provision for homeless people in Europe: Regulation and funding implications for service development*, European Observatory on Homelessness, The Changing Role of Services Provision, Working Group 3, Brussels: FEANTSA.

Edgar, W., Anderson, I., Baptista, I., Wolf, J., Sapounakis, A. and Schoibl, H. (2004) *Service provision for homeless people in Europe: Organisational factors affecting the delivery of services for homeless people*, Brussels: FEANTSA.

Elander, I. and Fridolfsson, C. (2011) *Faith-based organisations and social exclusion in Sweden*, Leuven: Acco.

FEANTSA (Federation of National Organisations working with the Homeless) (2005) *ETHOS – European typology of homelessness and housing exclusion*, Brussels: FEANTSA.

Forrest, R. (1999) 'The new landscape of precariousness', in P. Kennett and A. Marsh (eds) *Homelessness: Exploring the new terrain*, Bristol: The Policy Press, pp 17-36.

Friedrichs, J. and Klöckner, J. (2011) *Faith-based organisations and social exclusion in Germany*, Leuven: Acco.

Government and four major cities (2006) *Strategy plan for social relief*, The Hague: Ministry of Health, Welfare and Sport.

Hayward, K. (2004) *City limits: Crime, consumer culture and the urban experience*, London: Glasshouse Press.

Helvie, C. and Kunstmann, W. (1999) *Homelessness in the United states, Europe, and Russia*, Westport, CT: Bergin & Garvey.

Hopper, K. (2003) *Reckoning with homelessness*, Ithaca, NY: Cornell University Press.

Jencks, C. (1995) *The homeless*, Cambridge, MA: Harvard University Press.

Johnsen, S. and Fitzpatrick, S. (2007) *The impact of enforcement on street users in England*, Bristol: The Policy Press.

Johnsen, S. with Fitzpatrick, S. (2009) *The role of faith-based organisations in the provision of services for homeless people: Summary of key findings*, York: Centre for Housing Policy, University of York.

Kal, D. (2001) *Kwartiermaken. Werken aan ruimte voor mensen met een psychiatrische achtergrond*, [*Creating space for people with a psychiatric background*] Amsterdam: Boom.

Kusmer, K. (2003) *Down and out, on the road. The homeless in American history*, New York: Oxford University Press.

Lees, L. (2008) 'Urban renaissance and the street: spaces of control and contestation', in N. Fyfe (ed) *Images of the street: Planning, identity and control in public space*, London: Routledge, pp 236–53.

Levinson, D. (2004) *Encyclopedia of homelessness*, London: Sage Publications.

Martin, A. (2003) 'From a higher cause: faith-based organisations approach affordable housing from a scriptural spirit, but otherwise they are not so different from any other nonprofit with a heart', *Journal of Housing and Community Development*, 60, issue 3 (May/June) pp 56–60.

May, J., Cloke, P. and Johnsen, S. (2005) 'Re-phasing neo-liberalism: New Labour and Britain's crisis of street homelessness', *Antipode*, vol 37, pp 703-30.

May, J., Cloke, P. and Johnsen, S. (2006) 'Shelter at margins: New Labour and the changing state of emergency accommodation for single homeless people in Britain', *Policy & Politics*, vol 34, pp 711-30.

Minnery, J. and Greenhalgh, E. (2007) 'Approaches to homelessness policy in Europe, the United States, and Australia', *Journal of Social Issues*, vol 63, no 3, pp 641-55.

Minton, A. (2009) *Ground control. Fear and happiness in the twenty-first-century city*, London: Penguin Books.

Mitchell, D. (2001) 'Postmodern geographical praxis? The postmodern impulse and the war against homeless people in the "post-justice" city', in C. Minca (ed) *Postmodern geography: Theory and praxis*, Oxford: Blackwell, pp 57-92.

Olsson, L.-E. and Nordfeldt, M. (2008) 'Homelessness and the tertiary welfare system in Sweden – the role of the welfare state and non-profit sector', *European Journal of Homelessness*, vol 2, pp 157-73.

POD Maatschappelijke Integratie (2007) *Gids voor daklozen*, [*Guide for the homeless, Programmatic Federal Service on social integration*] Brussel: POD Maatschappelijke Integratie.

Ruddick, S. (1996) *Young and homeless in Hollywood*, New York: Routledge.

Sen, M. (2011) *Faith-based organisations and social exclusion in Turkey*, Leuven: Acco.

Sibley, D. (1995) *Geographies of exclusion. Society and difference in the West*, London/New York: Routledge.

Smith, N. (1996) *The new urban frontier: Gentrification and the revanchist city*, London: Routledge.

Snel, E. and Engbersen, G. (2009) 'Social reconquest as a new policy paradigm: changing urban policies in the city of Rotterdam', in K. de Boyser, C. Dewilde, D. Dierckx and J. Friederichs (eds) *Between the social and the spatial: Exploring the multiple dimensions of poverty and social exclusion*, Farnham: Ashgate, pp 149–66.

Takahashi, L. (1998) *Homelessness, AIDS and stigmatization*, Oxford: Clarendon Press.

Toro, P. (2007) 'Toward an international understanding of homelessness', *Journal of Social Issues*, vol 63, pp 461-82.

Uitermark, J. and Duyvendak, J.W. (2008) 'Civilizing the city: populism and revanchist urbanism in Rotterdam', *Urban Studies*, vol 45, no 7, pp 1485-503.

van Doorn, L. (2004) *Botsende werkelijkheidsopvattingen: Institutionele ratio's versus de realiteit van de straat*, [*Conflicting views of reality: Institutional ratios versus the reality of the street*] Amsterdam: SWP.

Walliser, A. and Villanueva, S. (2011) *Faith-based organisations and social exclusion in Spain*, Leuven: Acco.

TEN

Turkish Islamic organisations: a comparative study in Germany, the Netherlands and Turkey

Jürgen Friedrichs, Jennifer Klöckner, Mustafa Şen and Nynke de Witte

Introduction

Five million migrants from Turkey live in European countries and their number has continued to increase; Turks are the largest immigrant group in both Germany and the Netherlands. However, both countries differ markedly in their integration strategies; these strategies and their social and political implications are assessed in this chapter. While in Germany the main issue for Islamic organisations has been to get legally accepted as a religion, in the Netherlands, *Diyanet* and *Millî Görüş* are accepted as religions and both are part of the Contact Body Muslims and Government (*Contactorgaan Moslims en Overheid*, CMO). How does this have an impact on the strategies and activities of Islamic faith-based organisations (FBOs) in the two countries? And how are the FBOs related to their organisations in Turkey?

To answer these questions, we first present data on the number of Muslims in the three countries and a breakdown by Islamic Schools of religion. The next section compares migrant organisations in Germany and the Netherlands by analysing 23 interviews with organisations' representatives along with additional material on the FBOs. We include 47 interviews conducted in Turkey, describing their aims, the types and range of welfare services delivered and the legal status of these organisations in Germany and the Netherlands. We then discuss the problem of migrant organisations as religious organisations. The relation of these organisations to Turkey and Turkish policy is examined in the third section. We specifically study the links and influence between European *Millî Görüş* and *Diyanet*, and the relationship of *Millî Görüş* with the Justice and Development Party (JDP) in Turkey. A major question underlying these analyses is whether migrant problems are transformed into religious problems, and this is discussed in the fourth section.

We summarise our findings in comparative tables throughout this chapter, and suggest explanations for the differences observed. Based on these findings, in a final section we derive several policy implications, particularly with respect to a better recognition of Islamic organisations in Germany (following the Dutch model) and a party-independent welfare system in Turkey.

Turkish Muslims in Germany and the Netherlands

Compared to other European countries, Germany has a large Muslim population (three million) and the largest population of Turkish immigrants (1.7 million) in Europe (Maréchal et al, 2003; BMF, 2009; Haug et al, 2009, p 81; cf Friedrichs and Klöckner, 2011) see Table 10.1. According to data from the National Bureau for Statistics ((Statistics Netherlands, 2008, 2009), approximately 850,000 Muslims live in the Netherlands, representing 5.8 per cent of the population. Approximately 323,000 of the Dutch Muslim population has a Turkish (21 per cent) and 264,000 a Moroccan or Surinamese (both 19 per cent) migration background (Forum, 2008, pp 7, 12).

Table 10.1: Foreign-born in Germany and the Netherlands, 1990, 2004 and 2008

Country	Year	Population in 000s	Non-national population,[a] in 000s	%	Country of largest group of foreign citizens
Germany	2008	82,098	7,246	8.8	Turkey
	2004	75,190	7,342	8.9	Turkey
	1990	74,267	4,846	6.1	Turkey
Netherlands	2008	16,486	1,809	11.0	Turkey
	2004	15,556	0,702	4.3	Turkey
	1990	14,251	0,642	4.3	Turkey

Notes: [a] Only non-German citizenship, 1 January 2009.

Sources: Eurostat (2006); BMF (2009); Forum (2008, p 7); Statistics Netherlands (2008); Gijsberts and Dagevos (2009, p 40)

As a result, Germany and the Netherlands host many financially strong Islamic organisations (Topuz, 2003; cf Friedrichs and Klöckner, 2011). Turkish Islamic organisations have predominantly settled in North Rhine-Westphalia, the main reason being the concentration of the Turkish population there (Zentralinstitut Islam Archiv Deutschland Stiftung eV, 2006; Hero et al, 2008). In large Dutch cities like Amsterdam, Rotterdam, The Hague and Utrecht, more than 10 per cent of the inhabitants are Muslim.

Thirty-two per cent of all Turkish organisations in the Netherlands are affiliated to Islam. Different authors estimate that about 206 out of 365 to 245 out of 453 Turkish Islamic organisations to be mosque associations (Heelsum et al, 2004, p 3; Bernts et al, 2006, p 118). *Kerkgenootschap*, however, a legal entity church society, is open to all religious communities; unlike Jewish organisations, Islamic organisations have never established themselves as such (Waardenburg, 2001, p 21). They are either foundations or associations, operating under civil law, just

Table 10.2: Muslims in Germany and the Netherlands, by school of religion, 2006

	Germany[c]	The Netherlands
Total	4,300,000	857,000[a]
Sunnites	74.1%	60.3%[b]
Shiites	7.1%	3.8%
Alevis	12.7%	3.4%
Iranian Imamites and Turkish Shiites	no data	30.6%
Ahmadi-Muslims	1.7%	1.5%
Sufis/Mystics	0.1%	no data
Other	4.0%	no data

Notes: [a] van Herten and Otten (2007, p 51); cf Forum (2008, p 12). [b] Own calculations, based on the Survey Integratie Minderheden 2006; only Muslim respondents are included. [c] Haug et al (2009)

Source: Zentralinstitut Islam Archiv Deutschland Stiftung eV (2006)

like church societies. Germany has about 2,500 mosques serving social, cultural and even political or ideological functions (Rohe, 2008, p 53; Tezcan, 2008). Only 11.4 per cent of the organisations are just focused on Turkey while 59.1 per cent of the organisations focus their members' lives on Germany (Halm and Sauer, 2007, p 10).

In Turkey, official statistical data on the distribution of religious beliefs do not exist. However, the state elite and conservative politicians are eager to maintain that 99 per cent of the Turkish population are Muslims. This figure implies that all Turkish citizens are Muslims who interpret and practise Islam in the same way, but researchers point out that only 80-85 per cent are Sunnites of the Hannefi religious school, 15-20 per cent are Alevis, 0.2 per cent are Christians (100,000) and 0.04 per cent are Jews (25,000) (Steinbach, 2002; Spuler-Stegemann, 2005). German and Dutch data reflect this religious diversity of Turkish migrants, although most of the Turkish official religious institutions, including *Diyanet*, religious-track imam-hatip schools, compulsory religious courses at primary and secondary schools, official Qur'an courses and Divinity Faculties are based on the Sunni-Hanefi belief and practice and are funded by the state.

In Germany, Islamic organisations have about 377,500 members; in 2006 the largest are the Islamic Council (147,000 members), DITIB (117,000) and VIKZ (35,000) (Zentralinstitut Islam Archiv, 2006). The largest Dutch organisations are Foundation Platform Islamic Organisations Rijnmond (SPIOR), comprising 65 organisations (no membership data supplied), the CMO (560,000 members) and the CGI (115,000) (Netzeitung, 2006).

The crucial difference between German and Dutch organisations is that the two largest German organisations are Turkish. The dominance of the Turkish minority over all other minority ethnic groups hinders implementing one Islamic representation in Germany and the Netherlands. In Germany in particular official

Table 10.3: Muslim population in Germany and the Netherlands, by country of origin, 2007

Country of origin	Germany		The Netherlands[a]	
	Number	%	Number	%
Turkey	1,506,410	68.0	323,000	38.0
Morocco	32,609	1.5	264,000	31.1
Surinam	–	–	34,000	4.0
Iraq	44,248	2.0	27,000	3.2
Afghanistan	34,885	1.6	31,000	3.6
Iran	32,915	1.5	12,000	1.2
Somalia	–	–	20,000	2.4
Yugoslavia	346,917	15.7	–	–
Other	216,421	9.8	139,000	16.5
Total	2,214,405	100	850,000	100

Note: [a] 'After 2007 CBS, Dutch central office for statistical research, adjusted the method by which it calculated the number of Muslims in the Netherlands. This can explain the decrease in the estimated number of Muslims in the Netherlands between 2004 and 2007' (Forum, 2008, p 12).

Sources: Forum (2008, p 12); BAMF (2009)

recognition is required as the corporate body of public law, but without a legal structure, Islamic organisations are excluded from, for example, government funding, employment of civil servants and tax exemptions. The major problem is that the different organisations are unable to agree on one representative person or organisation, and Shiite and Sunni Muslims from Arabia and Turkey in particular compete with each other. Other religions and life convictions, for example, Christian churches, Jewish communities in Germany and in the Humanistic Society and Hindu community in the Netherlands already have such interlocutors, who are members of the integration board or committees (for example, Contact in Government Affairs [Contact in Overheidszaken, CIO], the Netherlands).

A good example for the Turkish Muslims' supremacy in Germany is implementation of departments and chairs of Islamic theology at universities to educate teachers of Islamic religious education and imams. Arab Muslim representatives are sceptical of an agreement between the Departments of Education of the German Länder and Turkish Islam organisations because the curriculum for such would otherwise be a 'Turkish' one. At first sight, such a suspicion does not seem justified, since the great majority of Muslims in Germany are Sunnites (cf Table 10.2). Apparently it is not a debate about religious schools, but about the impact of Turkish versus other Islamic countries on the institutionalisation of Islam in Germany.

Historical background of labour migration to Germany and the Netherlands

After the Socialist Unity Party of Germany (SED) built the Berlin Wall on 13 August in 1961, the labour immigration of Eastern Europe immediately stopped (Hunn, 2005; Knortz, 2008). For economic recovery, Western European countries were forced to attract a labour force from outside their countries.

Hence in 1961, the so-called *Gastarbeiter-Verträge* (guestworkers' contracts) were signed between Turkey and the German Federal Government[1] (Rieker, 2003; BAMF, 2008). During the oil crisis in 1973 and 1974, the contract ended and only the guestworkers' families were allowed to enter the country (Rieker, 2003; BAMF, 2008). Due to worse living standards and political unrest in Turkey, Turkish guestworkers led their families to Germany, instead of going back to their countries of origin, as originally planned ('the rotation principle').

While the status of the guestworkers changed to being immigrants, when they realised that they would not return to their home countries, German integration policies did not respond. Rather, they continued to adhere to 'the rotation principle'. Language skills, education as well as social mixing with the receiving (German) society was anything but ideal. When many manufacturing companies had to close down, predominantly unskilled guestworkers became unemployed. Neighbourhoods adjacent to production sites with a large share of the migrant population became deprived, and the residential segregation of poverty increased (Friedrichs, 1988; Friedrichs and Triemer, 2009).

Hence, the demand for cultural and social institutions as well as houses of worship increased, and the first Turkish Islamic organisations were local initiatives of the guestworkers. Small mosque communities and clubs were established with the objective of promoting and fulfilling Turkish needs concerning everyday life, religion and a sense of home. The establishment of Turkish Islamic organisations was not unaffected by political developments in Turkey, however. Quickly, political ambitions and lobbying became more important.

When civic organisations in Turkey were banned in the 1980s, oppositional and marginal groups started organisations abroad, competing for power in the growing Turkish communities in Western Europe. The interference of the Turkish government and Turkish religious-ideological movements in the organisation process resulted in the ideological fragmentation of Turkish Islamic organisations (Rath and Meyer, 1997, pp 390-1; Sunier, 1999, pp 73-4). The building of mosques and religious organisations became an expression of competition between different religious schools (Sunier, 1996). As a result, most Turkish mosques, as well as (related) youth and women organisations, are linked to the various national umbrella organisations of, for example, *Diyanet*, *Millî Görüş* or *Süleymancilar*.

The following section pertains to the political background of the two FBOs, *Diyanet* and *Millî Görüs*, on which the study is focused.

Comparing Islamic organisations in Germany and the Netherlands

While today national umbrella organisations are mainly engaged in capacity building and political advocacy, local organisations (primarily mosques and affiliated youth and women organisations) offer a wide range of services, including welfare, to their members. Although initially mosques had mainly a religious function, after family reunification, they gradually broadened their activities (see, for instance, Canatan et al, 2003, 2005). They created social and cultural activities, Islamic education for children, charity and established women groups and youth branches. Additionally, the organisation of and participation in inter-cultural and inter-religious activities has been added to this list in recent years.

Our analyses are based on broad literature research, statistical data and 70 face-to-face semi-structured interviews with top representatives of Islamic organisations in the three countries, conducted in 2008 and 2009. The interviews were part of the European Union (EU)-financed FACIT project.

General characteristics of the German and Dutch situation

There are large differences between mosques in terms of the range of activities they organise. In a study among 120 mosques in the Netherlands, 22 per cent were only active in the religious sphere, while 44 per cent pursued social activities in a variety of social domains and 34 per cent in specific social domains (Canatan et al, 2005). Focusing on the situation in Rotterdam, Canatan et al (2003) argued that differences between mosques were largely determined by the age of the members of the board (first generation immigrants viewed the mosque primarily as a house of worship), cultural and religious factors (mosques with a Turkish or Pakistani background more often played a social role) and the imams' attitudes. A report on the social role of mosques in Amsterdam by Driessen et al (2004) concluded that there were no large differences between social activities of the mosques. They also pointed out that most social activities were aimed at the self-help and emancipation of group members, while less attention was paid to participation and integration in society. An exception was the large-scale participation of mosques in inter-religious dialogue networks. According to the report, active cooperation with welfare organisations or local authorities was also incidental (Driessen et al, 2004).

Although most Dutch Turkish Islamic organisations do not provide general welfare services, they often function as intermediary organisations among migrant communities and welfare organisations. The interviews with Turkish mosques also confirmed the finding that in addition to being a house of worship, mosques often functioned as informal meeting places where mutual aid was organised, for example, financial support for a funeral, fundraising in case of nature disasters, information on provisions for older people, child rearing, school choices for children, employment, welfare services, elections or educational support. Several interviewees mentioned the importance of mosques for older people, who sojourned in the communities on a daily basis. Local authorities and welfare organisations also increasingly sought to cooperate with mosque associations and women organisations in order to reach and inform their rank and file.

Researchers in the Netherlands and Belgium found that *Millî Görüş* mosques were involved in a wider range of social activities than other Turkish and Moroccan mosques (van Bruinessen, 2004b). Large differences between *Millî Görüş* and *Diyanet* mosques did not emerge from our interviews. However, they indicate that the extent to which mosques organised social and cultural activities seemed to depend largely on the social capital and governmental subsidies available in the organisation (like Dutch language education or homework assistance). Interviews with *Diyanet* and *Millî Görüş* mosques in Amsterdam revealed that concerns about the building and reparation of the mosque received most attention from board members that constrained them to spend time and money. Many interviewees also expressed concerns about the education and recruitment of new board members, as well as the difficulty of binding young people to mosques. Women's organisations seemed to have fewer problems attracting new (active) members. Most mosque associations we interviewed did not receive subsidies for their social activities. While some regretted the lack of funding, others explicitly refrained from applying for subsidies.

After five years of residence in the Netherlands and eight years in Germany, immigrants receive active and passive voting rights. Hence, mosques are instrumental in the political mobilisation of Muslims at a local level. Sometimes mosque leaders (usually board members) invite representatives of local political parties to present their programmes before local elections. Some mosque leaders act as local representatives of Muslims, either as candidates for political parties or independently. Our fieldwork indicated that *Millî Görüş* mosques were more ambitious to be politically active then *Diyanet* mosques that claimed to refrain from political issues. In addition to organising debates on Turkish and local Dutch politics, *Millî Görüş* mosques were also involved in organising demonstrations and petitions against, for example, new immigration laws or the war in Bosnia.

Millî Görüş in Germany and the Netherlands

Millî Görüş (IGMG) is not committed to the official Turkish Islam. In 1975, the movement started its activities in Rotterdam (henceforth for the Netherlands, *Millî Görüş*), and in 1976 the Islamic Community of *Millî Görüş* (IGMG Germany) was founded as an offspring of the association the Turkish Union of Europe, with a strong focus on political issues in Turkey.

IGMG is the largest Muslim community in Europe, with 300,000 members, and also the largest in Germany, with 87,000 members and 323 mosques (in 2006). IGMG integrates about 10 per cent of Muslims in Germany. There are 600 member associations of IGMG in Europe and 274 in Germany. *Millî Görüş*, the 'National Vision', referring to a 'religious perspective', is an Islamic social and political movement in Turkey with several branches in Europe (Bernts et al, 2006, p 120). In contrast to *Diyanet*, *Millî Görüş* forces Muslims to observe Islamic rules in general, and advocates Islam against immoral capitalism (Landman, 1992, p 120). IGMG had intensive links to Necmettin Erbakan, leader of the Welfare Party of the Turkish government that tried to fight against the secularisation of Islamic countries (especially Turkey), allegedly caused by the European Market (Landman, 1992; van Bruinessen, 2004a). In 1984, the member organisation ICCB (Association of Islamic Clubs and Congregations) formed a separate radical Islamic group which was prohibited in 2001, and the fundamentalist leader Cemalettin Kaplan was deported to Turkey without possibility of parole (BVerwG, judgment of 27 November 2002, 6 A 4.02 [see www.aufenthaltstitel.de/stichwort/bverwg. html]; BMF, 1999) (Werle and Kreile, 1987; Schiffauer, 2000; Seidel et al, 2000).

Hence, for years IGMG has been observed by the Federal Office for the Protection of the Constitution and was classified as anti-constitutional and anti-Semitic (Topuz, 2003; BMF, 2009). In 2008, this charge was revised by the Federal Administrative Court in Leipzig, because the Federal Office for the Protection of the Constitution could not prove any Islamist action (*Die Welt*, 2008). Today, it is still supposed that IGMG gets financial support by radical Islamic states. With the generational member change from the first immigrants to migrants of the second and third generations, the close bonds to Turkey have diluted. However, in December 2009, the IGMG headquarters in Kerpen (near Cologne) was searched by the police because members of the management were suspected of embezzling charitable donations.

In contrast to the German organisation, *Millî Görüş* Netherlands formed separate northern and southern associations, and had to defend themselves against fundamentalist reprovals, although less so than in Germany. In 1975, the *Millî Görüş* movement started its activities in the Netherlands in Rotterdam and since 1987 it has been represented by the Dutch Islamic Federation (NIF) (Waardenburg, 2001, p 18). In 1997, due to internal power struggles and disagreements about the overall mission of the organisation (focusing more on Turkish politics or integration in the Netherlands), the organisation split up. As a result, *Millî Görüş* now has two umbrella organisations in the Netherlands. While the northern branch, Milli Görüs Noord-Nederlands (MGNN) focuses explicitly on the integration, emancipation and participation of their members in Dutch society, the southern branch (NIF) is more conservative and aims at supporting and representing its members, who are encouraged to maintain their cultural-religious identity.[2] After the attempt to gain power had failed, *Millî Görüş* has become more involved in issues related to the integration of their members. The northern branch has been engaged in various government-subsidised projects, including projects about creating awareness of honour killings and domestic violence, the prevention of radicalisation, participation of Muslim women in executive functions, training of imams, and so on. Representatives of MGNN have also regularly been invited by ministers to discuss integration-related issues. NIF is a member of the Consultation Body Turkey (IOT), and both the northern and southern branches are part of the CMO.

The formerly close relations between the northern branch and public authorities have deteriorated over the last few years as a result of conflicts concerning the ambitious plan to build a new mosque in Amsterdam (the Westermosque, named after the close-by Westerchurch), including housing, offices and parking facilities. What seemed to become a success of state–religion cooperation ended in a deadlock, when conflict arose over the ground deal (*gronddeal*), both within the municipal council and the *Millî Görüş* movement. Internal disagreement within the movement resulted in changes in the leadership of the northern branch. In 2006, the German headquarters dismissed the board of MGNN, which had become known for its progressive ideas and openness towards Dutch society. Negotiations concerning the mosque building failed. The government's main concern was the negative influence of the conservative European headquarters on the progressive Dutch *Millî Görüş* (cf Lindo, 2008). However, in response to parliament questions about the German influence on changes in the leadership of MGNN, the Minister of Integration stated that these concerns were largely ungrounded.

In an investigation for the Ministry of Housing, Neighbourhoods and Integration on the aims and activities of *Millî Görüş* Netherlands, Lindo (2008) draws similar conclusions. Although the European headquarters are involved in accepting and swearing in new leaders, they do not select candidates who are selected by members of local mosque boards. The author also refutes accusations of radicalisation and the alleged Janus face of the movement, which is the common view in Germany. Rather he points out that there are some leaders within the movement – especially from the first generation of migrants – with more orthodox attitudes than the majority (Lindo, 2008, pp 44-5). Although individual *Millî Görüş* members have been victims, and individual board members were involved as intermediaries, the Authority for Financial Markets concluded that *Millî Görüş* organisations as such were not involved in any illegal financial transactions (Lindo, 2008, pp 9-10).

Diyanet in Germany and the Netherlands

Most Turkish Islamic organisations are part of the Turkish *Diyanet İşleri Başkanlığı* (DIB), the Steering Committee of Religious Affairs in Turkey. In 1982, *Diyanet İşleri Türk İslam* Birliği (DiTiB) (Turkish Islamic Union of the Institute for Religions) was founded in Berlin including 15 registered mosques as a regional formation of DIB. Its two Dutch umbrella organisations are TICF (*Turks Islamitische Culturele Federatie*) and ISN (*Islamitische Stichting Nederland*). TICF was founded in 1979 to spread Islamic culture and to act as an umbrella organisation of Turkish mosque associations.[3]

With these foundations the Turkish government reacted to the formation of religious associations, some of them supported by radical, anti-laicistic and anti-kemalistic groups from Turkey. Therefore, *Diyanet* acts as representation of the official Turkish state policy and the kemalistic framework in the EU. Currently,

Diyanet is – in some references – meant to be the largest Islamic group, and cooperates closely with the governmental Presidium of Religious Affairs in Turkey.

Whereas TICF has 140 local member associations, ISN owns – on behalf of DIB – the Dutch *Diyanet* mosques (den Exter and Hessels, 2003, p 6). In 2003, there were 151 *Diyanet* mosques in the Netherlands (Bernts et al, 2006, p 118). ISN is directly connected to the Turkish government (via the embassy), and TICF depicts itself as a non-political, independent service organisation. According to the respondents in the FACIT survey, TICF aims to facilitate the integration of its members in Dutch society while retaining Turkish Islamic identity. TICF organises meetings to exchange information with their member organisations about current issues, coordinates a funeral fund (to repatriate the deceased to Turkey) and participates in the Consultation Body Turkey (*Inspraakorgaan Turkije*, IOT), and CMO.

Currently, *Diyanet* Germany comprises 889 member associations, controls more than 800 mosques and has about 117,000 members (Zentralinstitut Islam Archiv Deutschland Stiftung eV, 2006). Their tasks are similar to the Dutch organisations: funeral services and organising pilgrimages to Mecca and Qur'an courses are also offered including religious education. In both countries, imams are employed by the Turkish government. They work for four years abroad and are then sent back and replaced. Hence, these civil servants are often not familiar with life in other countries and the specific problems of the Muslim minority. Furthermore, their language skills are limited, although DIB recently prolonged foreign language training in Turkey and meanwhile the Turkish government is also promoting the training of imams in the host countries (Boender, 1999).

Diyanet claims that the German public does not know about the amount of its welfare activities, and although it cooperates with Christian FBOs concerning inter-faith dialogue and the integration of Turkish immigrants, they compete in some domains, for example, in running nurseries – Turkish parents prefer to place their children in Muslim nurseries, representatives claimed. However, *Diyanet's* social services provisions are limited because of a lack of governmental funds. Hence, *Diyanet* claims that Christian organisations hinder establishing such facilities. *Diyanet* depends on private donations, mobilised with reference to religious obligations and loyalty especially during special religious days, like Ramadan. In this respect, *Diyanet* mobilises some economic resources that otherwise could not have been mobilised. There is also competition between *Diyanet* and *Millî Görüş* for leadership of Sunni Muslims (see Problems of recognitions).

Welfare provision and services of Islamic organisations in the three countries

Although there are many FBOs in Turkey, the Sunni FBOs have dominated the field of social assistance for the poor. Their welfare provisions are more developed and well organised and the government is close to Sunni Islam that facilitates their work. The largest FBO is *Deniz Feneri Yardımlaşma ve Dayanışma Derneği* (Light House Aid and Solidarity Association). In 1996, during Ramadan, it was first started as a special television programme, namely 'City and Ramadan'. The major aim was to collect donations and to help the poor. The programme was broadcast on 'Kanal 7', one of the most influential Islamist–conservative television stations, found by leaders of the Welfare Party supported by Recep Tayyip Erdoğan, the former mayor of the Greater Istanbul Municipality. Due to the high demand of the audience who were eager to donate and to get support, it was moved to a weekly show named 'Deniz Feneri' (Light House). In 1998, it was registered as an association in Istanbul. Until 2009, Light House supported 500,000 families (equivalent to more than two million people) by providing food, shelter and money for healthcare and education. In addition to these activities, the organisation runs guest houses, public soup kitchens and occupational courses, runs projects such as 1001 Children Wishes, Water is Civilisation, Save a Life, Money-box for Little Donors, Social Support, Education Aid for Primary Schools, Health for Little Eyes, Hot Food and many more. It also provides social assistance in the form of foreign aid to poor Muslim countries such as Ethiopia, Iran, Indonesia and Lebanon. The association has been trying to expand its activities, although there are some suspicions about its link to *Deniz Feneri* in Germany. Some managers of *Deniz Feneri eV* were sentenced to three to five years' imprisonment due to illegal money transfer to Turkey. However, Light House was the first association to collaborate with *Millî Görüş* and mobilised donations of Islamists and pious people to combat poverty. After the split between the traditionalist and reformist wings of *Millî Görüş*, it has developed close relations with the JDP government and JDP-run municipalities.

Cansuyu is another FBO that is active in the field of social assistance, and was founded in 2005 in Ankara by former bureaucrats, mayors, deputies and ministers and activists of the Felicity Party (*Saadet Partisi*). *Cansuyu*'s activities are mainly focused on health, housing, education and employment, but, like other Sunni FBOs, during the month of Ramadan its activities increase. In 2008, during Ramadan, *Cansuyu* helped 170,000 people by providing donations and food. The organisation is predominantly funded by private organisations and members of organisations and has a pronounced Islamist discourse and apparent links to *Millî Görüş*. It also works nationwide in 36 Muslim countries, in particular Pakistan, Afghanistan and Bangladesh. However, in contrast to Light House, *Cansuyu* is less well-structured.

In 2002, similar to Light House, *Kimse Yok Mu* ('Is there anybody to help') was started as a television programme. It was broadcast by a television station, Samanyolu, run by followers of the Fethullah Gülen community, one of the most influential Turkish Islamist religious communities with its transnational business, media and private school networks. In 2004, the television show led to the setting up of a welfare association. *Kimse Yok Mu* focuses on collecting money, in-kind benefits and helping the poor. Its main aim is to become a bridge between the rich and the poor, and this is the main difference in contrast to other FBOs. Today, it is one of the most influential FBOs in Turkey and runs offices in many Western European, American, Canadian and Australian cities where immigrants from Turkey live. It also provides foreign aid to Muslim countries, in particular Bangladesh, Pakistan and the Sudan. Similar to other FBOs, it has also put special emphasis on religious events and ceremonies, for example, distributing free food during Ramadan and financing circumcision campaigns for poor boys. In addition to these activities, the association donates school materials to poor families and repairs houses destroyed by natural disasters. One of its leading projects is 'Sister Family' that aims to courage well-off families to support poor families. This project was meant to create the spirit of brotherhood experienced during the time of the 'Messengership of Prophet Muhammad'.

As a public institution, *Diyanet* also has a foundation, namely, the Diyanet Foundation, established on 13 March 1975 by a group of professionals. The organisation works both on the national and the international scale. In 1977, the organisation had achieved a tax exemption and also the right to collect money without any prior permission from the authorities. Its official aims are to help *Diyanet* in representing and teaching the principles of Islam, to help build mosques and to repair them if needed, and to help convey the donations to the poor and needy. It also helps *Diyanet*'s imams and provides scholarships to imam-hatip students.

Problems of recognition, equal treatment and religious freedom

Following Rath et al (2001), the degree and form of institutionalisation of Islam in Western Europe can be understood as the outcome of interactions between Muslim initiatives and the receiving society (including legislation, judiciary, government and organisations).[4] This framework can be applied to explain some of the similarities and differences in the collective action of Turkish Islamic organisations and the efforts to create a Muslim umbrella organisation in the Netherlands and Germany.

Different political opportunity structures have resulted in remarkable differences between the two countries. In 2007, only 35.1 per cent of the Turks in Germany acquired citizenship, as opposed to 72.8 per cent of the Turks in the Netherlands (2010) (Eurostat, 2007). Germany has the lowest rate of naturalisations in the entire Europe (Eurostat, 2007). This fact is based on different migrant and religious policies, for example, referring to religion–state relations.

In this context, Vermeulen (2005, p 90) demonstrates that the more favourable opportunity structures in the Netherlands have led to a much larger number of organisations per 1,000 Turkish inhabitants. Several studies have also pointed out that the Netherlands has been more accommodating to Muslims' religious needs than Germany (Rath et al, 2001; Fetzer and Soper, 2005; Koenig, 2005).[5] Although both Germany and the Netherlands are known as the corporatist types of welfare states, divergent state–religion practices and citizenship and integration policies have provided different political opportunities for Muslims' collective action and the institutionalisation of Islam. Two major reasons account for this difference.

In terms of historical state–religion relations, the Netherlands developed from a relatively tolerant polity dominated by the Calvinist church to a 'pillarised' society (Yukleyen, 2010); since the 1960s, secularisation has put this pillarised system under pressure and led to the constitutional separation of the state and church in 1983, and the pillarisation legacy provided favourable opportunities for Muslims to establish mosques, state-financed Muslim Islamic schools and broadcasting organisations (Rath et al, 2001).[6] In order to guarantee the religious freedom of Muslims, between 1976 and 1983, two temporary grant schemes were available for the establishment of places of worship for Muslims (Rath et al, 2001, pp 45-7). In 1983, the constitutional separation of state and church prevented further public financing of religion, and improved the bargaining position of Muslims. In 1983, ministers entered into discussions with several representatives of Christian churches and of Humanist, Hindu and Muslim groups, to determine how state–religion issues should be dealt with in a new era of state–religion relations. According to Rath et al (2001, p 35), 'The participation of Muslims in these discussions can be regarded as an important milestone in the actual recognition of Islam.' Unlike Germany, the Netherlands has no system of formal legal recognition of religions, because the state intends to be neutral and equal treatment prohibits a system of selective recognition of organised religions. Rather, recognition of Islam in the Netherlands takes place in the form of recognising an interlocutor for Muslims (which are currently CMO and CGI, see page 224). In addition, in the areas of education (faith-based schools), spiritual care and public broadcasting, formal recognition of faith-based organisations takes place through specific legislation.

Integration policies, especially minorities policy (Ministerie van Binnenlandse Zaken, 1983), have also provided opportunities for Islamic organisations in the Netherlands. The minorities policy was developed in the early 1980s and aimed at the emancipation of minority ethnic groups, who were stimulated to retain their cultural and religious identity. As Islamic organisations were considered important partners for the implementation of the new policy, the Department of Internal Affairs initiated a dialogue with Islamic organisations to establish a National Advice and Consultation Structure consisting of sub-committees of minority ethnic groups. Via the minorities policy different Islamic FBOs were included in consultative structures to represent community interests (Turkish Islamic organisations in the Consultation Platform for Turks, IOT, established in 1991). It resulted in structural cooperation between Turkish groups that formerly competed and also provided Turkish Islamic organisations with funding possibilities in some municipalities. The consultation structure set up for the purpose of the minorities policies also proved instrumental for the national government to get in contact with the most important Islamic organisations in times of crisis (for example, the Rushdie affair, the Gulf War, the murder of Theo Van Gogh etc). Although in the 1990s the minorities policy was replaced by new integration policies focused on the individual integration of migrants, Islamic organisations are still eligible for funding and part of consultation structures in some municipalities.

In contrast, German government (even in 2011) finds it hard to officially recognise Islam, one issue being the way some Islamic organisations deal with fundamentalists. Another issue is that the German government requires one representative as a negotiation partner regardless of the different origins and congregations of Muslims, for example, Arabs, former Yugoslavians and Turks, Sunni, Shiite and Alevi. Islam lacks religious leaders and baptisms, which was requested as a basis for member registration, inturn that impedes supplying valid membership figures. Furthermore, topics such as the wearing of headscarves and inequality are still being debated, and specific regulations, such as wearing headscarves in school, have to be passed by the *Länder* and not the national government.

The German official registration of religious denominations as 'cooperate bodies of public law' (*Körperschaft öffentlichen Rechts*) is combined with many advantages, for example, government-paid clergymen (*alim*), religious education at schools, Islamic theology implemented at German universities and exemption from corporate tax. This status is given to the Catholic church, the Greek Orthodox church, the Protestant church and the Jewish community.

Hence, the issue for Muslims in Germany is not whether the state should accommodate religion in public institutions but whether the state will expand its informal religious establishment to include Islam (Soper and Fetzer, 2007). Van Bruinessen (2004a) documents that European societies impose different ways of asserting Muslim identity. In Germany, the Court of Law is a major arena of communication, while in the Netherlands there is a permanent process of negotiation and gradual adaptation. Moreover, contrary to the Netherlands, Germany did not view itself as a country of immigration until the late 1990s. Corresponding to German citizenship law – until 1999 based on *ius sanguinis* – Islam has been dealt with for a long time as a foreign religion, and German authorities cooperated mainly with the Turkish *Diyanet* (Odmalm, 2009).

Sunier (1999, p 81) has argued that branches of the *Millî Görüş* movement adopted a much more radical and anti-Western discourse in Germany than in the Netherlands, due to the lack of communication networks and the unwillingness of German authorities to cooperate with them. In the Netherlands, *Millî Görüş* (especially the northern branch) has developed more independence from political and religious influences from both Turkey and Germany (Vermeulen, 2005, p 73). Odmalm (2009) similarly argues that Turks in the Netherlands have enjoyed fairly inclusive state policies and benefited from a corporatist tradition in policy making, while the lack of such formal platforms of participation in Germany have redirected participation of Turks to the supranational level.

Although these divergent political opportunity structures might explain some differences between Turkish Islamic organisations in the Netherlands and Germany, political opportunity structures do change over time. In this context we might look at European legislation regarding religious freedom and anti-discrimination (see, for instance, Ferrari, 2002; Koenig, 2005), recent changes in citizenship legislation (the introduction of civic integration requirements for naturalisation in both the

Netherlands and Germany) and the securitisation of Islam post-9/11 (also Avcı, 2006; Haddad and Golson, 2007).

Østergaard-Nielsen (2001) points out that the landscape of Turkish political, ethnic and religious movements in the Netherlands and Germany is remarkably similar despite the different political opportunity structures. In both countries the organising process of Turkish Muslim immigrants has been strongly influenced by ideological cleavages imported from Turkey. According to Doomernik (1991, pp 97-8), however, initially *Diyanet* was not as influential in Germany as in the Netherlands, mainly because *Millî Görüş* and other groups were more active in Germany and *Diyanet* came later. Both countries have struggled (and are still struggling) with the creation of a national umbrella organisation representing Muslims. Several authors have pointed out that the diversity of Muslims in Western Europe (in terms of origins, ethnicity, language and religious beliefs) and the fact that (Sunni) Islam has no tradition of being a hierarchical centralised organised religion (Vertovec and Peach, 1997; Ferrari, 2005; Warner and Wenner, 2006) have hampered the formation of Muslim national umbrella organisations in Western Europe. However, while in Germany Turkish Muslims are by far the largest Muslim group, in the Netherlands they are – albeit the largest – one group among others, which might have stimulated or even forced collaboration.

Links of Dutch and German organisations to Turkey

It is a well-known fact that the majority of Turkish migrants in Germany and the Netherlands as well as in other Western European countries have always maintained dense, multifaceted and continuous relations with Turkey. Above all, almost of them have preserved their ties with relatives left behind. Moreover, all Turkish migrant (religious or non-religious) organisations have had close relations with their counterparts in Turkey (see Friedrichs and Klöckner, 2011, p 47; see also, Abdullah, 1981; Lemmen, 2001).

ISN (*Diyanet*) is closely linked to the Turkish government, and administered mainly by embassy personnel. The Turkish *Diyanet* sends imams and literature to Turkish mosques in the Netherlands and has also started so-called imam-hatip education for Dutch Turks in Turkey (Waardenburg, 2001, p 72). *Millî Görüş* has close relations with the headquarters in Cologne, which determines the religious agenda of the movement and coordinates collective religious activities.

Thus, we conclude that all Turkish religious and political groups can be found in Western European countries. Nonetheless, from the outset Turkish governments have not developed well-defined, comprehensive and long-term policies with regards to the problems and demands of Turkish immigrants in Western European countries. They have seen international migration as a solution for the reduction of the unemployment rate and considered worker remittances as an important source for financing the chronic foreign currency deficits of the Turkish economy. In other words, during the 1960s and 1970s, Turkish governments did not develop a systematic attempt to reinforce links between Turkish immigrant organisations and Turkey. On the other hand, until the 1980s, Turkish religious organisations were not powerful and well organised. Most of the Turkish immigrant organisations were led by leftist and socialist groups and generally focused on the social-economic problems of migrant workers. However, two developments were crucial in diverting the Turkish state's attention to Turkish immigrants and their organisations. First, the Iranian revolution in 1979 gave a powerful impetus to the mobilisation of Islamist and fundamentalist groups in Turkey as well as in Western Europe. It not only radically changed the international environment, but also became a model for Islamist and fundamentalist groups worldwide. The new regime in Iran supported fundamentalist groups in other countries to disseminate its ideology and widen its international influence. Furthermore, the invasion of Afghanistan by the Soviet Red Army in 1979 and the Afghan Jihad led by the Saudis contributed to the radicalisation and internationalisation of Islamist movements. These two international developments also had a remarkable impact on Islamic organisations in Turkey as well as in Western Europe. But under the military regime of 1980, it was relatively easy to control the radicalisation of Islamist groups in Turkey. Indeed, the military regime used two strategies at the same time. It promoted the interpretation of Sunni Islam through the official religious bodies and covertly cooperated with specific religious groups, but attempted to control political activities of radicalised Islamist groups. Thus, the question was to control and block the activities of Turkish Islamist organisations in Germany and other Western European countries.

Second, after the 1980 military coup in Turkey, thousands of leftists and socialists had to escape from Turkey. Most became refugees in Western Europe. They attempted to mobilise Turkish migrant workers against the Turkish military regime. Indeed, allied with leftist and socialist groups in the host countries, they organised mass demonstrations, public panels, forums and other activities to protest against the military regime in Turkey.

These two developments, the radicalisation of Turkish Islamist groups and the activities of leftist and socialist refugees in the Western European countries, were deemed dangerous by the military regime of 1980-83, which was keen on hindering the rising influence of Islamist and leftist organisations among Turkish immigrants. The main solution of the military rule was to send *Diyanet*'s imams to Germany and other Western countries where Turkish immigrants had begun to become permanent residents. After the military regime, civilian governments have also maintained this policy of sending *Diyanet*'s imams to Western Europe. Within 20 years, *Diyanet* has become one of the largest and most powerful Turkish Islamic organisations in Western Europe. From the outset, the main aim of *Diyanet*'s activities in Western European countries has been to foster the loyalty of Turkish immigrants to Turkey. In the post-9/11 world, the Turkish state has begun to use *Diyanet* as a foreign policy tool. Through *Diyanet*'s activities, it has also attempted to promote Turkish Islam as a model for Muslims in Europe. Therefore, *Diyanet*'s branches in Germany and the Netherlands can be seen as an extension of the Turkish state (Avcı, 2004, p 207; Çitak, 2010, p 620).

Since the 1970s, the term 'Millî Görüş' has been used to identify the religious-political movement founded and led by Necmettin Erbakan and his close associates in Turkey. Since its inception, *Millî Görüş* has established a series of Islamist parties: the National Order Party (*Millî Nizam Partisi*), founded in 1969 and closed in 1971 by the Constitutional Court, the National Salvation Party (*Millî Selamet Partisi*), founded in 1972 and closed in 1980 by the military regime. However, during the 1970s, the National Salvation Party stayed in power for more than four years as a coalition partner in three governments. It was the only party whose term in power was longer than other parties. With the transition to civilian rule in 1983, Erbakan's close associates founded the Welfare Party (*Refah Partisi*). It stayed in power for over a year as the main coalition partner with the centre-right party in the mid-1990s.

In the 1994 municipal elections, the Welfare Party won 19.7 per cent of the national votes and took control of the mayor's office in 28 large cities, including Istanbul and Ankara. A year before its dissolution in 1998, the *Millî Görüş* leaders founded the Virtue Party (*Fazilet Partisi*). But in 2001 it was also closed by the Constitutional Court. After its closure, *Millî Görüş* was divided into two: the traditionalists and the reformists. In 2001, the traditionalists founded the Felicity Party (*Saadet Partisi*) led by Erbakan and his close friends. However, in 2001, the reformists collaborated with some prominent figures from centre-right parties led by Recep Tayyip Erdoğan and Abdullah Gül and established the Justice and Development Party (JDP) (*Adalet ve Kalkınma Partisi*). From the outset, this party has defined its identity as conservative democratic to distance itself from the Islamist stance of *Millî Görüş*. Since 2002, JDP has been in power and has also run the majority of municipalities, including Istanbul and Ankara.

During the 1950s, Erbakan studied mechanical engineering in Germany. He displayed a special interest in Turkish immigrants abroad and closely directed the development of *Millî Görüş* branches in Germany and the Netherlands. For instance, between 1996 and 2002, Sabri Erbakan, his nephew, led German *Millî Görüş*. Indeed, European *Millî Görüş* has always maintained organic links to the *Millî Görüş* parties led by Erbakan. In particular in the 1980s, European *Millî Görüş* had taken an important role in sustaining the electoral base of the Welfare Party. The party received financial support and *Millî Görüş* actively participated in its electoral campaigns as well. Furthermore, in the 1995 and 1999 general elections, German *Millî Görüş*'s leading figures became candidates of the *Millî Görüş* parties for the Turkish parliament and some of them became MPs.

The split between traditionalists and reformists in Turkey has also concerned European *Millî Görüş* branches, especially in the Netherlands. But European *Millî Görüş* branches are, to a large extent, loyal to Erbakan and have sustained organic links to the Felicity Party. Nevertheless, the JDP government is also willing to maintain good and close relations with European *Millî Görüş*. Indeed, in 2003, the then foreign minister Abdullah Gül formally advised Turkish embassies to cooperate with *Millî Görüş* in Europe. This made European *Millî Görüş* a more 'acceptable partner for the Turkish state' and also turned the relationship between

Millî Görüş and *Diyanet* into less of an 'adversarial' relationship (Avcı, 2005, pp 207, 210).

Rath and Meyer (1997, p 392) point out that since the end of the 1980s the relation between Islamic organisations and religious movements in the countries of origin have loosened considerably, as second generation immigrants took over leadership.

Summary and policy implications

Comparing Islamic organisations indicates the extent of the institutionalisation of Islam to be a crucial condition, as the different results from Germany and the Netherlands clearly indicate. The Netherlands have made much more progress in accepting Islam and Islamic organisations representing the Islam (and not only Turkish residents) community and has agreed to Islamic education in schools. Ironically, Germany has no comparable structure (although the Alevis are accepted and achieved to have Islamic school courses). The government has to deal with surrogates, such as the Islamic Conference. Founded in 2006, it comprises federal, regional and local authorities, "it is considered as the most important forum between the German state and Muslims living in Germany" (DIK 2012). Yet, the question remains, why is it so difficult to create a unified body representing all Islamic Schools of religion?

Thus, in the Netherlands, the situation for Islamic religion and for acceptance is much more legally institutionalised than in Germany. The Netherlands includes Islamic organisations as possible partners in local social policies; they have successfully applied multicultural policy. They have Islam organisations such as CMO, with which the government is able to discuss policy issues. From this we may infer a much broader acceptance of Islam and Muslims in the Netherlands (Yukleyen, 2010). However, the Dutch population seems to be split over integration issues. In June 2009, the country was shocked when the right-wing and anti-Islam politician Geert Wilders gained 17 per cent of the votes for the European parliament elections. The unexpected result imposed a discussion on what was 'Dutch' and how tolerant the citizens of the country were. Would this bring about a change in assimilation policy, as Vasta (2007) argues? This issue anticipated the debate initiated by the French President one year later on 'identité française'. A similar discussion emerged in 2010 in Denmark about 'Danishness'. Behind a veil of tolerance and seemingly achieved integration the government claims, and most Dutch believe to exist, that there are anti-ethnic movements of discontent, only seldom uttered in public but that come up in elections by votes for right-wing parties – resorting to a potential loss of national identity – be it Dutch, French, German or another identity. But this process works on both sides. Islamic organisations cater for Muslims in a European country and have to adopt their strategies to their host countries, eventually reorienting their identity, the result probably being a 'modernised' or 'European Islam' (cf Nielsen, 1999; Modood et al, 2006; Nökel and Tezcan, 2005). Yukleyen (2010, p 448) states, 'the constitutional protection of religious freedoms and the simultaneous intervention into the internal affairs of Muslims has proven a dilemma – than it is only part of the problem.' Honour killing, forced marriages, male violence in marriages or non-participation in school swimming courses interfere with (not only) the German constitution and press Islamic organisations to adopt more tolerant values. In their careful discussion of Islam positions and integration policies in Europe, Yazbeck and Golson (2007, p 497) conclude, 'the internal makeup of European Islam ultimately emerges out of Muslim initiative, while the secular state reserves only the right to set the external limits of group activities in keeping with legal standards.'

In Germany, Islam has to be officially recognised, although not as a church, which serves as a criterion for recognition, but Islam is a part of society. This would be the precondition for several changes in the status of Islam. First, Islamic organisations could be included into the German system of welfare organisations, which implies that they get refunded for at least part of the services they deliver. Moreover, it would allow better catering for the interests and demands of the Turkish population. Second, it would promote the demand for the university education of Islam teachers and in the long run the education of future imam teachers, instead of 'importing' them from Turkey. These imams would know more about the German society and therefore be better prepared to deal with the Turkish German population and their demands.

However, another major obstacle has to be overcome, as successfully done in Austria: to reconcile Turkish and Arab Islam associations, a divide which still hampers establishing a unified Islam body, which will function as an Islamic representative and deal with German administrations at the city, regional and national level.

With respect to Turkey, we arrive at two policy implications. The major task is to establish a welfare state independent of parties. We assume a learning process of Turkish FBOs in Germany and the Netherlands of how to transfer new techniques and arguments to Turkey. The second is to assist Islamic organisations in gaining recognition and professionalism. It may be the role of Turkish Islamic FBOs in the so-called integration of Turkish immigrants into German and Dutch societies.

Notes

[1] For the same reason, shortage of labour, the Netherlands signed recruitment contracts in the 1960s with countries from Southern Europe, then with Turkey and Morocco.

[2] On the website www.milligorus.nl/ it can be read that MGNN aims to represent the religious and social interests of Turkish Muslims in North Netherlands and to stimulate their integration, emancipation and participation in Dutch society by supporting activities of individual members.

[3] The DIB-related organisations in Germany and the Netherlands are further called *Diyanet*; the Committee of Religious Affairs in Turkey is further called DIB.

[4] Rath et al (2001) describe the responses of the receiving society in terms of the active promotion of and support for the formation of new Muslim institutions, passive and more or less neutral attitudes, and active opposition towards religious claims and organisations (see, for example, Rath et al, 2001, pp 10-11).

[5] Koenig (2005) has explained the variance in the accommodation of Islam in the UK, France and Germany by divergent institutional environments, which, according to him, are the result of historical paths of state and nation building. In their analysis of the accommodation of Islam in Britain, France and Germany, Fetzer and Soper (2005) focus on the importance of historical state–church relations to explain differences in the accommodation of Islam.

[6] In spite of the importance of the legacy of religious pillarisation, an Islamic pillar did not develop. There is, for instance, no Islamic newspaper, hospitals, trade union or political party or. There has been no Islamic welfare organisation either, apart from the Foundation Welfare for Muslims established in 1975 in the context of categorical welfare policies aimed at the Surinamese community in Amsterdam.

References

Avcı, G. (2006) 'Comparing integration policies and outcomes: Turks in the Netherlands and Germany', *Turkish Studies*, vol 7, no 1, pp 67-84.

Avcı, Z. (2005) 'Religion, transnationalism and Turks in Europe', *Turkish Studies*, vol 6, no 1, pp 201-13.

Bernts, T., de Jong, G. and Yar, H. (2006) 'Een religieuze atlas van Nederland', [*A religious atlas of the Netherlands*] in W.B.H.J. van de Donk, A.P. Jonkers, G.J. Kronjee and R.J.J.M. Plum (eds) *Geloven in het publieke domein: Verkenningen van een dubbele transformative*, [*Religion in the public domain: explorations of a double transformation*] Amsterdam: Amsterdam University Press/Wetenschappelijke Raad voor het Regeringsbeleid WRR, pp 89-138.

BMF (Bundesamt für Migration und Flüchtlinge) (1999) *Verfassungsschutzbericht 1999*, [*Report of the Federal Office for the Protection of the Constitution 1999*] Berlin. (www.bmi.bund.de/publikationen/in_spezialpublikationen.html).

BMF (2009) *Ausländerzahlen 2008* [*Non-German Population Data 2008*] (www.bamf.de/cln_101/nn_442496/SharedDocs/Anlagen/DE/DasBAMF/Downloads/Statistik/statistik-anlage-teil-2-auslaendezahlen-auflage14,templateId=raw,property=publicationFile.pdf/statistik-anlage-teil-2-auslaendezahlen-auflage14.pdf).

Boender, W. (1999) *Imams in the Netherlands*, C.I.E. Newsletter 1, pp 23–28.

Canatan, K., Oudijk, C.H. and Ljamai, A. (2003) *De maatschappelijke rol van de Rotterdamse moskeeën* [*The social role of the mosques in Rotterdam*] Rotterdam: Centrum voor Onderzoek en statistiek.

Canatan, K., Popovic, M. and Edinga, R. (2005) *Maatschappelijk actief in moskeeverband: Een verkennend onderzoek naar de maatschappelijke activiteiten van, en het vrijwilligerswerk binnen moskeeorganisaties en het gemeentelijk beleid ten aanzien van moskeeorganisaties,* [*Active citizenship in the context mosques: An exploratory study on the social activities of and voluntary work in and mosques within the municipal policy of mosque organizations*] 's-Hertogenbosch: IHSAN.

Çitak, Z. (2010) 'Between "Turkish Islam" and "French Islam": the role of the Diyanet in the Conseil Français du Culte Musulman', *Journal of Ethnic and Racial Studies,* vol 36, no 4, pp 619-34.

den Exter, J. and Hessels, T. (2003) 'Organisaties van minderheden' [Organisation of minorities], in J. Overdijk-Francis, H. Smeets, C. Tazelaar and J. Verheyden, *Handboek Minderheden,* [*Minorities handbook*] Houten: Bohn Stafleu Van Loghum, pp 1-34.

Die Welt (2008) 'Umstrittener Verein Millî Görüş siegt vor Gericht' [(Disputed Organisation Milli Görüs wins court case) (www.welt.de/politik/article2020862/Umstrittener_Verein_Millî_Goerues_siegt_vor_Gericht.html).

DIK (2012) *Tasks and objectives* (http://www.deutsche-islam-konferenz.de/cln_227/nn_1917164/SubSites/DIK/EN/AufgabenZiele/Inhalte/inhalte-node.html?__nnn=true, 12.6.2012).

Doomernik, J. (1991) *Turkse moskeeën en maatschappelijke participatie: De institutionalisering van de Turkse Islam in Nederland en de Duitse Bondsrepubliek,* [*Turkish mosques and social participation: the institutionalization of Turkish Islam in the Netherlands and the German Federal Republic*] Amsterdam: Amsterdam University Press.

Driessen, D., van der Werf, M. and Boulal, A. (2004) *Laat het van twee kanten komen: eindrapportage van een (quick scan) van de maatschappelijke rol van moskeeën in Amsterdam,* Amsterdam: Nieuwe Maan Communicatie Adviesgroep.

Eurostat (2006) *Statistik kurzgefasst. Bevölkerung und soziale Bedingungen* [*Statistics in brief. Population and social conditions*] www.eds-destatis.de/de/downloads/sif/nk_06_08.pdf, 25.11.2009.

Eurostat (2007) *Bevölkerung* [*Population*] http://epp.eurostat.ec.europa.eu/portal/page/portal/population/introduction, 1.6.2012

Fetzer, J.S. and Soper, J.C. (2005) *Muslims and the state in Britain, France, and Germany,* Cambridge: Cambridge University Press.

Ferrari, S. (2002) 'Islam and the western European model of church–state relations', in W.A. Shadid and P.S. van Koningsveld (eds) *Religious freedom and the neutrality of the state: Responses to the presence of Islam in the European Union,* Leuven: Peeters.

Ferrari, S. (2005) 'The secularity of the state and the shaping of Muslim representative organisations in Western Europe', in J. Cesari and S. McLoughlin (eds) *European Muslims and the secular state,* Aldershot: Ashgate.

Forum (2008) *The position of Muslims in the Netherlands: Facts and figures,* Utrecht: Forum.

Friedrichs, J. (1988) 'Makro- und mikrosoziologische Theorien der Segregation', [Macro- and micro-sociological theories of segregation] *Soziologische Stadtforschung. Kölner Zeitschrift für Soziologie und Sozialpsychologie,* vol 29, pp 56-77.

Friedrichs, J. and Triemer, S. (2009) *Gespaltene Städte? Soziale und ethnische Segregation in deutschen Großstädten* [*Split cities? Social and ethnic segregation in large German cities*], Wiesbaden: VS Verlag für Sozialwissenschaften (GWV).

Friedrichs, J. and Klöckner, J. (2011) *Faith-based organisations and social exclusion in Germany*, Vol 2, Leuven: Acco.

Gijsberts, M. and Dagevos, J. (2010) *At home in the Netherlands? Trends in integration of non-western migrants*, The Hague: The Netherlands Institute for Social Research.

Haddad, Y.Y. and Golson, T. (2007) 'Overhauling Islam: representation, construction, and cooption of "moderate Islam" in Western Europe', *Journal of Church and State*, vol 49, no 3, pp 487-516.

Halm, D. and Sauer, M. (2007) *Bürgerschaftliches Engagement von Türkinnen und Türken in Deutschland* [*Volunteering of Turks in Germany*], Wiesbaden: VS Verlag für Sozialwissenschaften.

Haug, S., Müssig, S. and Stichs, A. (2009) *Muslimisches Leben in Deutschland. Im Auftrag der Deutschen Islam Konferenz* (www.bamf.de/SharedDocs/Anlagen/DE/Publikationen/Forschungsberichte/fb06-muslimisches-leben.pdf?__blob=publicationFile) Accessed 30 August 2012.

Hero, M., V. Krech. and Zander, H. (eds) (2008) *Religiöse Vielfalt in Nordrhein-Westfalen* [Religious diversity in North-Rhine Westfalia), Paderborn: Schöningh.

Hunn, K. (2005) '*Nächstes Jahr kehren wir zurück...*' *Die Geschichte der türkischen 'Gastarbeiter' in der Bundesrepublik* [*'Next year we will go back" ... The history of the Turkish 'guestworkers' in Germany*], Göttingen: Wallstein Verlag.

Koenig, M. (2005) 'Incorporating Muslim migrants in Western nation states. A comparison of the United Kingdom, France, and Germany', *Journal of International Migration and Integration*, vol 6, no 2, pp 219-34.

Knortz, H. (2008) *Diplomatische Tauschgeschäfte. 'Gastarbeiter' in der westdeutschen Diplomatie und Beschäftigungspolitik 1953-1973* [*Diplomatic barter trade. 'Guestworkers' in West German diplomacy and employment policy, 1953-1973*], Köln: Böhlau Verlag.

Landman, N. (1992) *Van Mat tot Minaret*, VU Uitgeverij.

Lindo, F. (2008) 'Activiteiten en doelstellingen van Nederlandse organisaties gelieerd aan Millî Görüş', Onderzoek in opdracht van de minister voor Wonen, Wijken en Integratie, 14 oktober, Instituut voor Migratie- en Etnische Studies (IMES), Universiteit van Amsterdam.

Lemmen, T. (2001) *Muslime in Deutschland. Eine Herausforderung für Kirche und Gesellschaft* [*Muslims in Germany. A challenge for church and society*], Baden-Baden: Nomos.

Maréchal, B., Allievi, S., Dassetto, F. and Nielsen, J. (eds) (2003) *Muslims in the enlarged Europe*, Leiden, Boston: Brill.

Maussen, M. (2006) *Ruimte voor de islam? Stedelijk beleid, voorzieningen, organisaties* [*Space for Islam? Urban policy, facilities, organizations*], Apeldoorn/Antwerpen: Het Spinhuis.

Ministerie van Binnenlandse Zaken (1983) *Minderhedennota* [*Minorities Memorandum*], Den Haag: Staatsuitgeverij [Also in TK 1982-83, 16102, nr 21].

Modood, T., Trianafyllidou, A. and Zapata-Barrero, R. (eds) (2006) *Multiculturalism, Muslims and citizenship: A European approach*, New York: Routledge.

Netzeitung (2006) *Muslime in Europa* [*Muslims in Europe*] (www.netzeitung.de/sport/443264.html).

Nielsen, J.S. (1999) *Towards a European Islam*, Basingstoke: Macmillan.

Nökel, S. and Tezcan, L. (eds) (2005) *Islam and the new Europe: Continuities, changes, confrontations*, Piscataway, NJ: Transaction Publishers.

Odmalm, P. (2009) 'Turkish organisations in Europe: how national contexts provide different avenues for participation', *Turkish Studies*, vol 10, no 2, pp 149-63.

Østergaard-Nielsen, E. (2001) 'Transnational political practices and the receiving state: Turks and Kurds in Germany and the Netherlands', *Global Networks. A Journal of Transnational Affairs*, vol 1, no 3, pp 261-82.

Rath, J. and Meyer, A. (1997) 'The establishment of Islamic Institutions in a de-pillarizing society', *Tijdschrift voor Economische en Sociale Geografie*, vol 88, no 4, pp 389-95.

Rath, J., Penninx, R., Groenendijk, K. and Meyer, A. (2001) *Western Europe and its Islam*, Leiden: Brill Publishers.

Remid (2009) *Religionen in Deutschland: Mitgliederzahlen* [*Religions in Germany: Membership data*] (www.remid.de/remid_info_zahlen.htm).

Rieker, Y. (2003) *Ein Stück Heimat findet man ja immer. Die italienische Einwanderung in die Bundesrepublik* [*A piece of home you always find. Italian Migration to Germany*], Essen: Klartext.

Schiffauer, W. (2000) *Die Gottesmänner. Türkische Islamisten in Deutschland* [*God's Men: Turkish Islamists in Germany*], Frankfurt/Main: Suhrkamp.

Seidel, E., Dantschke, C. and Yildirim, A. (2000) 'Politik im Namen Allahs', [Politics in the Name of Allah] in O. Ceyhun (ed) *Der Islamismus – Eine Herausforderung für Europa* [*Islamism – A challenge for Europe*], Brüssel: MdEP.

Soper, J.C. and Fetzer, J. (2007) 'Religious institutions, church–state history and Muslim mobilisation in Britain, France and Germany', *Journal of Ethnic and Migration Studies*, vol 33, no 6, pp 933-44.

Spuler-Stegemann, U. (2005) 'Türkei', [Turkey] in W. Ende and U. Steinbach (eds) *Der Islam in der Gegenwart. 5. Aktualis*, Aufl, München: Beck, pp 229-46.

Statistics Netherlands, Voorburg/Heerlen (2008) *Yearbook 2008* (www.cbs.nl/NR/rdonlyres/163C8CBE-01F8-43DD-9B96-921425A4D1EE/0/2008a3pub.pdf).

Statistics Netherlands (2009) 'More than 850 thousand Muslims in the Netherlands' (www.cbs.nl/en-GB/menu/themas/vrije-tijd-cultuur/publicaties/artikelen/archief/2007/2007-2278-wm.htm).

Steinbach, U. (2002) *Islam in der Türkei*, [*Islam in Turkey*] Bonn: Bundeszentrale für politische Bildung, Informationen zur politischen Bildung, Heft 277.

Sunier, T. (1996) *Islam in beweging, Turkse jongeren en islamitische organisaties*, Amsterdam: Het Spinhuis.

Sunier, T. (1999) 'Muslim migrants, Muslim citizens. Islam and Dutch society', *Netherlands' Journal of Social Sciences*, vol 35, pp 69-82.

Tezcan, L. (2005) DITIB – eine Institution zwischen allen Stühlen (DITIB – An Organisation Sitting on the Fence), Bonn: Heinrich-Böll-Stiftung, www.migration-boell.de/web/integration/47_385.asp, 21.2.2011.

Topuz, G. (2003) *Entwicklung und Organisation von Milli Görüs in Deutschland (Formation and organisation of Milli Görüs in Germany)*, Kölner Arbeitspapiere zur internationalen Politik. www.holding-zedeler.de/htm/IMG_%20und_einsammeln.pdf, 14.3.2011.

van Bruinessen, M. (2004a) 'Millî Görüş in Western Europe', ISIM newsletter, 14 June.

van Bruinessen, M. (2004b) 'Millî Görüş in Western Europe', ISIM workshop, Leiden, 9 January, www.hum.uu.nl/medewerkers/m.vanbruinessen/conferences/Milli_Gorus_workshop_report.htm

van Heelsum, A., Fennema, M. and Tillie, J. (2004) 'Islamitische organisaties in Nederland', [Islamic organisations in the Netherlands] in K. Phalet and J. ter Wal (eds) *Moslim in Nederland*, Den Haag: Sociaal en Cultureel Planbureau.

van Herten, M. and Otten, F. (2007) *Naar een nieuwe schatting van het islamietten in Nederland*, [*Towards a new estimate of Islamic networks in the Netherlands*] Centraal Bureau voor de Statistiek (www.cbs.nl/NR/rdonlyres/ACE89EBE-0785-4664-9973-A6A00A457A55/0/2007k3b15p48art.pdf).

Vasta, E. (2007) 'From ethnic minorities to ethnic majority policy: multiculturalism and the shift to assimilation in the Netherlands', *Ethnic and Racial Studies*, vol 30, pp 713-40.

Vermeulen, F. (2005) *The immigrant organising process: The emergence and persistence of Turkish immigrant organisations in Amsterdam and Berlin and Surinamese organisations in Amsterdam, 1960-2000*, Amsterdam: IMES.

Vertovec, S. and Peach, C. (eds) (1997) *Islam in Europe. The politics of religion and community*, Houndmills: Macmillan.

Waardenburg, J.D.J. (2001) *Institutionele vormgeving van de Islam in Nederland gezien in Europees perspectief*, [*Institutional design of Islam in the Netherlands seen in a European perspective*] Den Haag: WRR Werkdocumenten, nr W118.

Warner, C.M. and Wenner, M.W. (2006) 'Religion and the political organization of Muslims in Europe', *Perspectives on Politics*, vol 4, no 3, pp 457-79.

Werle, R. and Kreile, R. (1987) *Renaissance des Islam. Das Beispiel Türkei*, [*Islam renaissance: The example Turkey*] Hamburg: Junius.

Yazbeck, H.Y. and Golson, T. (2007) 'Overhauling Islam: representation, construction, and cooption of "moderate Islam" in Western Europe', *Journal of Church & State*, vol 49, no 3, pp 487-515.

Yukleyen, A. (2010) 'State policies and Islam in Europe: Millî Görüş in Germany and the Netherlands', *Journal of Ethnic and Migration Studies*, vol 36, no 3, pp 445-63.

Zentralinstitut Islam-Archiv-Deutschland e.V. (2006) *Dokumentation No 1/2006, Frühjahrsumfrage, Neue Daten über den Islam in Deutschland* [*(Documentation No 1/2006, Spring Survey, New Data on Islam in Germany)*].

ELEVEN

Convictional communities

Samuel Thomas

In the context of the UK this chapter explores particular Christian faith-permeated practices in socioeconomically deprived areas. The chapter engages with forms of praxis that are born out of a critical dissidence with the way faith is often (not) translated into action and is at times physically distant from 'nearly forgotten places' (Thompson, 2010, p 120).

The importance of this chapter is to highlight an emerging turn in some faith-based organisational practice. While most faith-based organisations (FBOs) establish an organisational presence among the socially marginalised, there has recently been a move towards a more incarnational personal presence among such people (Cloke, 2010). This faith-motivated praxis involves choosing to live in among the excluded, serving as a neighbour rather than as a volunteer or worker, who vocationally breezes in and out of these areas.

There are three sections to this chapter. The first outlines how particular reflexive critiques have shaped portions of the Christian church to consider how it should re-engage and re-connect with socioeconomically deprived geographic communities. Drawing on three short case studies I examine how Christians in the UK have responded differently to these criticisms. The second section gives an account of the key discourses that structure this diverse range of faith-permeated practices: incarnation, community and mission. These discourses help collectively make sense of the vast array of faith-permeated practices discussed in the first section. Making sense of these discourses also draws out their motivational distinctiveness in comparison to their non-faith-based non-governmental organisation (NGO) counterparts. Drawing on a more in-depth case study, the third section highlights how these discourses are variously translated into action and embedded into a local geographic context. This brings light to some of the ways in which faith communities engage with local geographies and are enmeshed into emergent ethical spaces.

Critiquing the Christian church

Many critical questions have been asked of how the Christian faith should be practised in the light of the socioeconomic and political needs of surrounding communities. A good number of these criticisms have been from outside of faith networks (see Allahyari, 2000), while others have emanated from within (see Frost, 2006). Recently the resurgent critique that has prompted the Western church to question how it relates to 'the poor' has come from within (see Wilson, 2005; Claibourne, 2006; Bishop, 2007). Particular faith practitioners have questioned how urban Christian faith communities and FBOs should be structured, where they should be placed and what values should be central (see Frost, 2006; Graham and Low, 2009). To provide greater context and to elicit some of the passion that drives the forms of praxis at the centre of discussion in this chapter it is appropriate to dwell on this critique. In this instance, I consider the critical contribution of Gary Bishop, a faith-based practitioner working for The Salvation Army in the UK.

The critique by Bishop (2007), in his book *Darkest England: And the way back in*, suggests a two fold contradiction in what the Christian faith so often upholds as its central narratives. In the context of his own denominational movement, The Salvation Army, he writes that what has emerged is both a physical distance between churches and the marginalised, and a particular way of engaging with the marginalised, that is temporary and mediated through organisational and project-based contexts. He explains that the physical distance between the Western church and the poor has been exacerbated by the increasing wealth of those who practice Christianity. He highlights how The Salvation Army has grown from a 19th-century movement to a 21st-century respectable organisation, broadly being subject to an upward shift in socioeconomic terms. The gulf between the church and the marginalised has been further emphasised by the geographical relocation of many larger church congregations into out-of-town or industrial warehouses (see Connell, 2005; Warf and Winsberg, 2010), and the location of many FBO and church buildings onto the fringes of prime space away from major geographic pockets of deprivation. For Bishop the effect of these changes has been for Christian congregations to enter into areas of deprivation in a breeze-in/breeze-out fashion, shaping the way in which they relate to marginal others. In one sense charity has become the churches' mediator, while in another sense physical distance has become its comfort. What has emerged in the process is a set of dislocated and delocalised corporate expressions of the Christian faith, whereby more often than not, members of the Christian faith at best do things *for* others rather than *with* others (Auge, 1998).

Bishop is certain that in contrast to these distant and delocalised expressions of the Christian faith what would be most effective is to *journey back in*, consciously choosing to live within these areas of socioeconomic deprivation. This, he believes, would result in 'becoming part of these communities, making real friendships with people that may seem very different to us at the onset but allowing them to shape and change us so that we can become at home in their native territory' (2007, p 60). He hopes that this would result in an asymmetrical relationship with others, opening up 'a level of relationship with local people that is difficult to achieve when you only *do things for* the community' (2007, p 65; emphasis added).

These challenges have also been echoed by a number of prominent Christian activists in the US (see, for example, Sider, 2005; Claibourne, 2006). Claibourne (2006), an American Christian author and activist, argues that the hypocrisy and complacent indifference with which Christians treat Jesus' teachings on the marginalised has depersonalised poverty and has created relational and in some cases spatial and emotional distance from the marginalised. He claims that this has resulted in the ossification of personal responsibility to the marginalised.

The interventions of both Bishop (2007) and Claibourne (2006) reflect a wider discontentment with the geographic placement and practices of the church, and these challenges have provoked innovative responses. There is now a re-emergent movement of Christians willing to be placed within marginal landscapes and a supportive social network wanting to generously redistribute resources – particularly volunteers, time and money – to support others who have been in place all along. Across the complexity of this re-emergent movement is the call for an intentional *incarnational* presence that seeks to permanently place faith-motivated individuals or groups more permanently alongside those experiencing poverty or social exclusion.

Relocation of individuals, groups and churches

Efforts to relocate and incarnationally dwell with marginal others have broadly taken three forms. Although in some cases there is a sense of hybridity between how these forms of response are shaped, in what follows I am not so much suggesting a model or spectrum that defines the shape of relocation but aiming to draw out key differences in approach.

It is appropriate at this point to note that bucking the wider sociological trend, men appear to be as likely to be involved in these expressions of Christian faith-based action as women. In contrast to the wider gender trend that points to greater levels of involvement in both faith communities (see Woodhead, 2002, 2007) and in acts of volunteering by women (Wilson, 2000), these incarnational expressions of the Christian faith in marginal, socioeconomically deprived areas appear to be widely balanced in their gender make-up. There is not the scope in this chapter to delve in detail into the reasons for this gender balance, but one can assume that questions of personal safety are one of the significant factors that limit the number of single women who volunteer to relocate onto these estates in comparison to the number of single men.

In terms of the three forms of action that dominate incarnational expressions of the Christian faith on marginal socioeconomically deprived estates, the first is made up of faith-inspired *individuals*. These faith-inspired individuals intentionally relocate and live in areas of socioeconomic deprivation with the purpose and conviction of seeing positive transformation in these communities. These individuals may engage with the wider neighbourhood through community organising, purposefully participating in collective action with others of goodwill, while attentively listening to the particular needs of the area. Below is a typical example presented in the case study of Tom.[1]

Case study 1: Tom

Tom Cleft works as a regional manager for a Christian charity. He is a well-educated professional with a well-paid job. He could choose to live in suburbia but instead has chosen to live on the Axel Estate in Roehampton.

Prompted by his Christian faith he has moved onto the estate. He lives in Rivermead House in a two-bedroom flat, which he shares with a friend. There have been plans to demolish Rivermead House, but nothing definite has been decided and so residents are currently living with uncertainty, facing constant battles with the local council to persuade them to maintain the building. Tom has become something of a spokesperson for Rivermead House. He spends time visiting neighbours to canvas their views on what needs mending and liaises with the council. These issues bother Tom. His concern is for his fellow neighbours and their children. The lifts break down regularly and people treat the lifts like public urinals. The telecom system frequently does not work. Drug users ring all the buzzers until someone lets them in and then they deal drugs on the stairwell. Becoming a local resident has led Tom to campaign against these issues. Living in Rivermead House these issues have become personal for him.

Tom volunteers for another local charity mentoring several young people on the estate. He encourages each young person to achieve their own goals and is witnessing them take small steps towards these targets. Some are going to the gym, eating a better diet; others are less stressed and are drinking less. Some are applying to university.

Not all things are so positive for Tom. He has had to make some big personal sacrifices – his quality of life and his relationships could be better if he chose to live somewhere else. His family doesn't enjoy coming to visit and his fiancée Ruth does not feel safe visiting. But for Tom, living on the estate, he is less preoccupied with mortgages, career and success; the estate presents more immediate and communal concerns and he can't help but get involved.

Source: Personal interview, March 2010

Tom's example illustrates how his choice to relocate has led him to seek out positive transformation on the estate. His openness to being shaped by the narratives and events that he encounters through being with others has led him to become enfolded into the fabric of what is already hope seeking on the estate. Moving beyond the example of Tom there are groups of faith-inspired people, here termed *communities of intention*, which relocate. These *communities of intention* are informally linked with one another but often unaffiliated from any particular Christian denomination or established church. The example of Dave and Lucy highlights how these communities of intention start.

Case study 2: Dave and Lucy

Dave and his wife Lucy live in inner-city Manchester. Dave finished university in Manchester five years ago. Together with a group of friends they intentionally moved into an area they once avoided as students. Dave would have only come to into contact with the area through voluntary work with a local homeless organisation. He now lives in the area and works full time for the same charity.

From time to time Dave and Lucy hospitably house an asylum-seeker in connection with a citywide asylum-seeker charity. They regularly meet with other friends who have made the neighbourhood their home. This community of intention is not associated with any particular formal church. As a group of friends with a common faith and the same passion for the area they see themselves as a faith community wishing to make a difference in the local area. Drawing on their own Christian faith they re-imagine what the area could be like: a place with less poverty and racial conflict, a greater number of jobs for local people and a decline in mental health issues.

Source: Personal interview, April 2010

The example of Dave and Lucy indicates how *communities of intention* are informally structured and highlights the nature of their character. Founded on a passion for a particular area of the city and a hopeful participation within it, the example of Dave and Lucy elucidates how *communities of intention* seek to re-imagine socioeconomically deprived areas. Being bound together by a similar set of convictions, the case of Dave and Lucy also illustrates how communities of intention form, and gives an account of the purpose of their intentional relocation and gathering as a group.

In comparison to the examples of Tom, Dave and Lucy, the most structured accounts of relocation come in the form of 'church plants'. These seek to see a form of church established in the local neighbourhood. These *expressions of church* may not be as formally recognisable as their traditional affiliated counterparts but are in any case linked to both a wider network of similar expressions of 'doing church' and a support network of more traditional denominational churches – from which financial and social capital is often resourced. In the case of the UK, many of the major traditional denominations have in some way embraced supporting and overseeing these initiatives. The Baptist (see Urban Expression at www.urbanexpression.org.uk), The Salvation Army (see 614UK at www2.salvationarmy.org.uk/uki/www_614UK.nsf), Methodist and the Anglican Church (see Fresh Expressions at www.freshexpressions.org.uk) have all become involved across the scope of the UK in these initiatives. In the UK the extent of this expression of church finds its place in most major urban conurbations and many more are being planned. Case study 3 outlines how Mike became involved in an incarnational 'church plant' linked with the Eden Network (see later).

Case study 3: Mike

Mike spent a year on a UK-based Christian Gap Year project connecting social action with a bible-based personal faith. Having completed this year out he felt the urgency and conviction to continue living out his faith in a way that directed him to one of the several Manchester-based Eden Projects. The Eden Project Network facilitated this process for him. This meant he could study at university while actively being involved in a local 'church plant'. The Eden Project church partner organisation, The Salvation Army, helped finance his degree in Youth Work and Community, and he moved onto a well-renowned housing estate where the church plant had just been started. He soon became a key volunteer for the Eden Project/Salvation Army partnership.

The 'church plant' was comprised of 10 other volunteers who had moved from more affluent areas to commit to living on the estate for at least two years. Motivated by Christian convictions, each volunteer wanted to actively share their own faith through both words and actions. Their aim was to embed themselves in the life of the estate and to help make it a more hopeful and harmonious place where they could. This meant that Mike commuted the 50 minutes to university and committed his spare time to running drop-in youth clubs. He has now finished his degree and still lives on the estate. He still volunteers for the Eden Project and plays an active role in the church plant. He has made the estate his home. He now sits on a local residents' association board and has an open door policy with the many youth who knock on his door.

Source: Personal interview, February 2010

In some cases a church 'presence' in areas of deprivation is nothing new, nor something that necessarily involves relocation or 'planting'. Across the UK there is an ongoing church presence and sense of incarnation that can be traced through a very longstanding commitment by the established church. This commitment is built on the heritage of the Church of England parish model, and seeks to remain in place, engaging deeply with local areas of socioeconomic deprivation (see The National Estate Churches Network, NECN, at www.nationalestatechurches.org). In many cases if it were not for these parish-based congregations then the wider churches' involvement in socioeconomically deprived areas would be significantly diminished, as partnership schemes and short-term projects would never get off the ground (Graham and Lowe, 2009).

Many relocation efforts are supported by FBOs and ecumenical networks. These organisations facilitate the relocation of Christian faith-inspired individuals, connecting them with wider groups of faith-motivated people who have the same conviction to relocate to live among the marginalised. These FBOs offer training and placements and involve varied time length commitments. In some cases these are shorter 'gap year' opportunities, providing a training ground for individuals to experience this type of localised involvement (see Mission Year at www.missionyear.org.uk; XLP at www.xlp.org.uk) while for other organisations the intention is a longer commitment from the outset (see Eden Network later).

In summary, incarnational forms of praxis are clearly structured and supported in different ways. The examples of Tom, Dave and Lucy, and Mike, have highlighted how this can be an individual initiative, the effort of informal community or part of 'church plant'. These different forms of incarnational witness (see the next section) are united by a common Christian conviction to become involved in the evolving narrative of each marginal context and faithfully participate in life alongside marginalised others. These convictional communities are structured around having a permanent local presence, that is intentionally directed in numerous ways towards engaging with the specific need of the area, listening, witnessing, discerning and responding. The three short case studies have highlighted how this is done differently in different places. For Tom this involved advocating on behalf of other residents in his block of flats, in the case of Dave and Lucy this meant personally responding to the migration issues and asylum-seekers in their area, while for Mike it meant helping run several youth drop-in clubs. All three of these examples draw on the discourses that I now turn to examine.

Incarnation, community and mission

In this section I discuss some of the key discourses that shape these faith-permeated practices illustrated above. These discourses reflexively shape the action practices of convictional communities and are therefore important in understanding the motivations of these groups. Making sense of these discourses draws out their motivational distinctiveness in comparison to their non-faith-based NGO counterparts.

Being incarnational

Christianity after Christendom (see Murray, 2011) is turning once again to consider the life and death of Jesus Christ in ways that re-centre the importance of Christ's incarnational witness (Guder, 2000). Christians who relocate to socioeconomically deprived areas of the UK are comparing the contemporary practices of the church, and therefore themselves, to those of Christ, and this is reflexively shaping their actions.

As I explored in the critiques of Bishop, there is a discontentment with the tendency of the church and Christians to be located among affluent areas, dwelling among the middle class. However, considering that the church is theologically representative of Christ's body, many involved in convictional communities are questioning the discrepancies between the biblical narratives of Christ and the practices of the church. As biblical narrative portrays the embodied life of Christ as often dwelling among, and with, the marginalised in society, convictional communities are reflexively asking how they can emulate such a lifestyle when it is, at times, not reflected in the contemporary church. It is clear that in light of these theological narratives a set of discursive tropes have come together around the narrative of Christ's incarnation. This has produced particular theo-ethical enactments of this narrative (see Cloke, 2009).

In the example of Eden, a network of convictional communities explored later in this chapter, the incarnation, or as Matt Wilson (2005, p 91) puts it, 'the arrival of Christ in Human history', has clearly shaped Eden's practices. Drawing a comparison between the church and the narratives of the incarnation has provided the main motivation for relocation efforts into areas of socioeconomic deprivation. Convictional communities, like Eden, have sought to follow the example of how Christ dwelt with, and among, the marginalised, as they turned to question how they may be shaped by how Christ lived, and what he said. As Wilson explains:

> We've spent a lot time looking at the way Eden is influenced by the physical reflection of who God is, represented in the arrival of Jesus in human history. Its also right for us to offer ourselves to be shaped by what Jesus said in his brief time here. (Wilson, 2005, p 91)

The discourse of the incarnation not only presents the church and individual Christians with a question of where they should live, it also challenges how they might live. In recent years Western Christianity has begun to return to questions of virtue and character (see Wright, 2010), and questions of virtuous living have been central to those who have chosen to relocate into marginalised areas. Drawing inspiration from the theological narratives of the incarnation has prompted Christians involved in convictional communities to faithfully pursue ways of embodying similar virtues. This is clearly illustrated in the example of Gareth, a convictional community leader, as he described what defines his faith and how he tries to live:

> 'What I see differently about faith is this downward mobility, which you see in an example like Jesus, take the bible passage: Philippians 2 verse 5: "let your mind be like Jesus, though he had equality with God he did not consider equality with God but made himself of no reputation, taking on the form of a servant and became obedient even to the point of death, therefore he was highly exalted." I quote that because I think that is absolutely central to what we do. In a society that says upward mobility is right, it is our neighbourhood that exists because of this. It is the people who have lost in that game.' (personal interview, October 2009)

For Gareth it is the narrative of the sacrificed and humble incarnate Christ that shapes the way he seeks to actively embody his Christian faith in the context he is embedded within. Gareth is convinced the reason behind why marginal neighbourhoods, like the one he has moved into, exist, is because society upholds and encourages a different set of virtues or values. In light of this upward mobility, Gareth seeks to follow the example of Christ as portrayed in the narrative of the incarnation, something he words as 'downward mobility'. Gareth's faithful following of the discourse of the incarnation could be seen as a counter-cultural ethic (see Cloke, 2009) opposed to the widely hegemonic perusal of wealth, individualism, gain and pleasure (see Ward, 2001). In this way the incarnational discourse is a narrative that presents a confrontation in its theo-ethical call to go beyond the self, embracing what Zizek (2000) accounts to be the 'subversive core' of Christianity, radically inseparable from Christianity's orthodoxy (Ward, 2001). For a Christian like Tom, presented in the first case study, pursuing incarnational living among the marginalised has practically involved him choosing to live in relatively low quality housing with little accessible amenities. In the context of the example of Mike (see Case study 3) his theo-ethical desire to identify with those whom society often neglects or marginalises is something he feels 'called' to do in light of the incarnation:

> 'The example we see in Christ is that he identified with the poor, the outcast and the vulnerable in society, and living incarnationally is about embracing the spirit of the incarnation, I feel called to identify with exactly the same people. Now don't get me wrong, this does not mean I romantically embrace poverty as a Godly thing to do, but it is a question of with whom I am hanging out with and how I spend my time. To do this I have to embrace a certain type of lifestyle, one that might not have all the middle class luxuries. Living like this does not seem something you would choose for yourself, but it is not all that bad.' (personal interview, March 2010)

For Mike, like Gareth, pursuing the discourse of the incarnation has involved certain lifestyle choices as well as a physical relocation. These lifestyle choices, moulded by reflexively questioning the 'spirit of the incarnation', produce pragmatic tensions. In practice the continual do-ability of this discursive logic, and the contextualisation of it in place, and through praxis, appears to be sometimes problematic. Self-sacrifice and humility can lead to burnout; the lack of organisational help can lead to dis-enchantment with the idea of incarnational living. This is illustrated when Ruth recalls her three years as part of a convictional community in Manchester, explaining her frustrations and reasons for leaving:

> 'It was really hard on the estate. It is probably the hardest one that there is and it was really intense. I think a lot of the team were really burnt out, a lot of other teams got abuse from the kids and that, broken into and stuff. We got our cars smashed up, a kid punched me in the face, had eggs thrown at us, fireworks through the door. I was an 18-year-old kid, looking after kids with some real issues, I did not know how to look after this guy who was a heroine addict. Having to endlessly go and look after his kids when he was in jail. We did not have any

resources or training and we were totally out of our depth, it just got too much.' (personal interview, February 2010)

Ruth's faith-motivated desire to be present with and among marginalised young people clearly led to a series of confrontations, feelings of incompetency and exhaustion. For convictional communities, working out how to be a part of the local neighbourhood community and discerning what to become involved in is structured by how they envisage their place in the 'community'.

Joining and creating community

Convictional communities come to terms with 'community' through their relational and participatory involvement. To clearly understand how convictional communities evoke the discourse of community it is best to think of the discourse as having at least a two-fold nature. First, convictional communities intentionally seek to become embedded into the wider geographic community and second, in some form, they act as communities in and of themselves.

The example of Mike (Case study 3) illustrates how community is actively joined. Mike wants to be a part of the local community, volunteering at the local statutory youth club, sitting on a local neighbourhood residents' association and actively opening his own home to local neighbours and youth of the estate. Mike's incarnational intentions led him to actively seek to be embedded in various formal and informal structures of the wider community. For Tom, participating in the local community made him aware of residential issues and he quickly turned his experiential frustrations into personal attempts at advocating on behalf of other residents over living conditions, raising concern over injustices in local council provision.

Both examples illustrate how advocacy, participation and hospitality become important aspects of convictional community attempts to become embedded in local neighbourhood community landscapes. In other case examples participation has led to an involvement in forms of community organising and welfare with the aim of seeking common good for the neighbourhood (Bretherton, 2010). The capacity for this common good to increase in the community is also envisaged and worked out through convictional community volunteers actively seeking jobs in local services, using their skills to increase the welfare and well-being of the area. When services and vocational participation are not available, convictional community members often create a range of community-centred projects. Very often these soon become projects collaboratively run with others who are not directly involved in the convictional community.

Alongside efforts to become embedded into the neighbourhood community, convictional communities can be seen as communities in and of their own right. Lucy and Dave (Case study 2) gather together with other Christians who have relocated into the area, informally drawing together a community of faith that is structured by a set of core Christian beliefs. For Dave and Lucy this understanding of community involves an articulation of distinctiveness but not separation. As Dave explains:

> 'We believe in gathering together with other Christians from across the neighbourhood, it creates a sense of togetherness, you're not doing this on your own. Doing all this gets lonely and tiring, relocating is not that easy and so gathering together gives us time to celebrate our faith, worship and take stock of what we feel God is doing in the neighbourhood. It is not a holy huddle, we don't want to be separate from others who don't share our Christian beliefs, we just believe that this time of gathering is an encouragement and actively enables us to feel refreshed, continuing to be present here.' (personal interview, April 2010)

Many convictional communities involve some level of creating community through shared living arrangements, sharing meals, and in some cases, a shared economic purse. In contrast to both faith-motivated 'community living' arrangements and 'intentional communities' that are separate from the wider geographic neighbourhoods and not necessarily in areas of deprivation, convictional communities are present for others, seeking to have intentionally permeable boundaries between themselves and others in the neighbourhood. This is reflected in both Mark and Tom's involvement in wider community concerns and how Dave and Lucy have opened up their home to support asylum-seekers.

Drawing together these two different articulations of the discourse of community, we may be prone to question how the two overlap. In particular we may want to question how confessional faith is shared with others. We should necessarily ask how convictional communities engage with the wider geographic neighbourhood in proselytising acts, seeking not to simply serve the wider community but to 'church' them. In other words, questioning how convictional communities go about seeking to see non-believers in the surrounding neighbourhood take up a confessional faith similar to their own. Different members of convictional communities elicit this act of 'sharing faith' in different ways. Furthermore, different convictional communities, with their own organisational cultures and theological standing, facilitate this process of sharing and explaining faith differently. Accordingly some groups will be explicit about their faith and others will take a more implicit approach (see Baker, 2008). This depends on how the discourse of mission is interpreted.

Doing mission

Convictional communities see their incarnational practices of relocation, service and engagement with others in the local community as part of the discourse of mission. In line with this, some Christian commentators have labelled convictional communities as missional communities (see Bessenecker, 2006). Contemporary secular interpretations of 'mission' equate this with a wholly negative process of proselytisation (see Hacket, 2008). However, following the argument of Bosch (1991), this would mistakably translate the process of mission to be a process with the single intention of seeking to convert others to hold a confessional belief in the doctrines and creeds of the Christian church. Bosch (1991) outlines that 'mission', in its holistic sense, is an enactment and lived participation in a particular set of theological narratives, seeking to see the material and spiritual transformation of present contexts and geographies, not simply converts. Convictional communities can be described as seeking to take part in this sense of holistic mission. Furthermore, in line with Thiessen's philosophical defence of ethical proselytising (2011), maybe rather than seeing the act of persuading an other to see one's own faith-based beliefs as true as outright immoral, the more pertinent and critical question should be one that focuses in depth on how the believer goes about seeking to see others converted to their own belief system. Perhaps this way academic interrogations of faith-based praxis that are part and parcel of so-called Christian mission might be less likely to be subject to essentialist strategies that in turn deem all acts of such faith-based proselytisation, or persuasion, as outright immoral. Although, as Thiessen (2011) acknowledges, Christians throughout history have been guilty of gross misconduct in the name of sharing their faith (for an ably documented account of the Spanish conquest of America, see Rivera, 1992; for a historical catalogue of Christian failures in proselytising, see Megivern, 1967), perhaps it is due time that we deconstruct the overtly simplistic accounts that claim that persuading others to the point of religious conversion is wholly arrogant, the cause of religious intolerance and violence, and invalid by the nature of their inability to give complete rational explanations for the account of their faith (Thiessen, 2011). Taking a more careful look at the intersection between what is being shared and how it is being shared will naturally need to be built on certain criteria. This needs to be criteria that acknowledges in the encounter the concern for the dignity and care of the other while also being critical of when such acts of proselytisation involve coercion, both in a physical, social and psychological sense (see Thiessen, 2011).

Christians share their faith through acts of service and an engagement with others with different motivations (see Cloke et al, 2007). Some acts of service may seem like performances of 'moral selving' (Allahyari, 2000), interpreted as personal acts of virtuous self-betterment, while in other contexts faith-motivated acts of service may come with certain strings attached (see Cloke et al, 2005, 2007; Hackett, 2008). Other research has tentatively questioned how Christian praxis may involve no strings attached, placing as much an emphasis on faith in practice as it does on faith through dogma (see Cloke, 2010; Cloke and Beaumont, 2012). In this vein, the potential for faith to be translated into practice in either way means that to understand how convictional communities seek to serve and engage with wider neighbourhood communities we must be attentive to how faithful purposefulness is enacted in different styles of 'doing mission' and 'service'. To best question how mission is performed and how the politics and poetics of care are negotiated we need to make sense of the performativities of convictional communities through the conceptualisation of self–other relations.

Interrogating performances of mission in this way will open up an analysis of how difference might be imperialistically assimilated. Such colonial faith practices may have their outworkings in the assimilation of cultural differences, gender differences or religious differences, with little regard to diversity (see Volf, 1996). On the other hand, seeking to understand mission through the conceptual framework of self–other relations may bring to light faith practices that actively attempt to go beyond the self (Cloke, 2002), developing a sensitivity to otherness that includes both a sense of the other and for the other (see Auge, 1998). These performances of faith praxis might 'involve the ability to receive the specificity of the other and to be generous in the context of that specificity rather than in the context of the self' (Cloke, 2005, p 398), moving towards receptive forms of generosity that include a theo-ethical notion of embrace (Volf, 1996).

As religion has the capability to appear at odds with itself (Cloke, 2010), motivating acts of terror and acts of kindness, examining the Janus face of religion (de Vries, 2006) is crucial in the context of the practices of convictional communities. Religion has the capacity to spawn lovers of the impossible, capable of spilling out their passion into situations of social, economic or political need, yet it also has the tendency for its adherents to confuse themselves with God and to compromise the liberties of people who disagree with them (Caputo, 2001). Not neglecting this reality, vigilance and criticality must be employed when questioning how faithful purposefulness, or mission, in its holistic sense, is enacted in convictional communities. I return later to consider this in context of the last case study.

Eden Network/Salvation Army 614

The last section of the chapter shifts from an analysis of the discursive arena to one of the praxis-based arena. It aims to bring greater understanding of the place of these different discourses in the place of one case study. This will help to formulate a contextually informed picture of the real work of these discursive fixtures. In doing so it will bring light to some of the ways in which convictional communities engage with local geographies and are enmeshed into emergent ethical spaces.

Eden Hill Top is one of the three 'Eden' convictional communities in North East Greater Manchester. There are presently seven other similar communities spread across Greater Manchester. Eden Hill Top is a joint venture between both the Eden Network and The Salvation Army 614UK network. Both networks are 'missional' in their intention, 'incarnational' in their approach and 'community'-focused in their engagement. They are both about the proclamation of the Christian faith and the practice of it through an incarnational approach. For the Eden Network this is clearly expressed in their mandate 'to go to the most challenging urban areas and share God's life changing love in word and action' (see Eden Network at www.eden-network.org).

614UK is 'a network and strategy for planting Salvation Army teams in some of the most deprived neighbourhoods within the United Kingdom and Ireland' (www2.salvationarmy.org.uk/uki/www_614uk.nsf). In the schema presented in the first section of this chapter The Salvation Army 614UK projects could be seen to best fit under the label of denominational 'church plants'. The 614UK network identifies areas of high multiple deprivation (what it terms the 'forgotten 5%') and recruits teams of people who will move into the area to live and work. It iterates that it does 'not believe the answer to be to import service programme, rather it is about a commitment to a certain way of living out God's story which is all about favouring the poor, living in the neighbourhood, experiencing transformation and building community' (www2.salvationarmy.org.uk/uki/www_614uk.nsf). For these groups '614UK is not only about living in these areas out of God's compassion for these places' but because they 'believe the Bible re-imagines something different for these neighbourhoods'. Beyond the involvement with the Eden Hill Top community, the 614UK network helps oversee six other similar communities around the UK.

Eden Hill Top's co-partner organisation, the Eden Network, is similarly a relational support network that establishes and builds the capacity of teams of volunteers that similarly intentionally move in to socioeconomically deprived neighbourhoods. In terms of the schema presented in the first section it could best be described as an *ecumenical network* facilitating the development of convictional communities. The Eden Network oversees a network of convictional communities that are partnered with local churches. The core of Eden Network's philosophy is that:

> ... everyone shares an ownership of Eden's core value: making a redemptive home right in the heart of a difficult community. To this they are "totally devoted, deliberately choosing to live an alternative lifestyle in the face of some of the highest crime, deprivation, drug, alcohol, teen pregnancy and unemployment rates in the country". (Wilson, 2005, p 32)

Delivering a series of services across the council estates and inner-city areas of both the North West and the South East of England, their ethos is underpinned by the decision to 'choose to live in the most difficult areas, sharing the problems of those growing up there, and ministering to their needs' (http://eden-network.org/).

Eden Hill Top and incarnational living

For Eden Hill Top to be incarnational has involved, first, the choice of many of the initial volunteers to relocate to the immediate area. For many of these volunteers it has meant sacrificing other opportunities, turning down job prospects or places at high profile universities.

As volunteers move into the local area a certain *exposure* takes place (see Beaumont and Dias, 2008). The lack of facilities, resources and diminished standards of living often forms the seedbed for action. Many individual members of Eden Hill Top are *affected* by the stories of relative hardship and deprivation that they witness. In effect these encounters empathetically draw Eden volunteers closer to the wider community, binding them to individuals and consolidating a concern for their well-being. Similar to the accounts of the *Oudewijken Pastoraat* [Old Pastoral Districts] in the Netherlands, just 'being there' creates a people-centred approach rather than a solely problem-solving culture (Beaumont and Dias, 2008, p 387). This people-focused approach means it is commonplace for volunteers and staff of Eden Hill Top to be deeply affected by the testimonials, narratives and daily witnessed lived accounts of people living in the areas.

One example of this affective change or exposure is in the account of an Eden volunteer named Claire. Having spent a lot of her spare time on the estate tutoring one young person, she felt urgently challenged by the way the educational system seemed to fail some students caught up in a myriad of other social issues:

> '... it was just something that I was really annoyed about, particularly Sharon, who was completely off the rails.... I taught her A-level biology for a bit, 'cos she failed.... Well she did not do very well in her GCSEs, and then I was like ... well I will teach you some biology, then we will see how we go ... then she would turn up every week ... we would talk about it for 40 minutes, she would go away and she would do no work all week and she would just reproduce it, like half stoned, it was just incredible ... the whole system does not really work for those kids, so it was a bit of a niggle really and I did not know what to do....' (personal interview, April 2010)

Claire's sentiments were also affected when she was deeply troubled by the inadequacy of healthcare in the local neighbourhood. This drove her to acknowledge a deep-seated personal anger of the inadequate local healthcare, and the complacent and apathetical acceptance of substandard access to care, as she explains:

> 'I was really angry about the healthcare my neighbours and the people I knew were getting, ... and everybody knew that the doctors were crap and they gave prescriptions for ridiculous things, and they were referred on ... and just the general view, but nobody could do anything about it....' (personal interview, April 2010)

Her anger with the structural injustice embedded in the provision of both local educational and healthcare provision finally led her to sacrifice completing her own medical degree to set up a health company. She set aside her personal ambitions to pursue the well-being of the wider neighbourhood in order to actively provide better healthcare for her neighbours. Claire saw this as part and parcel of practising a sense of incarnation, developing a gracious self-giving sense of selfhood that prioritised the well-being of others before her own career success.

For Susan, another volunteer, modelling the discourse of the incarnation led her to intentionally work in the local secondary school. This opened her up to develop an attitude of concern and discontent against a school system that repeatedly labelled certain 'sink students' devoid of making it through, and consequently of less value, somehow deserving less attention in the school community.

Eden Hill Top and community

As Eden has its roots in working with young people, it is not difficult to imagine that many of the responses that structure Eden Hill Top's involvement in local community focuses around and on youth. And the partnership with The Salvation Army means that some of the volunteers drafted through The Salvation Army draw on their church-based experience of working as informal youth workers in the church ministry, while others put to use their professional skills as trained youth workers.

Through being deeply affected by the structural injustices that persist in both the neighbourhood and among the local public services, Claire and Susan went on to develop various inclusionary initiatives. For Claire this developed into an initiative that partners young people in the local comprehensive school with local pupils from the privately paid school in the same area. This initiative has snowballed into both a social responsibility initiative and a tutoring programme to widen the chances of their participation in tertiary education. In turn this initiative aims to begin to redeem the ghettoised nature of the estate through bridging young people of different economic backgrounds.

In contrast to Claire, Susan responded to her feelings of disaffection and disapproval by wanting to change the school system from within. Susan worked alongside the full-time Eden youth worker to imbue hope into situations that can at times be awash with neoliberal target-based league tables and tokenistic qualifications (Hursch, 2005). With the help of Phil, the youth worker, she started responding to this malaise of concern by delivering a targeted curriculum and investing extra time in and out of school in the lives of these young people. Using Phil's previous occupational skills as a chef they delivered a cookery class to encourage and engage with these individuals and matched this with a school-timetabled set of lessons to build their confidence as learners.

Matching these responses with the examples of how both Susan and Claire became aware of the level of need, as they were exposed to people's stories and lives, hints towards how many initiatives are set up as a direct result of the intersubjective encounters and experiences with individual young people in the neighbourhood. In some cases, however, initiatives have simply been a response to *plug a gap* in youth club provision. For Eden Hill Top this took the form of catering for an underrepresented age range on a night of the week when there was no statutory provision.

It is important to note that these spaces of provision are often co-constituted by the relational engagement of staff and volunteer workers (see Conradson, 2003) with young people. In effect this often transforms particular mirco-geographies of the estate into positively affective environments in which the psychogeographies or the embodied experience of certain spaces are translated as open, friendly, welcoming and peaceful – localised spaces of hospitality (see Cloke et al, 2008). This is clearly seen in the account of a local police community support officer (PCSO), Amanda, describing a youth drop-in club that Eden Hill Top provides:

> '… it is always very welcoming when you come in, and to be honest with you, Frank really makes me laugh, it's just personalities, and I get on well with Dave as well, and even though they are a faith-based group, in that the Eden project is run by The Salvation Army, they don't throw the church in your face or anything like that, they don't try and change you, you are what you are, they treat every person as you are what you are … and I do believe that the kids have more respect here and stuff like that. When you are in the youth club [statutory provision], you are dealing with issues and when I come here I can relax and I can play pool, there is just no issues … it's dead chilled, I could sit on the couch and the kids would come round me, you see if I sat in there [statutory provision], you would not have any kids round you, you gotta go to the kids, here the kids will come to you, speak to you, it is kinda a lot more chilled atmosphere, it is a lot more like family, you know what I mean?' (personal interview, April 2010)

Along with describing how the drop-in club makes her feel a welcomed visitor, feeling comfortable with being a PCSO in this amicable setting, Amanda gives an account of the lack of 'church in your face' as no one is out to 'try and change you'. Here it seems faith is not coercively presented in the form of a proselytising force but as a connective set of performative enactments that gives a 'family' feel and generates an atmosphere of respect and tranquility.

Alongside creating spaces of hospitality, through which youth and other statutory workers can harmoniously interact together, Eden Hill Top has put in place many measures to effectively build spaces of partnership. This has been done through building imaginative resonance of what the estate could become. Practically this has involved organising 'visioning days' to collaboratively bring together different local activists, third sector organisations and statutory organisations to collectively re-imagine the estate. Deliberately this has involved attempting to re-narrate the estate through a media project venture with young people. Here the intention is to collectively give space to the hopeful and positive stories already emerging from within the neighbourhood, countering the effect of wider negative media discourses.

Rather pragmatic in nature, these partnerships are often created with the impetus of building capacity for action, by increasing access to financial and social capital. This has often been built on the back of a common rationale and a good relationship. In the case of the youth sector involvement, Eden Hill Top's partnerships have officially and unofficially developed with other organisations that seek to have a positive impact on the lives of young people. These range from partnerships with the police, the youth inclusion programme and local schools. Most of the time these are not set up as a means to an end (for example, to reduce anti-social behaviour) but to give more space to develop greater relationships with both the young people and the partnering staff members of other organisations. In turn this has fed back into the ability for Eden Hill Top to collaboratively build spaces and practices of hospitability and mutability on the estate.

Just as the example of the youth worker, Phil, highlights, some members of convictional communities like Eden Hill Top draw on their professional youth work skills to make a difference through provision and partnership; other volunteers, like Claire, have drawn on a combination of their discontent with the inadequacy of healthcare provision and their own interest in health and medical care to renew local healthcare with a focus on excellence and justice. For the healthcare charity that emerged, the opportunity to do medical care presented itself differently in the persistent and tiresome attempts to battle against the bureaucracies and target-based culture that sees results, figures and statistics put before the locally contextualised lives of those they seek to care for. Tackling the market-based culture that pervades neoliberal healthcare (see Gould and Gould, 2001; Henderson and Petersen, 2002), the company has constantly sought to move beyond mandatory targets to prioritise effective change and increased well-being in the community.

Eden Hill Top and mission

Eden Hill Top has intentionally involved itself in the community through volunteers and staff workers dwelling and living among those they wish to serve. However, as a community of faith, this is purposeful part of their sense of mission. In recollection of the second section, Eden Hill Top seeks to holistically practice mission, not equating mission simply with conversion or sharing faith (evangelism) but with all aspects of participation in the geographic community. Here I bring together a brief discussion of how Eden Hill Top volunteers, as part of a convictional community, explicitly aim to share their Christian faith.

In practice this means that alongside participating in the wider community through building spaces of provision, enlarging spaces of partnership and creating spaces of hospitality, Eden Hill Top actively creates spaces in which they can share their Christian faith. These spaces are openly labelled and signalled for those who, of their own choice, wish to question and come to terms with the Christian faith.

These are structured around inviting youth to collaboratively organised evangelical church events in the City of Manchester, while on the estate itself these take the form of evening *discussion groups* and Sunday morning *gatherings* with the whole convictional community.

These forms of engagement could be critically labelled as 'spaces of proselytisation'; however, as these are clearly signalled spaces in which service users can additionally choose to participate without major strings attached, it is more viable to suggest that these are seen as explicit 'spaces of active faith' (see Chapter Three, this volume). This is not to suggest that there are no strings attached, but as in Amanda's narrative, the local PCSO, the flavour of these faith practices and acts of sharing are not ones that give an indication of the convictional community wishing to 'change you' or to 'put church in your face'.

Conclusion

This chapter has reviewed some of the Christian critiques that have prompted the re-engagement of certain portions of the Christian church with areas of high socioeconomic deprivation. These critiques highlighted how dissatisfaction with faith-motivated dislocated and delocalised breeze-in/breeze-out approaches have prompted Christians to relocate to these 'nearly forgotten places' (Thompson, 2010). These efforts of relocation have been structured in multiple ways: seeing individuals, groups, church plants and ecumenical networks facilitate and become enrolled in this intentional relocation. The second section made sense of these diverse and differently structured forms of Christian faith praxis by discussing the major themes that discursively underpin these forms of praxis. Drawing out how incarnation, community and mission are all central concerns to these convictional communities, it highlighted how convictional communities seek to participate in an holistic sense of mission in these areas of high deprivation. This sense of participation, or mission, is structured around physical relocation and embodied virtuous acts of sacrifice and humility. The chapter has highlighted how a two-fold understanding of community tends to be discursively assembled and is intentionally overlapping. In this sense convictional communities see themselves as faith communities embedded and participating in various ways in the wider geographic community. Drawing on Eden Hill Top as a case study, it has shown how these discursive characteristics are worked out in the context of one localised example. Relocation causes faith-inspired people to be affected in various ways as they are exposed to the relative hardship and deprivation. This in turn prompts a response to actively engage in working towards a common good in the community (Bretherton, 2010) through building space for partnership, plugging welfare gaps and bringing spaces of hospitality into being. In seeking to see the faith community enlarged, convictional communities, such as the Eden Hill Top project, actively provide space in which they can share their faith. The way in which this is done varies between each convictional community, but as in the case of Eden Hill Top, this has the potential to be non-threatening, nonintrusive and non-coercive, largely shared through embodied acts of good will and personal sacrifice, with space for additional voluntary participation in signalled spaces that explicitly explore the Christian faith.

In the UK, convictional communities are emerging in different forms, and it is clear that the scale of this *incarnational* form of action is prevalent within many major urban UK landscapes. In searching to find similar cases in other European countries discussed in this book, an examination of socioeconomically deprived urban landscapes would soon show comparative examples. There will be faith-motivated people who have relocated to intentionally dwell among, and with, the socially excluded in more permanent ways. To unearth these comparative examples future research needs to look beyond the confines of traditional models of FBOs and faith-motivated charity and search to closely examine local faith networks.

Note

[1] For the purpose of this publication all individuals and organisations involved in the interview process have been given pseudonyms.

References

Allahyari, R. (2000) *Visions of charity: Volunteer workers and moral community*, Berkeley, CA: University of California Press.

Auge, M (1998) *A sense for the other*, Stanford, CA: Stanford University Press.

Baker, C. (2008) 'Seeking hope in the indifferent city: faith-based contributions to spaces of productions to spaces of production and meaning in the postsecular city', Paper, Association of American Geographers Annual Meeting, Boston, 2008.

Beaumont, J. and Dias, C. (2008) 'Faith based organizations and urban social justice in the Netherlands', *Tijdschrift voor Economische en Sociale Geografie*, vol 99, no 4, pp 382-92.

Bessenecker, S. (2006) *The new friars*, Downers Grove, IL: Intervarsity Press.

Bishop, G. (2007) *Darkest England: And the way back in*, London: Authentic Media.

Bosch, D. (1991) *Transforming mission: Paradigm shifts in theology of mission*, New York, NY: Orbis.

Bretherton, L. (2010) *Christianity and contemporary politics: The conditions and possibilities of faithful witness*, London: Wiley-Blackwell.

Caputo, J (2001) *On religion*, London: Routledge.

Claibourne, S. (2006) *The irresistible revolution: Living as an ordinary radical*, Michigan, MI: Zondervan.

Cloke, P. (2010) 'Theoethics and radical faith based praxis in the postsecular city', in A.L. Molendijk, J. Beaumont and C. Jedan (eds) *Exploring the postsecular: The religious, the political and the urban*, International Studies in Religion, 13, Leiden/Boston: Brill.

Cloke, P., Johnsen, S. and May, J. (2005) 'Exploring ethos? Discourses of charity in the provision of emergency services for homeless people', *Environment and Planning A*, vol 37, pp 385-402.

Cloke, P., Johnsen, S. and May, J. (2007) 'Ethical citizenship? Volunteers and the ethics of providing services for homeless people', *Geoforum*, vol 38, pp 1089-101.

Cloke, P., May, J. and Johnsen, S. (2008) 'Performativity and effect in the homeless city', *Environment and Planning D*, vol 26, pp 241-63.

Connell, J. (2005) 'Hillsong: a megachurch in the Sydney suburbs', *Australian Geographer*, vol 36, no 3, pp 315-32.

Conradson, D. (2003) 'Doing organisational space: practices of voluntary welfare in the city', *Environment and Planning A*, vol 35, pp 1975-92.

de Vries, H. (2006) 'Introduction: Before, around and beyond the theologico-political', in H. de Vries and L. Sullivan (eds) *Political theologies: Public religions in a postsecular world*, New York: University of Fordam Press, pp 1-90.

Frost, M. (2006) *Exiles: Living missionally in a post-Christian culture*, Peabody, MA: Hendrickson.

Hursch, D. (2005) 'Neoliberalism, markets and accountability: transforming and undermining democracy in the United States and England', *Policy Futures in Education*, vol 3, no 1, pp 3-15.

Gould, N. and Gould, E. (2001) 'Health as a consumption object: research notes and preliminary investigation', *International Journal of Consumer Studies*, vol 25, no 2, pp 90-101.

Graham, E. and Lowe, L. (2009) *What makes a good city? Public theology and the urban church*, London: Draton, Longman and Todd Ltd.

Guder, D. (2000) *The continuing conversion of the church*, Grand Rapids, MI: Eerdmans.

Hackett, R. (2008) *Proselytisation revisited: Rights talk, free markets and cultural wars*, London: Equinox.

Henderson, S. and Petersen, A. (2002) *Consuming health: The commodification of health care*, London: Routledge.

Murray, S (2011) *Post-Christendom: Church and Mission in a strange new world (After Christendom)* Milton Keynes: Authentic Media.

Rivera, L.N. (1992) *A violent evangelism: The political and religious conquest of Americas*, Louisville, KY: John Knox Press.

Sider, R. (2005) *Rich Christians in an age of hunger*, Nashville, TN: Nelson.

Thiessen, E. (2011) *The ethics of evangelism: A philosophical defense of proselytizing and persuasion*, London: Paternoster.

Thompson, A. (2010) 'Eden Fitton Hill: demonstrating and becoming in Oldham', in A. Davey (ed) *Crossover city*, London: Mowbray, pp 120–25.

Volf, M. (1996) *Exclusion and embrace: A theological exploration of identity, otherness and reconciliation*, Nashville, TN: Abingdon Press.

Ward, G. (2001) 'Suffering and incarnation', in G. Ward (ed) *The Blackwell companion to postmodern theology*, Oxford: Blackwell Publishing, pp 192-208.

Warf, B. and Winsberg, M. (2010) 'Geographies of megachurches in the United States', *Journal of Cultural Geography*, vol 27, no 1 pp 33-51.

Wilson, J. (2000) 'Volunteering', *Annual Review of Sociology*, vol 26 pp 215-40.

Wilson, M. (2005) *Eden: Called to the streets*, London: Kingsway Publications.

Woodhead, L. (2002) 'Women and religion', in *Religions in the modern world: Traditions and transformations*, London: Routledge, pp 332-56.

Woodhead, L. (2007) 'Gender differences in religious practice and significance', in *The Sage handbook of the sociology of religion*, Los Angeles, CA, London, New Delhi, Singapore: Sage Publications, pp 550-70.

Wright, T. (2010) *Virtue reborn*, London: SPCK.

Zizek, S. (2000) *The fragile absolute: Or, why is the Christian legacy worth fighting for?*, London: Verso.

Personal interviews

T. Cleft, volunteer survey, interviewed by S. Thomas, Manchester, UK, 19 March 2010

A. Fields, PSCO interview, interviewed by S. Thomas, Manchester, UK, 21 April 2010

M. Parson, volunteer survey, interviewed by S. Thomas, Manchester, UK, 15 February 2010

D. Pike and L. Pike, volunteer survey, interviewed by S. Thomas, Manchester, UK, 23 April 2010

G. Stone, FACIT cross-comparative survey, interviewed by S. Thomas, Bristol, UK, 9 October 2009

C. Wash, volunteer survey, interviewed by S. Thomas, Manchester, UK, 20 April 2010

TWELVE

Conclusion: the faith-based organisation phenomenon

Paul Cloke and Justin Beaumont

We would like to conclude with a summary of the central themes of state/society/religion relations addressed by the contributions in this volume. We allude to the *faith-based organisation (FBO) phenomenon* as a notion or idea that has evoked a series of dilemmas but that also signifies a fascinating and still relatively under-explored area of research in Europe today. In the second section of this conclusion we discuss eight propositions that will potentially drive new research in European FBOs and the struggle against poverty, exclusion and injustice in the future.

Changing state/society/religion relations

In recent history there have been a series of key moments in which religious groups and faith-motivated individuals have played a prominent role in tackling issues of social welfare and justice at national as well as local levels. Prior to the 19th century in the UK, for example, it was generally held as axiomatic that charitable welfare was the domain of individuals and private corporations. The state was considered as neither an appropriate nor an efficient source of aid for those in poverty. It was during this century that Christian liberal philanthropists began to come to the fore, combining their desire to see people saved by a new relationship with Jesus Christ with a belief that such salvation had to be accompanied by changes to the impoverished and unjust conditions of everyday life.

RobertWhelan (1996) charts the impacts of this Christian charity at two scales. First, he notes the rapid rise of localised rudimentary welfare services run by Christian organisations and individuals for the socially excluded people of the day: shelters for homeless people, soup kitchens for the poor and needy, employment training for the unskilled, places of care for orphaned or abandoned children, and many other manifestations of Christian charity that emerged during this time. Second, he highlights the contribution of particular high-profile Christian philanthropists, who used their wealth and influence to improve the everyday material circumstances of poor and excluded people in an essential coalescence of religious faith and social welfare. The cast is well known: the Earl of Shaftesbury became the conscience of the nation over issues of slavery and injustice; Thomas Barnardo established a series of charitable organisations to provide housing, education and care for children in poverty; William Booth's Salvation Army tended to the most marginalised and impoverished people in society; and William Lever and William Cadbury pioneered 'model' workplaces and community facilities for their employees. These religious charitable developments were not without controversy – especially given the intertwining of the twin goals of providing for people's material circumstances and saving their souls – but they sparked a sea-change in the wider culture of welfare and charity of the times.

During the 20th century, it became increasingly accepted that the state needed to become involved in regulating and regularising these welfare services, and with the development of the welfare state, and its inherent replacement of charity with taxation, the prominence of welfare services delivered by religious organisations generally diminished. This is not to suggest that the organisations concerned, and their contributions to charitable welfare, somehow disappeared; The Salvation Army and Barnardo's, for example, have sustained important welfare services to the present day, and elsewhere in Europe the enduring cultural (and sometimes political) position of the Catholic church has ensured a continuing role in the provision of welfare services. However, the expectation that religious agencies would be a leading player in national regimes of care and justice generally became an anachronism in the increasing secularised era of state welfare.

Until now.... Over the last two or three decades, there has been a curious re-emergence of faith-motivated people establishing shelters for the homeless, soup kitchens for the hungry and employment training for the unskilled, along with services to deal with issues that have become prevalent in this day and age – rehabilitation for those addicted to drugs and sanctuary for the seemingly 'unwanted strangers' seeking asylum and better life opportunities through migration. Rather than depicting this re-emergence as a simple return to the circumstances of a bygone age, the European Union (EU) 7th Framework Programme FACIT project has focused on the contemporary circumstances of what we consider to be a highly significant aspect of the latest phase of the shifting relations between religion, state and society. FBOs appear once again to be important players in the welfare landscape, as the contribution of longstanding religious agencies alongside the work being carried out by a fleet of new made-for-purpose organisations is being acknowledged as integral to some arenas of care and welfare.

The FBO phenomenon, therefore, both deserves attention, and poses questions. Certainly, the wheel of state/society/religion relations seems to have turned somewhat, but how significant is the wider role of religion in contemporary society? Charles Taylor (2007) has painted a picture of the widespread resurgence of religion as a return to a more sacred and enchanting world buttressed by a firm belief in the possibilities of transcendence. He points to a rebuttal of what he sees as a secularist bias, and a discursive and practical rejection of the fractured mentalities of the previously secular age. Yet in many European countries, this resurgence of religion seems questionable, with studies of religious adherence (see, for example, Davie et al, 2003; Davie, 2007; Beckworth and Demerath III, 2007) suggesting that regular attendance in Protestant and Catholic churches is falling, despite what is becoming , perhaps, a broader cultural fascination with 'the spiritual'. So

Jürgen Habermas (2010) speaks instead of an *impression* of religious resurgence, built on three foundations: the advance throughout the world of orthodox and conservative religious organisations, including Hinduism and Buddhism as well as the monotheistic religions; the radicalised fundamentalism of the most rapidly growing religious movements, for example, the dynamic growth of Pentecostalism in Latin America and of Islam in sub-Saharan Africa; and the potential for innate violence over religious causes displayed in the practices and outcomes of Islamic terrorism. In these ways, Habermas argues, public consciousness is adjusting to the continuing existence of religion in the secular social setting. And we would want to add the FBO phenomenon into this mix; as the increasingly prominent role placed by faith-motivated individuals and organisations in providing care and welfare and in promoting issues of justice becomes increasingly apparent in contemporary society, so the impression of the activities and achievements of religion in the public sphere begins to change.

Once again, there is a growing recognition (see Chapter Five, this volume) that the most pressing problems of social exclusion and marginalisation in the most difficult neighbourhoods of our cities are as often as not being responded to by religious people – Jack Caputo (2001, p 92) calls them 'the better angels of our nature.' Volunteers, members of caring professions with deeply held religious convictions, Christian, Jewish and Islamic, women and men, different backgrounds and ethnicities, are all out there in the marginalised spaces of the city serving the homeless, the stranger and others who have been excluded from or by the formal welfare state.

It is important to acknowledge this presence without romanticising it. Controversy remains, not least because the secular instincts of many social analysts (and especially many academic social analysts) remain resolutely opposed to any formal social role for religion, and vehemently assertive of the capacity of religion to cause rather than respond progressively to social problems. Far from being the better angels of our nature, these faith-motivated people can be represented as amateurish do-gooders, engaging in moral selving so as to boost their own identities and subjectivities. They are assumed to be dupes of neoliberal governmentality, unthinkingly colluding in the wider project of the shrinkage and privatisation of the state, and unable to administer more than a sticking plaster to the deep-seated ailments of a post-welfare, post-justice society that requires major political surgery. Clearly some (but certainly not all) of the services operated by FBOs on shoestring charitable budgets and with the help of less than fully trained volunteers will risk being assessed as amateurish. Undoubtedly there are dilemmas to be faced in accepting the strings attached to government funding while wanting to maintain the integrity and motivation of a faith-motivated approach. Clearly unwanted proselytisation of vulnerable service clients is ethically inappropriate. But do these assumptions summarise adequately the role, performance and achievements of FBOs in their pursuit of welfare and justice in the city? Could there be an alternative reading here, involving the deployment of theo-ethically driven faith motivation as a sensitive and progressive resistance to the failings of neoliberal governmentality? In this book we have delved into some of these questions, grappling with the difficulties of cross-national comparison in the European context, but fascinated by the obvious significance of the current FBO phenomenon. In what follows, we summarise and assess some of the main findings that flow from our research, formulating them into eight propositions.

1. An understanding of secularism is essential for grasping the differences between European contexts and the place of faith-based organisations within them

In Chapter Two, this volume, there is an important emphasis on the need to understand the *public sphere* in order to account for any transition in state–religion relations involving the political impact of specific FBO activities. 'Secular' is routinely understood in terms of the political separation of church and state, but our research has underlined that the secular is itself inseparable from the wider contextual concerns – including religious and ideological dimensions – with which it interacts. Thus to assume that, say, Belgium, France, the Netherlands and the UK are somehow inherently secular nations in which religiously motivated FBO activity is suddenly appearing is to ignore the evidence that different states have demonstrated historically varying positions on secularism, and that FBOs themselves usually exhibit different kinds of partnership between church, state and the voluntary sector. In other words, there is no one model of secularism against which the impact and influence of FBOs in general can be contradistinguished, and FBOs are already implicated in the particular state/society/religion relations of the national context concerned.

Whereas we acknowledge that public imagination and consciousness of the political rationalities that unfold from religious activity are often shaped by the assumption that particular space specificities – such as the fundamentalist right-wing Christianity of the US – will uniformly prevail, we want to emphasise that the interconnection between religious activity and the public sphere will be context-dependent (see Chapter One, this volume). Different state/society/religion relations prevail across Europe, with different historical path-dependencies at work. Although the cultural and interpretative power of the ideas of *ancient regime* continues to perpetuate assumptions about how the political left eschews religion in favour of secular public autonomy, while the political right cosies up to religion as a bastion of conservatism and tradition, such assumptions should not be permitted to overshadow the very important contextual variations that occur around FBO activities in different nations. It has indeed been suggested elsewhere (Zizek and Milbank, 2009; Cloke, 2010; McLennan, 2011) that some leading leftist thinkers in continental Europe have been evoking religious ideas of hope and love as sources of understanding and envisioning for alternative and progressive ideas for addressing how hospitality might be mixed in with difference in postmodern settings. Care needs to be taken, then, when drawing conclusions about the fundamental nature and purpose of FBO activities in different settings.

2. Faith-based organisations can be affirmed as legitimate and potentially creative and progressive political forces in the public sphere

Throughout the book we have provided evidence in various cultural and religious contexts that FBOs are capable of performing beneficial social and political roles in the contemporary city. Whether it is as the better angels of our nature, seeking out opportunities to serve marginalised people whose situations are not dealt with by more formal welfare safety nets, or whether it is fostering integrative and hospitable relations between different ethnic and religious groups in particular places, FBOs are present in many urban settings as an often unseen, but generally active, force for positive welfare outcomes. We emphasise here that there are of course non-governmental organisations (NGOs) not motivated by faith that are also active in these spheres. The claim is not, then, one of exclusivity, but one of significance. Faith motivation forms a significant part of the reason why people get involved in caring for the poor and needy, and (see Chapter Three, this volume) they often find common ethical ground with other similarly active people whose participation has nothing to do with religious motivation. In addition, we suggest that FBOs can represent religious activity in the public sphere that should not necessarily be decried as automatically proselytising; our evidence suggests that FBOs should not be somehow assumed as ideologically coercive. There will always be a continuum here between religious service 'without strings' and involvement that seeks to express the values, ethics and moralities of the religion concerned. However, to dismiss all FBO activity as somehow tainted by proselytising self-interest is not only to ignore the 'without' strings service and care offered in FBO contexts, but it is also to discount the much longer standing religious underpinnings of progressive political events and actions (see Habermas, 2006).

To some extent, the potential for progressive and creative FBO activity is best expressed in contexts where actions speak louder than words, where high-minded and fundamentalist expressions of moral and political certainty are replaced by religious activity that is open to being moulded through *praxis* (see Chapter Five, this volume). So, for example, alongside what is sometimes assumed to be a hegemonic and fundamentally oppositional discourse between the followers of Christ and Islam that contributes to the insidious rise of Islamophobia in the public domain, we need to note the occurrence of inter-religious collaboration, for example, in the prompting of moderate discussion of the perceived threat of terrorist activity, in the forging of community organisation to press for employment and anti-poverty goals that work across different ethnicities and religions, and in the humane and politically progressive welfare of asylum-seekers and undocumented migrants. Here we see a sense of progressive political performance which is not being imposed by external secular forces on religion, but which rather is emanating from within a faith-motivated desire to take action against the pressing problems affecting urban populations. Again, we do not claim that all FBOs are willing to move away from fundamentalist positionalities, but we do suggest that the presence of some FBOs in the public sphere highlights issues of social exclusion and introduces challenging notions of ethical citizenship into the public consciousness.

3. Faith-based organisations occupy complex spaces within neoliberalism

It is common to suppose that FBOs become easily incorporated into neoliberal politics, thereby helping to reproduce reactionary political agendas associated with the shrinking of the state, the privatisation of welfare and the strengthening of market logics (Peck and Tickell, 2002; Peck, 2006). In this way FBOs can become implicated in an economic system that actually produces exclusion and exacerbates social inequality. As can be seen from Chapters Two, Eight and also Eleven in this volume, such assumptions oversimplify and create a mistaken impression of both neoliberalism and the impact of faith-based delivery of social welfare. Neoliberalism is not simply circumscribed by privatisation, deregulation and the rolling out of *laissez faire* policies. Rather, it describes what is in effect an ideological shift in which the logics of market-driven competition that shape public conceptions of the citizen-subject as consumer, entrepreneur and responsible individual. Such a shift produces particular rationalities and technologies, some of which do indeed lead to the contractual partnership between government and particular FBOs in the provision of particular welfare services, and it is important to assess the possibility that such partnership can reproduce reactionary and conservative political agendas. However, it is equally important to recognise that what actually happens on the ground as part of a wide range of FBO activity – some of which involves contractual partnership and some of which do not – is contingent on the interaction between governmental rationalities and technologies and the ethical agency and performance of both FBO practitioners and their clients.

In particular, we suggest that some FBO activity may be regarded at least in part as moments of ethical citizenship (see Chapter Six, this volume) in which the reconfiguration and practice of urban welfare can encapsulate elements that are politically progressive rather than reactionary. Indeed, FBO activities can sometimes be understood to involve spaces in which there is a subversion of the very neoliberal tendencies that they are assumed to uphold. We have found evidence (see, for example, Chapter Eight, this volume) of FBO practitioners who, although in contractual partnership with government, are engaged in a revision of official policies and practices through the adoption of alternative strategies and technologies that modify the intended outcomes. We have also found evidence of FBOs who have established services beyond the formal welfare state and in so doing resist neoliberal tendencies by developing alternative technologies and practices to care for socially excluded people such as the minority ethnic immigrant and the homeless person (see Chapters Ten and Eleven, this volume).

In all of this, the *performance* of care is critical. FBOs will often operate outside of the traditional spaces of state-led governance, and in so doing they are capable of embodied and relational moments of caring subjectivity, expressed in conversations, in emotional connections, in the giving of time, in the formation of communities of care, and so on. Although these qualities are of course not restricted to faith-motivated people, the motivation of staff and volunteers in many of the FBOs studied were framed with reference to theological precepts of human dignity, compassion for the poor and a desire to bring freedom to the oppressed. These self-conscious ethics were often coupled with a wider organisational ethos incorporating different forms of eschatological hopefulness. We believe that it is significant to note that these theologically derived ethics as performed by FBO staff and volunteers frequently served as an alternative framework of care to that dictated by handed-down neoliberal frameworks of targets, restricted eligibility and social obligations on service clients.

4. The relations between faith-based organisations and the central and local state vary significantly in different contexts, affecting the precise roles performed therein

The evidence presented in this book suggests that there are important variations in relationships between FBOs and central and local government. Chapter Four, this volume, identifies two common contexts in which FBO activity has become important in providing welfare for the most vulnerable groups in society: first, situations in which the restructuring of welfare systems downloads responsibilities for welfare to for-profit or third sector organisations; and second, where international migration has led to new social challenges in the form of both the need for hospitable co-relations between different ethnic groups, and the more specific need for welfare provision for asylum-seekers and undocumented migrants, who often do not 'fit in' with conventional mechanisms of care and welfare. In both cases, there are significant variations in the particular contexts and circumstances that underpin FBO activity. Notably, different nations have varying histories of welfare state provision, and varying levels of devolution of welfare away from the central state and towards the local. So, for example, the UK government has been active in promoting and funding central state schemes for the welfare of rough sleepers, and so acts in partnership with local authorities to put in place a general response to the issues involved. Elsewhere (for example, Chapter Four, this volume, discusses Sweden, the Netherlands and Spain), the responsibility for dealing with rough sleepers has been devolved to the local state, creating potential for variations in the levels and types of responses involved. To some extent, then, FBO activity in Europe can be contextualised by the social demographics and political make-up of individual cities. There will be uneven geographies of in-migration, leading to differential awareness of and response to the welfare issues of people from minority ethnicities. There will be uneven geographies of local state propensity to embrace the marketisation of welfare – Chapter Four, this volume, for example, contrast the conservative political character of Madrid with the more leftist politics of Barcelona, and draws out important implications for how Catholic FBOs are regarded, and for how the use of for-profit organisations (as opposed to FBOs) is encouraged under more conservative political regimes.

So, FBO activity will be influenced significantly by the uneven geographical contexts in which it is located. Governments will turn to alternative organisations for complementary support when they experience economic restrictions that curtail their ability to provide welfare services, and different kinds of organisations will flourish in different local circumstances. For example, in some cases FBOs will have a longstanding and trusted position locally, and will therefore represent a favoured partner in such complementary welfare schemes, whereas elsewhere a more monetarist local state might prefer to turn to the for-profit sector for such schemes. Other social issues attract little public sector attention, and FBO activity in these cases often involves unincorporated services, circumventing formal (and sometimes legal) systems in order to support on-street homeless people, or undocumented migrants. An increasingly important element of FBO activity in some cities is the emergence of the socially active mosque, often operating in an environment of anti-Islamic sentiment, but nevertheless an important source of social support for Islamic communities in those cities that have experienced significant in-migration of Muslim people (see the example of the Stockholm mosque, as described in Chapter Four, this volume).

5. Faith-based organisations bring particular resources to the performance of care

As Dierckx et al argued in this volume (Chapter Seven), FBOs are often described in terms of apparently contradictory participatory qualities. On the one hand, they are potentially able to represent particular communities or population groups in which they have been historically embedded or with which they share common social or ethnic traits. Such representation can be beneficial in terms of public participation, not least in the poorer areas of cities. On the other hand, the religious nature of the value systems espoused by FBOs can render them as somewhat exclusive, potentially marginalising or failing to embrace those who do not share the value systems involved. As participatory agencies, therefore, FBOs receive a mixed press, based mainly on the conditionalities, or lack thereof, that are inherent in their *modus operandi*.

The particular qualities of FBOs that are significant in their performance of care may, however, stretch beyond these participatory issues. Where FBOs are incorporated as partners into formal state welfare systems, it often has as much to do with their resources as their participatory benefits. Religious groupings have access to charitable funding, pools of volunteer labour, existing echelons of leadership and well-established social networks within which particular applications of faith or ethics can be recommended. They perhaps buck the trend of shrinking social capital in the city, and offer a potential capacity for action which is unparalleled by other community aquifers of social action. These banks of resources are given further legitimacy where there has been a longstanding social presence in the city, either in particular neighbourhoods as islands of social activity or as deep-seated and trusted organisations with connections to particular groups of impoverished or marginalised people. As such, there can be some legitimacy for FBOs as incorporated welfare partners, but these same qualities also equip FBOs for unincorporated roles.

The Christian Council of Sweden's 'Easter Call' (see Chapters Four and Seven, this volume) illustrates how these self-same networks of leadership, resource and influence were used to issue FBO resistance to hard-line government policies relating to granting residence permits to asylum-seekers. 'The Call' was soon joined by other religious groups and non-religious NGOs, resulting in the granting of some 20,000 additional residence permits for asylum-seekers at that time. In one sense, then, FBOs benefit from organisational structures and resources that allow their positioning as either incorporated or unincorporated actors in welfare provision and politics in European cities. In this light, they present themselves as large, potentially powerful and well-resourced NGOs that happen to be connected to religious institutions. However, the results of our research suggest that their significance depends on more than this seemingly casual reference to religion and faith motivation.

6. Faith-motivation and theo-ethics underpin the distinctiveness of faith-based organisations

To some extent, FBOs have in the past been regarded as merely a subset of NGOs, sharing mostly the same qualities and positionings. Our research has shown, however, that the faith component of their work – the 'f' in FBO – has particular relevance to both the foundational and practical motivation for participation and the nature of the performance of care. The exploration of the ethical citizenship exhibited by volunteers working in services for homeless people in the UK (see Chapter Six, this volume) suggests not only that religious faith was one key reason for people to become involved, but also that it was the outworking of theological ethics associated with that faith that permeated the performance of volunteering in many cases. We would go so far as to suggest that the contemporary phenomenon of FBO involvement in providing welfare to urban socially excluded people has been fuelled by changes in the understanding of theological ethics that have resulted in a greater awareness of, and affiliation to, a more radical faith praxis (see Chapter Five, this volume).

Taking the changing theological landscape of Christian faith motivation as an example, we have traced a trend, even within long-present Christian FBOs, by which the theological underpinnings of FBO work seems to be changing with the times, perhaps reflecting the twin demands of post-Christendom and postmodernism on the need to find religious meaning in praxis rather than simply in theological discourse. Although there remains some adherence to the traditional evangelical opposition to social action, many contemporary evangelical Christians nowadays acknowledge both that caring for the poor, and standing up for justice for the oppressed, are entirely compatible with the biblical narrative, and that this discursive theological trait is best experienced by doing rather than talking about. This change has partly been prompted by the increasing take-up of transformational approaches by evangelical Christians, but may also be due to the rising popularity of the ideas pioneered by the radical orthodoxy movement in developing a form of 'socialism by grace' both by reconnecting postmodern Christianity with the critical theoretical insights of materialist socialism and by returning socialism to its Christian roots. The move towards Christian social action may also be traced to a more radical setting aside of certain knowledge about God as prompted by postsecular religion, which once again places the theological onus on participation in events of love and charity as a way of practising the love of God.

FBOs are therefore likely to be vehicles in which faith-motivated people can practise theo-ethical qualities, for example, agape and caritas, and where the performance of these qualities is likely to be valorised as a virtuous approach. In Chapter Eleven, this volume, we see another such translation of theo-ethical precepts into practical action in impoverished city spaces. Christian theology, especially through the narrative of Jesus Christ coming to earth and living among the poor and needy, raises the possibility of an incarnational approach to serving disadvantaged others, to be practised by living in among the poor and developing a sense of convictional community therein. As a significantly radical form of faith praxis, such convictional communities entail, as it does, the often purposefully sacrificial decision to dwell in spaces of poverty and marginalisation in order to serve from within the communities concerned. Such a strategy illustrates a significant linkage between the theological principle of incarnation, and the ethical practice of dwelling within spaces of need: 'I simply had to' and '[i]t had to be done', as one of the 'refugee hiders' in Sweden said during 'the Easter Call' (see Chapter Four, this volume).

In this and other ways, we can begin to argue that the 'f' in FBO makes a difference. Although in some ways FBOs look and act like NGOs, they are often founded on particular theological principles which are played out and performed according to religious translations of theological ethics into the ordinary ethics of caring for the stranger and providing welfare for the disadvantaged. These principles may or may not be distinctive from secular concerns (see below). But they form part of the essential personal and socially networked motivation for participation in welfare and care tasks, and they add colour and fragrance to the embodied relational moments of subjectivity that are produced through caring practices of caritas and agape.

7. Faith-based organisations can perform a significant role in the development of postsecular spaces of care and welfare in the city

Chapter Three, this volume, discussed postsecularism as the renewed visibility and consciousness of religion in contemporary society, and in particular in its politics and culture, and it should immediately be acknowledged that this idea of postsecularism can implicate a wide-ranging series of complex and dynamic relations between religion and other (for example, secular and humanist) positioning within the public sphere (see also Chapter One, this volume). The important argument here is that these changing relations have spatial as well as social implications, and the spaces of religion and society become transformed in place. Our research positions the FBO phenomenon at the heart of the emerging postsecular city. As the contribution of FBOs to welfare, community and inclusion becomes more recognised and appreciated, so their place in the public consciousness changes and the possibility arises of transformed relations between religion and society, as theo-ethics and a spiritual hopefulness are increasingly accepted as building blocks in a broader urbanism of hospitality and welfare, and as a rebuttal of the politics of revanchism.

Postsecular spaces will depend heavily on a mutual acceptance between religious and other groups of the possibility of working together. Habermas (2010, p 17) speaks of the 'reciprocal cognitive demands' that postsecular activity places on both religious and non-religious elements. Such demands imply not only a greater sense of tolerance between different groups and their worldviews, but also an acceptance of the possibility that the truth claims made in religious and non-religious contexts have some purchase across the religious divide. For religion to contribute to emergent postsecular rapprochement it must first ensure that the language and rationality of faith is translated effectively into the secular public sphere. Then, non-religious citizens must sign up to collaboration by adjusting to the presence of religious activity as a legitimate partner in the postsecular city. If these conditions are met, even in part, then valuable 'crossover narratives' (for example, around ethical themes such as caritas and agape) can occur around which collaborative social action can be formed. Our research suggests that FBOs are helping to develop such postsecular rapprochements both through their willingness to take action against social exclusion, and in their theologically rooted proclivity towards social inclusion. In bringing a style of ethical citizenship into the public domain, and thereby into the public consciousness, FBOs have helped to challenge the neoliberal gentrification of the public sphere and resisted the sweeping away of marginalisation from that sphere as if it were some kind of private concern.

The idea of emerging spaces of postsecular rapprochement in the contemporary city should be regarded with both caution and excitement. Caution is required because there is as yet no generalised evidence of wholesale acceptance of the mutual cognitive demands of religion and non-religion in the city. And we have emphasised above, context is important here; while some cities appear to present fruitful environments for cooperation and collaboration across religious divides, the position elsewhere provides less evidence of cognitive or practical reciprocity. It is certainly the case that some FBOs continue to operate within their own boundaries of moral code and social participation. Typically such organisations will ensure that staff and volunteers meet appropriate criteria of religious belief and adherence, and they will either serve their own ethnic/religious communities or they will make demands on their clients to fall in line with the religious framing of the services being provided. This *modus operandi* restricts both the practical possibilities of collaborating outside of the religious boundaries concerned, and of developing any mutual cognitive acceptance with non-religious elements of society.

There is, however, certainly evidence that other FBOs do present more fruitful sites of postsecular rapprochement. Here, neither the theo-ethical foundations of the organisation nor its policy towards staffing and client conditionality present barriers to cooperation with people who are not motivated by any faith. In the homelessness sector, for example (see Chapter Nine, this volume), FBOs are in some places the dominant agency of care and welfare, and they attract a range of different people as staff and volunteers, including those who are, and are not, faith-motivated. In such cases the crossover narratives of hospitality, unconditional love and charitable care seem to form a central focus for mutual action on the part of those who are and who are not faith-motivated that permits collaboration despite potentially divisive moral differences that could in other circumstances prevent any working together.

A similar emergence of postsecular activity can be recognised in the activities of groups such as London Citizens (see Chapter Three, this volume), where FBOs and representatives of different religious groups have joined together with trade unions, community groups and other political activists with no obvious religious motivation in order to campaign for the basic welfare and employment rights of citizens in a particular part of the city. Again, the working together of different religions and none signifies the potential for exciting postsecular spaces in the contemporary city.

8. The mutual cognitive demands of postsecularism apply equally to undertaking research on faith-based organisations

The FACIT project involved a number of different researchers from seven European nations, and the passage of the research reflects many of the features of the above discussion on postsecularism. Researchers brought different cultures and traditions of social science research to the table, representing not only specific disciplinary reflexivities and practices but also particular sociologies of scientific knowledge that served somehow to naturalise particular ontological and epistemological approaches. The ideas that were formative to the initiation and development of the project (see, for example, Beaumont, 2008a, 2008b, 2008c; see also Chapter One, this volume) came from a human geographer who was fascinated by how the political economy of the city was being challenged by the emergence of faith-motivated interventions to provide care and welfare. This seminal input was not itself faith-motivated, and could indeed have succumbed to what is a more general taboo in social science about being seen to deviate from an entrenched position of securing the secular basis of scholarship and research. However, such was the conviction that FBOs were becoming a significant actor not only on landscapes of urban welfare, that a clear strategy of cognitive reciprocity emerged in order to open out academic inquiry to include religious worldviews and the possibility that theological ethics have some purchase across the religious–secular divide.

This recognition that emerging postsecular circumstances in the city could only be grasped with an epistemology that mirrored these postsecular ideas was grasped at different stages throughout the project by other researchers, some of whom had connections with faith-motivated groups and were used to including faith perspectives in academic work, and others willing to 'embrace the unembraceable' by taking seriously the claims and faith practices of those religious people who were becoming part of the urban landscape of care and welfare. It would be fair to report that the uptake of such an epistemological direction was uneven, inevitably resulting in a variety of emphases and priorities across the research teams as they grappled with researching and assessing the contributions of FBOs. From a perspective founded on concepts of welfare and the state, FBOs appeared rather like any other NGO, with internal faith-based rationales and practices being secondary to the position and role of the organisation in wider networks of governance and policy. From the perspective of researchers with personal experience of particular faith cultures and of FBO involvement in particular spheres of care and welfare, the theo-ethical foundation of this participation became an easy focus to engage with.

In these circumstances, the research highlights the advantages and disadvantages of approaches involving *critical distance* and *critical proximity*. Of course, distance and proximity are not fixed positions; they are performed, and as such research performance can occupy distant and proximal positions (or indeed spaces in between the two) at the same time. However, critical distance provides academic detachment and seems to offer a neutral perspective and measurability but is prone to ideological or conceptual presupposition (for example, about the need to keep research secular) and can mask out recognition of activity and purpose that would be recognisable from the inside. Critical proximity in this case risks an underlying assumption about the legitimacy of religion in the public sphere, about the possibility of progressive as opposed to regressive or reactionary outcomes and that faith-based actions are intuitively 'for the good' of everyone. However, being willing to engage closely with faith group activity permits a sharper awareness of the networks and activities concerned, and perhaps also a critical perspective that discriminates between different religious or faith-based elements rather than regarding them as one homogeneous block. Neither distance nor proximity depends on faith adherence; they are simply different social science approaches that explain how a phenomenon such as FBOs can be positioned differently in the research process. As the research project progressed there was a general acceptance that FBOs could not simply be regarded as NGOs, and that the 'f' word in FBO had some additional relevance. As is evident in the written contributions to this book, however, there has been an inevitable unevenness in the degree to which FBOs represent a potentially significant marker of the emergence of spaces of postsecularism in the city, and in the endorsement of the need to deploy postsecular epistemologies in pursuit of this phenomenon.

References

Beaumont, J.R. (2008a) 'Dossier: faith-based organizations and human geography', *Tijdschrift voor Economishe en Sociale Geografie*, vol 99, no 4, pp 377-81.

Beaumont, J.R. (2008b) 'Faith action on urban social issues', *Urban Studies*, vol 45, no 10, pp 2019-34.

Beaumont, J.R. (2008c) 'Introduction: faith-based organizations and urban social issues', *Urban Studies*, vol 45, no 1, pp 2011-17.

Beckworth, J.A. and Demerath III, N.J. (eds) (2007) *The Sage handbook of the sociology of religion*, London: Sage Publications.

Caputo, J. (2001) *On religion*, London: Routledge.

Cloke, P. (2010) 'Theo-ethics and radical faith-based praxis in the postsecular city', in A.L. Molendijk, J. Beaumont and C. Jedan (eds) *Exploring the postsecular: The religious, the political and the urban*, Boston, MA/Leiden: Brill, pp 223-41.

Davie, G. (2007) *The sociology of religion*, London: Sage Publications.

Davie, G., Heelas, P. and Woodhead, L. (eds) (2003) *Predicting religion: Christian, secular and alternative futures*, Aldershot: Ashgate.

Habermas, J. (2006) 'Religion in the public sphere', *European Journal of Philosophy*, vol 14, pp 1-25.

Habermas, J. (2010) 'An awareness of what is missing', in J. Habermas et al, *An awareness of what is missing: Faith and reason in a postsecular age*, Cambridge: Polity Press, pp 15-23.

McLennan, G. (2011) 'Postsecular cities and radical critique: a philosophical sea change?', in J. Beaumont and C. Baker (eds) *Postsecular cities: Space, theory and practice*, London: Continuum, pp 15-30.

Peck, J. (2006) 'Liberating the city: between New York and New Orleans', *Urban Geography*, vol 27, no 8, pp 681-713.

Peck, J. and Tickell, A. (2002) 'Neoliberalizing space', *Antipode*, vol 34, no 3m pp 380-404.

Taylor, C. (2007) *A secular age*, Cambridge, MA: Harvard University Press.

Whelan, R. (1996) *The corrosion of charity*, London: Institute of Economic Affairs.

Zizek, S. and J. Milbank (2009) *The monstrosity of Christ: Paradox or dialectic?* (edited by Creston Davis), Cambridge, MA: The MIT Press.

Index

Note: Page numbers in italic type refer to tables; page numbers followed by 'n' suffix refer to notes.

A

accessibility of services 210–13
Action for Employment (A4e) 180
agape 118, 120
agency *see* individual agency
Alinsky, Saul 28n.16, 66
Allahyari, R. 132
altruism/selflessness 132, 137
Amin, A. 61, 70
Amnå, E. 169
ancien régime 41
Asad, Talal 40
assertive secularism 40, 41, 42–3, 47
Association of Islamic Clubs and
  Congregations (ICCB) 226
asylum-seekers 95–6, 166–7, 247

B

Baker, C. 20, 64
Barnes, M. 175–6
Beaumont, J.R. 20, 22, 25, 64
Bebbington, D. 107
Belgium
  FBO political participation in 162, 164, 165,
    167, 168
  homelessness services in 204, 206
  state-FBO relations in 165
Big Society 173, 179–80, 192n.3
Bishop, Gary 244
Blond, P. 114, 192n.2
Bode, Ingo 45, 49, 50
Bosch, D. 254
Brown, L.D. 156
Brueggemann, W. 112
Buber, M. 69–70
'Building Bridges in Burnley' programme 64

C

Cameron, Angus 45, 51–2
Cameron, David 51, 173
Campolo, Tony 121
Camus, Albert 2
Canatan, K. 157, 224
Cansuyu 18, 229
CAP (Church Action on Poverty) 187–8
capacity building 64, 156, *158*, 159–60
Caputo, John D. 118–20
care

performance of 143–5, 185–6, 270–1
  spaces of 64
  see also service delivery
CARF (Christian Aid and Resources
  Foundation) 13, 27n.6, 72–3
caritas 118, 120, 184
Caritas (German FBO) 45
Casanova, José 39, 45–6
case study comparison 8–9
Catholic Church, in Spain 88–9, 91
Catholic FBOs
  in Belgium 164
  in Spain 89, 90, 91–2
Chalke, Steve 108
Changemakers 194n.13
charity
  postsecular 128
  see also caritas; Christian charity
child sexual abuse 26n.1
Christian Aid and Resources Foundation
  (CARF) 13, 27n.6, 72–3
Christian challenges to neoliberal policy
  188–9
Christian charity
  development of 265–6
  see also caritas
Christian Church, critique of 243–5, 249
Christian Council of Sweden 96, 166, 167
Christian ethics 41–2, 111–12
Christian faith motivation 105–7, 120–3,
  273–4
  evangelicalism 107–13, 121
  poststructural religion 117–20, 122
  radical orthodoxy 113–17, 121–2
  and volunteering 135–6, 138
Christian FBOs, faith identity 12
Christian hope 112-13, 176, 192n.7
Christian virtue ethics 111–12
Christianity, and Muslim 'Other' 42
Church Action on Poverty (CAP) 187–8
'church plants' 247–8, 256
Church of Sweden 45, 92–3, 95, 167, 169
cities 7
  location of homelessness services in 211–12
  postsecular 60, 61–3
citizen participation
  motivation for 169
  see also volunteering
Citizens Organising Foundation (COF) 75n.7

W

Y

Z